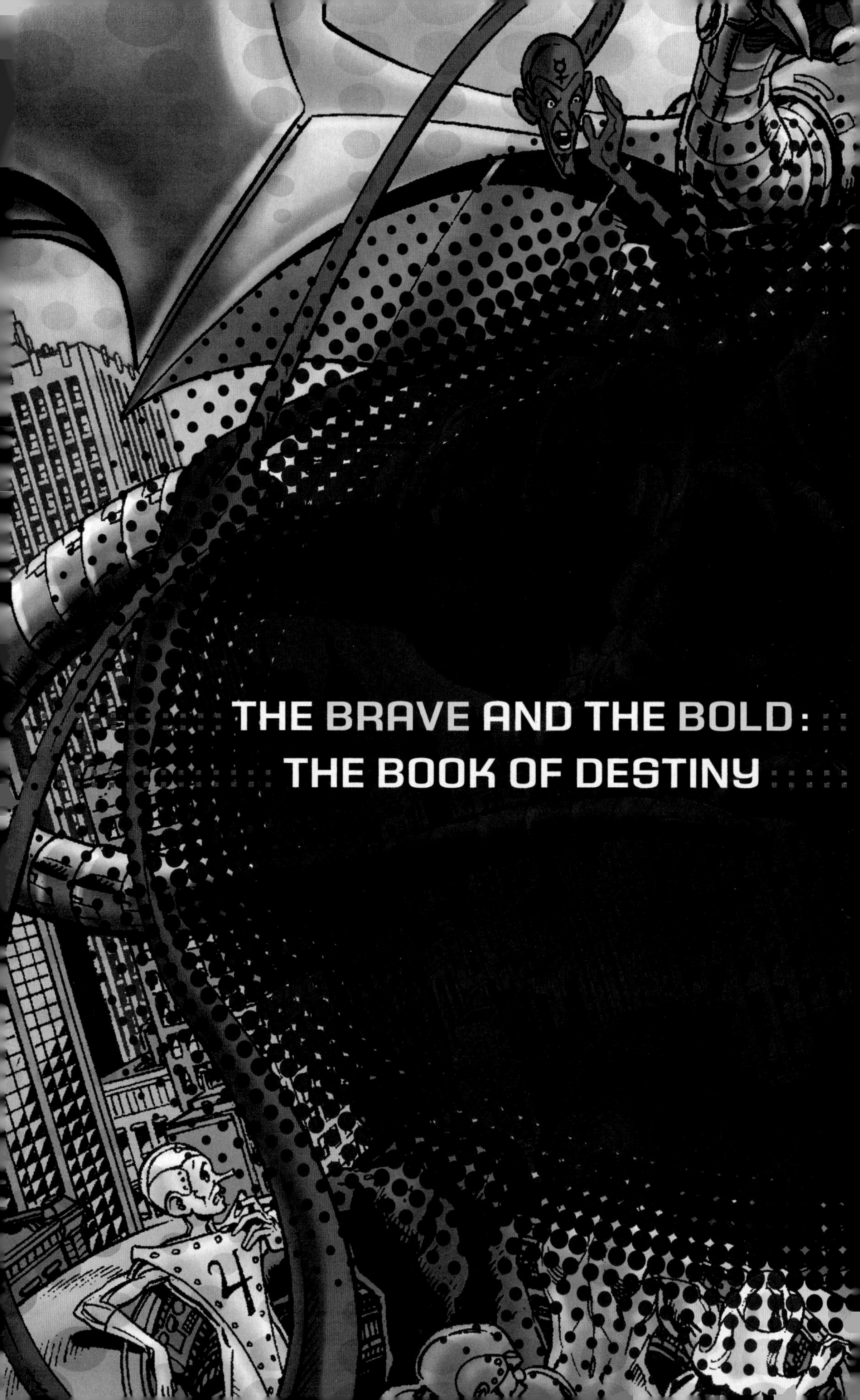

THE BRAVE AND THE BOLD: THE BOOK OF DESTINY

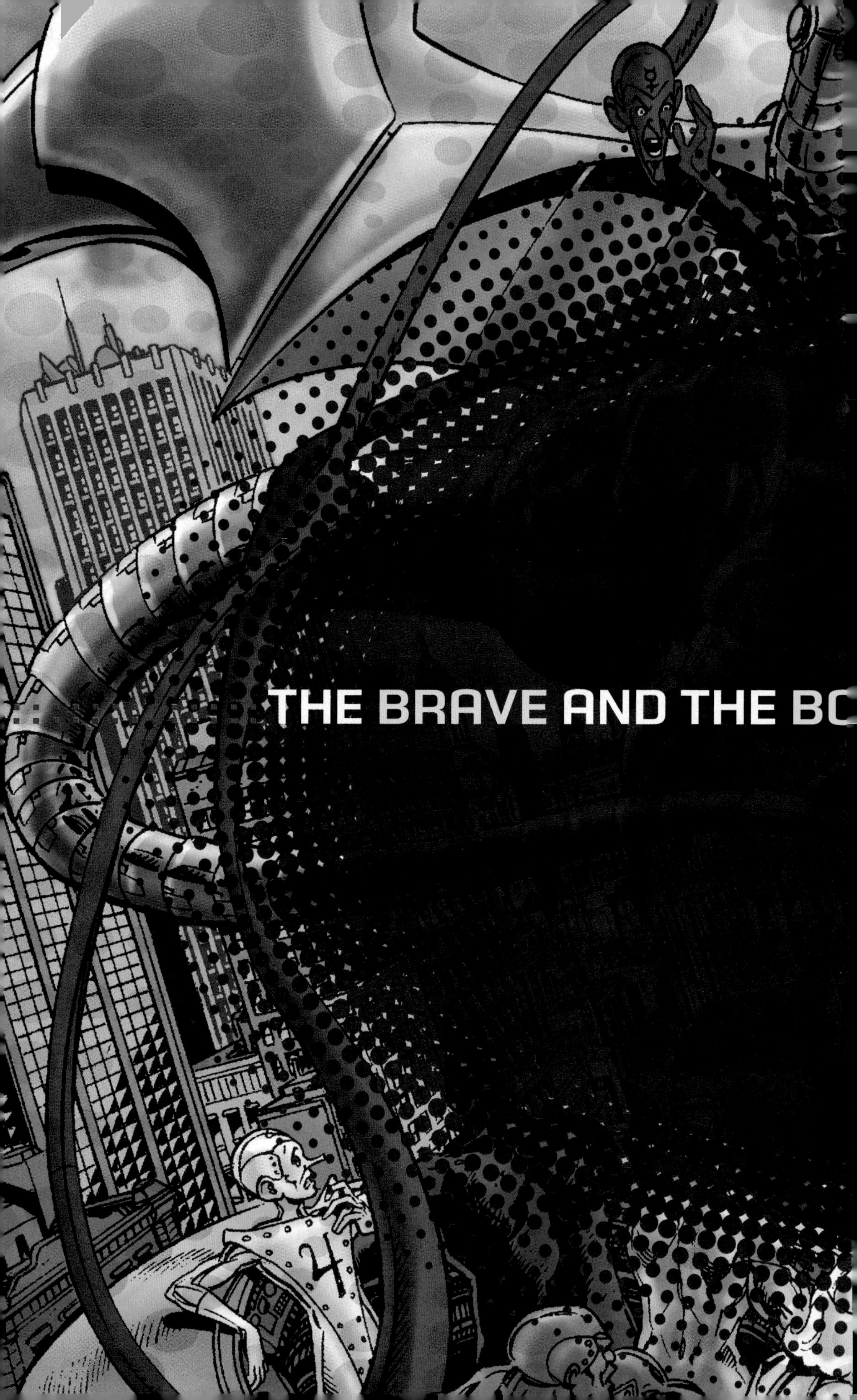
THE BRAVE AND THE B

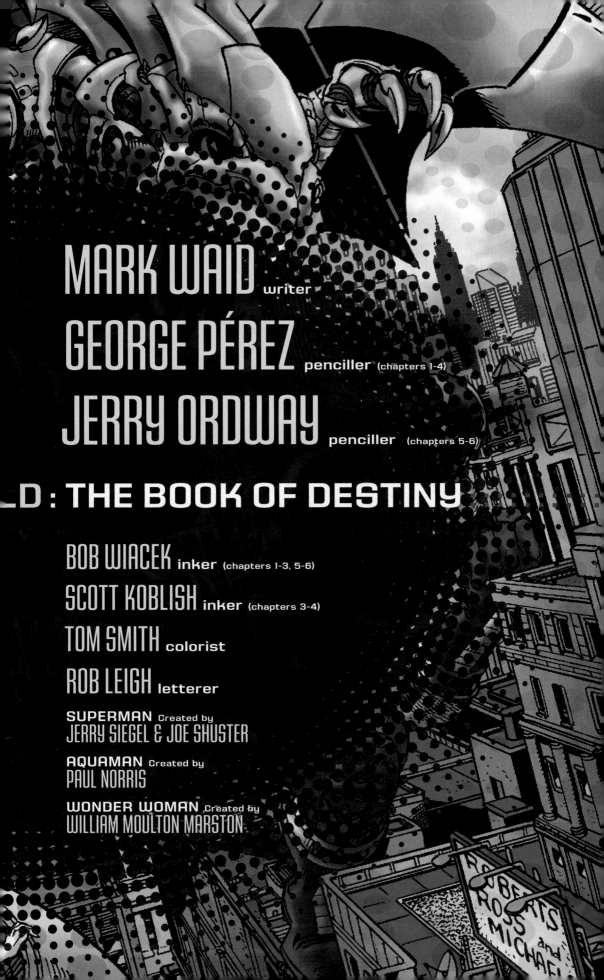

MARK WAID writer

GEORGE PÉREZ penciller (chapters 1-4)

JERRY ORDWAY penciller (chapters 5-6)

LD : THE BOOK OF DESTINY

BOB WIACEK inker (chapters 1-3, 5-6)

SCOTT KOBLISH inker (chapters 3-4)

TOM SMITH colorist

ROB LEIGH letterer

SUPERMAN Created by
JERRY SIEGEL & JOE SHUSTER

AQUAMAN Created by
PAUL NORRIS

WONDER WOMAN Created by
WILLIAM MOULTON MARSTON

Cover art by George Pérez and Tom Smith.

THE BRAVE AND THE BOLD: THE BOOK OF DESTINY
Published by DC Comics. Cover and compilation Copyright © 2008 DC Comics. All Rights
Reserved. Originally published in single magazine form in THE BRAVE AND THE BOLD 7-12.
Copyright © 2007, 2008 DC Comics. All Rights Reserved. All characters, their distinctive
likenesses and related elements featured in this publication are trademarks of DC Comics.
The stories, characters and incidents featured in this publication are entirely fictional. DC Comics
does not read or accept unsolicited submissions of ideas, stories or artwork.

DC Comics, 1700 Broadway, New York, NY 10019. | A Warner Bros. Entertainment Company.
Printed in Canada. First Printing. HC ISBN 13: 978-1-4012-1838-6 SC ISBN 13: 978-1-4012-1861-4

THE BOOK OF DESTINY contains the stories of every person and every event that ever happened... or ever will!

Except for those of four humans.

The lives of the Challengers of the Unknown no longer impact the book, but their epic adventures and everyone they connect with continually alter the future, and thus the tome is in a constant state of flux.

Destiny, the immortal keeper of the book, placed it in the care of the Challengers—charging them with the responsibility of stabilizing the timeline.

THE BRAVE AND THE BOLD

F
E
A
T
U
R
I
N
G

Rocketed as a child from the doomed planet Krypton, the infant Kal-El acquired great powers on Earth, where he fights for truth and justice as...
SUPERMAN

Born on the secret island of the legendary Amazons, Princess Diana draws upon the strength, stamina, wisdom and grace of the Greek gods to defend Man's World as...
WONDER WOMAN

The son of a surface man and a refugee from sunken Atlantis, Arthur Curry defends his undersea kingdom using his abilities to thrive underwater and command aquatic life as...
AQUAMAN

A speedster since childhood, third in the line of fastest men alive, Wally West now raises children of his own — Iris and Jai, whose genes are strangely altered by their father's super-speed!
THE FLASH

Carter Hall, reincarnated prince of ancient Egypt, flies using antigravity Nth Metal from the planet Thanagar and employs weapons of the past to protect Earth's future as...
HAWKMAN

Ryan Choi, longtime protégé of the missing professor Ray Palmer, inherited the white dwarf star-powered Bio-Belt Palmer used to control his size and weight and now follows in his mentor's super-heroic footsteps as...
THE ATOM

THE BOOK OF DESTINY

Survivor of the lost planet Krypton of another universe, cousin to a Superman not our own, Kara Zor-L fights for truth, justice and equality as...

POWER GIRL

Radiation from an ancient meteor transformed soldier-of-fortune Rex Mason into the bizarre Element Man, able to recombine his body's elements into any form as...

METAMORPHO

Lt. Clark Kent, astronaut from an anti-matter Earth where good and evil are reversed, uses alien-given super powers to rain criminal terror on his homeworld!

ULTRAMAN

Clad in magic armor of mysterious origin, humble stable boy Brian of Greystone defends his village from tyranny as the...

SILENT KNIGHT

Every time Robby Reed spins his alien H-Dial, it transforms him into a new and different champion of justice!

DIAL H FOR HERO

Robin! Kid Flash! Wonder Girl! Aqualad! The junior partners of the Justice League join forces to fight evil as the...

TEEN TITANS

FEATURING

Mutilated by catastrophes, Rita Farr, Larry Trainor and Cliff Steele came under the care of Professor Niles Caulder, who molded them into The World's Strangest Heroes...

THE DOOM PATROL

Brought together by certain doom, four brave men escaped miraculously and dedicated themselves to a second life! They are the death cheaters living on borrowed time...

CHALLENGERS OF THE UNKNOWN

Elements brought to robotic life with Responsometers, Dr. Will Magnus's inventions battle the bizarre as...

METAL MEN

BLACKHAWK

...fights World War II with his international band of high-flying aviators: André (France), Olaf (Sweden), Hendrickson (Netherlands), Stanislaus (Poland), Chop-Chop (China), Chuck (Texas) and Lady Blackhawk (the USA)!

Captain Rip Carter fights Axis soldiers with his international band of two-fisted kids: André (France), Jan (Netherlands), Alfie (England) and Brooklyn (take a guess)!

BOY COMMANDOS

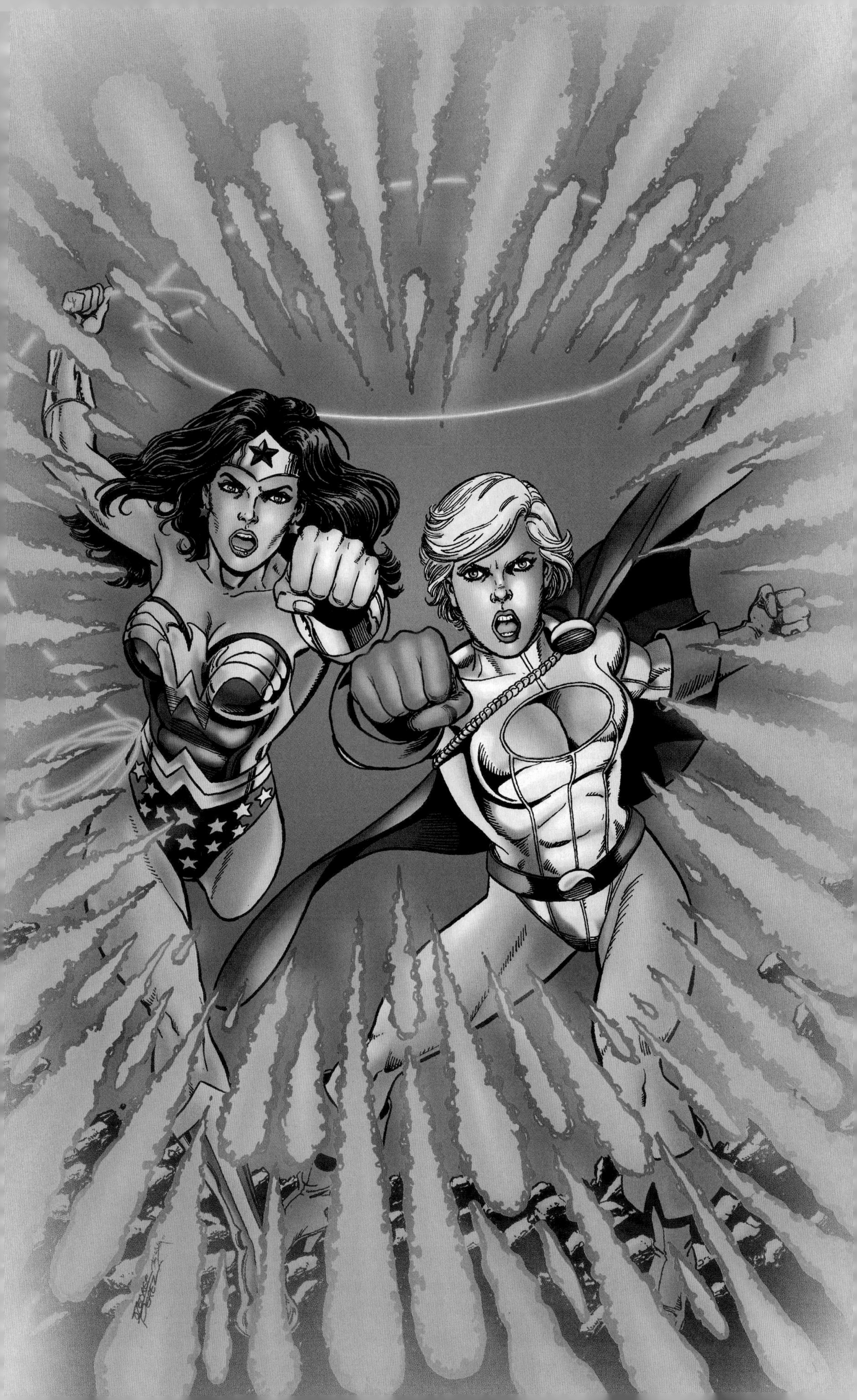

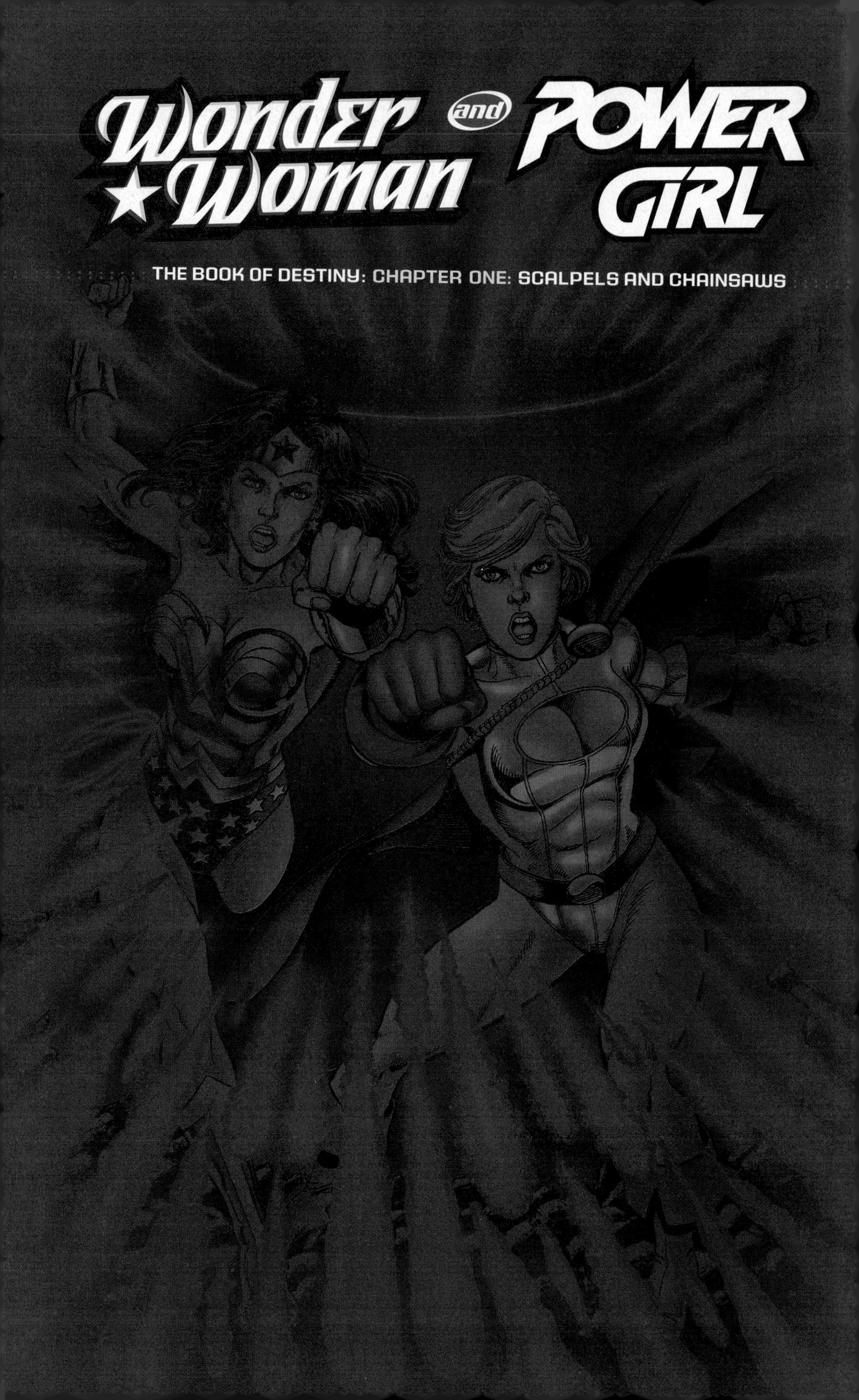
Wonder Woman
and
POWER GIRL
THE BOOK OF DESTINY: CHAPTER ONE: SCALPELS AND CHAINSAWS

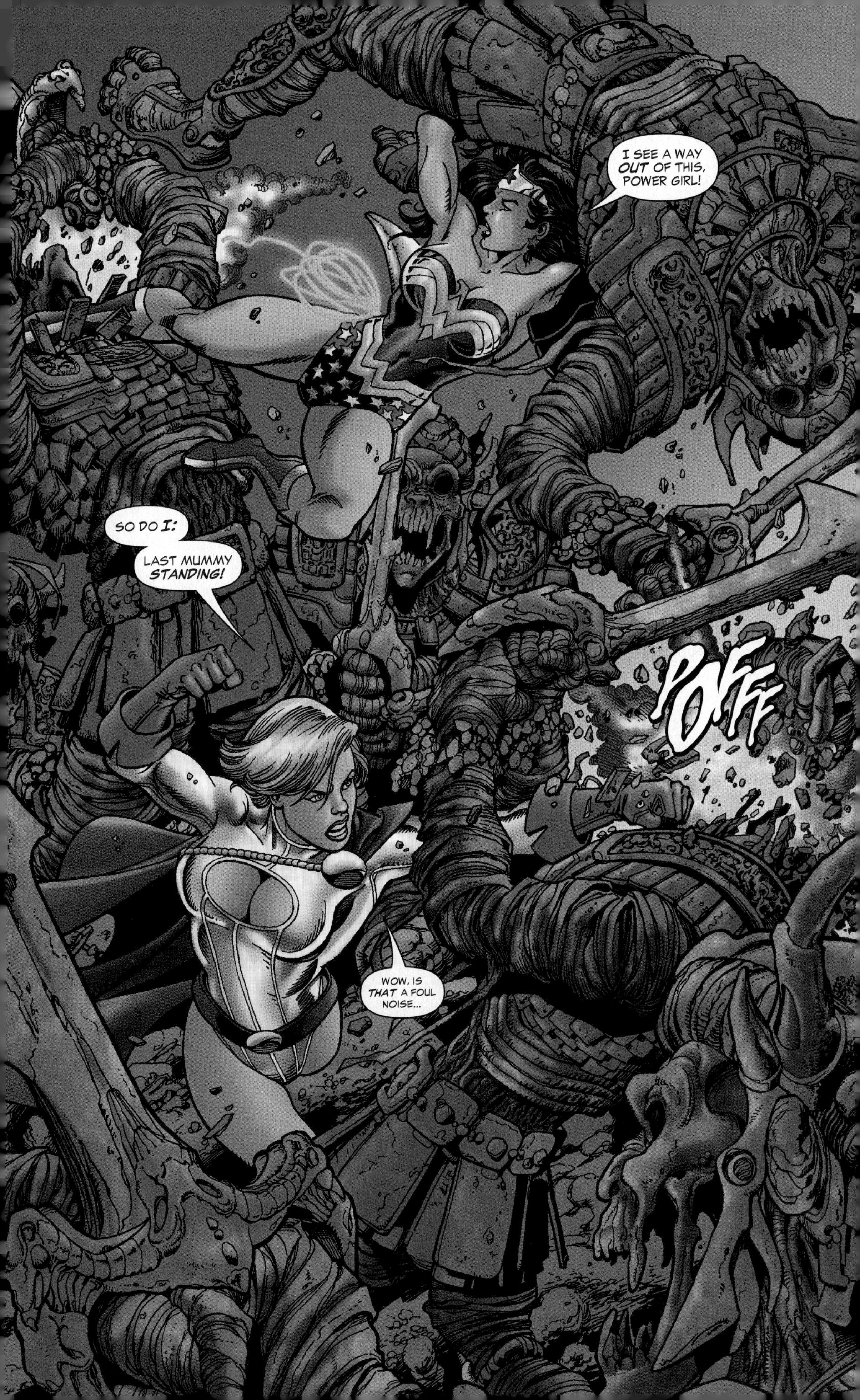
I SEE A WAY OUT OF THIS, POWER GIRL!
SO DO I:
LAST MUMMY STANDING!
POOFFF
WOW, IS THAT A FOUL NOISE...

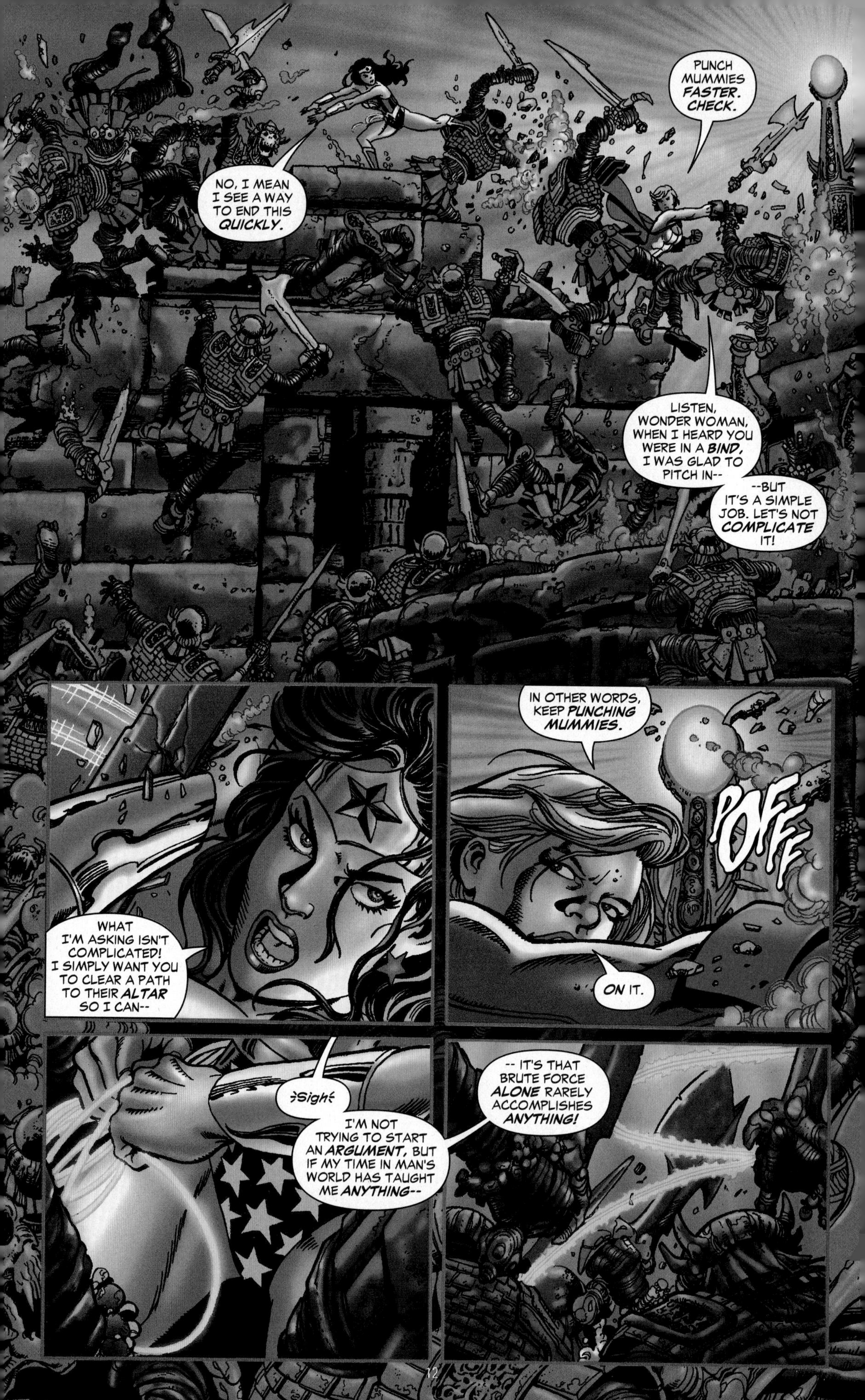

NO, I MEAN I SEE A WAY TO END THIS QUICKLY.
PUNCH MUMMIES FASTER. CHECK.
LISTEN, WONDER WOMAN, WHEN I HEARD YOU WERE IN A BIND, I WAS GLAD TO PITCH IN--
--BUT IT'S A SIMPLE JOB. LET'S NOT COMPLICATE IT!
WHAT I'M ASKING ISN'T COMPLICATED! I SIMPLY WANT YOU TO CLEAR A PATH TO THEIR ALTAR SO I CAN--
IN OTHER WORDS, KEEP PUNCHING MUMMIES.
POFFF
ON IT.
Sigh
I'M NOT TRYING TO START AN ARGUMENT, BUT IF MY TIME IN MAN'S WORLD HAS TAUGHT ME ANYTHING--
-- IT'S THAT BRUTE FORCE ALONE RARELY ACCOMPLISHES ANYTHING!

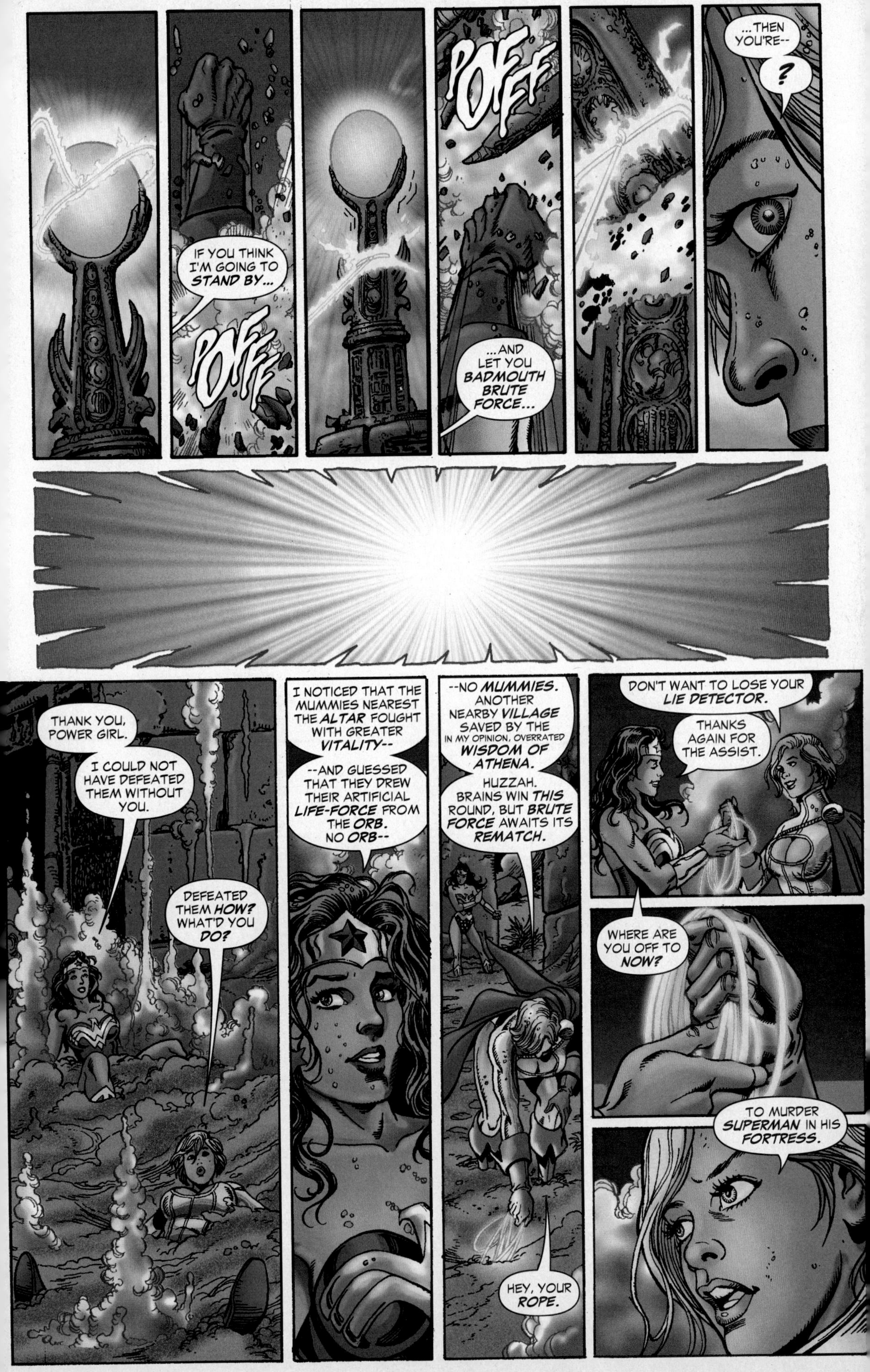
IF YOU THINK I'M GOING TO STAND BY...
POFFF
POFFF
...AND LET YOU BADMOUTH BRUTE FORCE...
...THEN YOU'RE--
?
THANK YOU, POWER GIRL.
I COULD NOT HAVE DEFEATED THEM WITHOUT YOU.
DEFEATED THEM HOW? WHAT'D YOU DO?
I NOTICED THAT THE MUMMIES NEAREST THE ALTAR FOUGHT WITH GREATER VITALITY--
--AND GUESSED THAT THEY DREW THEIR ARTIFICIAL LIFE-FORCE FROM THE ORB. NO ORB--
--NO MUMMIES. ANOTHER NEARBY VILLAGE SAVED BY THE IN MY OPINION, OVERRATED WISDOM OF ATHENA.
HUZZAH. BRAINS WIN THIS ROUND, BUT BRUTE FORCE AWAITS ITS REMATCH.
HEY, YOUR ROPE.
DON'T WANT TO LOSE YOUR LIE DETECTOR.
THANKS AGAIN FOR THE ASSIST.
WHERE ARE YOU OFF TO NOW?
TO MURDER SUPERMAN IN HIS FORTRESS.

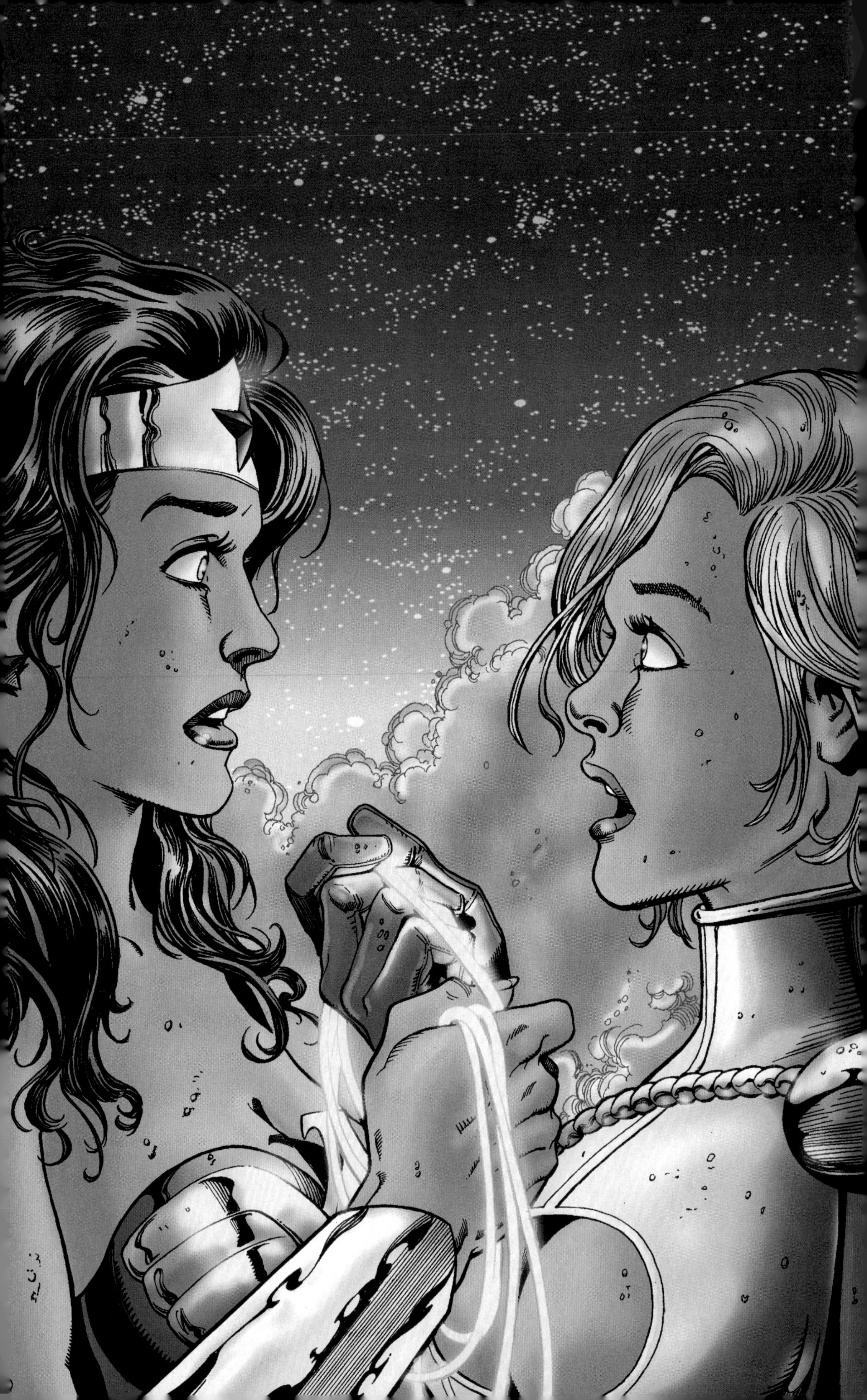

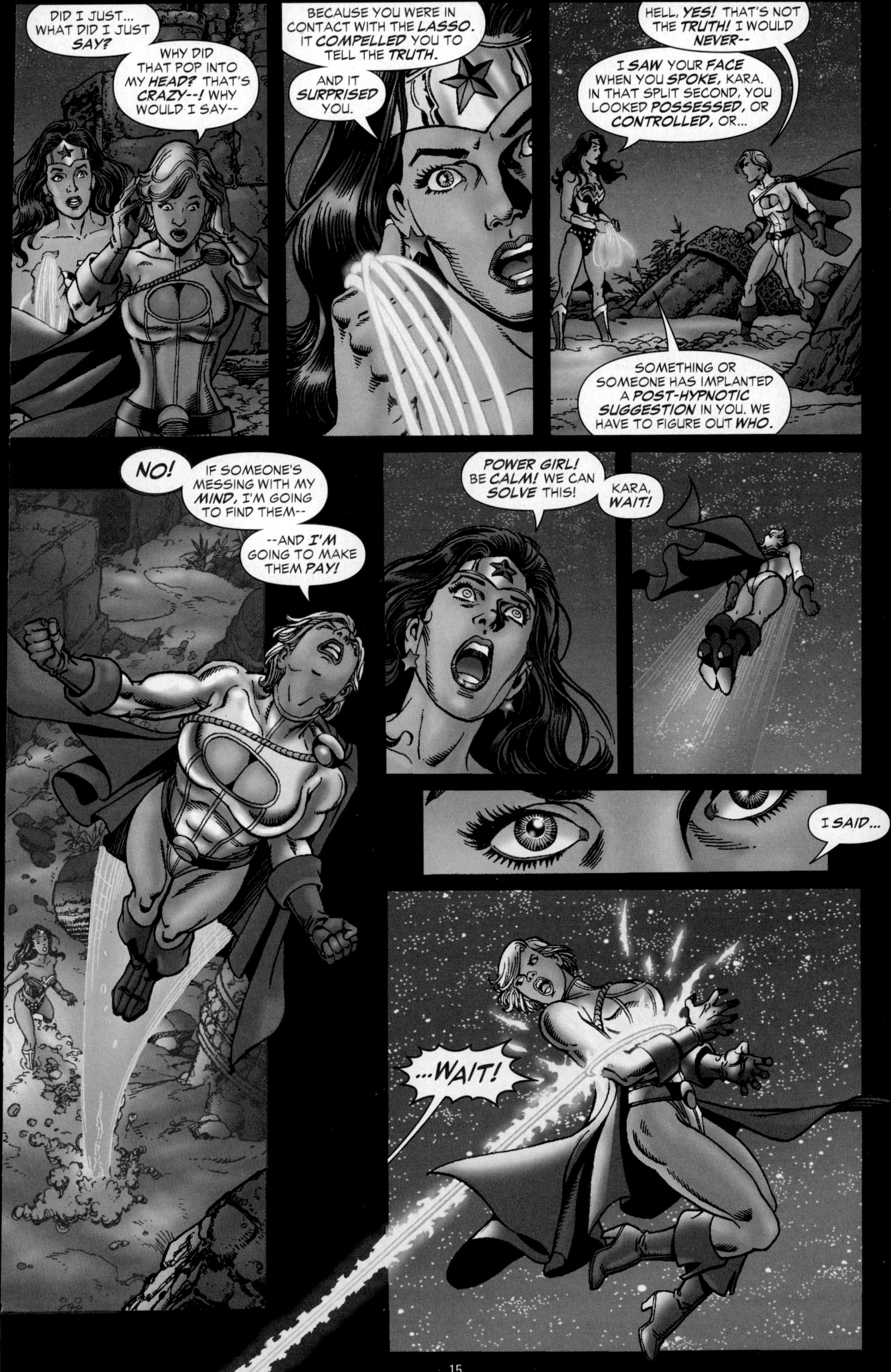
DID I JUST... WHAT DID I JUST SAY?
WHY DID THAT POP INTO MY HEAD? THAT'S CRAZY--! WHY WOULD I SAY--
BECAUSE YOU WERE IN CONTACT WITH THE LASSO. IT COMPELLED YOU TO TELL THE TRUTH.
AND IT SURPRISED YOU.
HELL, YES! THAT'S NOT THE TRUTH! I WOULD NEVER--
I SAW YOUR FACE WHEN YOU SPOKE, KARA. IN THAT SPLIT SECOND, YOU LOOKED POSSESSED, OR CONTROLLED, OR...
SOMETHING OR SOMEONE HAS IMPLANTED A POST-HYPNOTIC SUGGESTION IN YOU. WE HAVE TO FIGURE OUT WHO.
NO!
IF SOMEONE'S MESSING WITH MY MIND, I'M GOING TO FIND THEM--
--AND I'M GOING TO MAKE THEM PAY!
POWER GIRL! BE CALM! WE CAN SOLVE THIS!
KARA, WAIT!
I SAID...
...WAIT!

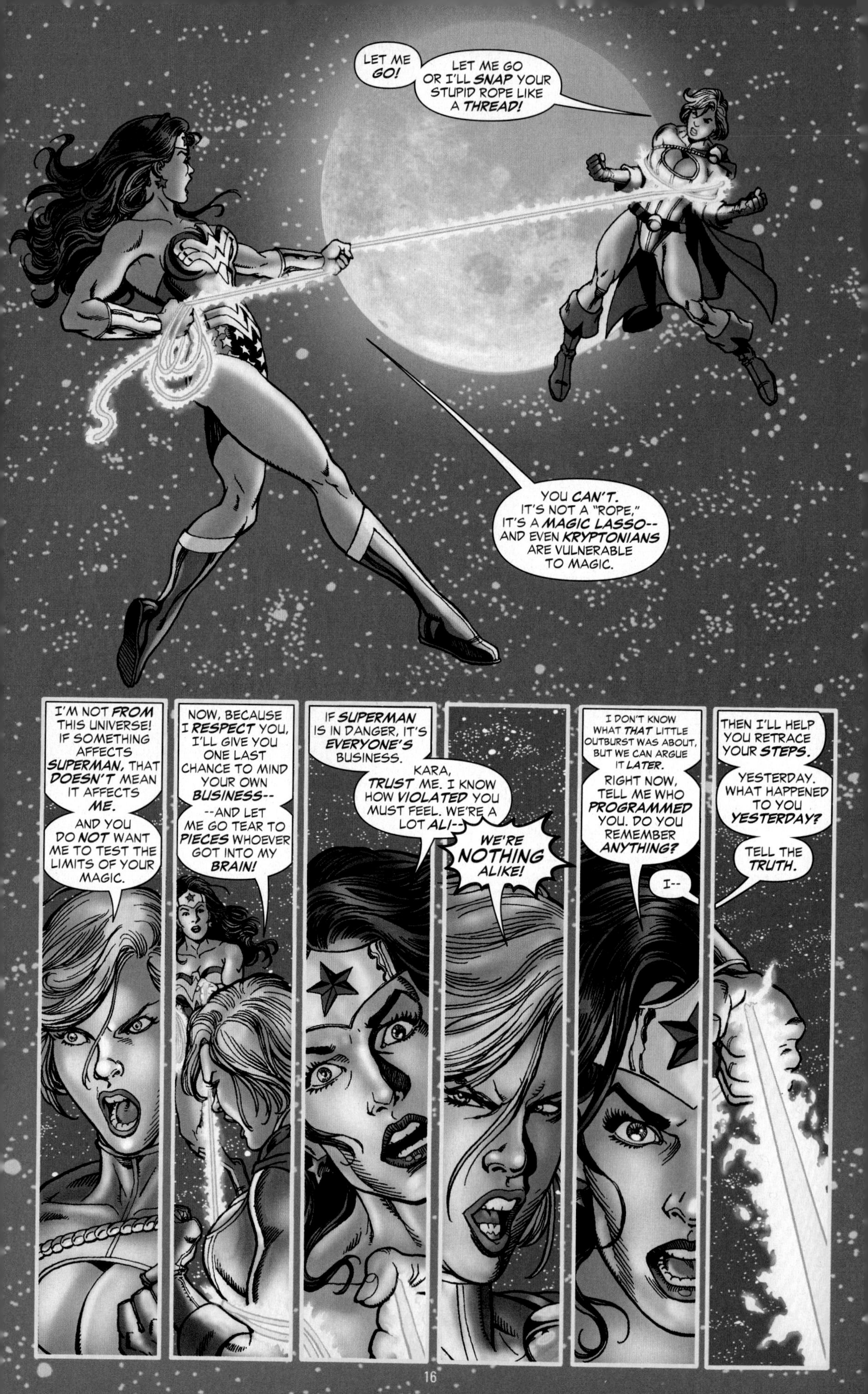
LET ME GO!
LET ME GO OR I'LL SNAP YOUR STUPID ROPE LIKE A THREAD!
YOU CAN'T. IT'S NOT A "ROPE," IT'S A MAGIC LASSO-- AND EVEN KRYPTONIANS ARE VULNERABLE TO MAGIC.
I'M NOT FROM THIS UNIVERSE! IF SOMETHING AFFECTS SUPERMAN, THAT DOESN'T MEAN IT AFFECTS ME.
AND YOU DO NOT WANT ME TO TEST THE LIMITS OF YOUR MAGIC.
NOW, BECAUSE I RESPECT YOU, I'LL GIVE YOU ONE LAST CHANCE TO MIND YOUR OWN BUSINESS--
--AND LET ME GO TEAR TO PIECES WHOEVER GOT INTO MY BRAIN!
IF SUPERMAN IS IN DANGER, IT'S EVERYONE'S BUSINESS.
KARA, TRUST ME. I KNOW HOW VIOLATED YOU MUST FEEL. WE'RE A LOT ALI--
WE'RE NOTHING ALIKE!
I DON'T KNOW WHAT THAT LITTLE OUTBURST WAS ABOUT, BUT WE CAN ARGUE IT LATER.
RIGHT NOW, TELL ME WHO PROGRAMMED YOU. DO YOU REMEMBER ANYTHING?
I--
THEN I'LL HELP YOU RETRACE YOUR STEPS.
YESTERDAY. WHAT HAPPENED TO YOU YESTERDAY?
TELL THE TRUTH.

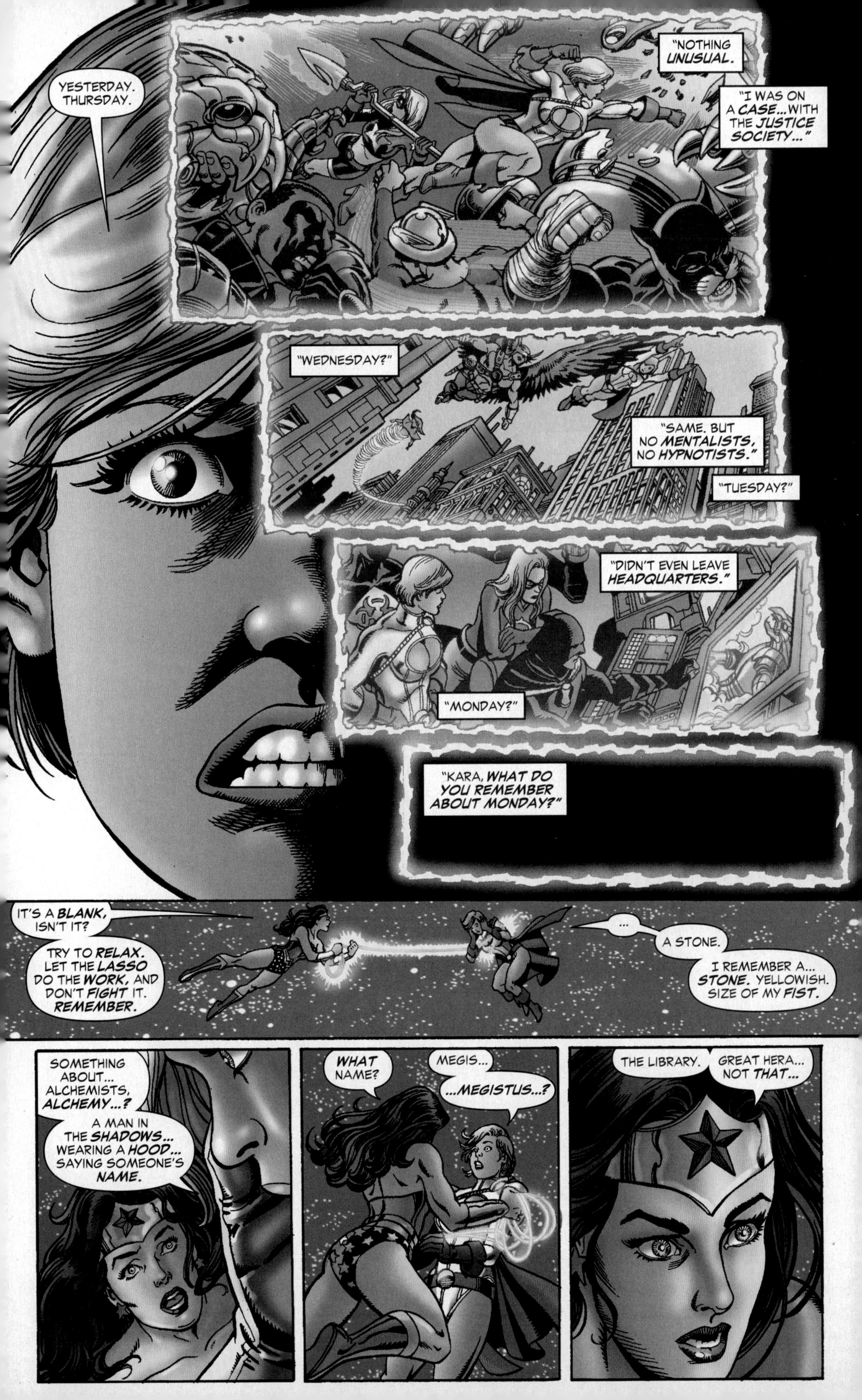
YESTERDAY. THURSDAY.
"NOTHING UNUSUAL.
"I WAS ON A CASE... WITH THE JUSTICE SOCIETY..."
"WEDNESDAY?"
"SAME. BUT NO MENTALISTS, NO HYPNOTISTS."
"TUESDAY?"
"DIDN'T EVEN LEAVE HEADQUARTERS."
"MONDAY?"
"KARA, WHAT DO YOU REMEMBER ABOUT MONDAY?"
IT'S A BLANK, ISN'T IT?
TRY TO RELAX. LET THE LASSO DO THE WORK, AND DON'T FIGHT IT. REMEMBER.
...
A STONE.
I REMEMBER A... STONE. YELLOWISH. SIZE OF MY FIST.
SOMETHING ABOUT... ALCHEMISTS, ALCHEMY...?
A MAN IN THE SHADOWS... WEARING A HOOD... SAYING SOMEONE'S NAME.
WHAT NAME?
MEGIS...
...MEGISTUS...?
THE LIBRARY.
GREAT HERA... NOT THAT...

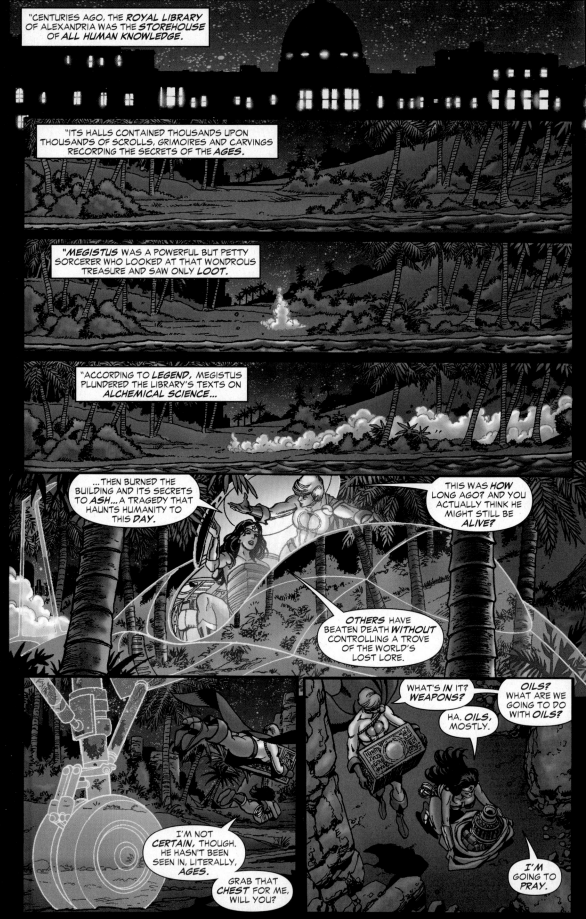

"CENTURIES AGO, THE *ROYAL LIBRARY* OF ALEXANDRIA WAS THE *STOREHOUSE* OF *ALL HUMAN KNOWLEDGE.*"

"ITS HALLS CONTAINED THOUSANDS UPON THOUSANDS OF SCROLLS, GRIMOIRES AND CARVINGS RECORDING THE SECRETS OF THE *AGES.*"

"*MEGISTUS* WAS A POWERFUL BUT PETTY SORCERER WHO LOOKED AT THAT WONDROUS TREASURE AND SAW ONLY *LOOT.*"

"ACCORDING TO *LEGEND,* MEGISTUS PLUNDERED THE LIBRARY'S TEXTS ON *ALCHEMICAL SCIENCE...*"

"...THEN BURNED THE BUILDING AND ITS SECRETS TO *ASH...* A TRAGEDY THAT HAUNTS HUMANITY TO THIS *DAY.*

THIS WAS *HOW* LONG AGO? AND YOU ACTUALLY THINK HE MIGHT STILL BE *ALIVE?*

OTHERS HAVE BEATEN DEATH *WITHOUT* CONTROLLING A TROVE OF THE WORLD'S LOST LORE.

I'M NOT *CERTAIN,* THOUGH. HE HASN'T BEEN SEEN IN, LITERALLY, *AGES.*

GRAB THAT *CHEST* FOR ME, WILL YOU?

WHAT'S *IN* IT? *WEAPONS?*

OILS? WHAT ARE WE GOING TO DO WITH OILS?

HA. *OILS,* MOSTLY.

I'M GOING TO PRAY.

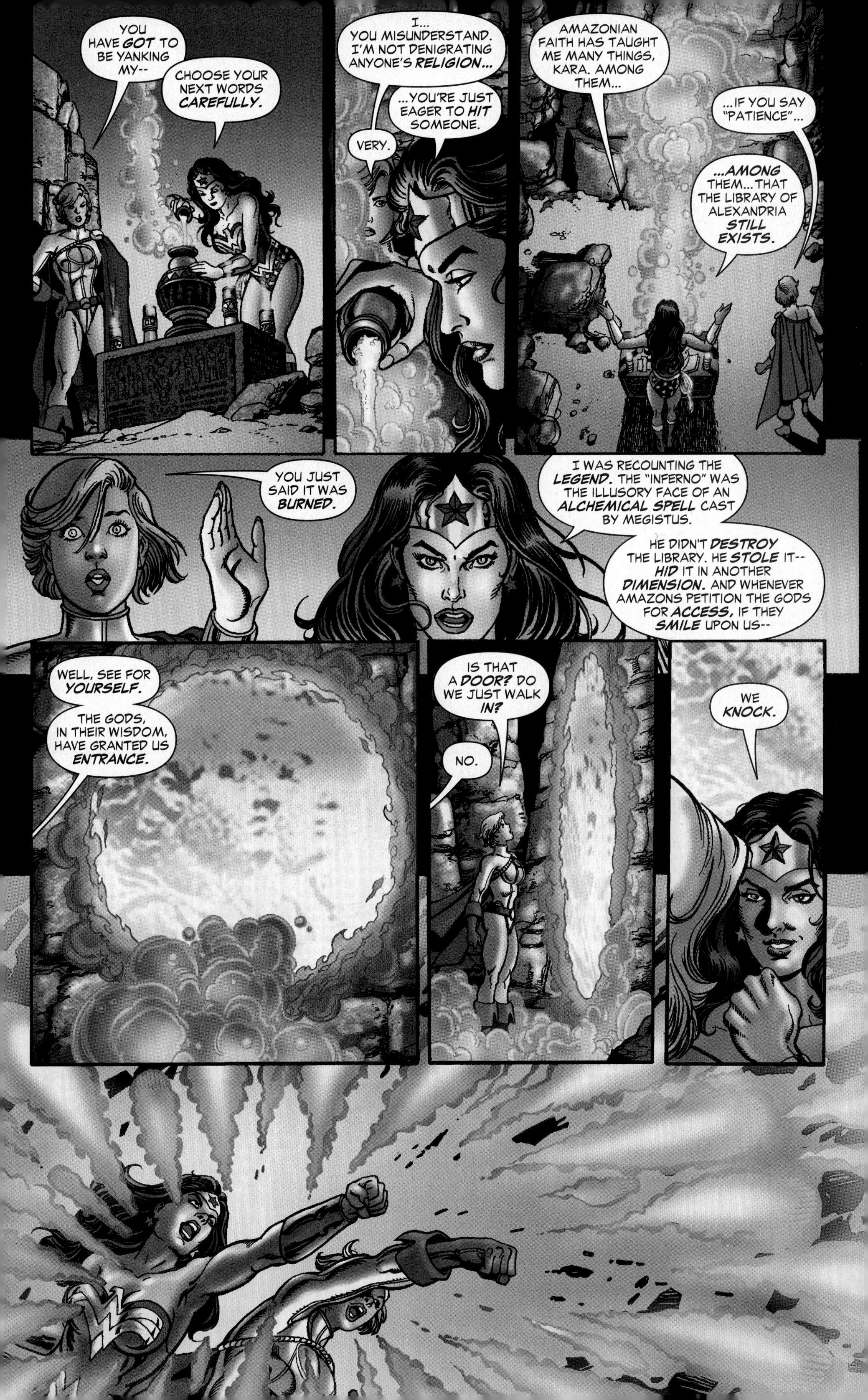

YOU HAVE GOT TO BE YANKING MY--
CHOOSE YOUR NEXT WORDS CAREFULLY.
I... YOU MISUNDERSTAND. I'M NOT DENIGRATING ANYONE'S RELIGION...
...YOU'RE JUST EAGER TO HIT SOMEONE.
VERY.
AMAZONIAN FAITH HAS TAUGHT ME MANY THINGS, KARA. AMONG THEM...
...IF YOU SAY "PATIENCE"...
...AMONG THEM...THAT THE LIBRARY OF ALEXANDRIA STILL EXISTS.
YOU JUST SAID IT WAS BURNED.
I WAS RECOUNTING THE LEGEND. THE "INFERNO" WAS THE ILLUSORY FACE OF AN ALCHEMICAL SPELL CAST BY MEGISTUS.
HE DIDN'T DESTROY THE LIBRARY. HE STOLE IT-- HID IT IN ANOTHER DIMENSION. AND WHENEVER AMAZONS PETITION THE GODS FOR ACCESS, IF THEY SMILE UPON US--
WELL, SEE FOR YOURSELF.
THE GODS, IN THEIR WISDOM, HAVE GRANTED US ENTRANCE.
IS THAT A DOOR? DO WE JUST WALK IN?
NO.
WE KNOCK.

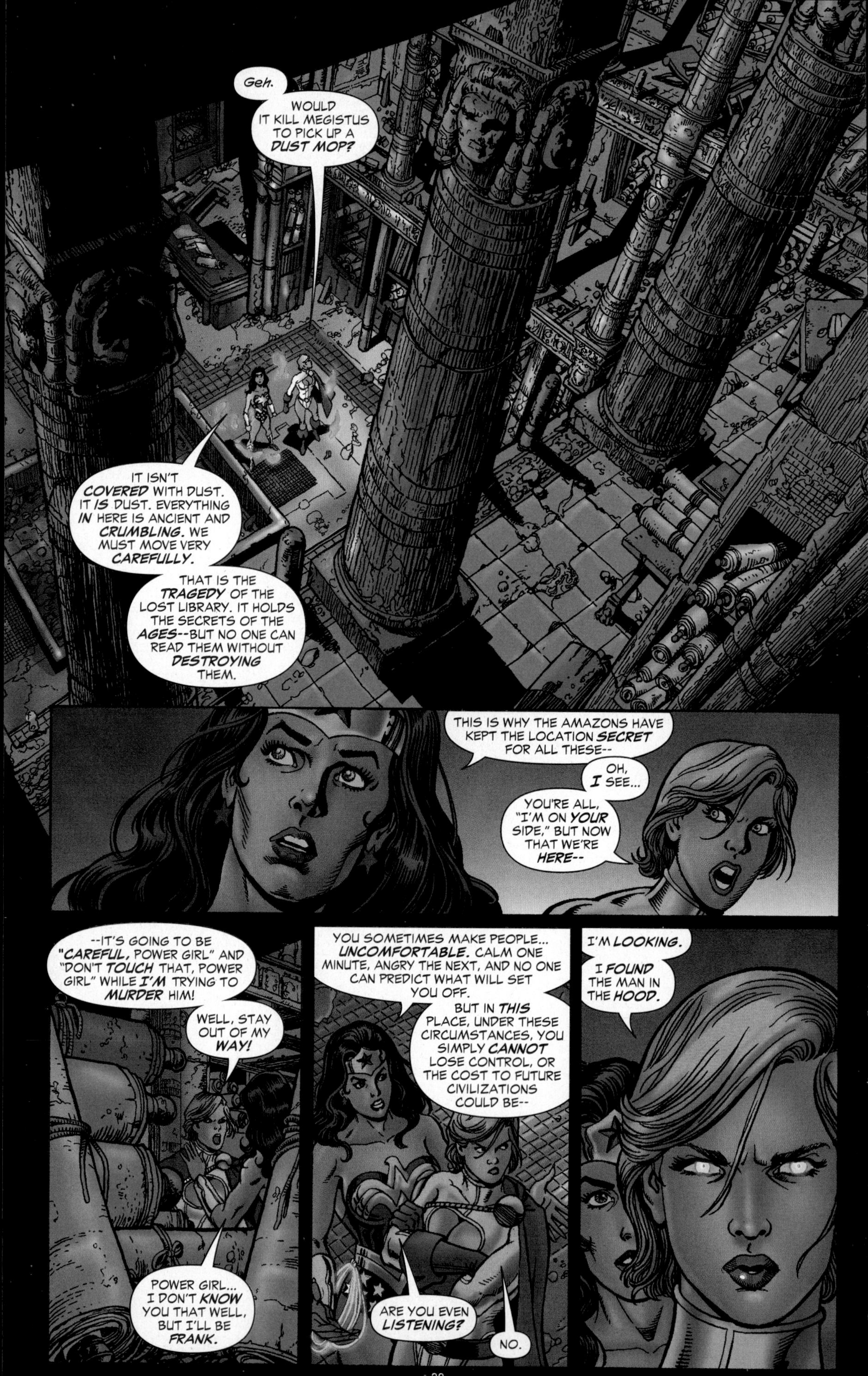
Geh.
WOULD IT KILL MEGISTUS TO PICK UP A DUST MOP?
IT ISN'T COVERED WITH DUST. IT IS DUST. EVERYTHING IN HERE IS ANCIENT AND CRUMBLING. WE MUST MOVE VERY CAREFULLY.
THAT IS THE TRAGEDY OF THE LOST LIBRARY. IT HOLDS THE SECRETS OF THE AGES--BUT NO ONE CAN READ THEM WITHOUT DESTROYING THEM.
THIS IS WHY THE AMAZONS HAVE KEPT THE LOCATION SECRET FOR ALL THESE--
OH, I SEE...
YOU'RE ALL, "I'M ON YOUR SIDE," BUT NOW THAT WE'RE HERE--
--IT'S GOING TO BE "CAREFUL, POWER GIRL" AND "DON'T TOUCH THAT, POWER GIRL" WHILE I'M TRYING TO MURDER HIM!
WELL, STAY OUT OF MY WAY!
POWER GIRL... I DON'T KNOW YOU THAT WELL, BUT I'LL BE FRANK.
YOU SOMETIMES MAKE PEOPLE... UNCOMFORTABLE. CALM ONE MINUTE, ANGRY THE NEXT, AND NO ONE CAN PREDICT WHAT WILL SET YOU OFF.
BUT IN THIS PLACE, UNDER THESE CIRCUMSTANCES, YOU SIMPLY CANNOT LOSE CONTROL, OR THE COST TO FUTURE CIVILIZATIONS COULD BE--
ARE YOU EVEN LISTENING?
NO.
I'M LOOKING.
I FOUND THE MAN IN THE HOOD.

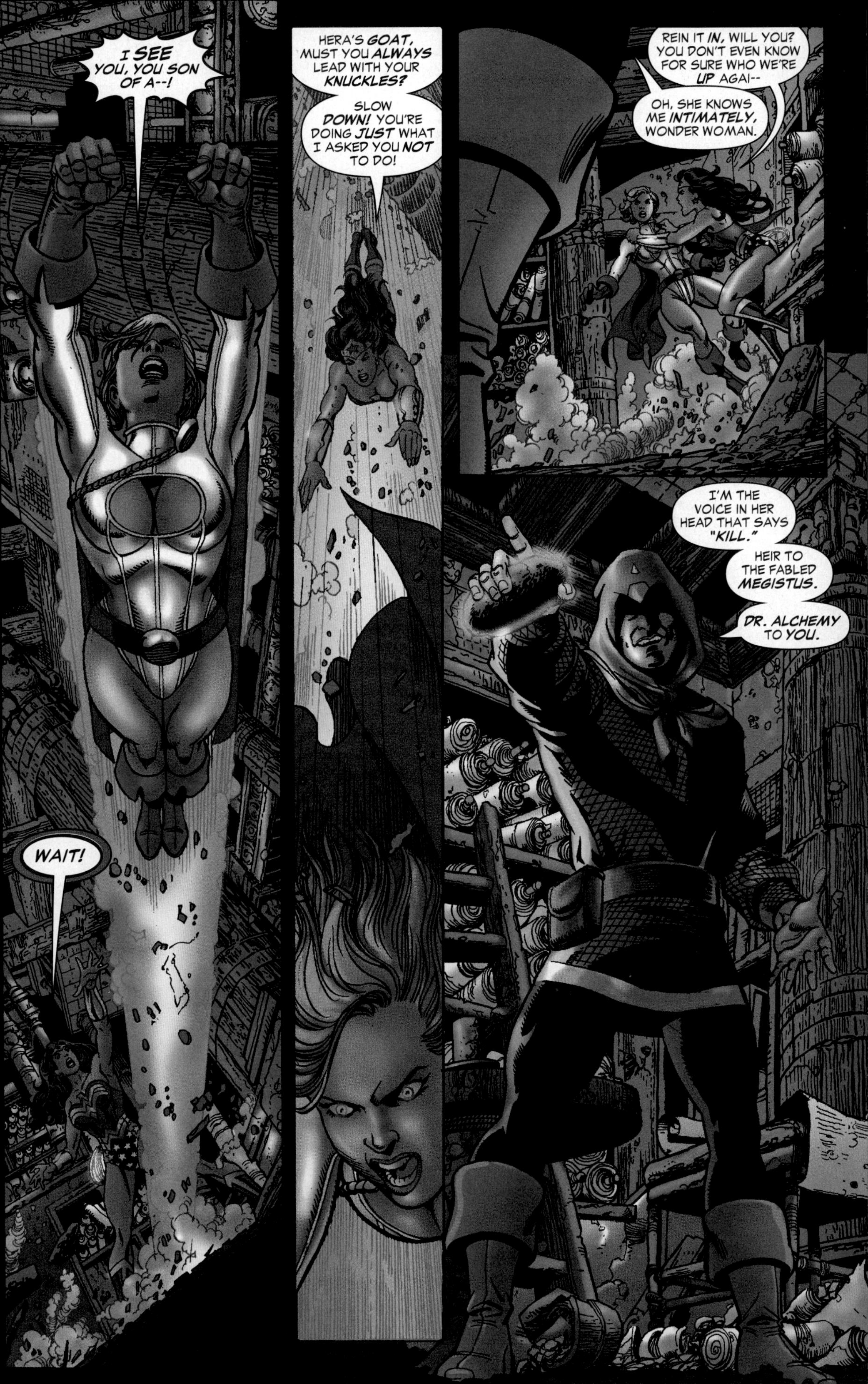
I SEE YOU, YOU SON OF A--!
WAIT!
HERA'S GOAT, MUST YOU ALWAYS LEAD WITH YOUR KNUCKLES?
SLOW DOWN! YOU'RE DOING JUST WHAT I ASKED YOU NOT TO DO!
REIN IT IN, WILL YOU? YOU DON'T EVEN KNOW FOR SURE WHO WE'RE UP AGAI--
OH, SHE KNOWS ME INTIMATELY, WONDER WOMAN.
I'M THE VOICE IN HER HEAD THAT SAYS "KILL."
HEIR TO THE FABLED MEGISTUS.
DR. ALCHEMY TO YOU.

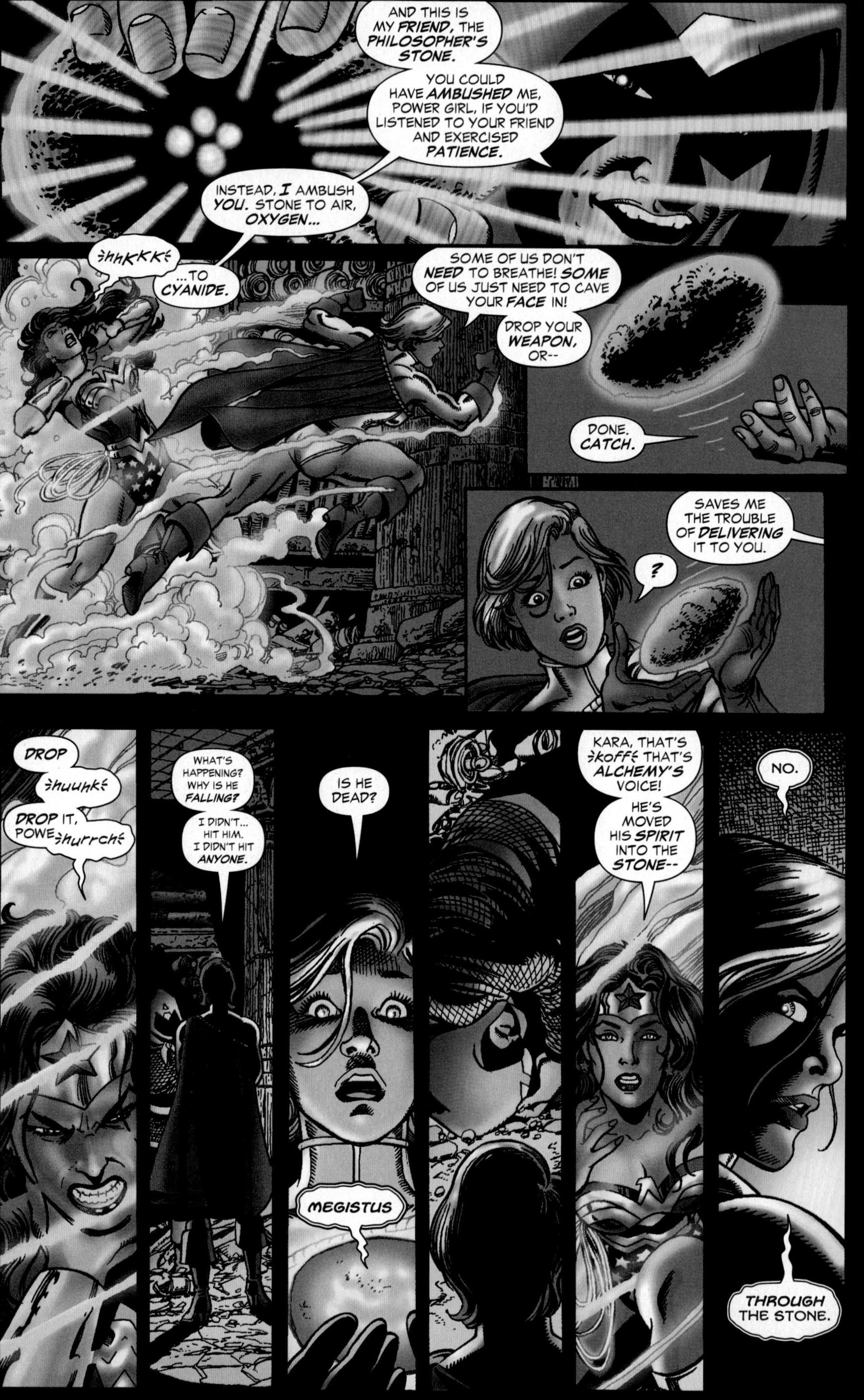
AND THIS IS MY FRIEND, THE PHILOSOPHER'S STONE.
YOU COULD HAVE AMBUSHED ME, POWER GIRL, IF YOU'D LISTENED TO YOUR FRIEND AND EXERCISED PATIENCE.
INSTEAD, I AMBUSH YOU. STONE TO AIR, OXYGEN...
...TO CYANIDE.
hhKKK
SOME OF US DON'T NEED TO BREATHE! SOME OF US JUST NEED TO CAVE YOUR FACE IN!
DROP YOUR WEAPON, OR--
DONE. CATCH.
SAVES ME THE TROUBLE OF DELIVERING IT TO YOU.
?
DROP
huuhk
DROP IT, POWE hurrch
WHAT'S HAPPENING? WHY IS HE FALLING?
I DIDN'T... HIT HIM. I DIDN'T HIT ANYONE.
IS HE DEAD?
MEGISTUS
KARA, THAT'S koff THAT'S ALCHEMY'S VOICE!
HE'S MOVED HIS SPIRIT INTO THE STONE--
NO.
THROUGH THE STONE.

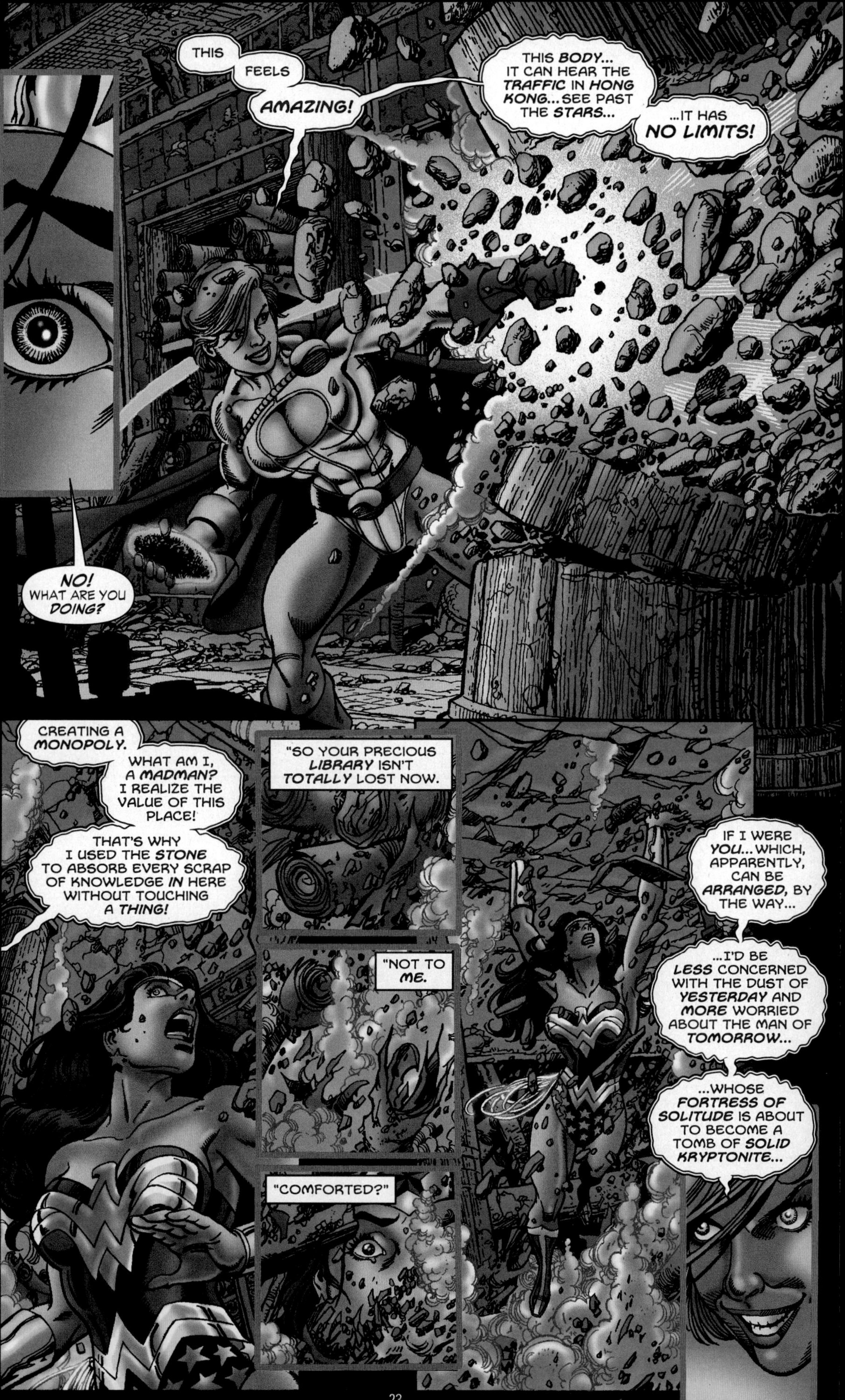
THIS
FEELS
AMAZING!
THIS BODY... IT CAN HEAR THE TRAFFIC IN HONG KONG... SEE PAST THE STARS...
...IT HAS NO LIMITS!
NO! WHAT ARE YOU DOING?
CREATING A MONOPOLY.
WHAT AM I, A MADMAN? I REALIZE THE VALUE OF THIS PLACE!
THAT'S WHY I USED THE STONE TO ABSORB EVERY SCRAP OF KNOWLEDGE IN HERE WITHOUT TOUCHING A THING!
"SO YOUR PRECIOUS LIBRARY ISN'T TOTALLY LOST NOW.
"NOT TO ME.
"COMFORTED?"
IF I WERE YOU... WHICH, APPARENTLY, CAN BE ARRANGED, BY THE WAY...
...I'D BE LESS CONCERNED WITH THE DUST OF YESTERDAY AND MORE WORRIED ABOUT THE MAN OF TOMORROW...
...WHOSE FORTRESS OF SOLITUDE IS ABOUT TO BECOME A TOMB OF SOLID KRYPTONITE...

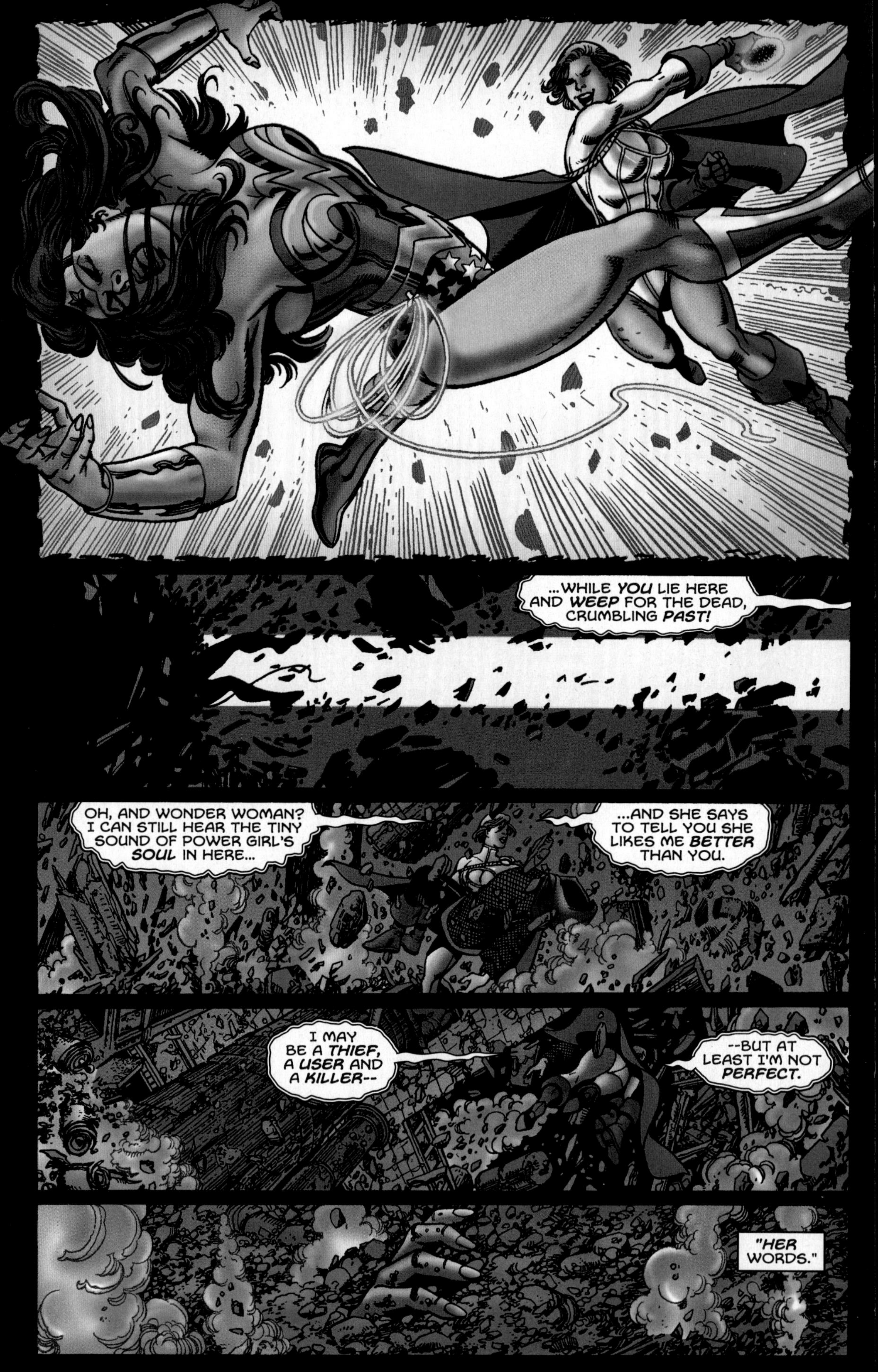
...WHILE YOU LIE HERE AND WEEP FOR THE DEAD, CRUMBLING PAST!
OH, AND WONDER WOMAN? I CAN STILL HEAR THE TINY SOUND OF POWER GIRL'S SOUL IN HERE...
...AND SHE SAYS TO TELL YOU SHE LIKES ME BETTER THAN YOU.
I MAY BE A THIEF, A USER AND A KILLER--
--BUT AT LEAST I'M NOT PERFECT.
"HER WORDS."

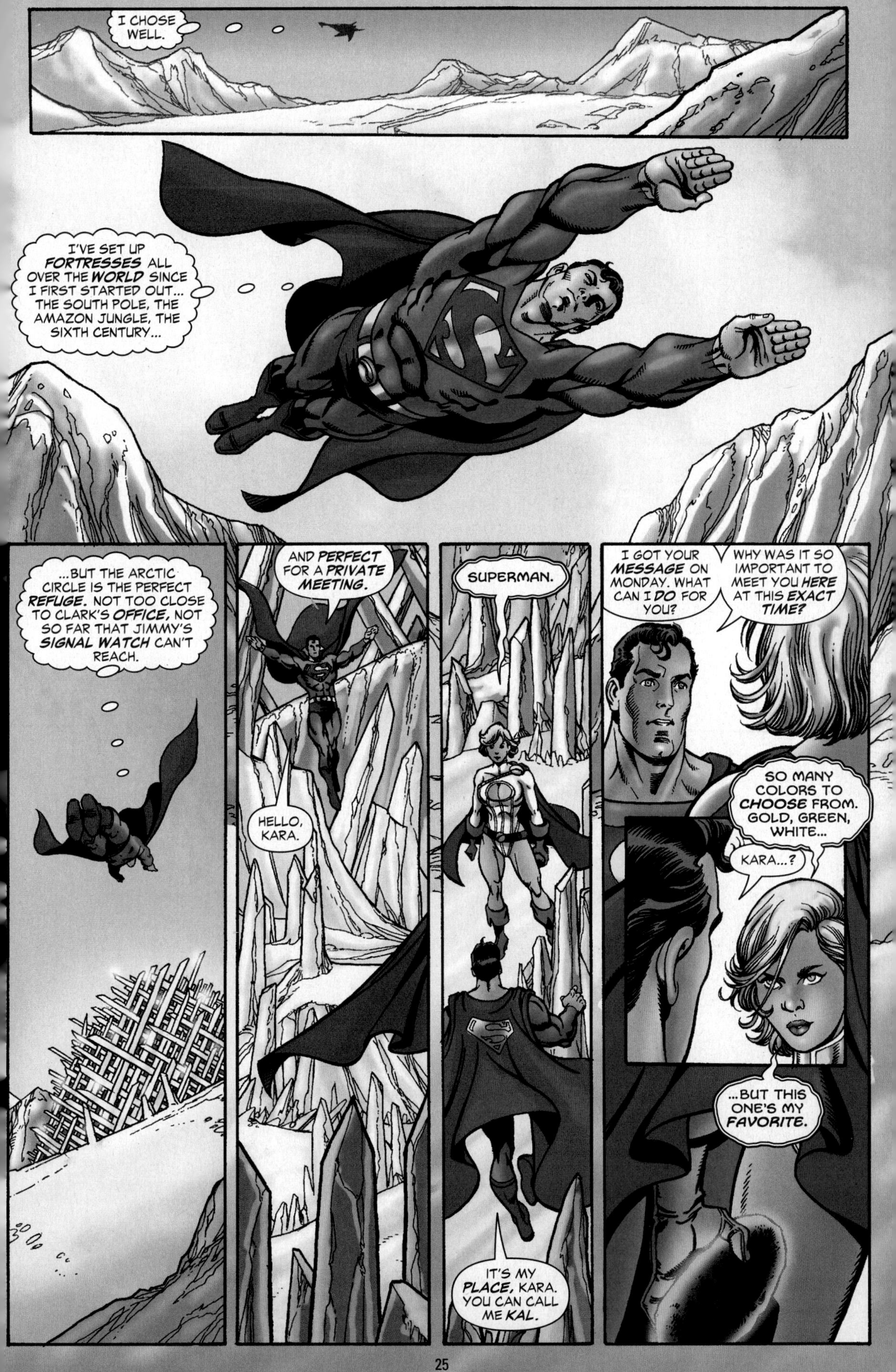
I CHOSE WELL.
I'VE SET UP FORTRESSES ALL OVER THE WORLD SINCE I FIRST STARTED OUT... THE SOUTH POLE, THE AMAZON JUNGLE, THE SIXTH CENTURY...
...BUT THE ARCTIC CIRCLE IS THE PERFECT REFUGE. NOT TOO CLOSE TO CLARK'S OFFICE, NOT SO FAR THAT JIMMY'S SIGNAL WATCH CAN'T REACH.
AND PERFECT FOR A PRIVATE MEETING.
HELLO, KARA.
SUPERMAN.
IT'S MY PLACE, KARA. YOU CAN CALL ME KAL.
I GOT YOUR MESSAGE ON MONDAY. WHAT CAN I DO FOR YOU?
WHY WAS IT SO IMPORTANT TO MEET YOU HERE AT THIS EXACT TIME?
SO MANY COLORS TO CHOOSE FROM. GOLD, GREEN, WHITE...
KARA...?
...BUT THIS ONE'S MY FAVORITE.

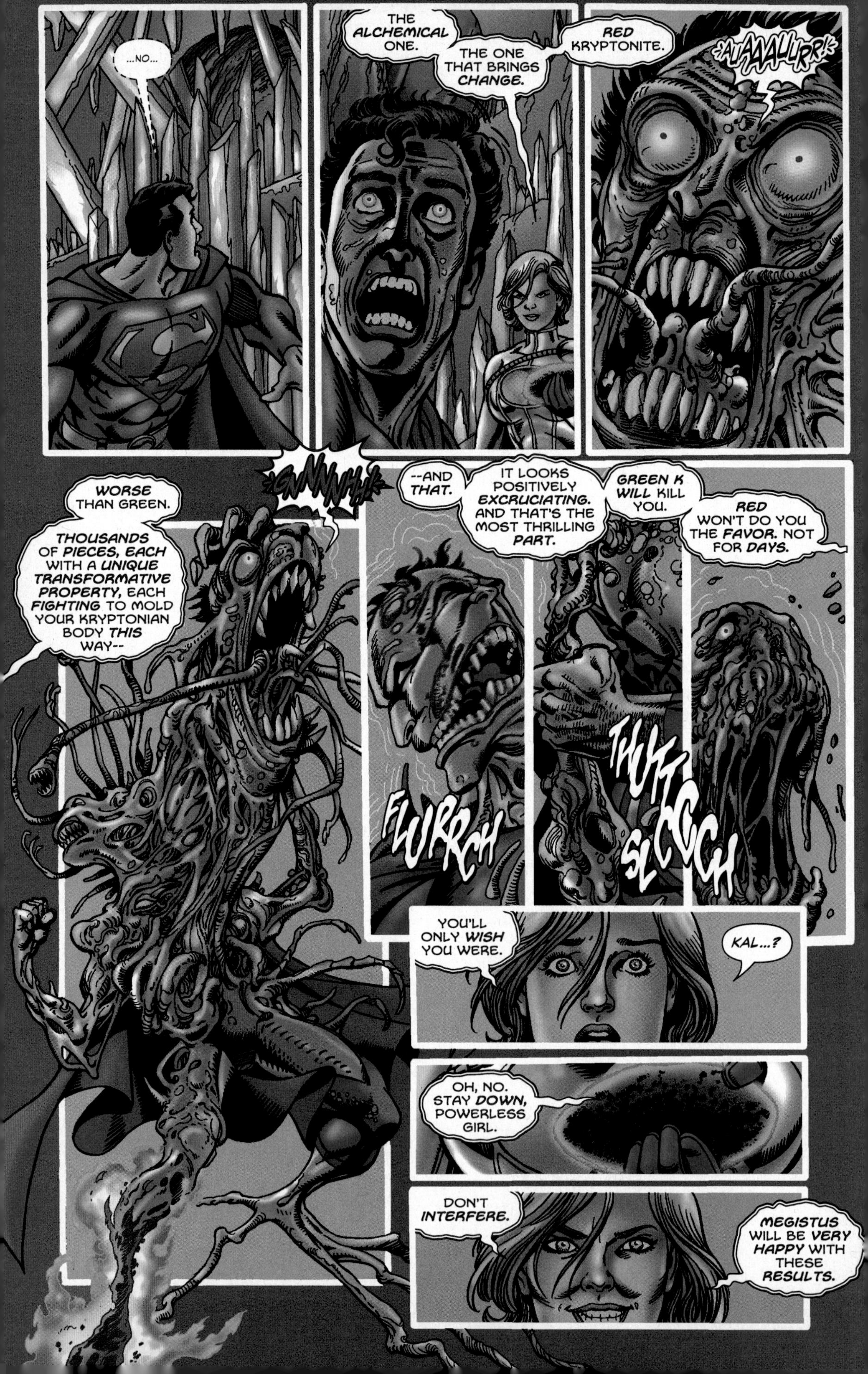

...NO...
THE ALCHEMICAL ONE.
THE ONE THAT BRINGS CHANGE.
RED KRYPTONITE.
AUAAAAUURR!
GNNNNH!
WORSE THAN GREEN.
THOUSANDS OF PIECES, EACH WITH A UNIQUE TRANSFORMATIVE PROPERTY, EACH FIGHTING TO MOLD YOUR KRYPTONIAN BODY THIS WAY--
--AND THAT.
IT LOOKS POSITIVELY EXCRUCIATING. AND THAT'S THE MOST THRILLING PART.
GREEN K WILL KILL YOU.
RED WON'T DO YOU THE FAVOR. NOT FOR DAYS.
FLURRCH
THUKKOOCH
SLCH
YOU'LL ONLY WISH YOU WERE.
KAL...?
OH, NO. STAY DOWN, POWERLESS GIRL.
DON'T INTERFERE.
MEGISTUS WILL BE VERY HAPPY WITH THESE RESULTS.

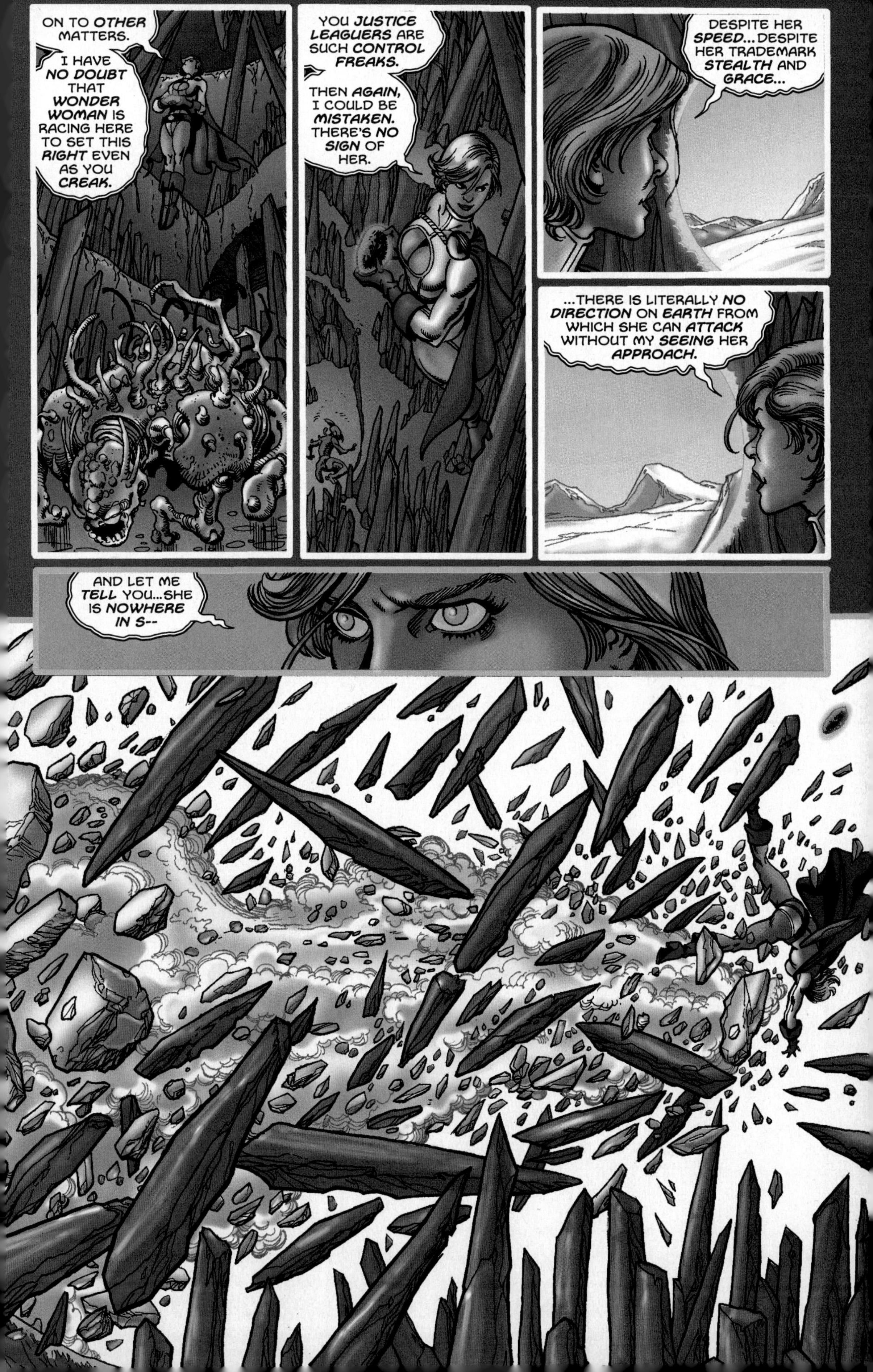
ON TO OTHER MATTERS.
I HAVE NO DOUBT THAT WONDER WOMAN IS RACING HERE TO SET THIS RIGHT EVEN AS YOU CREAK.
YOU JUSTICE LEAGUERS ARE SUCH CONTROL FREAKS.
THEN AGAIN, I COULD BE MISTAKEN. THERE'S NO SIGN OF HER.
DESPITE HER SPEED... DESPITE HER TRADEMARK STEALTH AND GRACE...
...THERE IS LITERALLY NO DIRECTION ON EARTH FROM WHICH SHE CAN ATTACK WITHOUT MY SEEING HER APPROACH.
AND LET ME TELL YOU...SHE IS NOWHERE IN S--

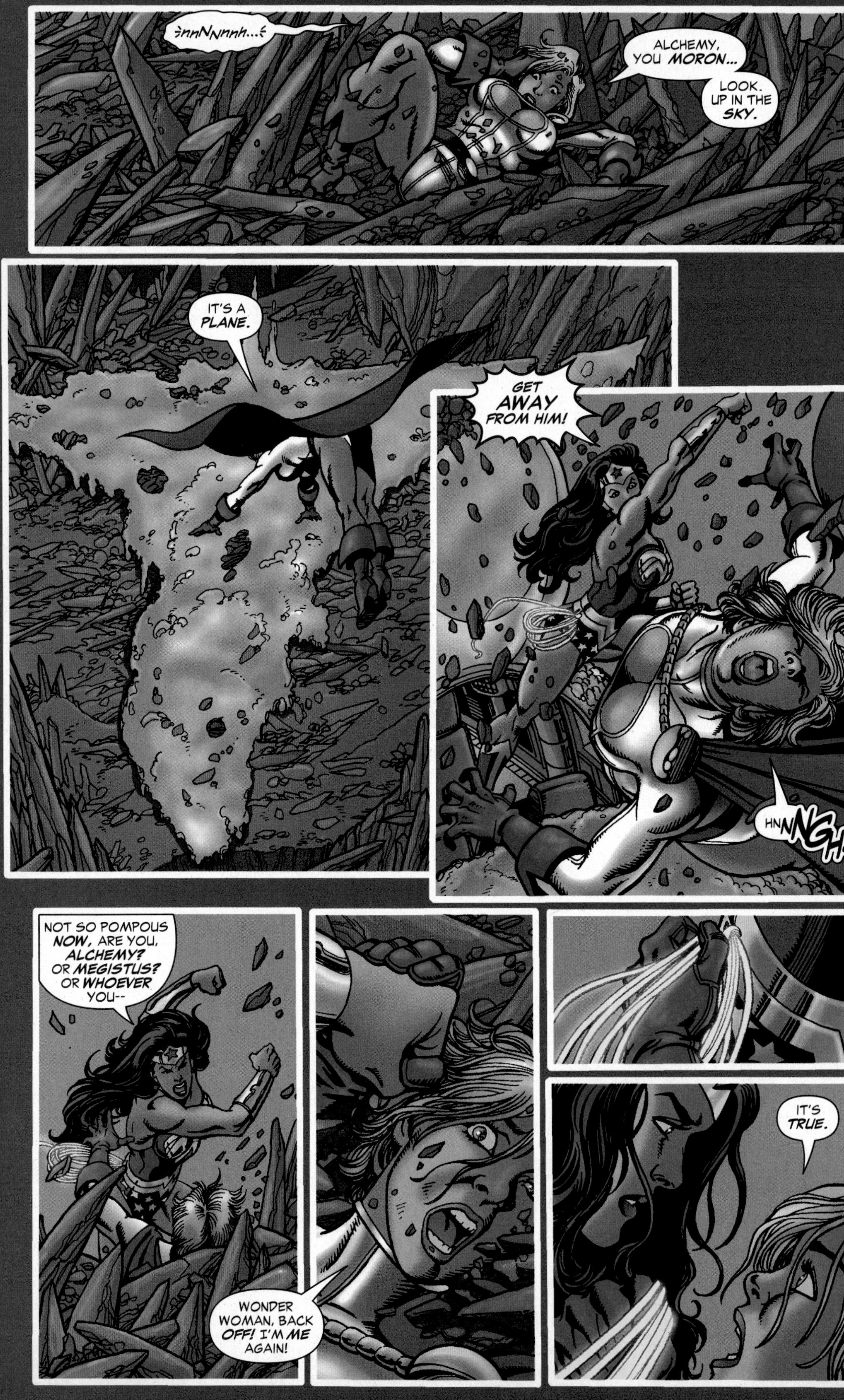
nnNnnnh...
ALCHEMY, YOU MORON...
LOOK. UP IN THE SKY.
IT'S A PLANE.
GET AWAY FROM HIM!
HNNNGH!
NOT SO POMPOUS NOW, ARE YOU, ALCHEMY? OR MEGISTUS? OR WHOEVER YOU--
WONDER WOMAN, BACK OFF! I'M ME AGAIN!
IT'S TRUE.

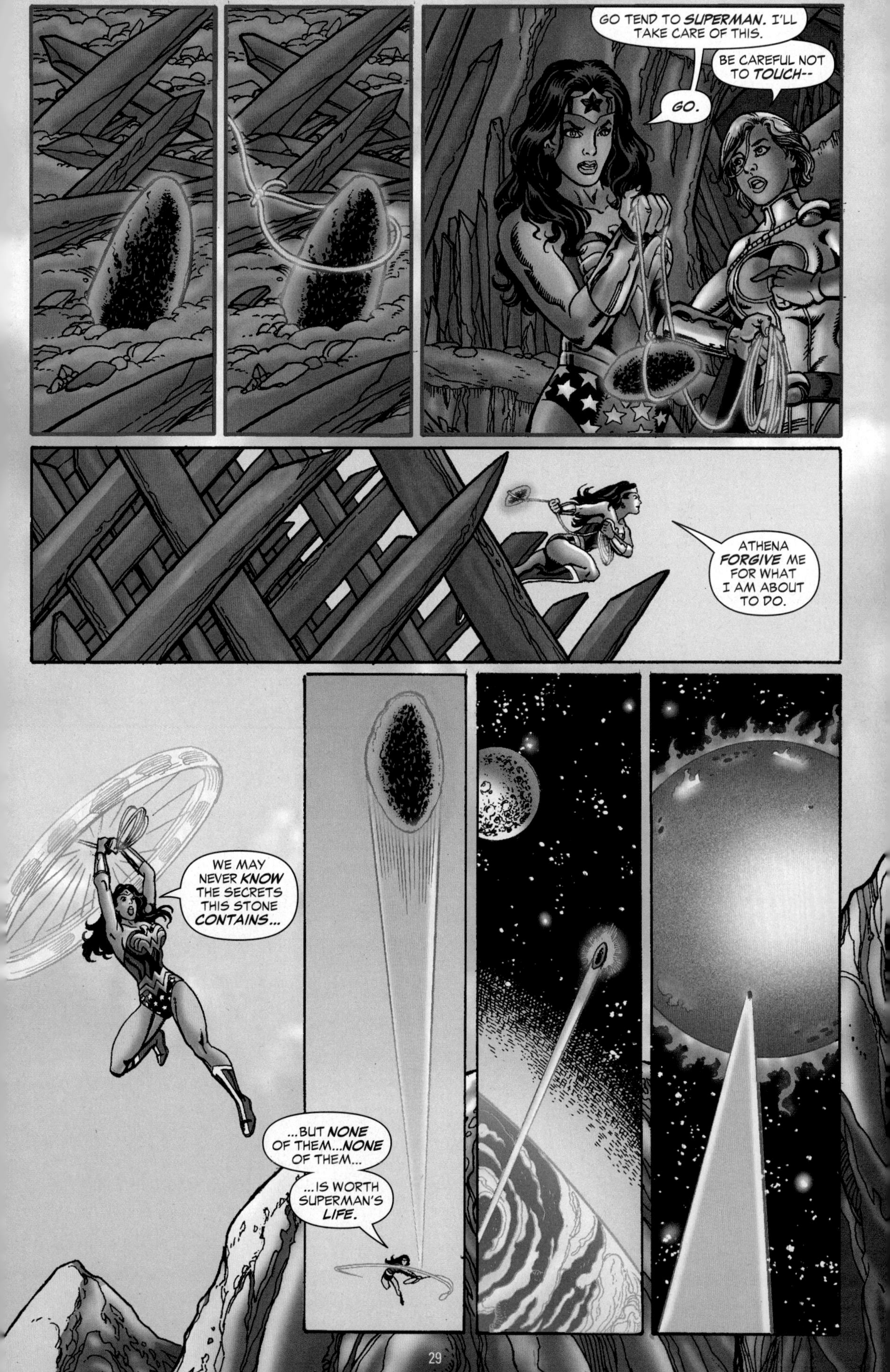
GO TEND TO SUPERMAN. I'LL TAKE CARE OF THIS.
BE CAREFUL NOT TO TOUCH--
GO.
ATHENA FORGIVE ME FOR WHAT I AM ABOUT TO DO.
WE MAY NEVER KNOW THE SECRETS THIS STONE CONTAINS...
...BUT NONE OF THEM...NONE OF THEM...
...IS WORTH SUPERMAN'S LIFE.

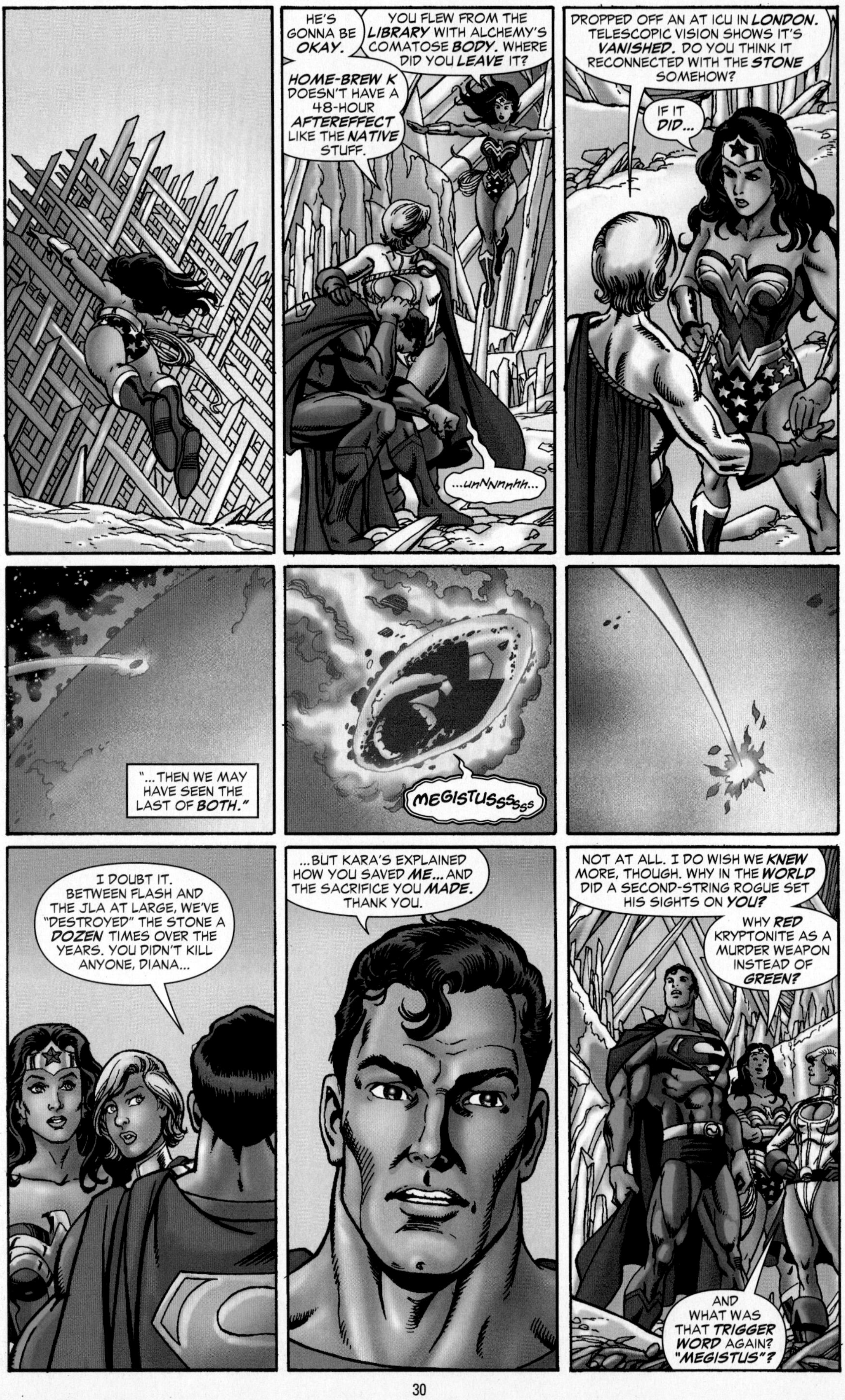
HE'S GONNA BE OKAY.
YOU FLEW FROM THE LIBRARY WITH ALCHEMY'S COMATOSE BODY. WHERE DID YOU LEAVE IT?
HOME-BREW K DOESN'T HAVE A 48-HOUR AFTEREFFECT LIKE THE NATIVE STUFF.
...unNNnnhh...
DROPPED OFF AN AT ICU IN LONDON. TELESCOPIC VISION SHOWS IT'S VANISHED. DO YOU THINK IT RECONNECTED WITH THE STONE SOMEHOW?
IF IT DID...
"...THEN WE MAY HAVE SEEN THE LAST OF BOTH."
MEGISTUSSsss
I DOUBT IT. BETWEEN FLASH AND THE JLA AT LARGE, WE'VE "DESTROYED" THE STONE A DOZEN TIMES OVER THE YEARS. YOU DIDN'T KILL ANYONE, DIANA...
...BUT KARA'S EXPLAINED HOW YOU SAVED ME... AND THE SACRIFICE YOU MADE. THANK YOU.
NOT AT ALL. I DO WISH WE KNEW MORE, THOUGH. WHY IN THE WORLD DID A SECOND-STRING ROGUE SET HIS SIGHTS ON YOU?
WHY RED KRYPTONITE AS A MURDER WEAPON INSTEAD OF GREEN?
AND WHAT WAS THAT TRIGGER WORD AGAIN? "MEGISTUS"?

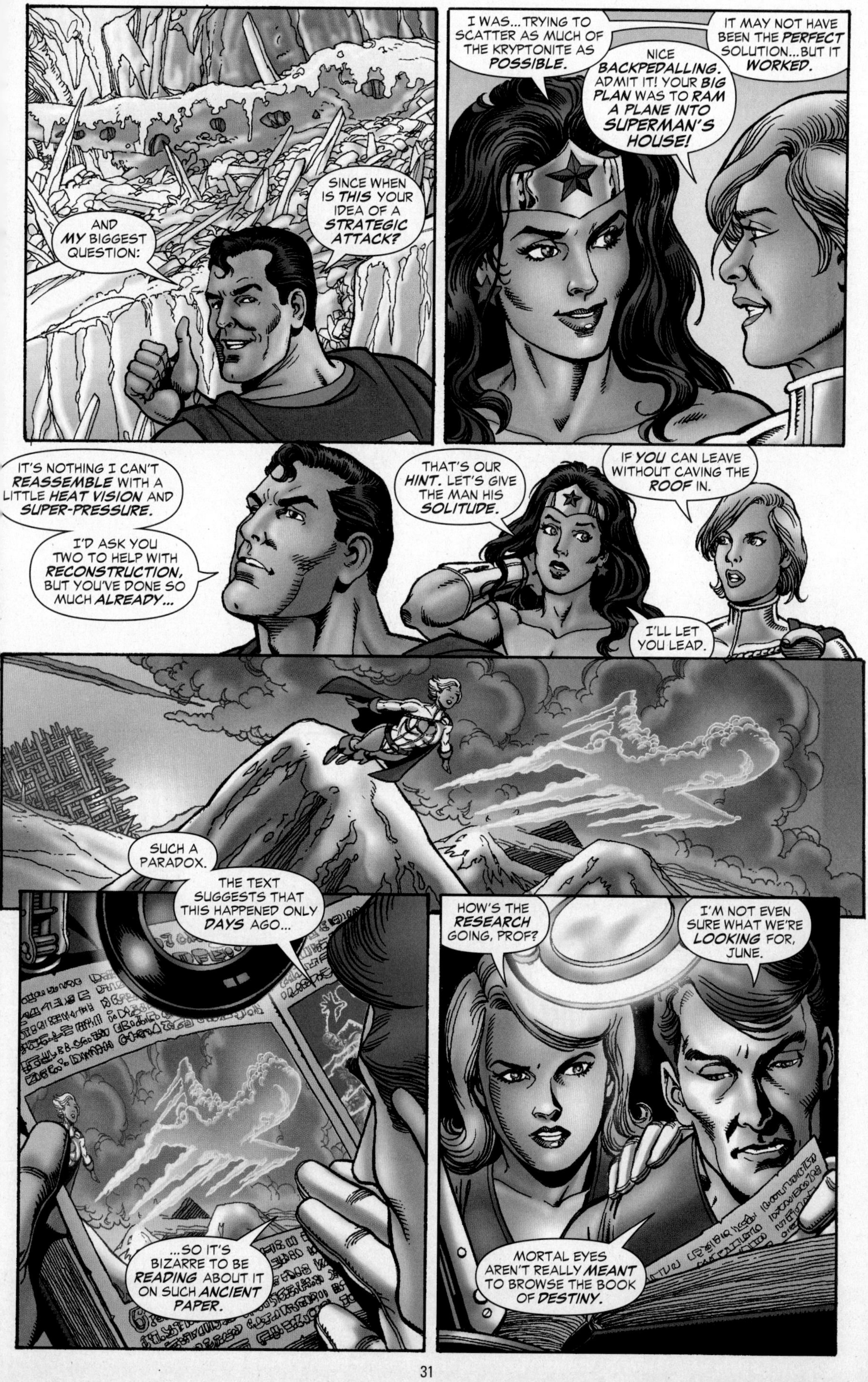
AND MY BIGGEST QUESTION:
SINCE WHEN IS THIS YOUR IDEA OF A STRATEGIC ATTACK?
I WAS...TRYING TO SCATTER AS MUCH OF THE KRYPTONITE AS POSSIBLE.
NICE BACKPEDALLING. ADMIT IT! YOUR BIG PLAN WAS TO RAM A PLANE INTO SUPERMAN'S HOUSE!
IT MAY NOT HAVE BEEN THE PERFECT SOLUTION...BUT IT WORKED.
IT'S NOTHING I CAN'T REASSEMBLE WITH A LITTLE HEAT VISION AND SUPER-PRESSURE.
I'D ASK YOU TWO TO HELP WITH RECONSTRUCTION, BUT YOU'VE DONE SO MUCH ALREADY...
THAT'S OUR HINT. LET'S GIVE THE MAN HIS SOLITUDE.
IF YOU CAN LEAVE WITHOUT CAVING THE ROOF IN.
I'LL LET YOU LEAD.
SUCH A PARADOX.
THE TEXT SUGGESTS THAT THIS HAPPENED ONLY DAYS AGO...
...SO IT'S BIZARRE TO BE READING ABOUT IT ON SUCH ANCIENT PAPER.
HOW'S THE RESEARCH GOING, PROF?
I'M NOT EVEN SURE WHAT WE'RE LOOKING FOR, JUNE.
MORTAL EYES AREN'T REALLY MEANT TO BROWSE THE BOOK OF DESTINY.

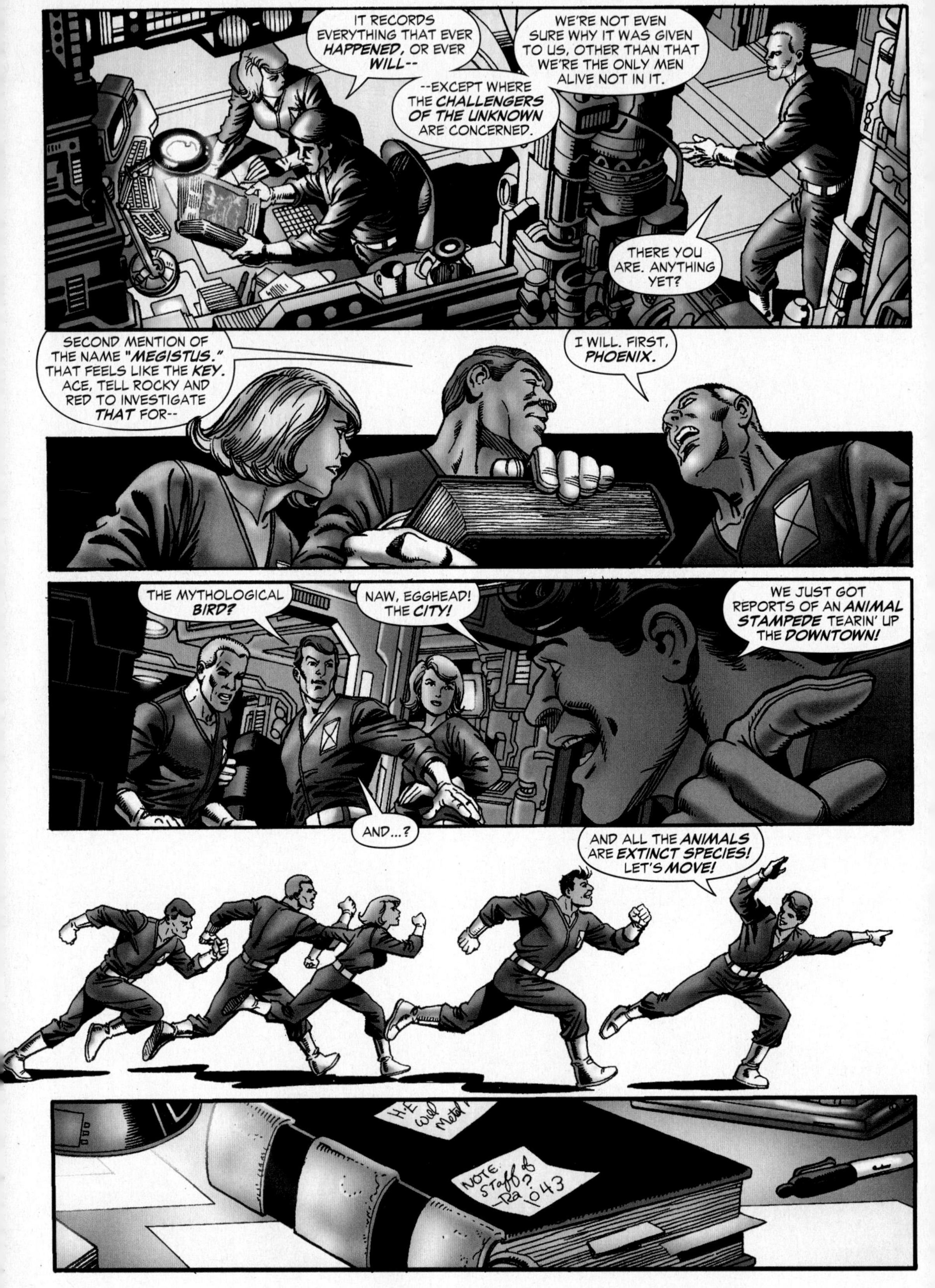
IT RECORDS EVERYTHING THAT EVER HAPPENED, OR EVER WILL--
WE'RE NOT EVEN SURE WHY IT WAS GIVEN TO US, OTHER THAN THAT WE'RE THE ONLY MEN ALIVE NOT IN IT.
--EXCEPT WHERE THE CHALLENGERS OF THE UNKNOWN ARE CONCERNED.
THERE YOU ARE. ANYTHING YET?
SECOND MENTION OF THE NAME "MEGISTUS." THAT FEELS LIKE THE KEY. ACE, TELL ROCKY AND RED TO INVESTIGATE THAT FOR--
I WILL. FIRST, PHOENIX.
THE MYTHOLOGICAL BIRD?
NAW, EGGHEAD! THE CITY!
WE JUST GOT REPORTS OF AN ANIMAL STAMPEDE TEARIN' UP THE DOWNTOWN!
AND...?
AND ALL THE ANIMALS ARE EXTINCT SPECIES! LET'S MOVE!
NOTE: Staff of Ra?

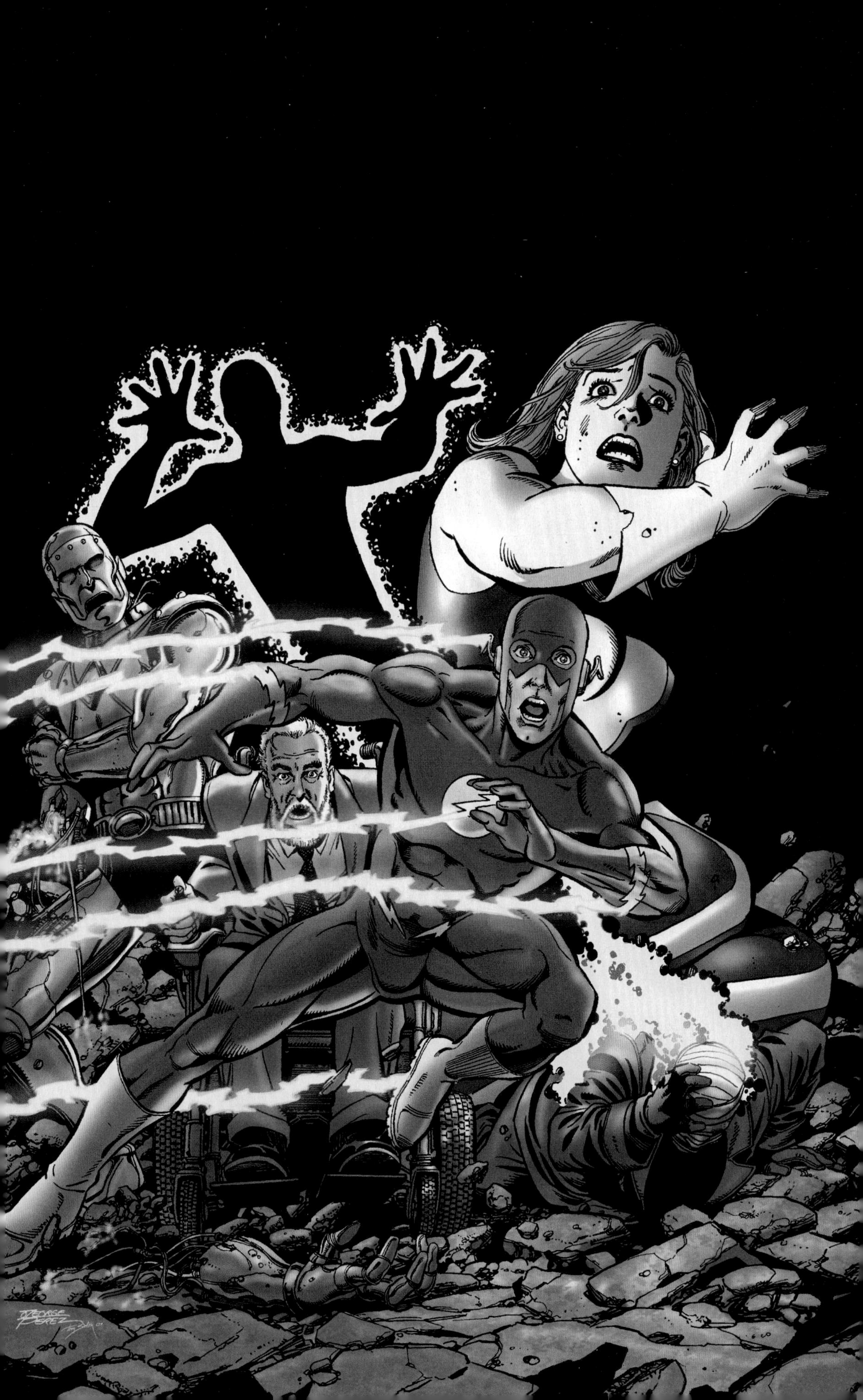

THE FLASH: THE FASTEST MAN ALIVE and DOOM PATROL

THE BOOK OF DESTINY: CHAPTER TWO: WALLY'S CHOICE

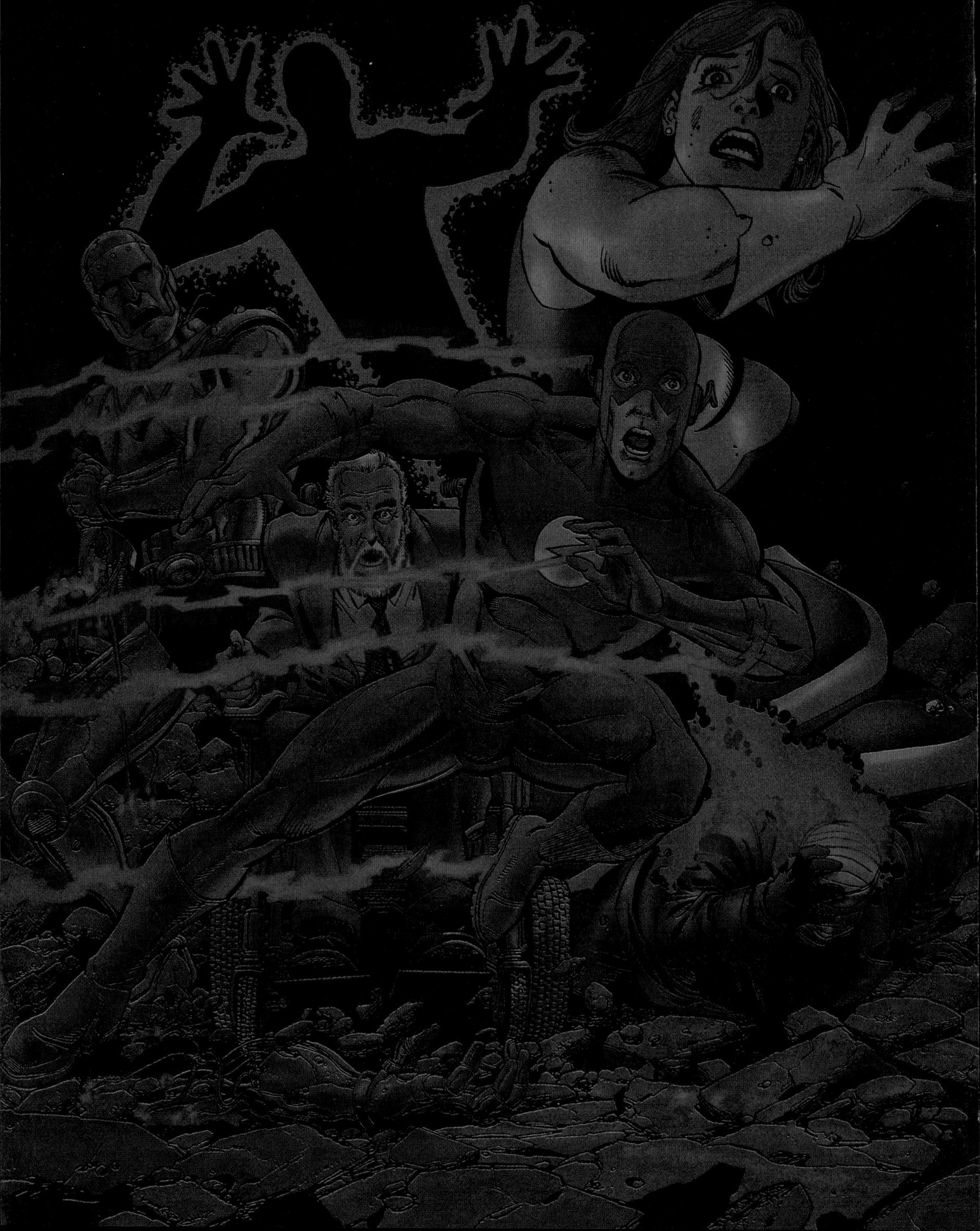

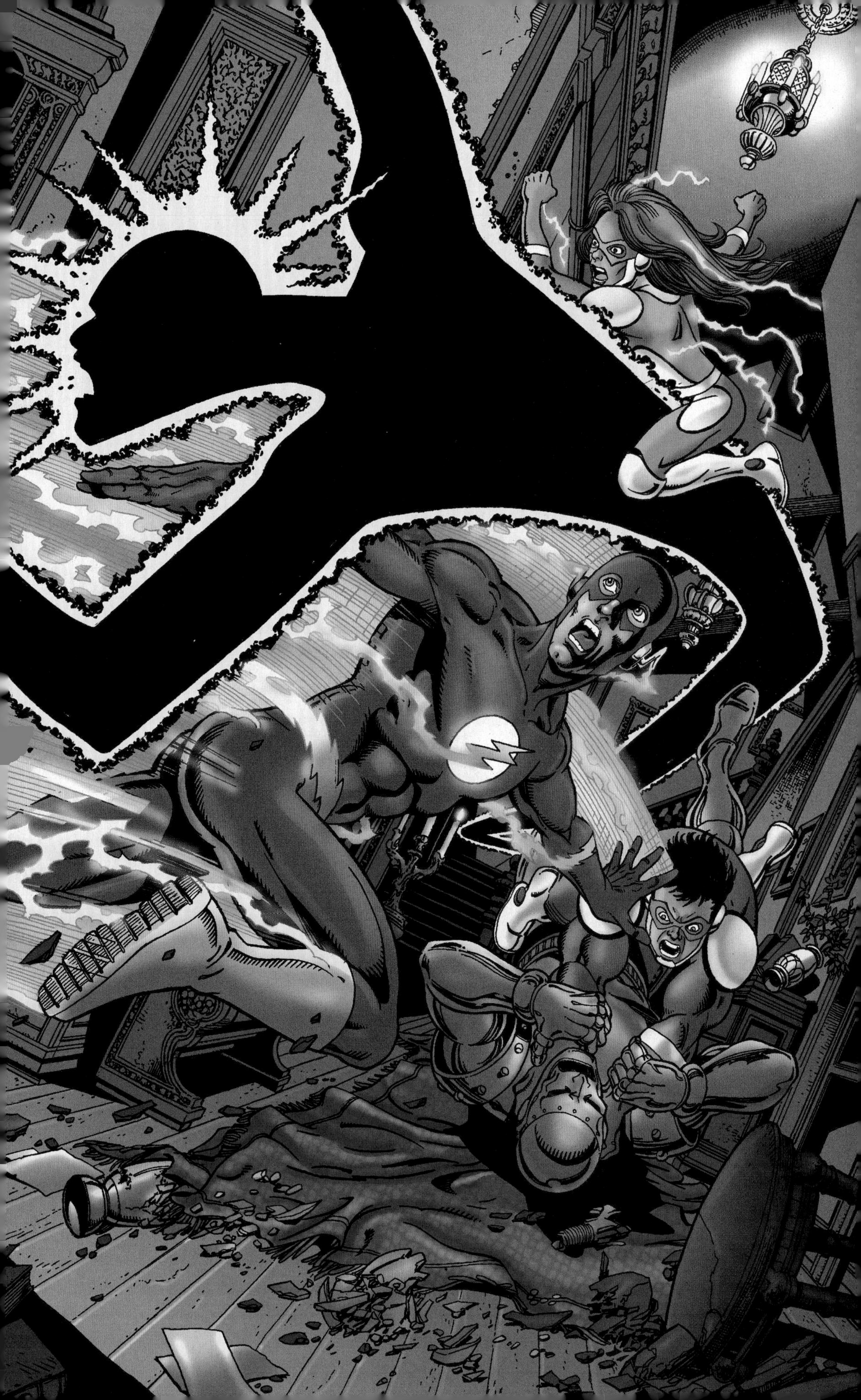

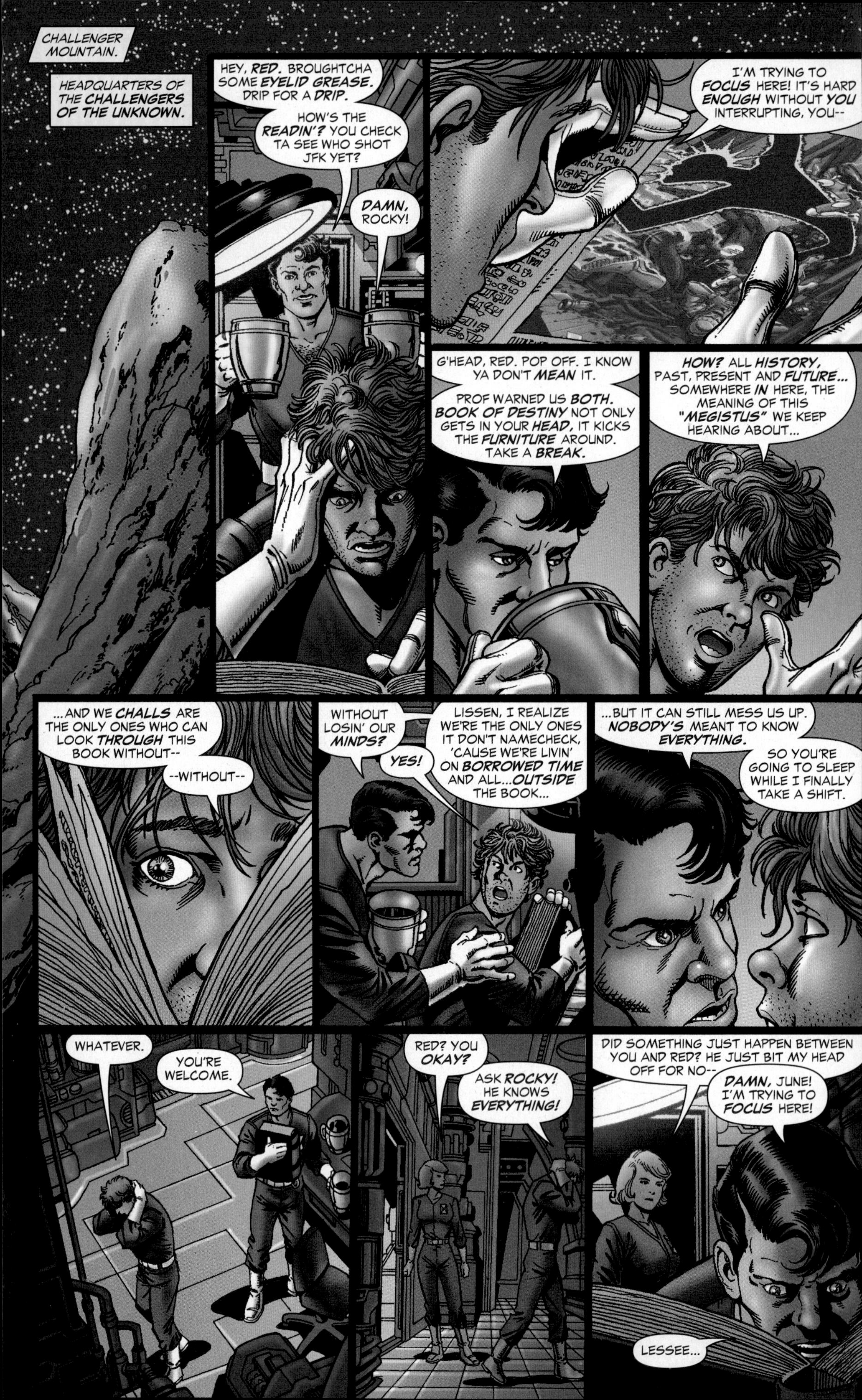
CHALLENGER MOUNTAIN.
HEADQUARTERS OF THE CHALLENGERS OF THE UNKNOWN.
HEY, RED. BROUGHTCHA SOME EYELID GREASE. DRIP FOR A DRIP.
HOW'S THE READIN'? YOU CHECK TA SEE WHO SHOT JFK YET?
DAMN, ROCKY!
I'M TRYING TO FOCUS HERE! IT'S HARD ENOUGH WITHOUT YOU INTERRUPTING, YOU--
G'HEAD, RED. POP OFF. I KNOW YA DON'T MEAN IT.
PROF WARNED US BOTH. BOOK OF DESTINY NOT ONLY GETS IN YOUR HEAD, IT KICKS THE FURNITURE AROUND. TAKE A BREAK.
HOW? ALL HISTORY, PAST, PRESENT AND FUTURE... SOMEWHERE IN HERE, THE MEANING OF THIS "MEGISTUS" WE KEEP HEARING ABOUT...
...AND WE CHALLS ARE THE ONLY ONES WHO CAN LOOK THROUGH THIS BOOK WITHOUT--
--WITHOUT--
WITHOUT LOSIN' OUR MINDS?
YES!
LISSEN, I REALIZE WE'RE THE ONLY ONES IT DON'T NAMECHECK, 'CAUSE WE'RE LIVIN' ON BORROWED TIME AND ALL...OUTSIDE THE BOOK...
...BUT IT CAN STILL MESS US UP. NOBODY'S MEANT TO KNOW EVERYTHING.
SO YOU'RE GOING TO SLEEP WHILE I FINALLY TAKE A SHIFT.
WHATEVER.
YOU'RE WELCOME.
RED? YOU OKAY?
ASK ROCKY! HE KNOWS EVERYTHING!
DID SOMETHING JUST HAPPEN BETWEEN YOU AND RED? HE JUST BIT MY HEAD OFF FOR NO--
DAMN, JUNE! I'M TRYING TO FOCUS HERE!
LESSEE...

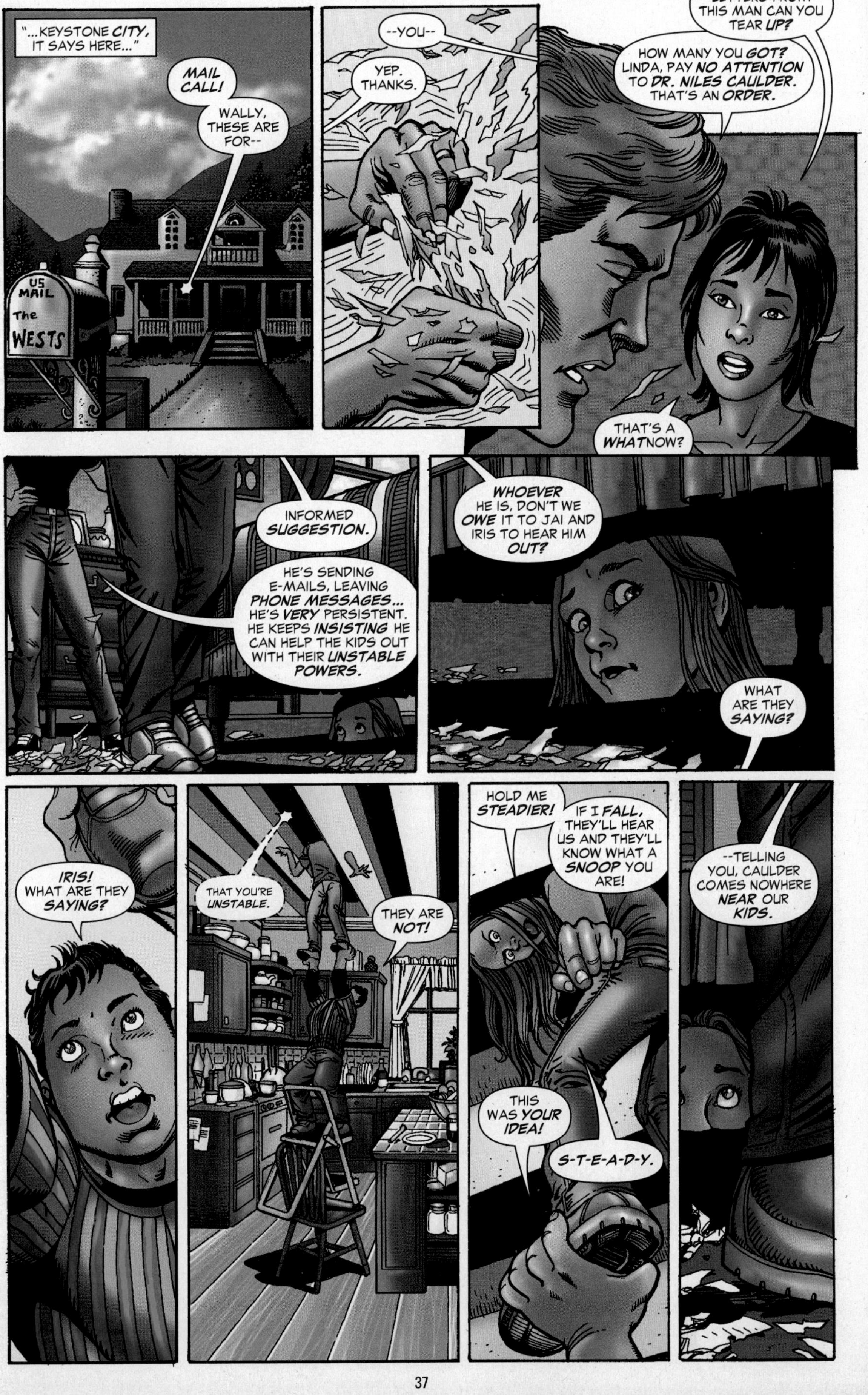
"...KEYSTONE CITY, IT SAYS HERE..."
MAIL CALL!
WALLY, THESE ARE FOR--
US MAIL The WESTS
--YOU--
YEP. THANKS.
HOW MANY LETTERS FROM THIS MAN CAN YOU TEAR UP?
HOW MANY YOU GOT? LINDA, PAY NO ATTENTION TO DR. NILES CAULDER. THAT'S AN ORDER.
THAT'S A WHATNOW?
INFORMED SUGGESTION.
HE'S SENDING E-MAILS, LEAVING PHONE MESSAGES... HE'S VERY PERSISTENT. HE KEEPS INSISTING HE CAN HELP THE KIDS OUT WITH THEIR UNSTABLE POWERS.
WHOEVER HE IS, DON'T WE OWE IT TO JAI AND IRIS TO HEAR HIM OUT?
WHAT ARE THEY SAYING?
IRIS! WHAT ARE THEY SAYING?
THAT YOU'RE UNSTABLE.
THEY ARE NOT!
HOLD ME STEADIER!
IF I FALL, THEY'LL HEAR US AND THEY'LL KNOW WHAT A SNOOP YOU ARE!
THIS WAS YOUR IDEA!
S-T-E-A-D-Y.
--TELLING YOU, CAULDER COMES NOWHERE NEAR OUR KIDS.

HE'S A **DOCTOR.**

SO WAS **FRANKENSTEIN.**

AND HE WAS LESS **MANIPULATIVE.** HONEY...

I DON'T UNDERSTAND. HE RUNS THE **DOOM PATROL,** RIGHT? AND YOU'VE SAID BEFORE THAT THEY'RE THE **GOOD GUYS...**

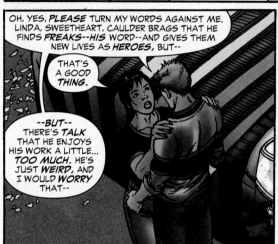

OH, YES, **PLEASE** TURN MY WORDS AGAINST ME. LINDA, SWEETHEART, CAULDER BRAGS THAT HE FINDS **FREAKS**--HIS WORD--AND GIVES THEM NEW LIVES AS **HEROES,** BUT--

THAT'S A GOOD **THING.**

--BUT-- THERE'S **TALK** THAT HE ENJOYS HIS WORK A LITTLE... **TOO MUCH.** HE'S JUST **WEIRD,** AND I WOULD **WORRY** THAT--

KRASH

NO! PLEASE--!

KIDS? YOU ALL RIGHT DOWN THERE?

FINE, DAD! JAI WAS JUST BEING **CLUMSY!**

HOW COME IT'S ALWAYS **MY** FAULT...?

WALLY, **PLEASE.** I'M SICK OF JUMPING AT EVERY **NOISE** THEY MAKE, THINKING "IS IT ANOTHER **MUTATION?** OR **WORSE?**" **I'M** THE ONE WATCHING THEIR **HEALTH,** AND I'M **BARELY** QUALIFIED. I NEED **HELP.**

YOU'RE RIGHT. I'M SORRY. LET'S HEAR CAULDER **OUT,** AND IF WE GET THE CRAWLIES FOR **ONE SECOND,** WE CAN BE **OUT** OF THERE.

I'LL CALL THE JLA AND ARRANGE A QUICK **TELEPORT** TO CAULDER'S **DIGS.**

LET'S SUIT **UP.**

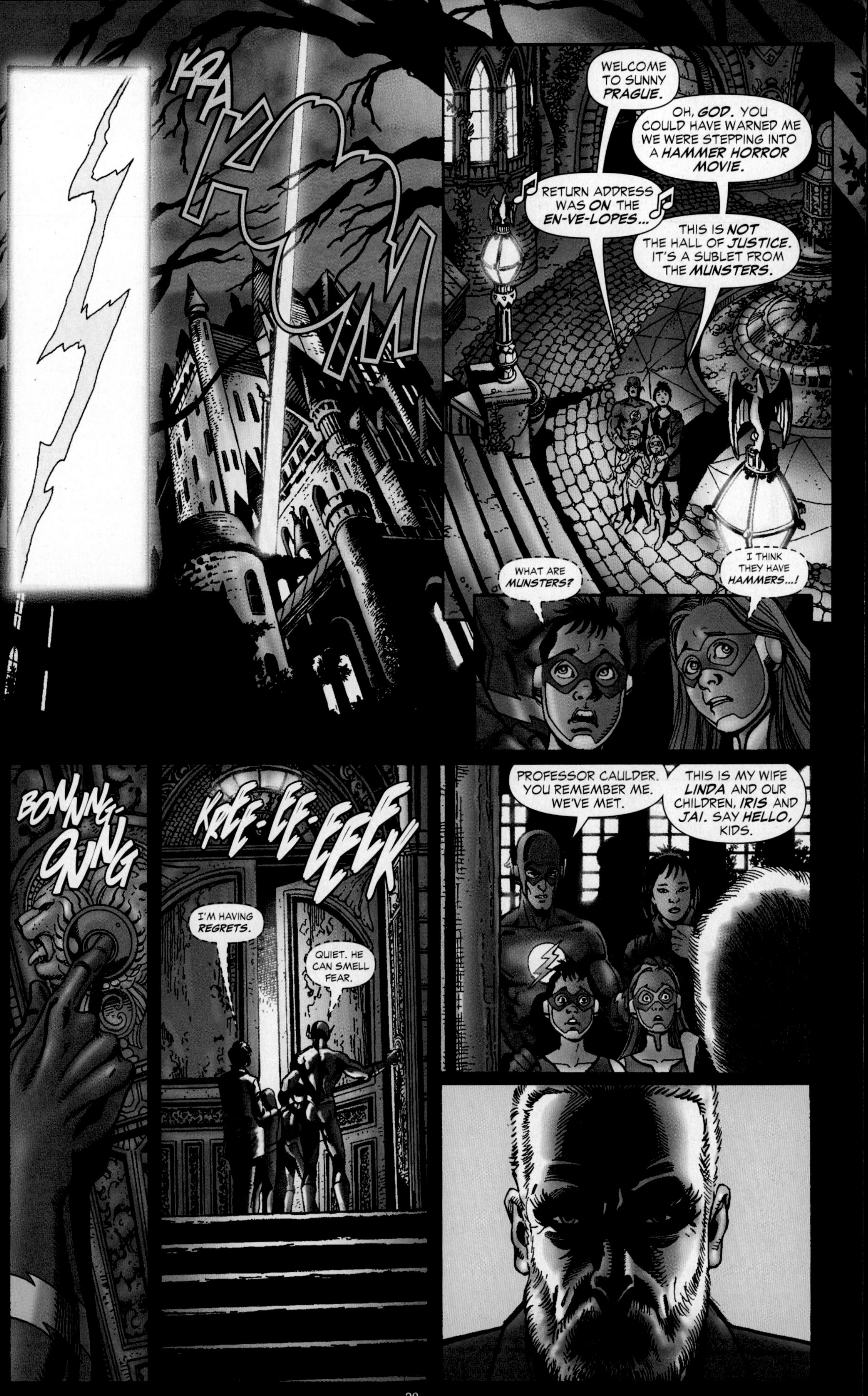
KRA KOOM
WELCOME TO SUNNY PRAGUE.
OH, GOD. YOU COULD HAVE WARNED ME WE WERE STEPPING INTO A HAMMER HORROR MOVIE.
RETURN ADDRESS WAS ON THE EN-VE-LOPES...
THIS IS NOT THE HALL OF JUSTICE. IT'S A SUBLET FROM THE MUNSTERS.
WHAT ARE MUNSTERS?
I THINK THEY HAVE HAMMERS...!
BONNNG-GUNG
KREE-EE-EEEK
I'M HAVING REGRETS.
QUIET. HE CAN SMELL FEAR.
PROFESSOR CAULDER. YOU REMEMBER ME. WE'VE MET.
THIS IS MY WIFE LINDA AND OUR CHILDREN, IRIS AND JAI. SAY HELLO, KIDS.

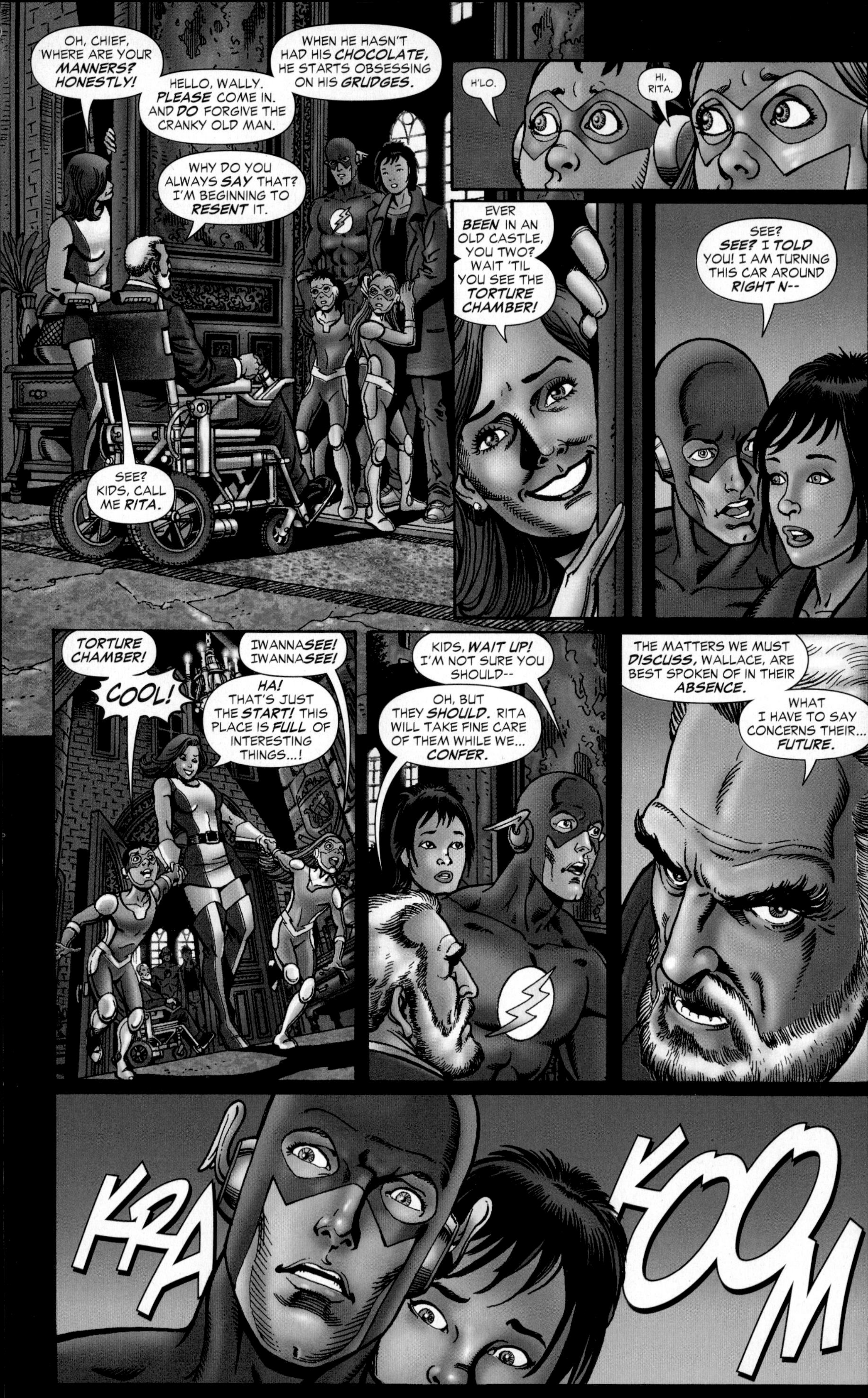
OH, CHIEF, WHERE ARE YOUR MANNERS? HONESTLY!
HELLO, WALLY. PLEASE COME IN. AND DO FORGIVE THE CRANKY OLD MAN.
WHEN HE HASN'T HAD HIS CHOCOLATE, HE STARTS OBSESSING ON HIS GRUDGES.
WHY DO YOU ALWAYS SAY THAT? I'M BEGINNING TO RESENT IT.
SEE? KIDS, CALL ME RITA.
H'LO.
HI, RITA.
EVER BEEN IN AN OLD CASTLE, YOU TWO? WAIT 'TIL YOU SEE THE TORTURE CHAMBER!
SEE? SEE? I TOLD YOU! I AM TURNING THIS CAR AROUND RIGHT N--
TORTURE CHAMBER!
COOL!
IWANNASEE! IWANNASEE!
HA! THAT'S JUST THE START! THIS PLACE IS FULL OF INTERESTING THINGS...!
KIDS, WAIT UP! I'M NOT SURE YOU SHOULD--
OH, BUT THEY SHOULD. RITA WILL TAKE FINE CARE OF THEM WHILE WE... CONFER.
THE MATTERS WE MUST DISCUSS, WALLACE, ARE BEST SPOKEN OF IN THEIR ABSENCE.
WHAT I HAVE TO SAY CONCERNS THEIR... FUTURE.
KRA
KOOM

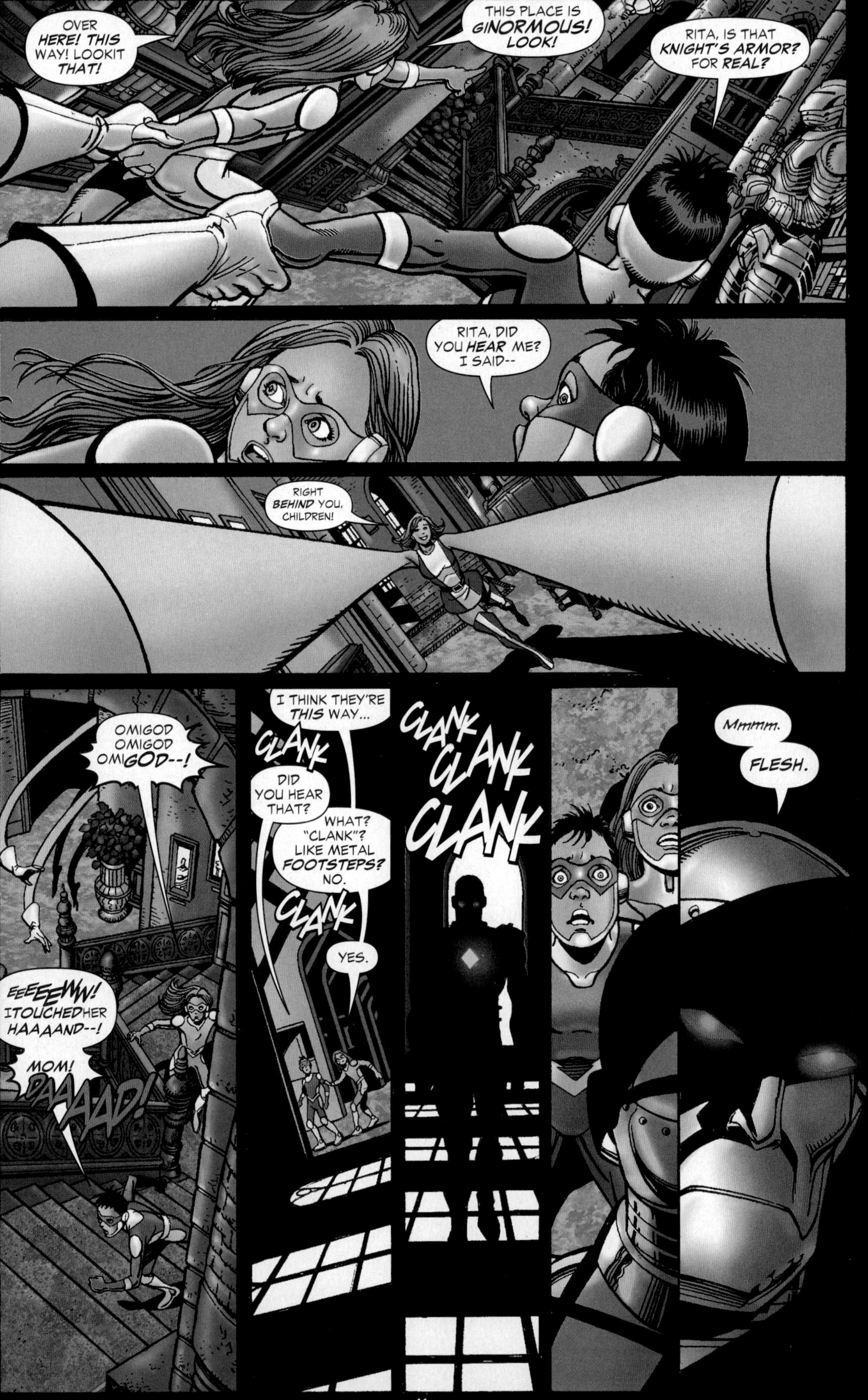

OVER HERE! THIS WAY! LOOKIT THAT!
THIS PLACE IS GINORMOUS! LOOK!
RITA, IS THAT KNIGHT'S ARMOR? FOR REAL?
RITA, DID YOU HEAR ME? I SAID--
RIGHT BEHIND YOU, CHILDREN!
OMIGOD OMIGOD OMIGOD--!
EEEEEWW! ITOUCHEDHER HAAAAND--!
MOM! DAAAAD!
I THINK THEY'RE THIS WAY...
CLANK
DID YOU HEAR THAT?
WHAT? "CLANK"? LIKE METAL FOOTSTEPS? NO.
CLANK
YES.
CLANK CLANK CLANK
Mmmm.
FLESH.

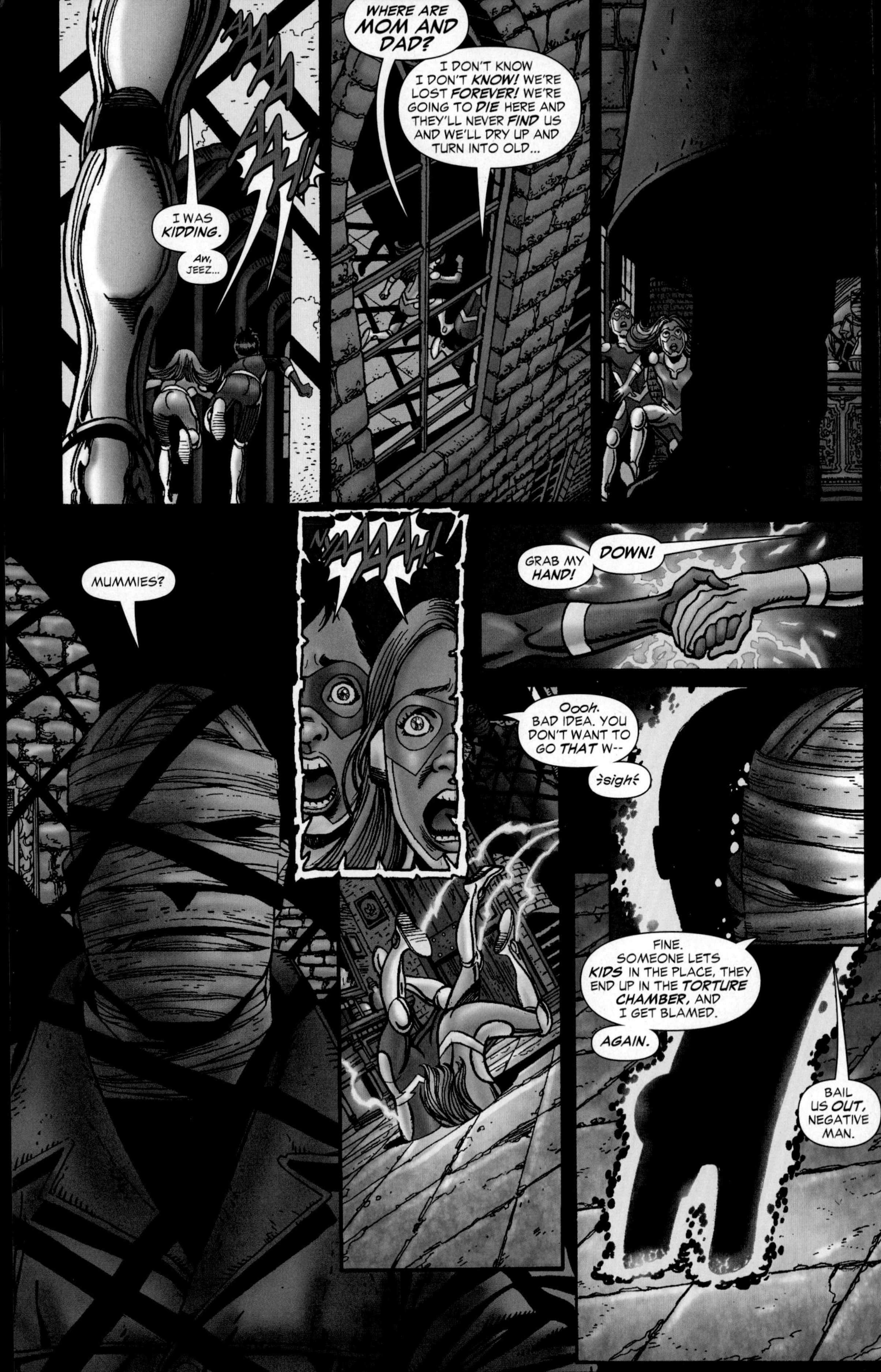
NYAAAAAH!
I WAS KIDDING.
AW, JEEZ...
WHERE ARE MOM AND DAD?
I DON'T KNOW I DON'T KNOW! WE'RE LOST FOREVER! WE'RE GOING TO DIE HERE AND THEY'LL NEVER FIND US AND WE'LL DRY UP AND TURN INTO OLD...
MUMMIES?
NYAAAAAH!
GRAB MY HAND!
DOWN!
Oooh. BAD IDEA. YOU DON'T WANT TO GO THAT W--
sigh
FINE. SOMEONE LETS KIDS IN THE PLACE, THEY END UP IN THE TORTURE CHAMBER, AND I GET BLAMED.
AGAIN.
BAIL US OUT, NEGATIVE MAN.

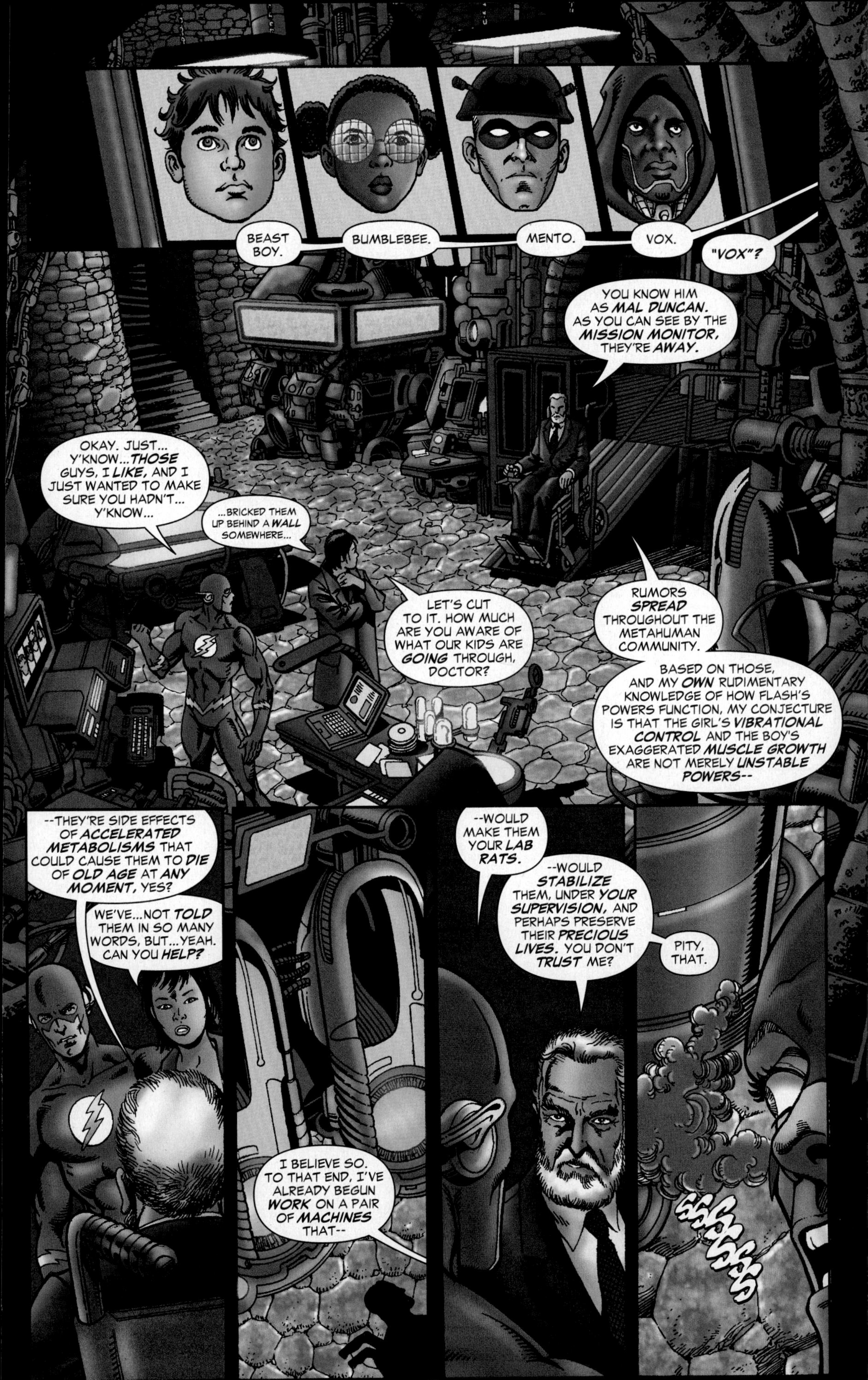
BEAST BOY.
BUMBLEBEE.
MENTO.
VOX.
"VOX"?
YOU KNOW HIM AS MAL DUNCAN. AS YOU CAN SEE BY THE MISSION MONITOR, THEY'RE AWAY.
OKAY. JUST... Y'KNOW...THOSE GUYS, I LIKE, AND I JUST WANTED TO MAKE SURE YOU HADN'T... Y'KNOW...
...BRICKED THEM UP BEHIND A WALL SOMEWHERE...
LET'S CUT TO IT. HOW MUCH ARE YOU AWARE OF WHAT OUR KIDS ARE GOING THROUGH, DOCTOR?
RUMORS SPREAD THROUGHOUT THE METAHUMAN COMMUNITY.
BASED ON THOSE, AND MY OWN RUDIMENTARY KNOWLEDGE OF HOW FLASH'S POWERS FUNCTION, MY CONJECTURE IS THAT THE GIRL'S VIBRATIONAL CONTROL AND THE BOY'S EXAGGERATED MUSCLE GROWTH ARE NOT MERELY UNSTABLE POWERS--
--THEY'RE SIDE EFFECTS OF ACCELERATED METABOLISMS THAT COULD CAUSE THEM TO DIE OF OLD AGE AT ANY MOMENT, YES?
WE'VE...NOT TOLD THEM IN SO MANY WORDS, BUT...YEAH. CAN YOU HELP?
I BELIEVE SO. TO THAT END, I'VE ALREADY BEGUN WORK ON A PAIR OF MACHINES THAT--
--WOULD MAKE THEM YOUR LAB RATS.
--WOULD STABILIZE THEM, UNDER YOUR SUPERVISION, AND PERHAPS PRESERVE THEIR PRECIOUS LIVES. YOU DON'T TRUST ME?
PITY, THAT.
SSSSSSSSS

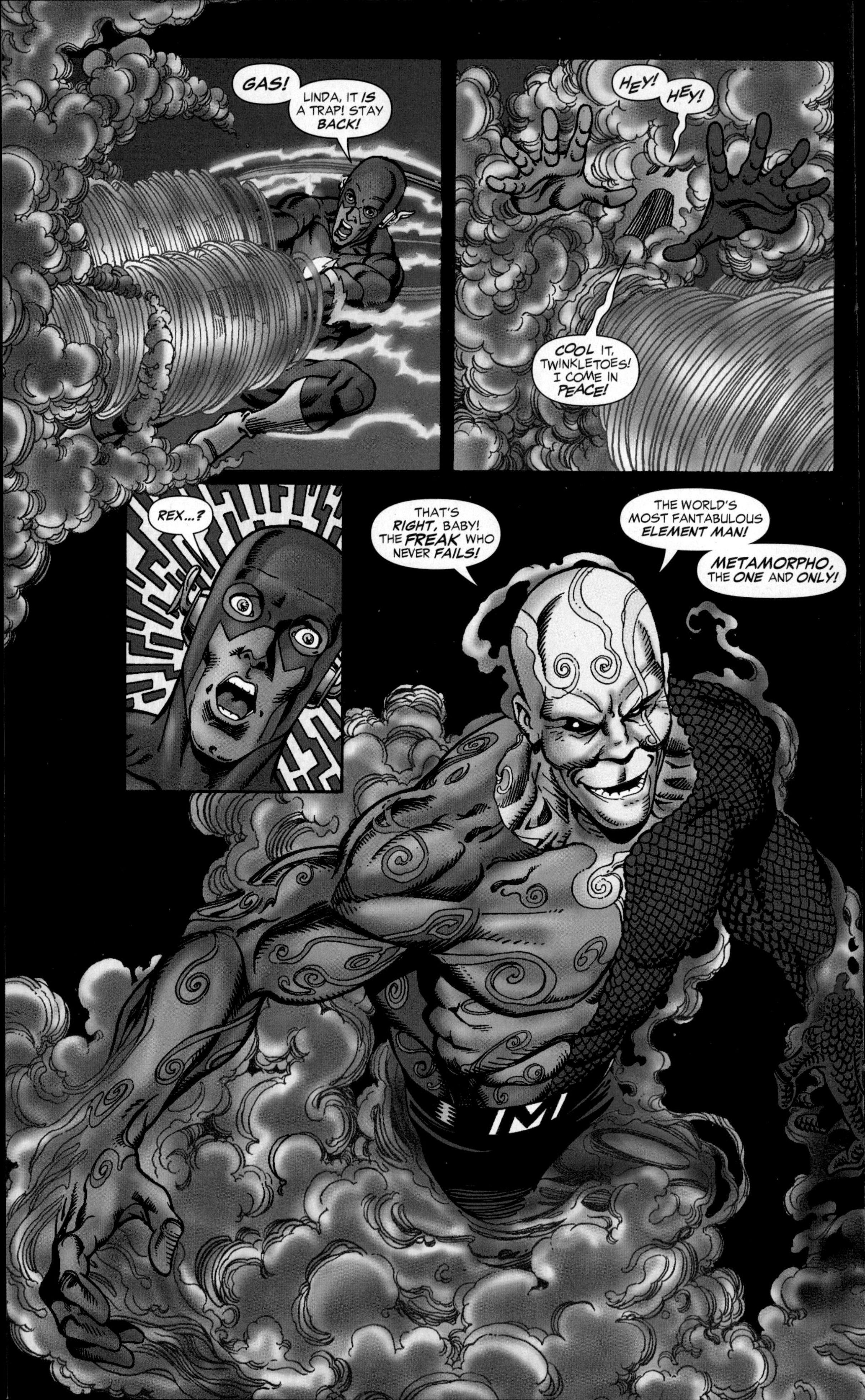

GAS!
LINDA, IT IS A TRAP! STAY BACK!
HEY! HEY!
COOL IT, TWINKLETOES! I COME IN PEACE!
REX...?
THAT'S RIGHT, BABY! THE FREAK WHO NEVER FAILS!
THE WORLD'S MOST FANTABULOUS ELEMENT MAN!
METAMORPHO, THE ONE AND ONLY!

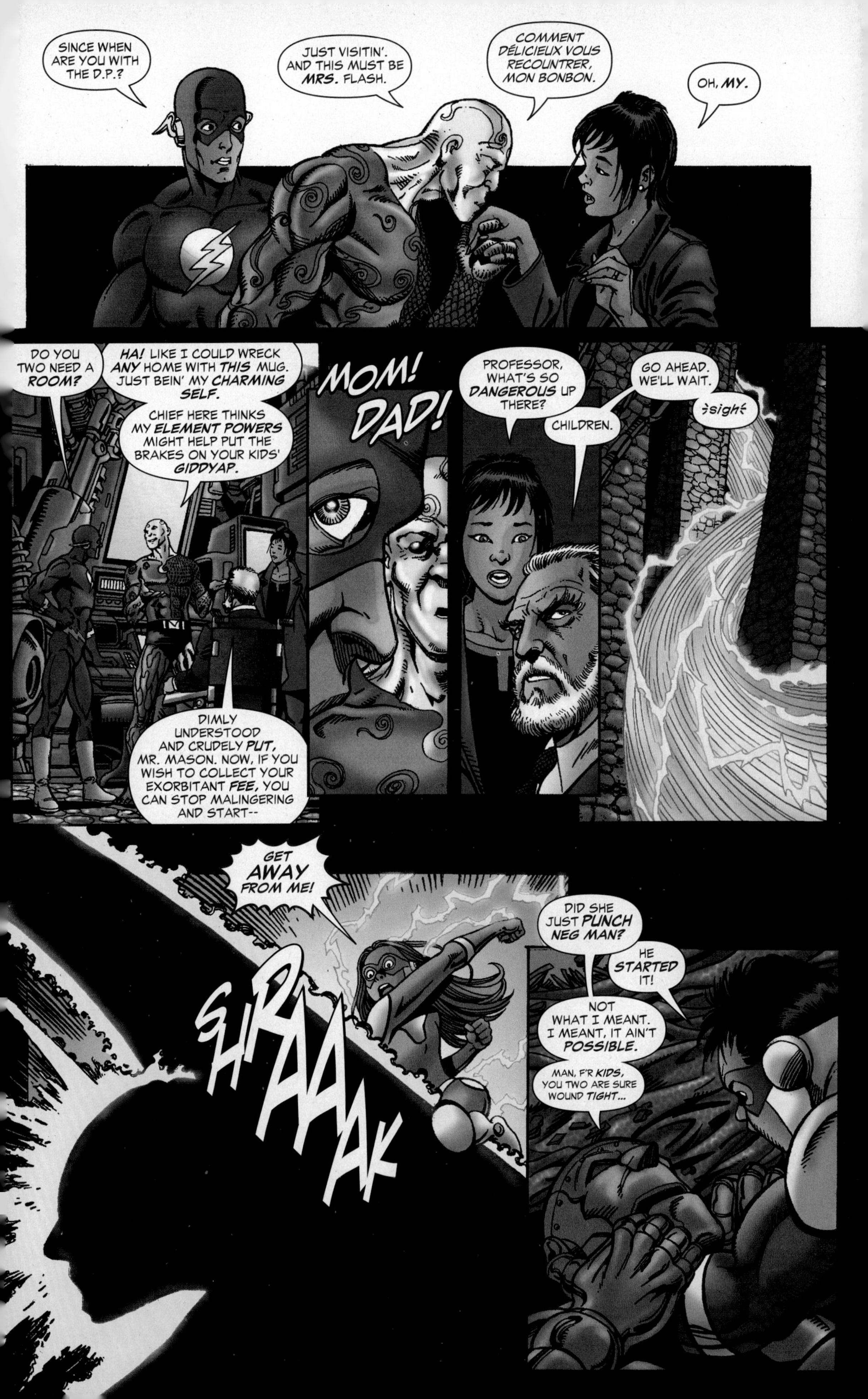

SINCE WHEN ARE YOU WITH THE D.P.?
JUST VISITIN'. AND THIS MUST BE MRS. FLASH.
COMMENT DÉLICIEUX VOUS RECOUNTRER, MON BONBON.
OH, MY.
DO YOU TWO NEED A ROOM?
HA! LIKE I COULD WRECK ANY HOME WITH THIS MUG. JUST BEIN' MY CHARMING SELF.
CHIEF HERE THINKS MY ELEMENT POWERS MIGHT HELP PUT THE BRAKES ON YOUR KIDS' GIDDYAP.
DIMLY UNDERSTOOD AND CRUDELY PUT, MR. MASON. NOW, IF YOU WISH TO COLLECT YOUR EXORBITANT FEE, YOU CAN STOP MALINGERING AND START--
MOM! DAD!
PROFESSOR, WHAT'S SO DANGEROUS UP THERE?
CHILDREN.
GO AHEAD. WE'LL WAIT.
sigh
GET AWAY FROM ME!
SHRAAAK
DID SHE JUST PUNCH NEG MAN?
HE STARTED IT!
NOT WHAT I MEANT. I MEANT, IT AIN'T POSSIBLE.
MAN, F'R KIDS, YOU TWO ARE SURE WOUND TIGHT...

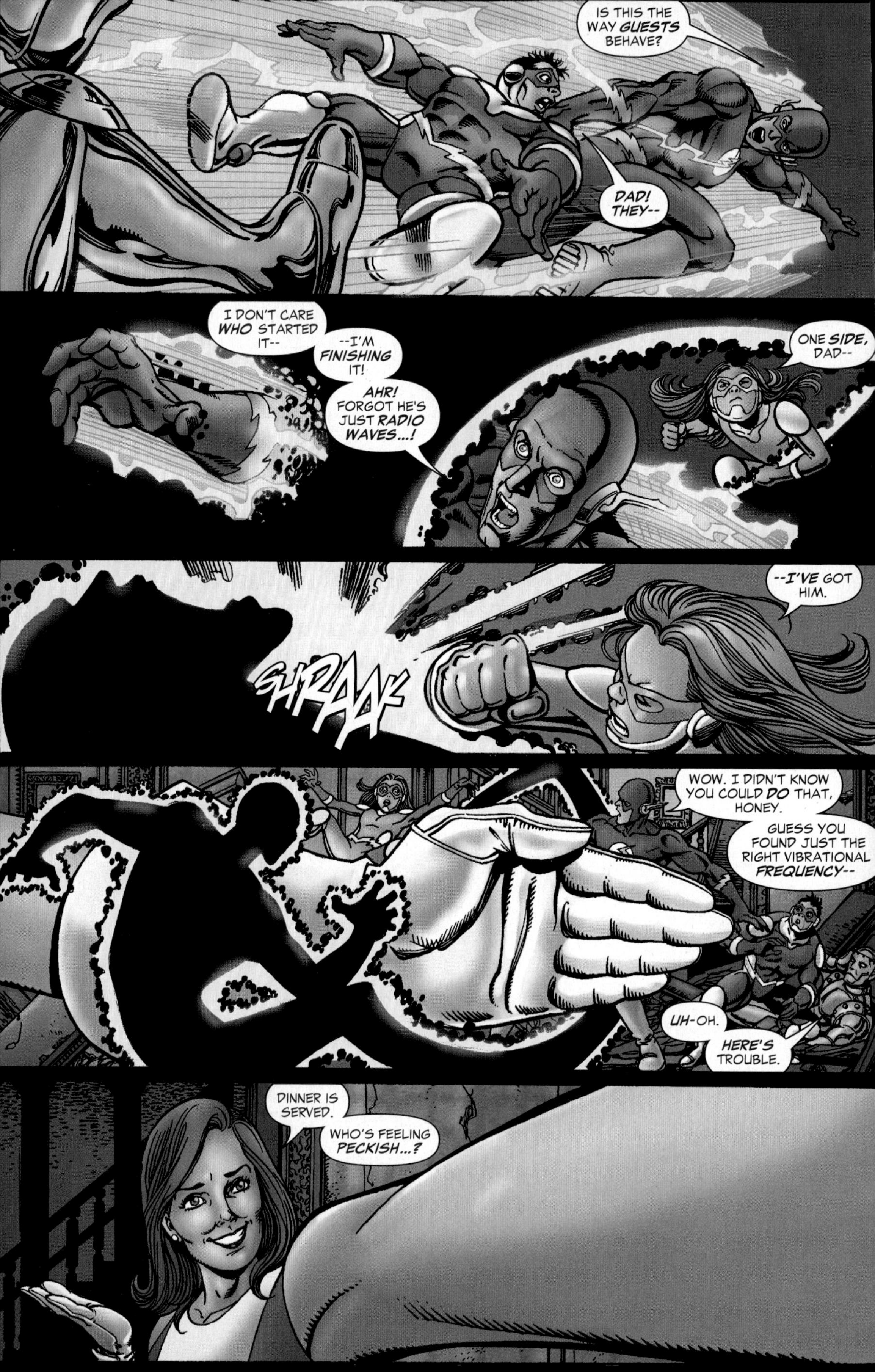
IS THIS THE WAY GUESTS BEHAVE?
DAD! THEY--
I DON'T CARE WHO STARTED IT--
--I'M FINISHING IT!
AHR! FORGOT HE'S JUST RADIO WAVES...!
ONE SIDE, DAD--
--I'VE GOT HIM.
SHRAAK
WOW. I DIDN'T KNOW YOU COULD DO THAT, HONEY.
GUESS YOU FOUND JUST THE RIGHT VIBRATIONAL FREQUENCY--
UH-OH.
HERE'S TROUBLE.
DINNER IS SERVED.
WHO'S FEELING PECKISH...?

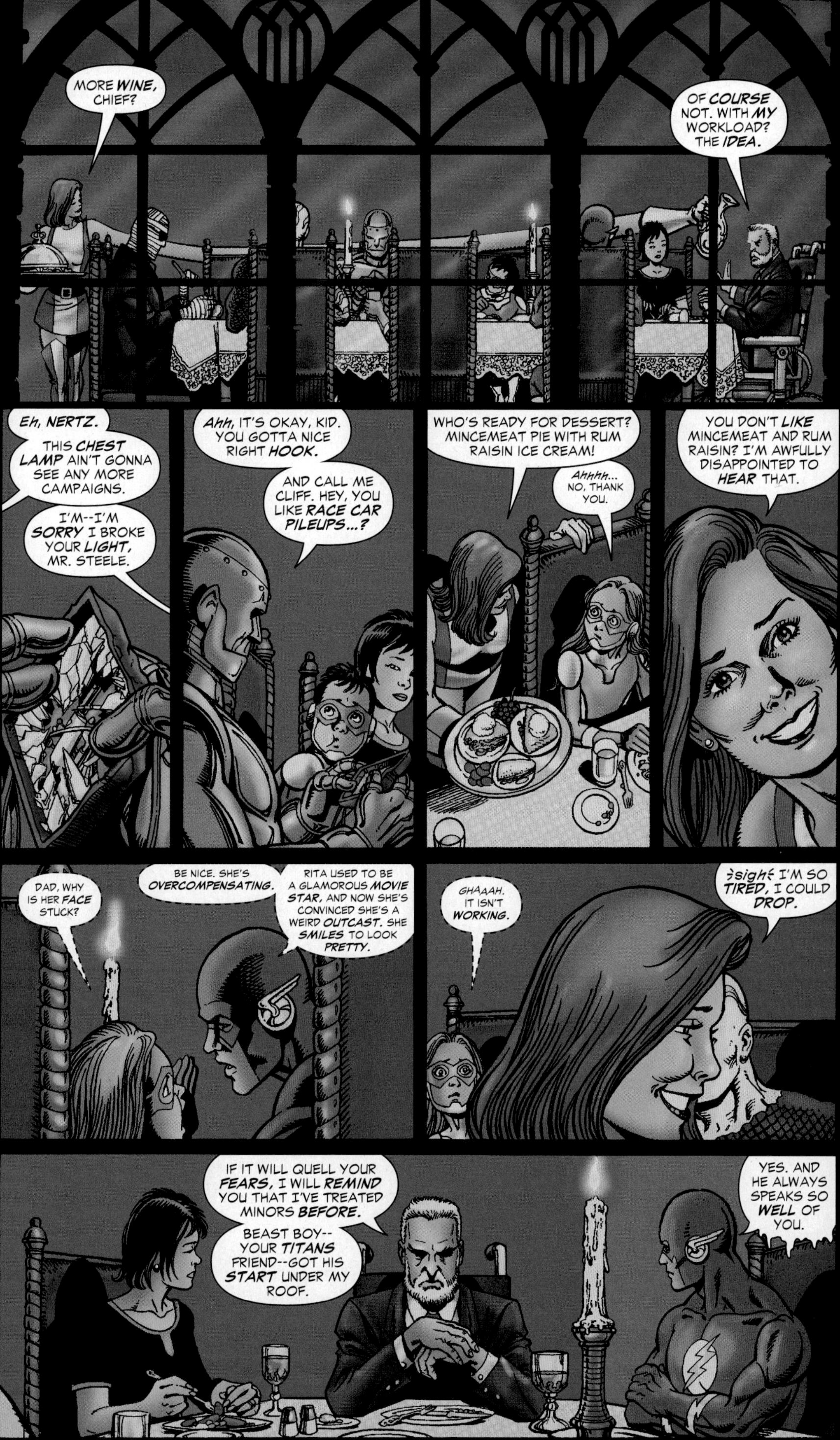

MORE WINE, CHIEF?
OF COURSE NOT. WITH MY WORKLOAD? THE IDEA.
Eh, NERTZ.
THIS CHEST LAMP AIN'T GONNA SEE ANY MORE CAMPAIGNS.
I'M--I'M SORRY I BROKE YOUR LIGHT, MR. STEELE.
Ahh, IT'S OKAY, KID. YOU GOTTA NICE RIGHT HOOK.
AND CALL ME CLIFF. HEY, YOU LIKE RACE CAR PILEUPS...?
WHO'S READY FOR DESSERT? MINCEMEAT PIE WITH RUM RAISIN ICE CREAM!
Ahhhh... NO, THANK YOU.
YOU DON'T LIKE MINCEMEAT AND RUM RAISIN? I'M AWFULLY DISAPPOINTED TO HEAR THAT.
DAD, WHY IS HER FACE STUCK?
BE NICE. SHE'S OVERCOMPENSATING.
RITA USED TO BE A GLAMOROUS MOVIE STAR, AND NOW SHE'S CONVINCED SHE'S A WEIRD OUTCAST. SHE SMILES TO LOOK PRETTY.
GHAAAH. IT ISN'T WORKING.
sigh I'M SO TIRED, I COULD DROP.
IF IT WILL QUELL YOUR FEARS, I WILL REMIND YOU THAT I'VE TREATED MINORS BEFORE.
BEAST BOY--YOUR TITANS FRIEND--GOT HIS START UNDER MY ROOF.
YES. AND HE ALWAYS SPEAKS SO WELL OF YOU.

AS HE *SHOULD.* I MANAGED TO MAP HIS FANTASTIC DNA WITHOUT WREAKING ANY-- *SLURP*

SLURP
SLURP *SLURP*

WE HAVE *COMPANY, LARRY.* MANNERS?

BEST I CAN DO WITH THESE *BANDAGES.* WOULD YOU RATHER I *UNWRAP* AND *IRRADIATE* EVERYONE?

CLIFF? AREN'T *YOU* EATING?

ALL THE *TIME, KID,* BUT NOT THE WAY *YOU* DO. WANNA *SEE?*

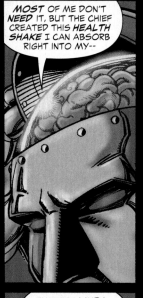

MOST OF ME DON'T *NEED* IT, BUT THE CHIEF CREATED THIS *HEALTH SHAKE* I CAN ABSORB RIGHT INTO MY--

BRAAAAN!

ENOUGH!

KLINNK

WHAT KIND OF *MON*--

--WHAT KIND OF *HEROES* ARE YOU? I THINK YOU *ENJOY* FRIGHTENING MY KIDS.

I'M WITH *LINDA.* LET'S JUST DO WHAT WE *CAME* HERE FOR AND GET *OUT.*

I *SINCERELY* APOLOGIZE FOR THE WAY YOU CHOOSE TO *REACT.* WE'LL BEGIN *IMMEDIATELY.*

READY, MR. MASON?

SURE. IF I WON'T *SCARE* ANYONE.

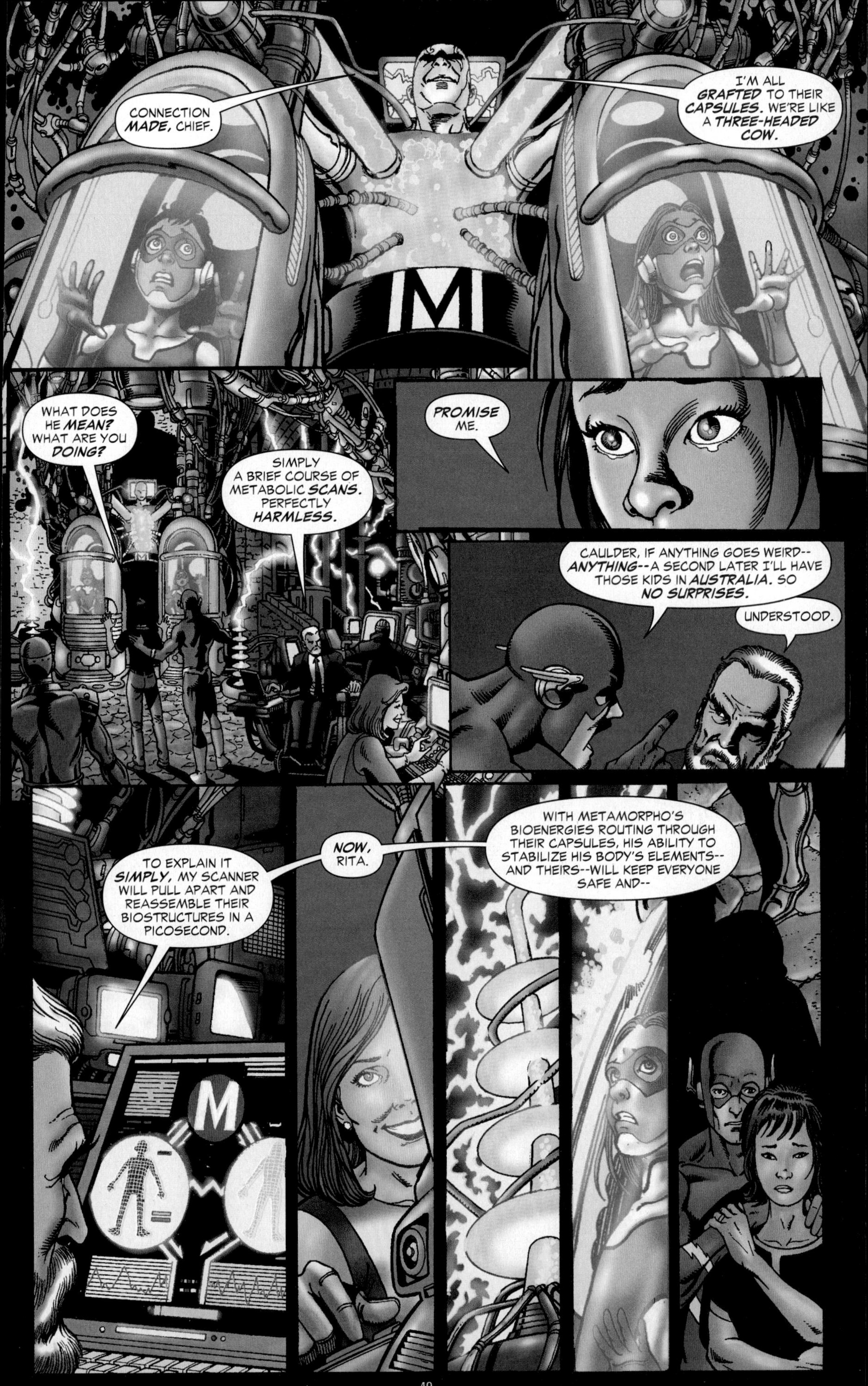

CONNECTION MADE, CHIEF.
I'M ALL GRAFTED TO THEIR CAPSULES. WE'RE LIKE A THREE-HEADED COW.
WHAT DOES HE MEAN? WHAT ARE YOU DOING?
SIMPLY A BRIEF COURSE OF METABOLIC SCANS. PERFECTLY HARMLESS.
PROMISE ME.
CAULDER, IF ANYTHING GOES WEIRD-- ANYTHING--A SECOND LATER I'LL HAVE THOSE KIDS IN AUSTRALIA. SO NO SURPRISES.
UNDERSTOOD.
TO EXPLAIN IT SIMPLY, MY SCANNER WILL PULL APART AND REASSEMBLE THEIR BIOSTRUCTURES IN A PICOSECOND.
NOW, RITA.
WITH METAMORPHO'S BIOENERGIES ROUTING THROUGH THEIR CAPSULES, HIS ABILITY TO STABILIZE HIS BODY'S ELEMENTS-- AND THEIRS--WILL KEEP EVERYONE SAFE AND--
M

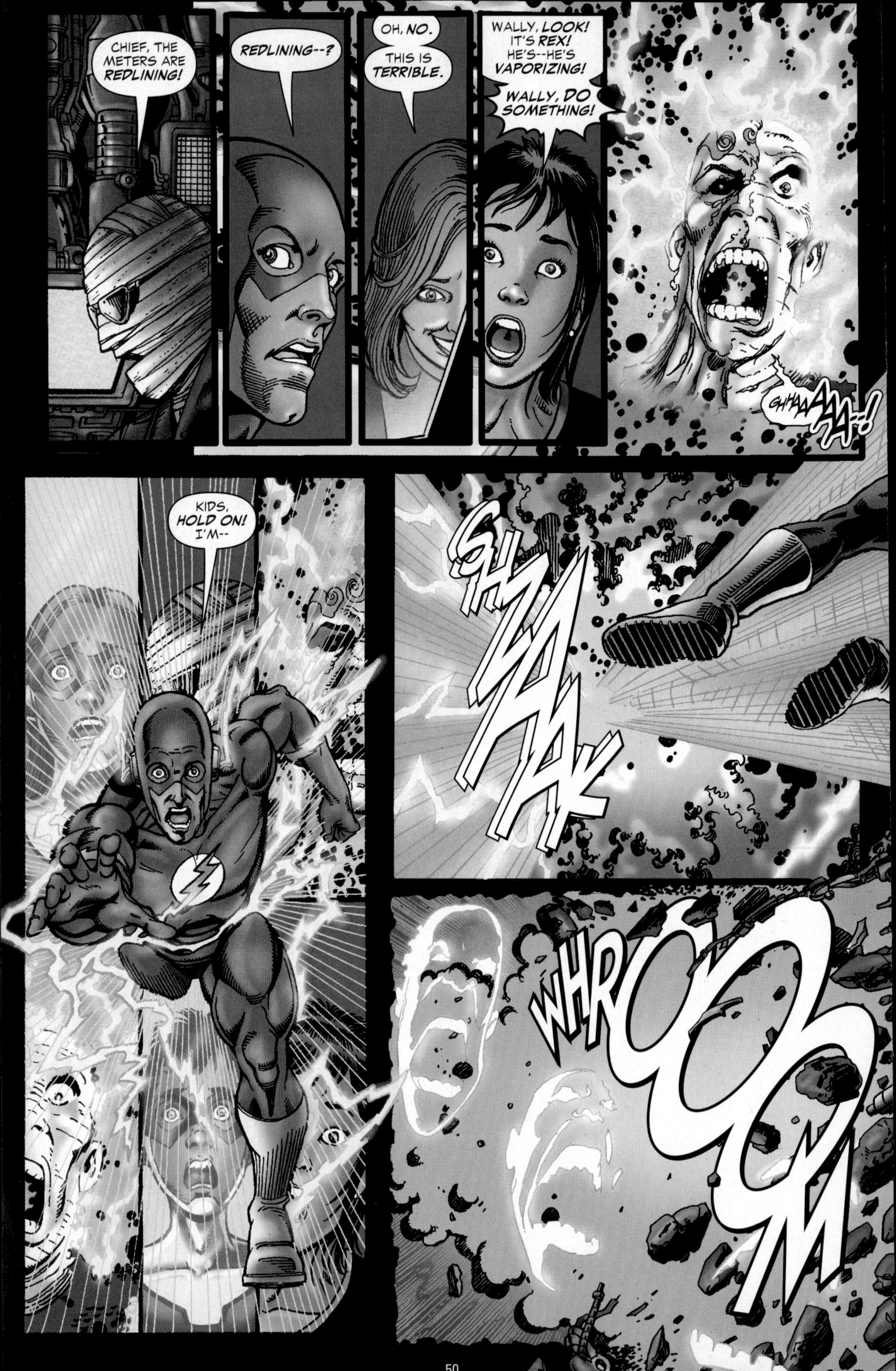
CHIEF, THE METERS ARE REDLINING!
REDLINING--?
OH, NO.
THIS IS TERRIBLE.
WALLY, LOOK! IT'S REX! HE'S--HE'S VAPORIZING!
WALLY, DO SOMETHING!
GHHAAAAAA--!
KIDS, HOLD ON! I'M--
SHZAK
WHROOOM

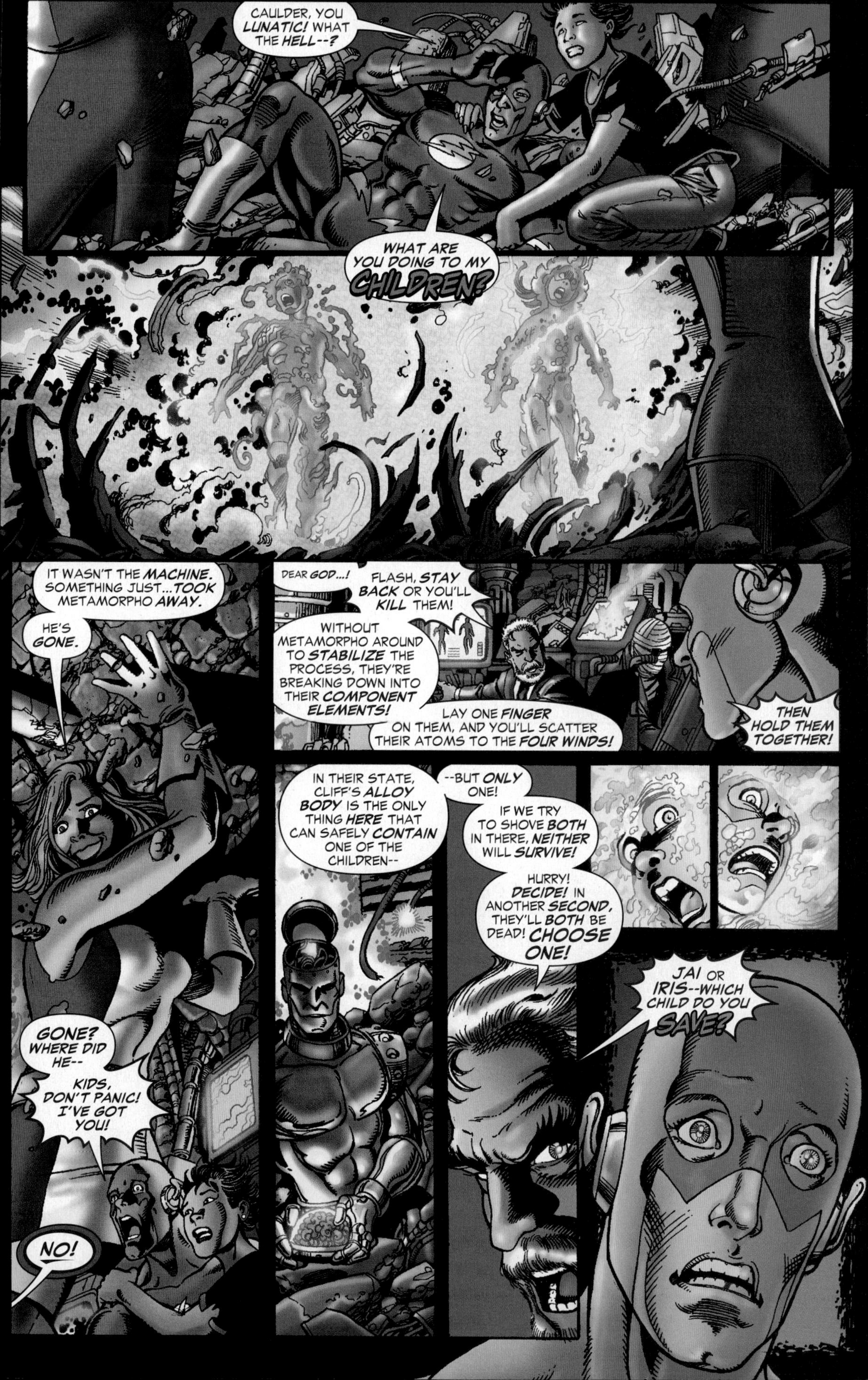
CAULDER, YOU LUNATIC! WHAT THE HELL--?
WHAT ARE YOU DOING TO MY CHILDREN?
IT WASN'T THE MACHINE. SOMETHING JUST...TOOK METAMORPHO AWAY.
HE'S GONE.
DEAR GOD...!
FLASH, STAY BACK OR YOU'LL KILL THEM!
WITHOUT METAMORPHO AROUND TO STABILIZE THE PROCESS, THEY'RE BREAKING DOWN INTO THEIR COMPONENT ELEMENTS!
LAY ONE FINGER ON THEM, AND YOU'LL SCATTER THEIR ATOMS TO THE FOUR WINDS!
THEN HOLD THEM TOGETHER!
IN THEIR STATE, CLIFF'S ALLOY BODY IS THE ONLY THING HERE THAT CAN SAFELY CONTAIN ONE OF THE CHILDREN--
--BUT ONLY ONE!
IF WE TRY TO SHOVE BOTH IN THERE, NEITHER WILL SURVIVE!
HURRY! DECIDE! IN ANOTHER SECOND, THEY'LL BOTH BE DEAD! CHOOSE ONE!
JAI OR IRIS--WHICH CHILD DO YOU SAVE?
GONE? WHERE DID HE--
KIDS, DON'T PANIC! I'VE GOT YOU!
NO!

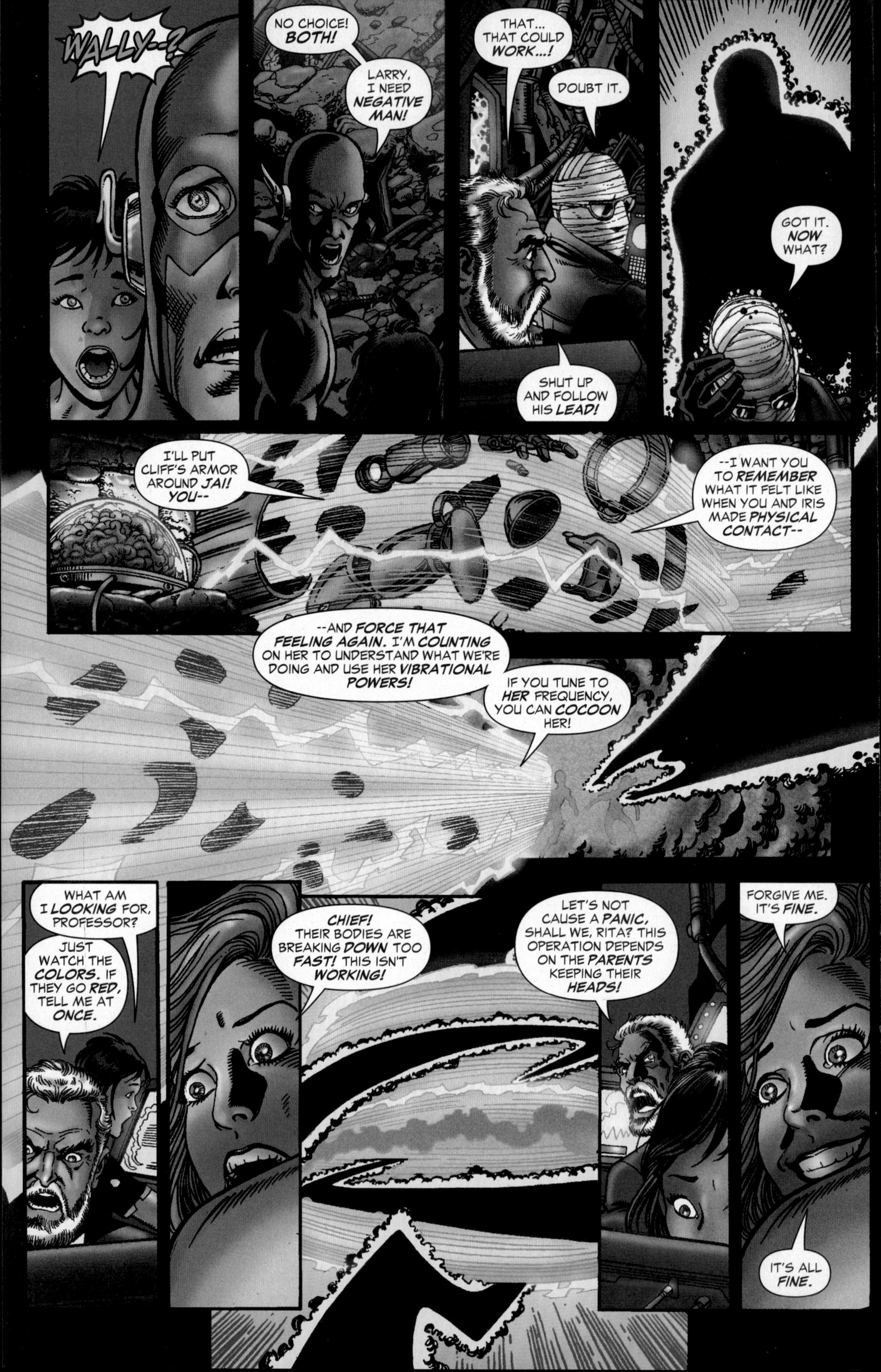
WALLY--?
NO CHOICE! BOTH!
LARRY, I NEED NEGATIVE MAN!
THAT... THAT COULD WORK...!
DOUBT IT.
SHUT UP AND FOLLOW HIS LEAD!
GOT IT. NOW WHAT?
I'LL PUT CLIFF'S ARMOR AROUND JAI! YOU--
--I WANT YOU TO REMEMBER WHAT IT FELT LIKE WHEN YOU AND IRIS MADE PHYSICAL CONTACT--
--AND FORCE THAT FEELING AGAIN. I'M COUNTING ON HER TO UNDERSTAND WHAT WE'RE DOING AND USE HER VIBRATIONAL POWERS!
IF YOU TUNE TO HER FREQUENCY, YOU CAN COCOON HER!
WHAT AM I LOOKING FOR, PROFESSOR?
JUST WATCH THE COLORS. IF THEY GO RED, TELL ME AT ONCE.
CHIEF! THEIR BODIES ARE BREAKING DOWN TOO FAST! THIS ISN'T WORKING!
LET'S NOT CAUSE A PANIC, SHALL WE, RITA? THIS OPERATION DEPENDS ON THE PARENTS KEEPING THEIR HEADS!
FORGIVE ME. IT'S FINE.
IT'S ALL FINE.

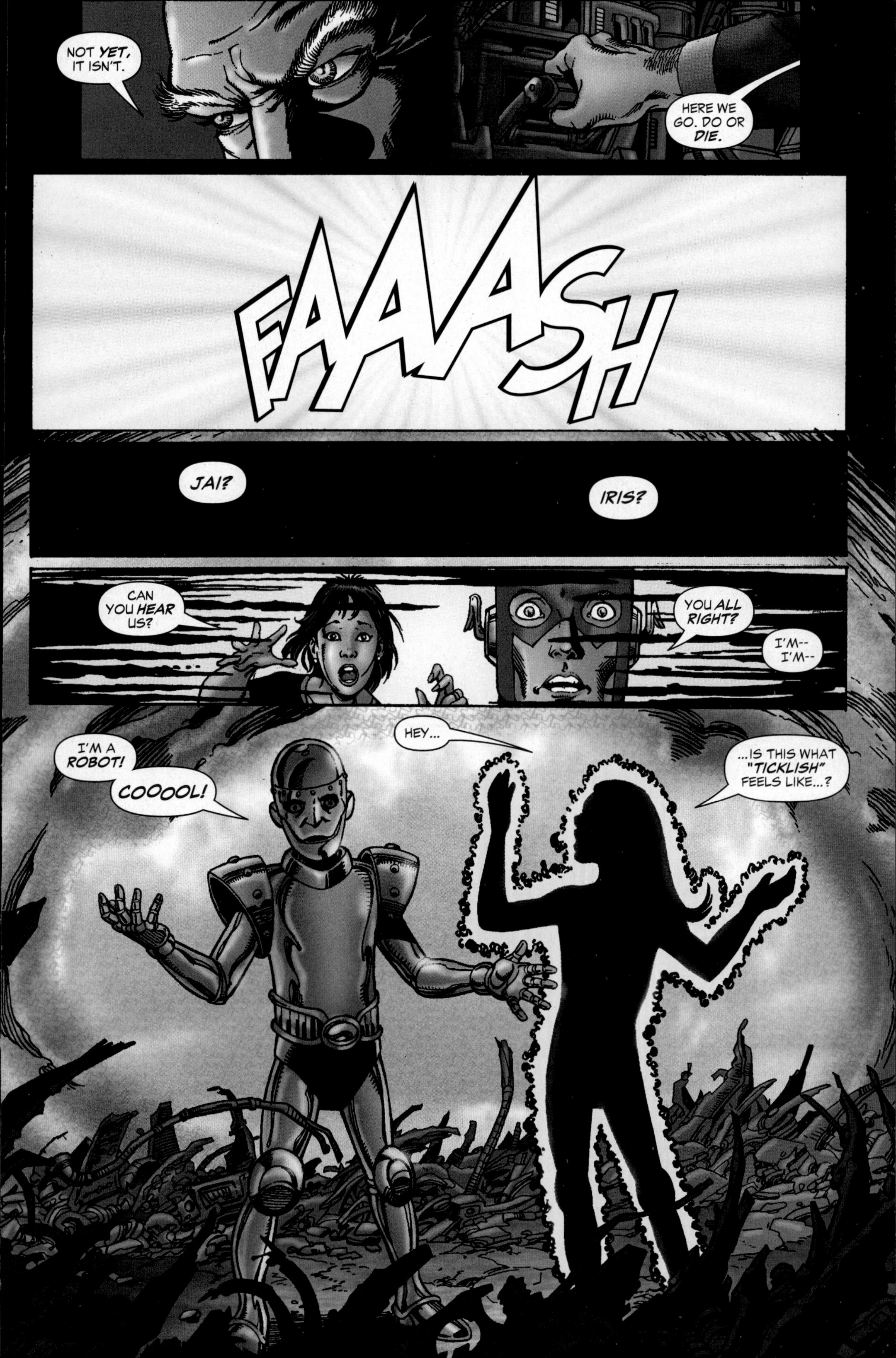
NOT YET, IT ISN'T.
HERE WE GO. DO OR DIE.
FAAASH
JAI?
IRIS?
CAN YOU HEAR US?
YOU ALL RIGHT?
I'M-- I'M--
I'M A ROBOT!
COOOOL!
HEY...
...IS THIS WHAT "TICKLISH" FEELS LIKE...?

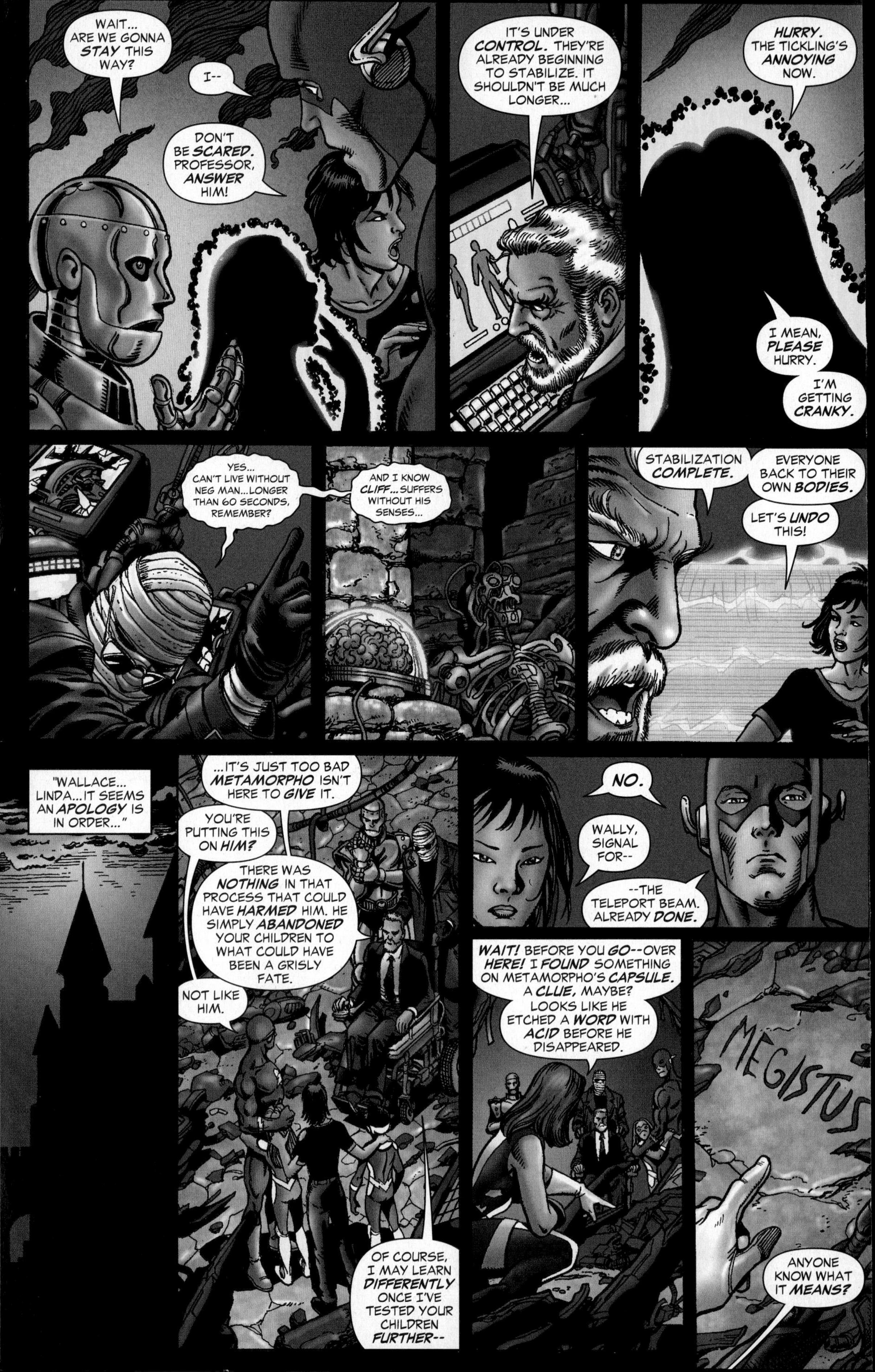

WAIT... ARE WE GONNA STAY THIS WAY?
I--
DON'T BE SCARED. PROFESSOR, ANSWER HIM!
IT'S UNDER CONTROL. THEY'RE ALREADY BEGINNING TO STABILIZE. IT SHOULDN'T BE MUCH LONGER...
HURRY. THE TICKLING'S ANNOYING NOW.
I MEAN, PLEASE HURRY.
I'M GETTING CRANKY.
YES... CAN'T LIVE WITHOUT NEG MAN...LONGER THAN 60 SECONDS, REMEMBER?
AND I KNOW CLIFF... SUFFERS WITHOUT HIS SENSES...
STABILIZATION COMPLETE.
EVERYONE BACK TO THEIR OWN BODIES.
LET'S UNDO THIS!
"WALLACE... LINDA...IT SEEMS AN APOLOGY IS IN ORDER..."
...IT'S JUST TOO BAD METAMORPHO ISN'T HERE TO GIVE IT.
YOU'RE PUTTING THIS ON HIM?
THERE WAS NOTHING IN THAT PROCESS THAT COULD HAVE HARMED HIM. HE SIMPLY ABANDONED YOUR CHILDREN TO WHAT COULD HAVE BEEN A GRISLY FATE.
NOT LIKE HIM.
OF COURSE, I MAY LEARN DIFFERENTLY ONCE I'VE TESTED YOUR CHILDREN FURTHER--
NO.
WALLY, SIGNAL FOR--
--THE TELEPORT BEAM. ALREADY DONE.
WAIT! BEFORE YOU GO--OVER HERE! I FOUND SOMETHING ON METAMORPHO'S CAPSULE. A CLUE, MAYBE? LOOKS LIKE HE ETCHED A WORD WITH ACID BEFORE HE DISAPPEARED.
MEGISTUS
ANYONE KNOW WHAT IT MEANS?

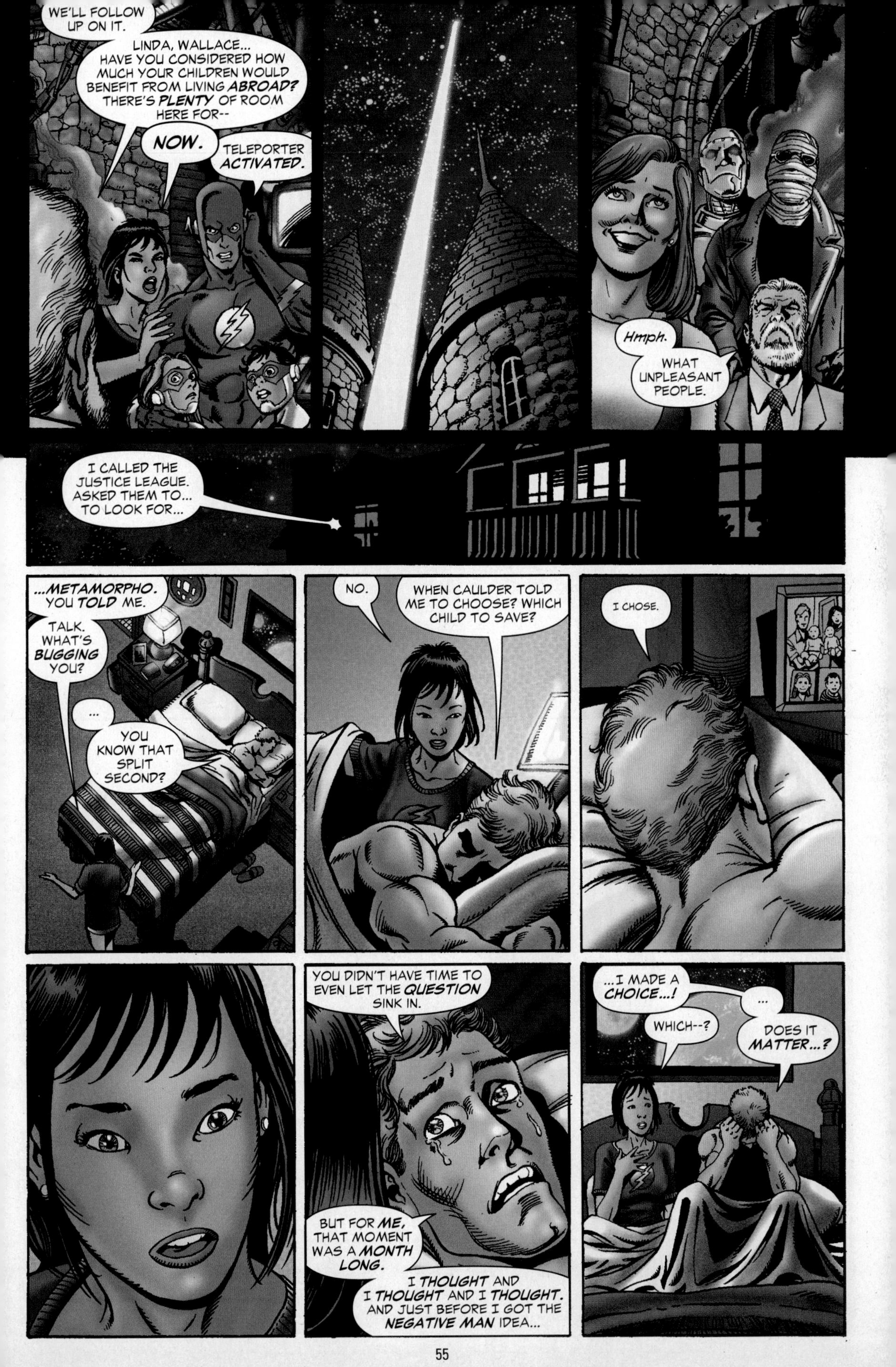

WE'LL FOLLOW UP ON IT.
LINDA, WALLACE... HAVE YOU CONSIDERED HOW MUCH YOUR CHILDREN WOULD BENEFIT FROM LIVING ABROAD? THERE'S PLENTY OF ROOM HERE FOR--
NOW.
TELEPORTER ACTIVATED.
Hmph.
WHAT UNPLEASANT PEOPLE.
I CALLED THE JUSTICE LEAGUE. ASKED THEM TO... TO LOOK FOR...
...METAMORPHO. YOU TOLD ME.
TALK. WHAT'S BUGGING YOU?
...
YOU KNOW THAT SPLIT SECOND?
NO.
WHEN CAULDER TOLD ME TO CHOOSE? WHICH CHILD TO SAVE?
I CHOSE.
YOU DIDN'T HAVE TIME TO EVEN LET THE QUESTION SINK IN.
BUT FOR ME, THAT MOMENT WAS A MONTH LONG.
I THOUGHT AND I THOUGHT AND I THOUGHT. AND JUST BEFORE I GOT THE NEGATIVE MAN IDEA...
...I MADE A CHOICE...!
WHICH--?
...
DOES IT MATTER...?

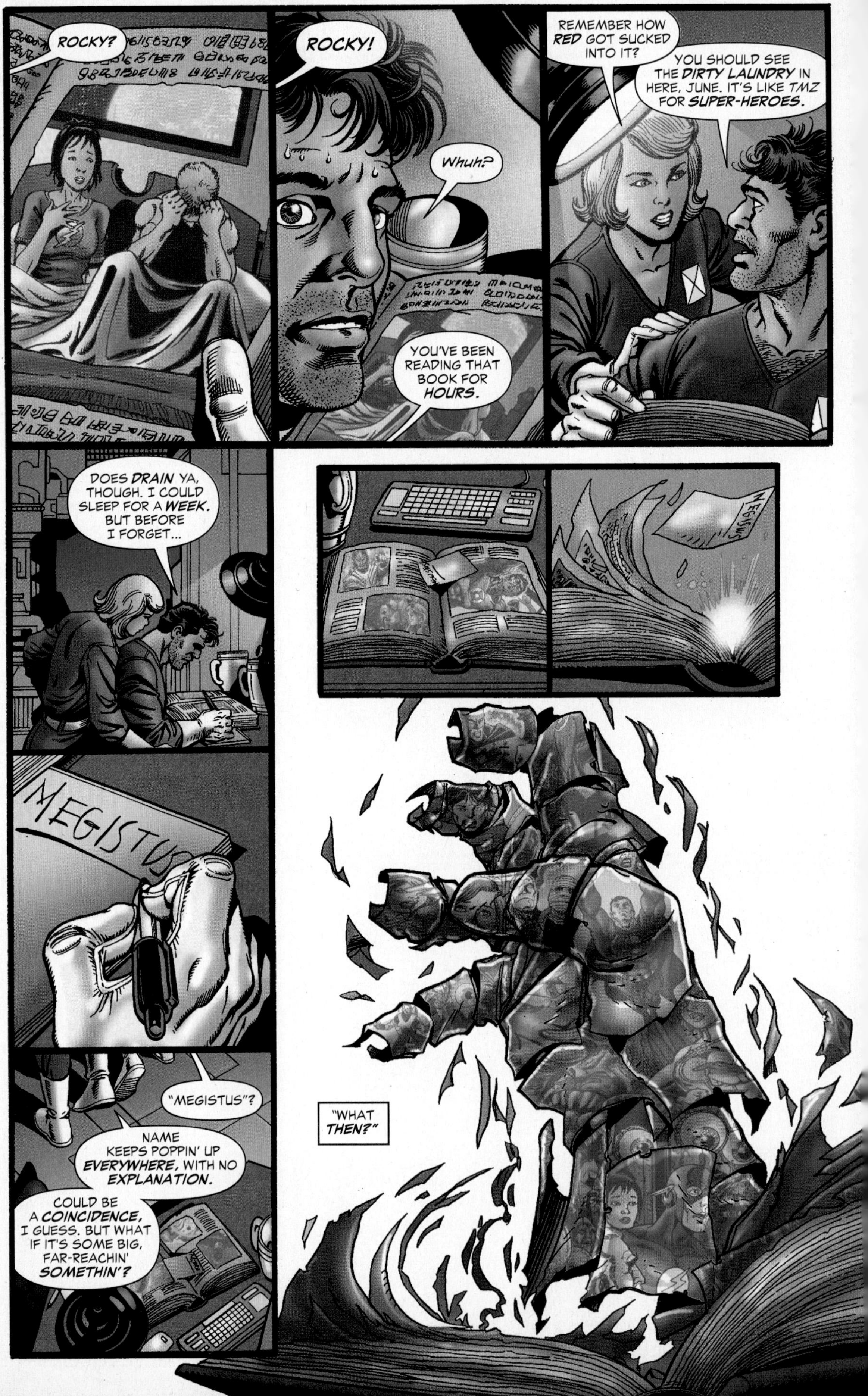

ROCKY?
ROCKY!
Whuh?
YOU'VE BEEN READING THAT BOOK FOR HOURS.
REMEMBER HOW RED GOT SUCKED INTO IT?
YOU SHOULD SEE THE DIRTY LAUNDRY IN HERE, JUNE. IT'S LIKE TMZ FOR SUPER-HEROES.
DOES DRAIN YA, THOUGH. I COULD SLEEP FOR A WEEK. BUT BEFORE I FORGET...
MEGISTUS
"MEGISTUS"?
NAME KEEPS POPPIN' UP EVERYWHERE, WITH NO EXPLANATION.
COULD BE A COINCIDENCE, I GUESS. BUT WHAT IF IT'S SOME BIG, FAR-REACHIN' SOMETHIN'?
"WHAT THEN?"

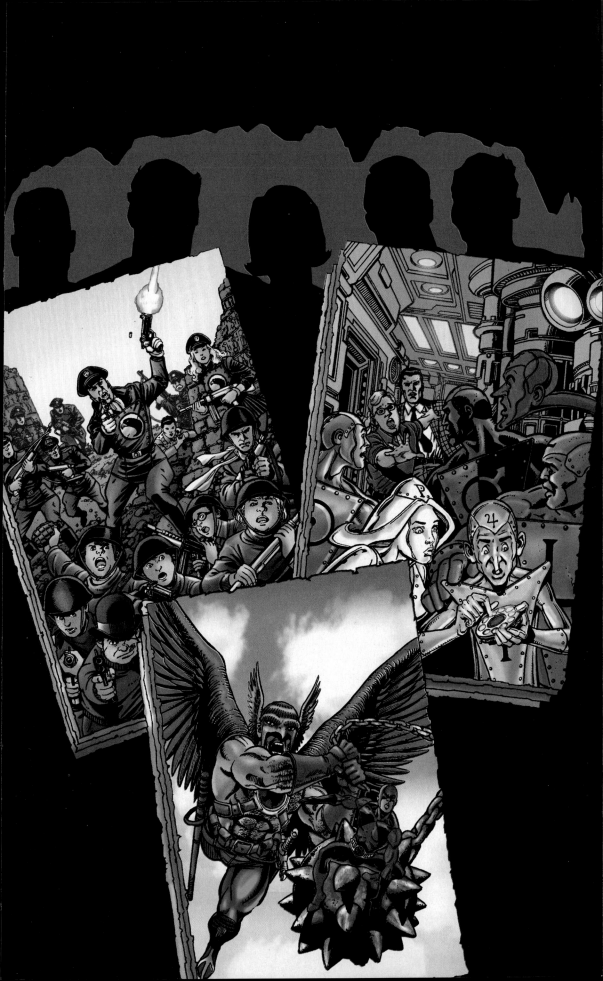

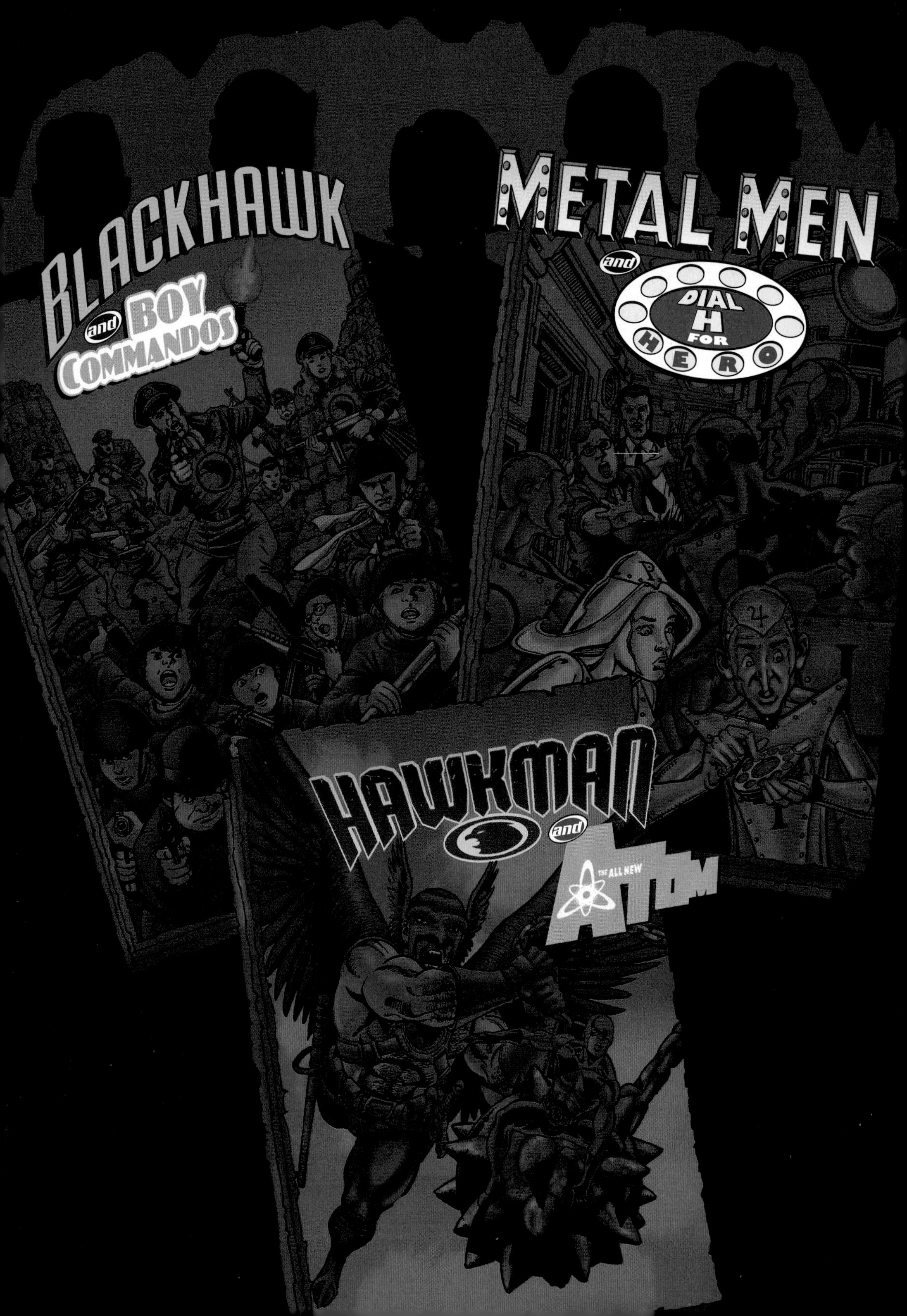
BLACKHAWK
and BOY COMMANDOS
METAL MEN
and
DIAL H FOR HERO
HAWKMAN
and
THE ALL NEW ATOM

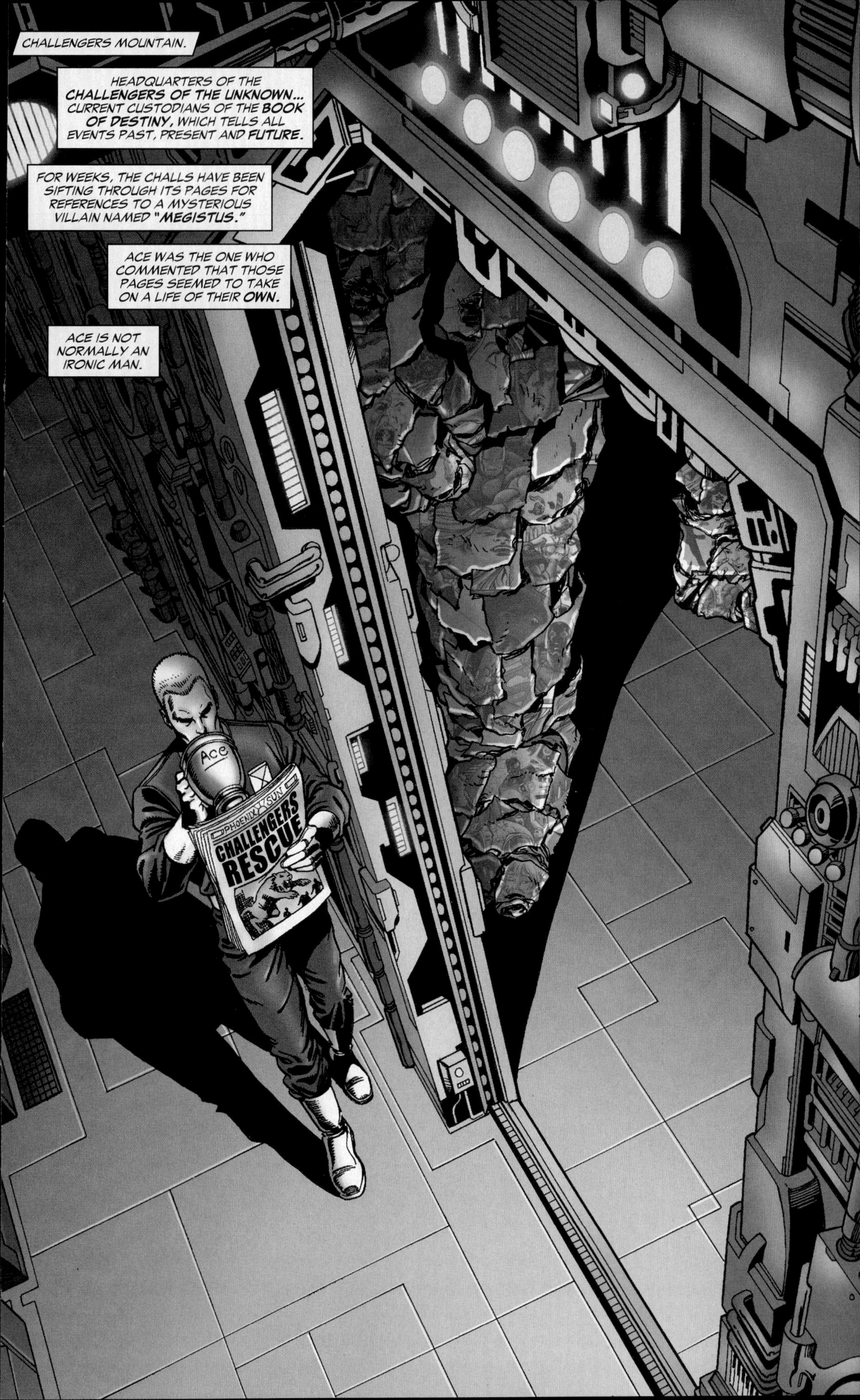
CHALLENGERS MOUNTAIN.
HEADQUARTERS OF THE CHALLENGERS OF THE UNKNOWN... CURRENT CUSTODIANS OF THE BOOK OF DESTINY, WHICH TELLS ALL EVENTS PAST, PRESENT AND FUTURE.
FOR WEEKS, THE CHALLS HAVE BEEN SIFTING THROUGH ITS PAGES FOR REFERENCES TO A MYSTERIOUS VILLAIN NAMED "MEGISTUS."
ACE WAS THE ONE WHO COMMENTED THAT THOSE PAGES SEEMED TO TAKE ON A LIFE OF THEIR OWN.
ACE IS NOT NORMALLY AN IRONIC MAN.
Ace
PHOENIX SUN
CHALLENGERS RESCUE

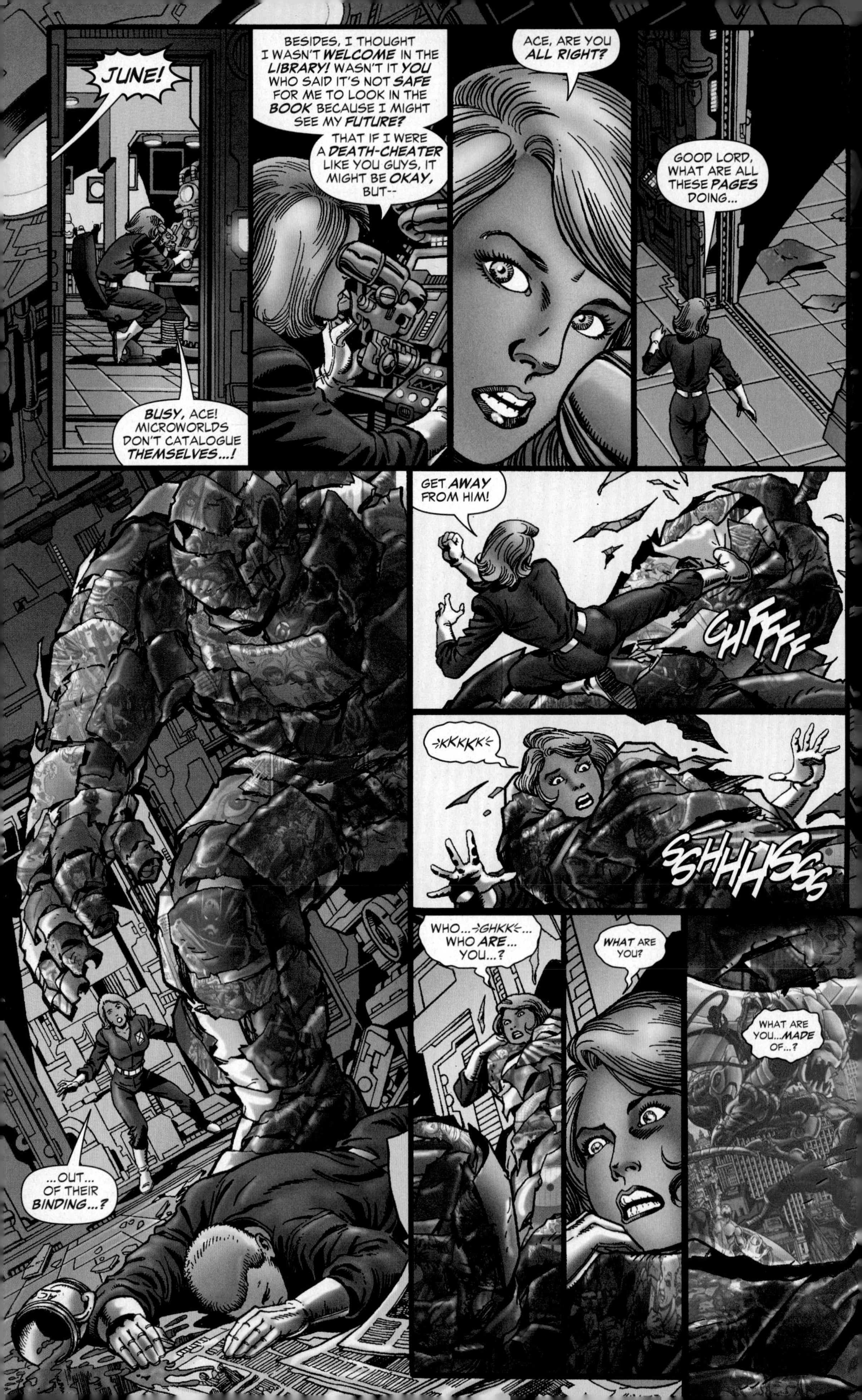
JUNE!
BUSY, ACE! MICROWORLDS DON'T CATALOGUE THEMSELVES...!
BESIDES, I THOUGHT I WASN'T WELCOME IN THE LIBRARY! WASN'T IT YOU WHO SAID IT'S NOT SAFE FOR ME TO LOOK IN THE BOOK BECAUSE I MIGHT SEE MY FUTURE?
THAT IF I WERE A DEATH-CHEATER LIKE YOU GUYS, IT MIGHT BE OKAY, BUT--
ACE, ARE YOU ALL RIGHT?
GOOD LORD, WHAT ARE ALL THESE PAGES DOING...
...OUT... OF THEIR BINDING...?
GET AWAY FROM HIM!
CHFFFFF
KKKKK
SSHHHISSSS
WHO... GHKK... WHO ARE... YOU...?
WHAT ARE YOU?
WHAT ARE YOU...MADE OF...?

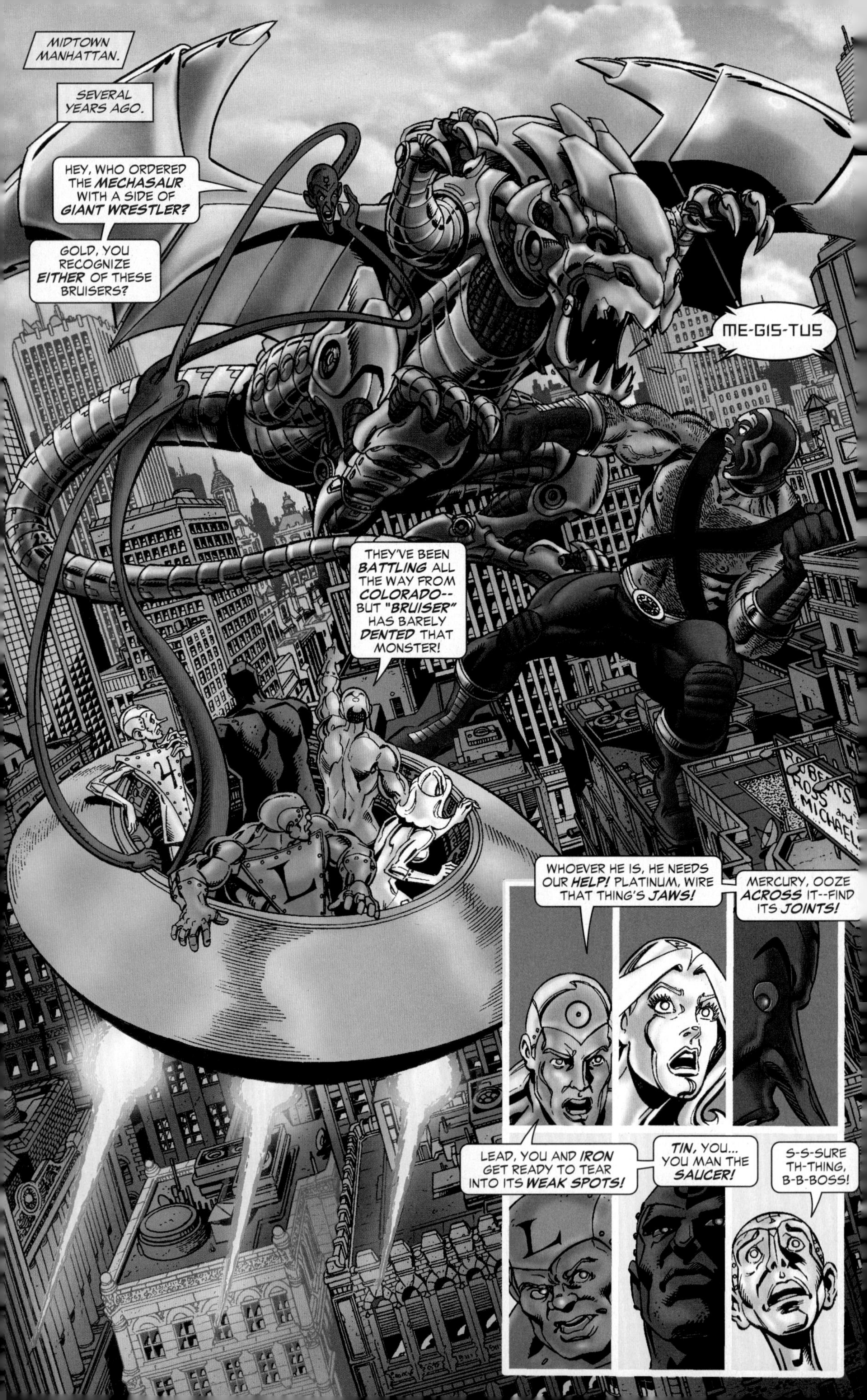
MIDTOWN MANHATTAN.
SEVERAL YEARS AGO.
HEY, WHO ORDERED THE MECHASAUR WITH A SIDE OF GIANT WRESTLER?
GOLD, YOU RECOGNIZE EITHER OF THESE BRUISERS?
ME-GIS-TUS
THEY'VE BEEN BATTLING ALL THE WAY FROM COLORADO-- BUT "BRUISER" HAS BARELY DENTED THAT MONSTER!
ROBERTS, ROSS and MICHAEL
WHOEVER HE IS, HE NEEDS OUR HELP! PLATINUM, WIRE THAT THING'S JAWS!
MERCURY, OOZE ACROSS IT--FIND ITS JOINTS!
LEAD, YOU AND IRON GET READY TO TEAR INTO ITS WEAK SPOTS!
TIN, YOU... YOU MAN THE SAUCER!
S-S-SURE TH-THING, B-B-BOSS!

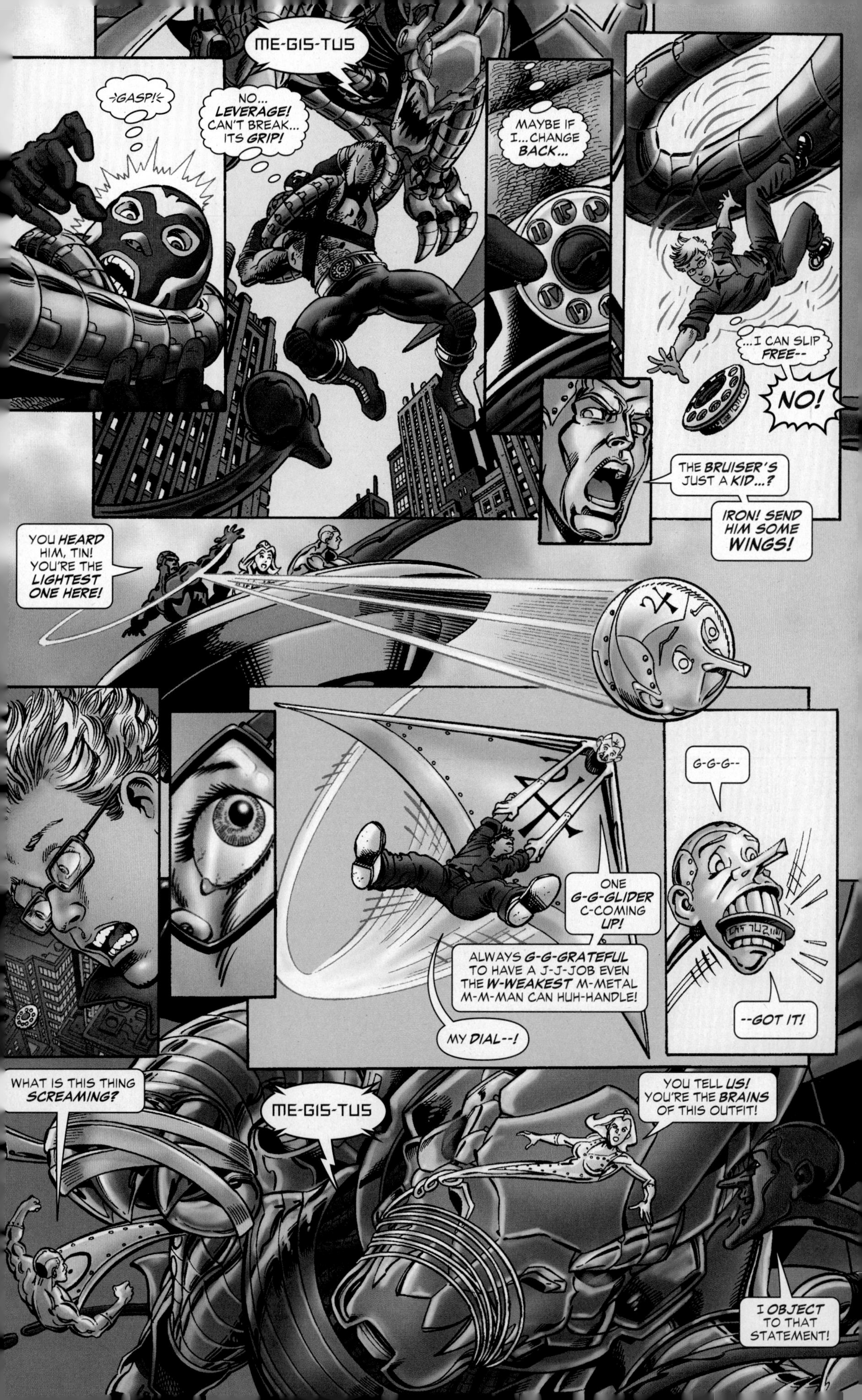
ME-GIS-TUS
-GASP!-
NO... LEVERAGE! CAN'T BREAK... ITS GRIP!
MAYBE IF I...CHANGE BACK...
...I CAN SLIP FREE--
NO!
THE BRUISER'S JUST A KID...?
IRON! SEND HIM SOME WINGS!
YOU HEARD HIM, TIN! YOU'RE THE LIGHTEST ONE HERE!
G-G-G--
ONE G-G-GLIDER C-COMING UP!
ALWAYS G-G-GRATEFUL TO HAVE A J-J-JOB EVEN THE W-WEAKEST M-METAL M-M-MAN CAN HUH-HANDLE!
MY DIAL--!
--GOT IT!
WHAT IS THIS THING SCREAMING?
ME-GIS-TUS
YOU TELL US! YOU'RE THE BRAINS OF THIS OUTFIT!
I OBJECT TO THAT STATEMENT!

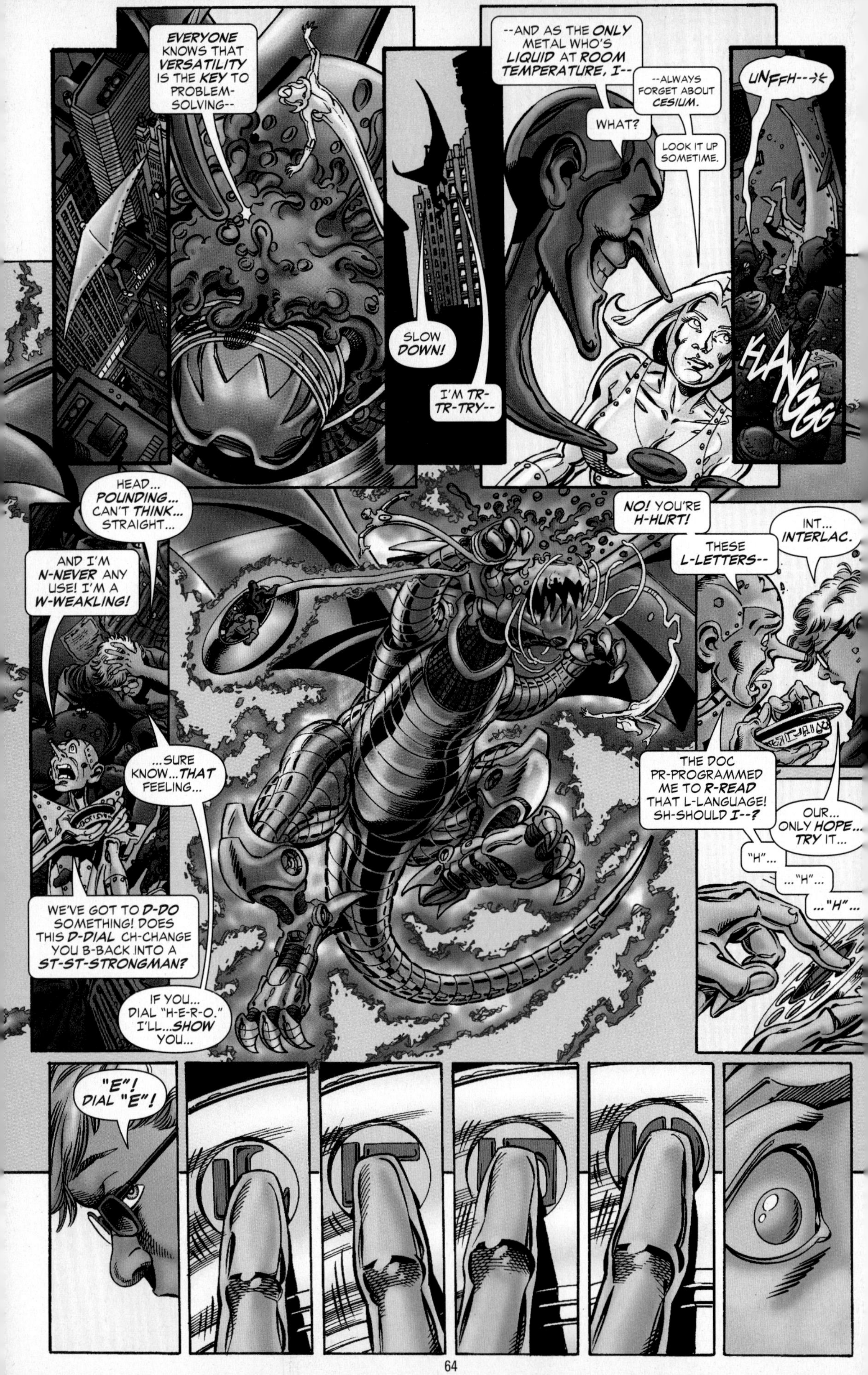
EVERYONE KNOWS THAT VERSATILITY IS THE KEY TO PROBLEM-SOLVING--
SLOW DOWN!
I'M TR-TR-TRY--
--AND AS THE ONLY METAL WHO'S LIQUID AT ROOM TEMPERATURE, I--
WHAT?
--ALWAYS FORGET ABOUT CESIUM.
LOOK IT UP SOMETIME.
UNFFH--
KLANGGG
HEAD... POUNDING... CAN'T THINK... STRAIGHT...
AND I'M N-NEVER ANY USE! I'M A W-WEAKLING!
...SURE KNOW...THAT FEELING...
WE'VE GOT TO D-DO SOMETHING! DOES THIS D-DIAL CH-CHANGE YOU B-BACK INTO A ST-ST-STRONGMAN?
IF YOU... DIAL "H-E-R-O." I'LL...SHOW YOU...
NO! YOU'RE H-HURT!
THESE L-LETTERS--
INT... INTERLAC.
THE DOC PR-PROGRAMMED ME TO R-READ THAT L-LANGUAGE! SH-SHOULD I--?
OUR... ONLY HOPE... TRY IT...
"H"...
..."H"...
..."H"...
"E"! DIAL "E"!

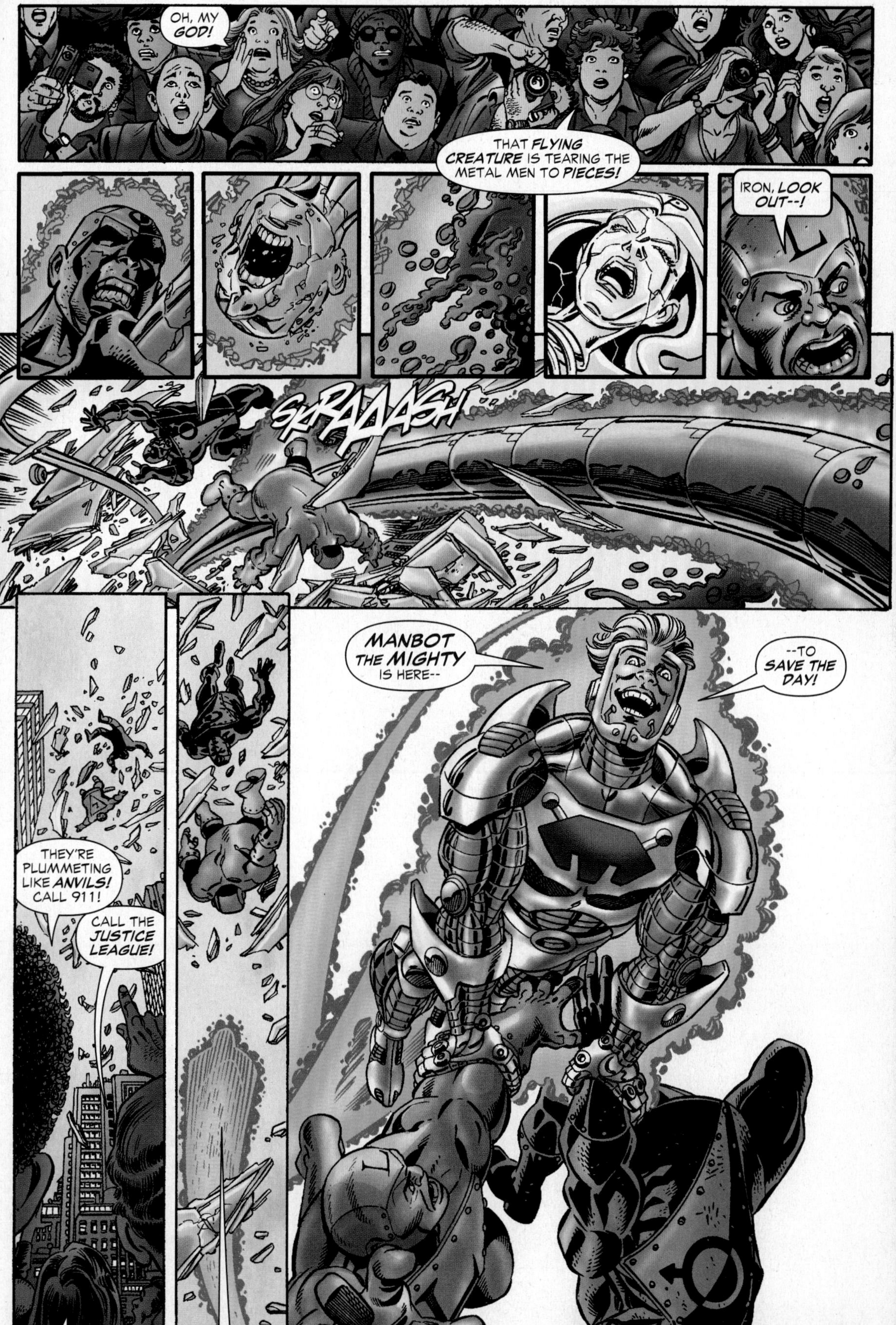
OH, MY GOD!
THAT FLYING CREATURE IS TEARING THE METAL MEN TO PIECES!
IRON, LOOK OUT--!
SKRAAAASH
THEY'RE PLUMMETING LIKE ANVILS! CALL 911!
CALL THE JUSTICE LEAGUE!
CALL ANYONE!
NO NEED, FOLKS!
MANBOT THE MIGHTY IS HERE--
--TO SAVE THE DAY!

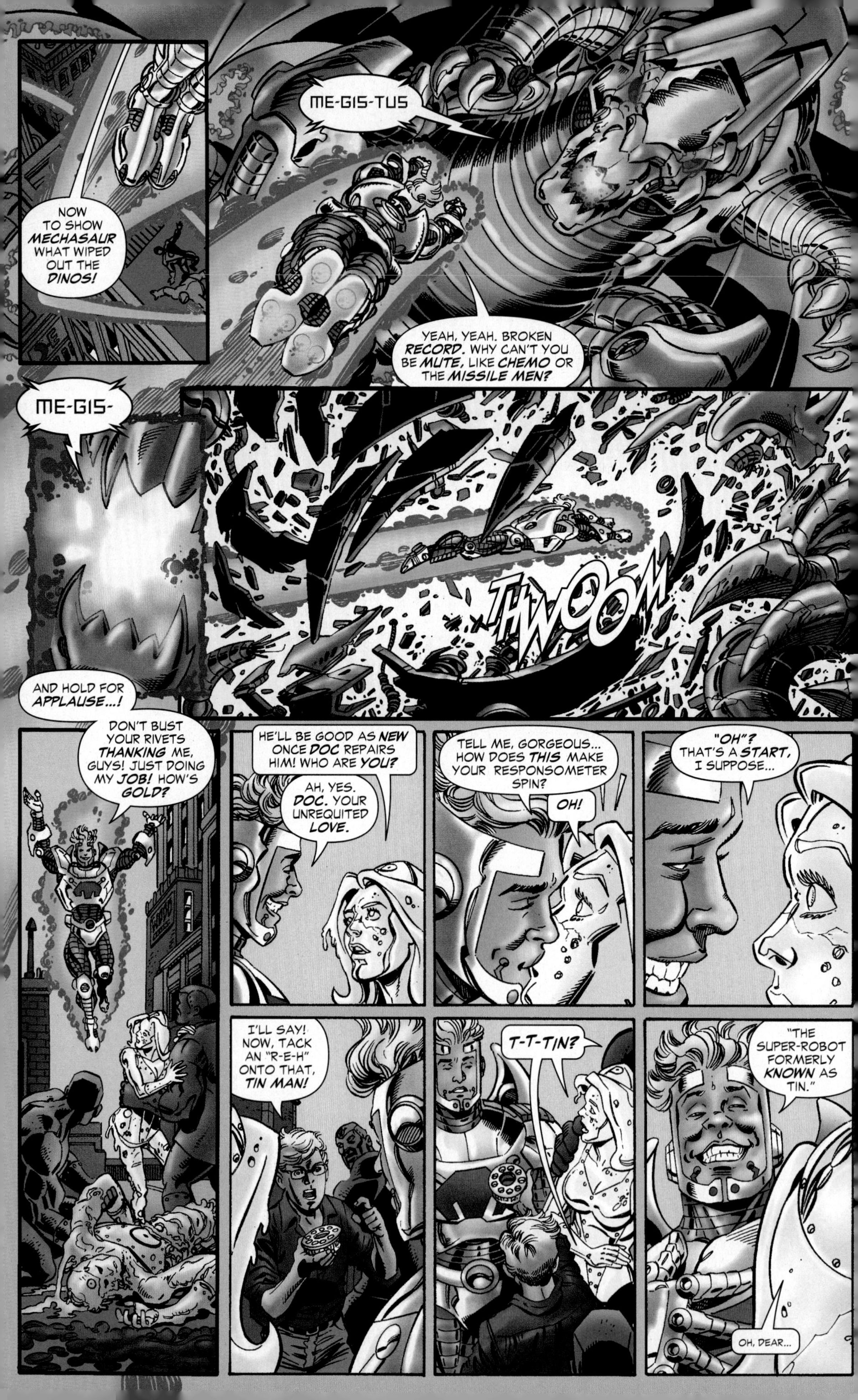
ME-GIS-TUS
NOW TO SHOW MECHASAUR WHAT WIPED OUT THE DINOS!
YEAH, YEAH. BROKEN RECORD. WHY CAN'T YOU BE MUTE, LIKE CHEMO OR THE MISSILE MEN?
ME-GIS-
THWOOM
AND HOLD FOR APPLAUSE...!
DON'T BUST YOUR RIVETS THANKING ME, GUYS! JUST DOING MY JOB! HOW'S GOLD?
HE'LL BE GOOD AS NEW ONCE DOC REPAIRS HIM! WHO ARE YOU?
AH, YES. DOC. YOUR UNREQUITED LOVE.
TELL ME, GORGEOUS... HOW DOES THIS MAKE YOUR RESPONSOMETER SPIN?
OH!
"OH"? THAT'S A START, I SUPPOSE...
I'LL SAY! NOW, TACK AN "R-E-H" ONTO THAT, TIN MAN!
T-T-TIN?
"THE SUPER-ROBOT FORMERLY KNOWN AS TIN."
OH, DEAR...

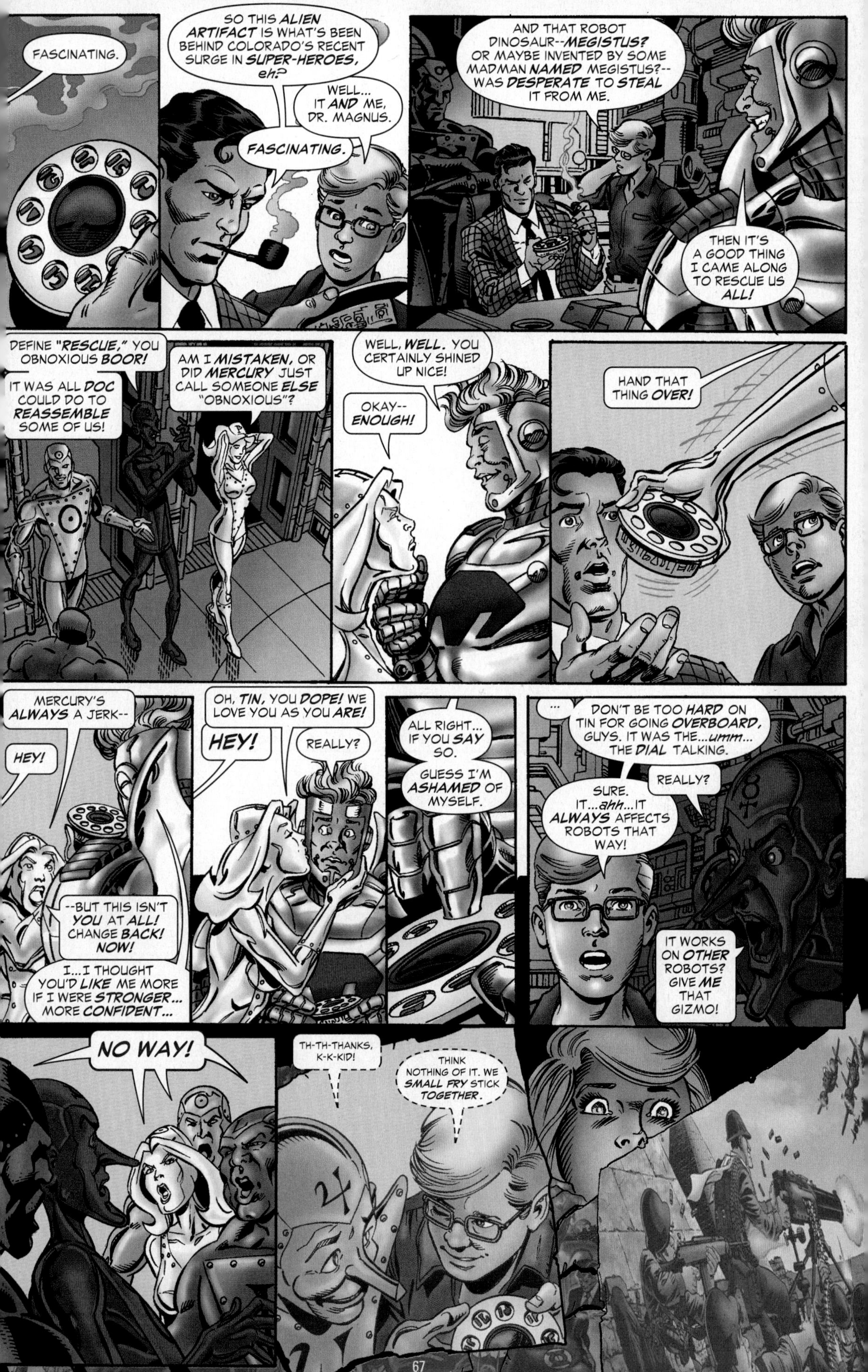
FASCINATING.
SO THIS ALIEN ARTIFACT IS WHAT'S BEEN BEHIND COLORADO'S RECENT SURGE IN SUPER-HEROES, eh?
WELL... IT AND ME, DR. MAGNUS.
FASCINATING.
AND THAT ROBOT DINOSAUR--MEGISTUS? OR MAYBE INVENTED BY SOME MADMAN NAMED MEGISTUS?--WAS DESPERATE TO STEAL IT FROM ME.
THEN IT'S A GOOD THING I CAME ALONG TO RESCUE US ALL!
DEFINE "RESCUE," YOU OBNOXIOUS BOOR!
IT WAS ALL DOC COULD DO TO REASSEMBLE SOME OF US!
AM I MISTAKEN, OR DID MERCURY JUST CALL SOMEONE ELSE "OBNOXIOUS"?
WELL, WELL. YOU CERTAINLY SHINED UP NICE!
OKAY-- ENOUGH!
HAND THAT THING OVER!
MERCURY'S ALWAYS A JERK--
HEY!
--BUT THIS ISN'T YOU AT ALL! CHANGE BACK! NOW!
I...I THOUGHT YOU'D LIKE ME MORE IF I WERE STRONGER... MORE CONFIDENT...
OH, TIN, YOU DOPE! WE LOVE YOU AS YOU ARE!
HEY!
REALLY?
ALL RIGHT... IF YOU SAY SO.
GUESS I'M ASHAMED OF MYSELF.
...
DON'T BE TOO HARD ON TIN FOR GOING OVERBOARD, GUYS. IT WAS THE...umm... THE DIAL TALKING.
REALLY?
SURE. IT...ahh...IT ALWAYS AFFECTS ROBOTS THAT WAY!
IT WORKS ON OTHER ROBOTS? GIVE ME THAT GIZMO!
NO WAY!
TH-TH-THANKS, K-K-KID!
THINK NOTHING OF IT. WE SMALL FRY STICK TOGETHER.

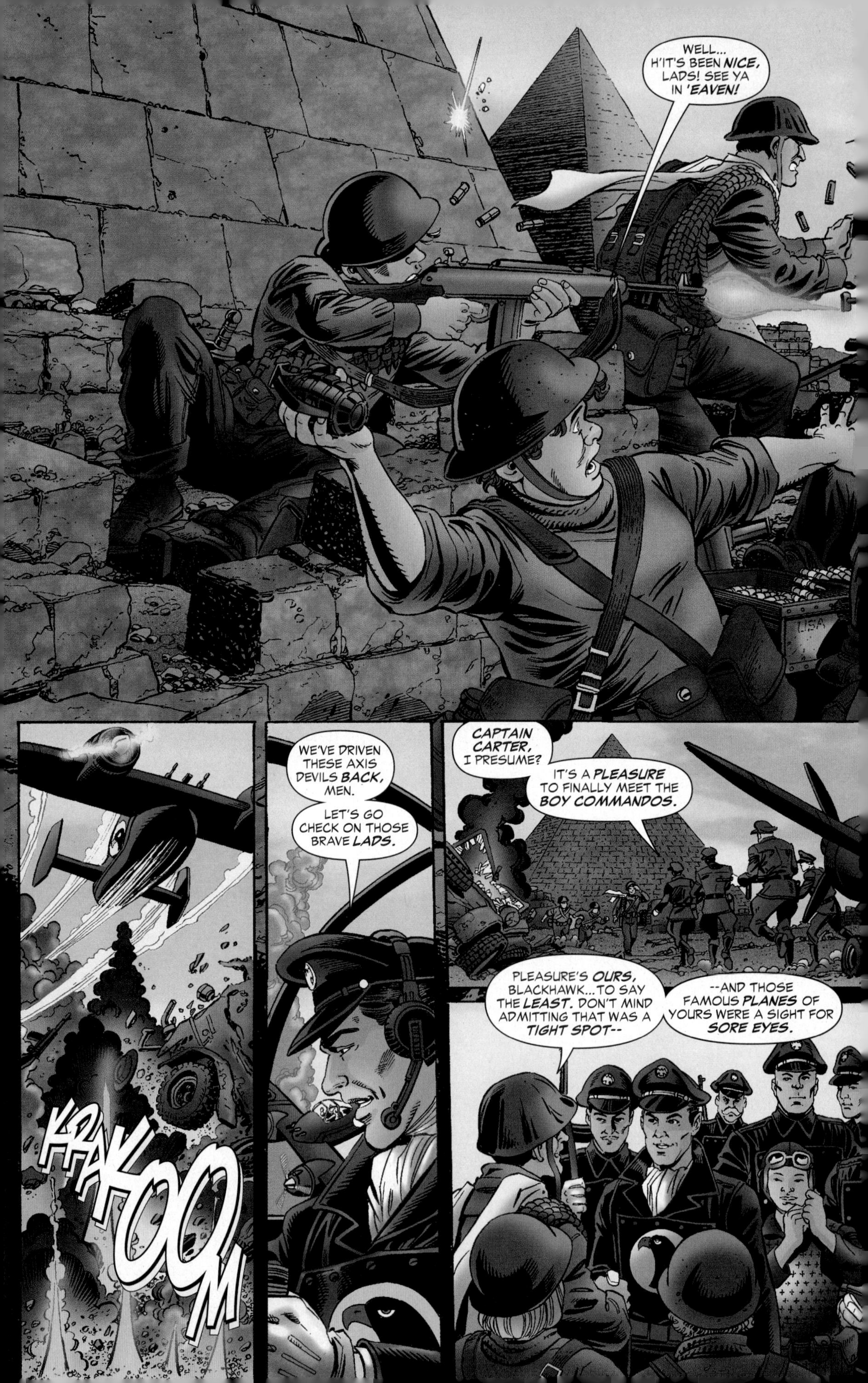

WELL... H'IT'S BEEN NICE, LADS! SEE YA IN 'EAVEN!
KRAKOOOM
WE'VE DRIVEN THESE AXIS DEVILS BACK, MEN.
LET'S GO CHECK ON THOSE BRAVE LADS.
CAPTAIN CARTER, I PRESUME?
IT'S A PLEASURE TO FINALLY MEET THE BOY COMMANDOS.
PLEASURE'S OURS, BLACKHAWK...TO SAY THE LEAST. DON'T MIND ADMITTING THAT WAS A TIGHT SPOT--
--AND THOSE FAMOUS PLANES OF YOURS WERE A SIGHT FOR SORE EYES.

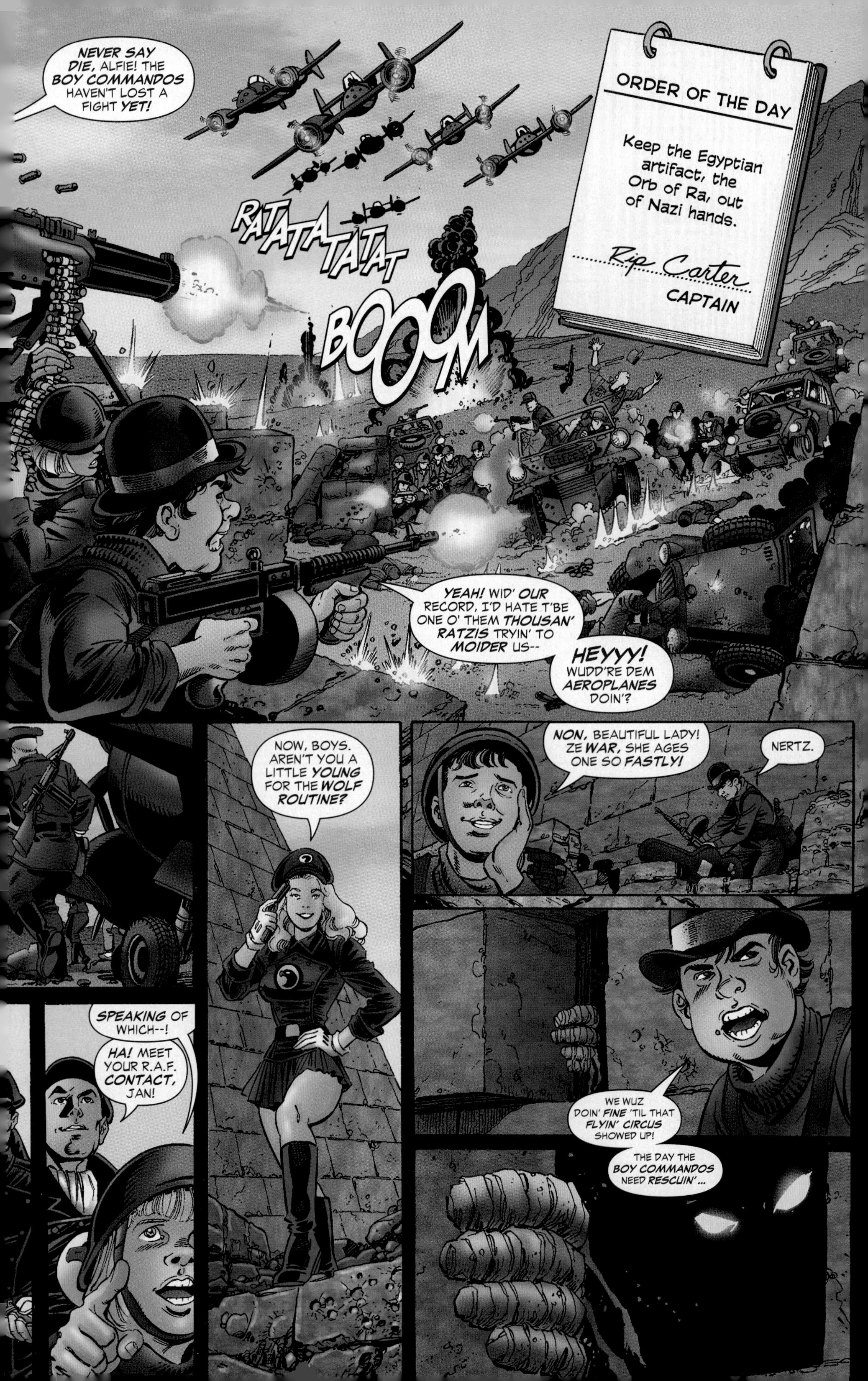
NEVER SAY DIE, ALFIE! THE BOY COMMANDOS HAVEN'T LOST A FIGHT YET!
ORDER OF THE DAY
Keep the Egyptian artifact, the Orb of Ra, out of Nazi hands.
Rip Carter
CAPTAIN
RATATATATAT
BOOOM
YEAH! WID' OUR RECORD, I'D HATE T'BE ONE O' THEM THOUSAN' RATZIS TRYIN' TO MOIDER US--
HEYYY! WUDD'RE DEM AEROPLANES DOIN'?
NOW, BOYS. AREN'T YOU A LITTLE YOUNG FOR THE WOLF ROUTINE?
NON, BEAUTIFUL LADY! ZE WAR, SHE AGES ONE SO FASTLY!
NERTZ.
SPEAKING OF WHICH--!
HA! MEET YOUR R.A.F. CONTACT, JAN!
WE WUZ DOIN' FINE 'TIL THAT FLYIN' CIRCUS SHOWED UP!
THE DAY THE BOY COMMANDOS NEED RESCUIN'...

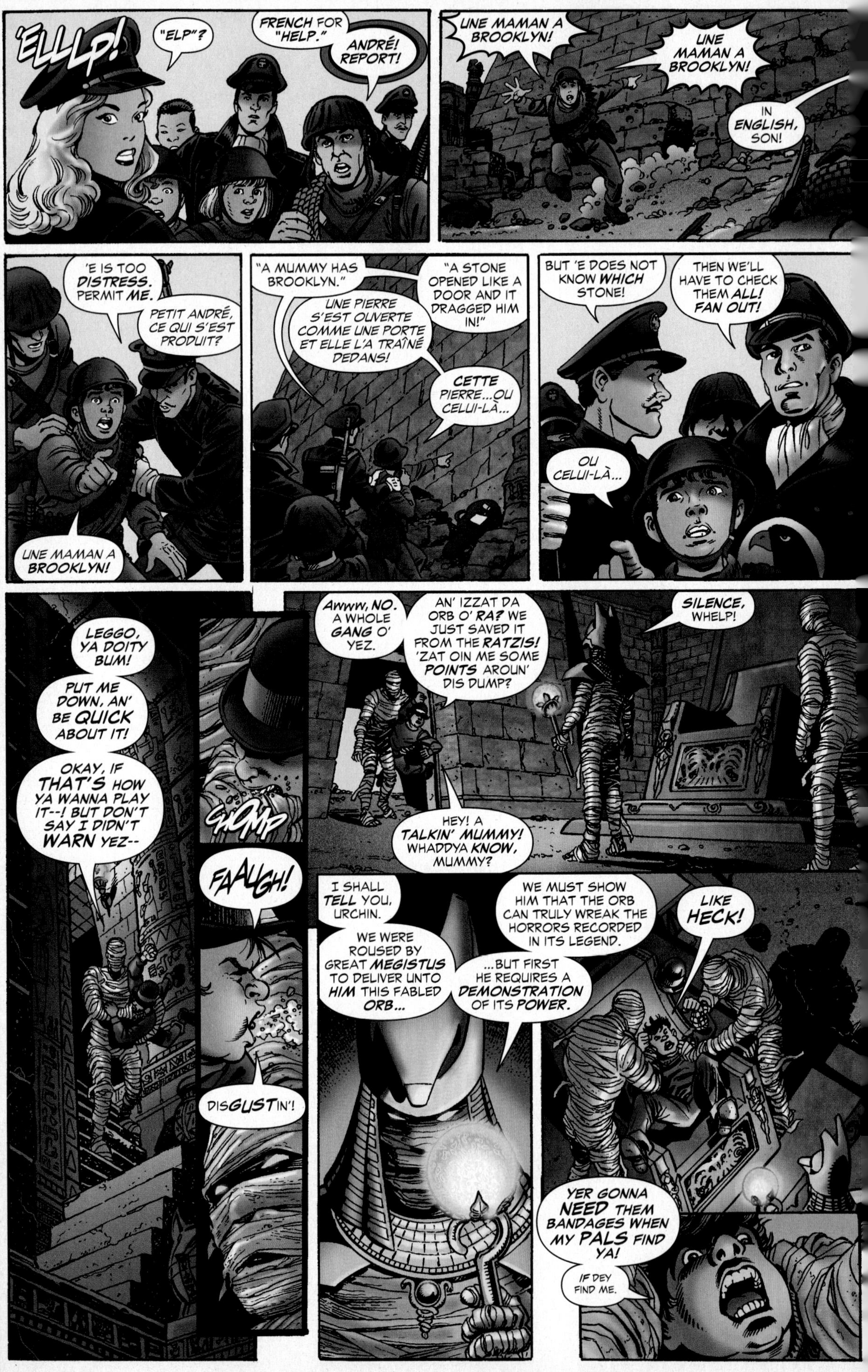
'ELLLP!
"ELP"?
FRENCH FOR "HELP."
ANDRÉ! REPORT!
UNE MAMAN A BROOKLYN!
UNE MAMAN A BROOKLYN!
IN ENGLISH, SON!
'E IS TOO DISTRESS. PERMIT ME.
PETIT ANDRÉ, CE QUI S'EST PRODUIT?
UNE MAMAN A BROOKLYN!
"A MUMMY HAS BROOKLYN."
UNE PIERRE S'EST OUVERTE COMME UNE PORTE ET ELLE L'A TRAÎNÉ DEDANS!
"A STONE OPENED LIKE A DOOR AND IT DRAGGED HIM IN!"
CETTE PIERRE...OU CELUI-LÀ...
BUT 'E DOES NOT KNOW WHICH STONE!
THEN WE'LL HAVE TO CHECK THEM ALL! FAN OUT!
OU CELUI-LÀ...
LEGGO, YA DOITY BUM!
PUT ME DOWN, AN' BE QUICK ABOUT IT!
OKAY, IF THAT'S HOW YA WANNA PLAY IT--! BUT DON'T SAY I DIDN'T WARN YEZ--
CHOMP
FAAUGH!
DISGUSTIN'!
AWWW, NO. A WHOLE GANG O' YEZ.
AN' IZZAT DA ORB O' RA? WE JUST SAVED IT FROM THE RATZIS! 'ZAT OIN ME SOME POINTS AROUN' DIS DUMP?
SILENCE, WHELP!
HEY! A TALKIN' MUMMY! WHADDYA KNOW, MUMMY?
I SHALL TELL YOU, URCHIN.
WE WERE ROUSED BY GREAT MEGISTUS TO DELIVER UNTO HIM THIS FABLED ORB...
WE MUST SHOW HIM THAT THE ORB CAN TRULY WREAK THE HORRORS RECORDED IN ITS LEGEND.
...BUT FIRST HE REQUIRES A DEMONSTRATION OF ITS POWER.
LIKE HECK!
YER GONNA NEED THEM BANDAGES WHEN MY PALS FIND YA!
IF DEY FIND ME.

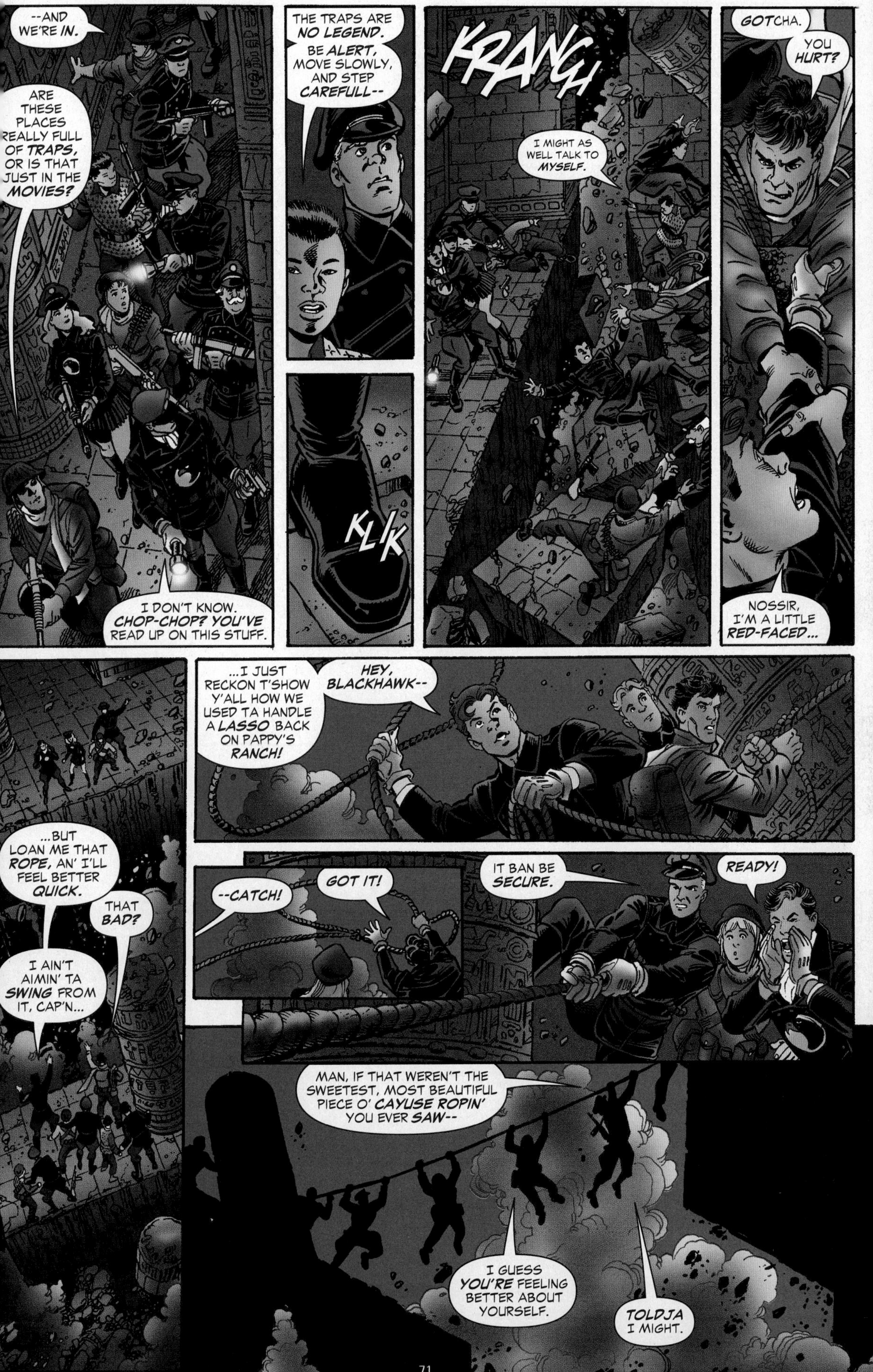
--AND WE'RE IN.
ARE THESE PLACES REALLY FULL OF TRAPS, OR IS THAT JUST IN THE MOVIES?
I DON'T KNOW. CHOP-CHOP? YOU'VE READ UP ON THIS STUFF.
THE TRAPS ARE NO LEGEND. BE ALERT, MOVE SLOWLY, AND STEP CAREFULL--
KLIK
KRANCH
I MIGHT AS WELL TALK TO MYSELF.
GOTCHA.
YOU HURT?
NOSSIR, I'M A LITTLE RED-FACED...
...BUT LOAN ME THAT ROPE, AN' I'LL FEEL BETTER QUICK.
THAT BAD?
I AIN'T AIMIN' TA SWING FROM IT, CAP'N...
...I JUST RECKON T'SHOW Y'ALL HOW WE USED TA HANDLE A LASSO BACK ON PAPPY'S RANCH!
HEY, BLACKHAWK--
--CATCH!
GOT IT!
IT BAN BE SECURE.
READY!
MAN, IF THAT WEREN'T THE SWEETEST, MOST BEAUTIFUL PIECE O' CAYUSE ROPIN' YOU EVER SAW--
I GUESS YOU'RE FEELING BETTER ABOUT YOURSELF.
TOLDJA I MIGHT.

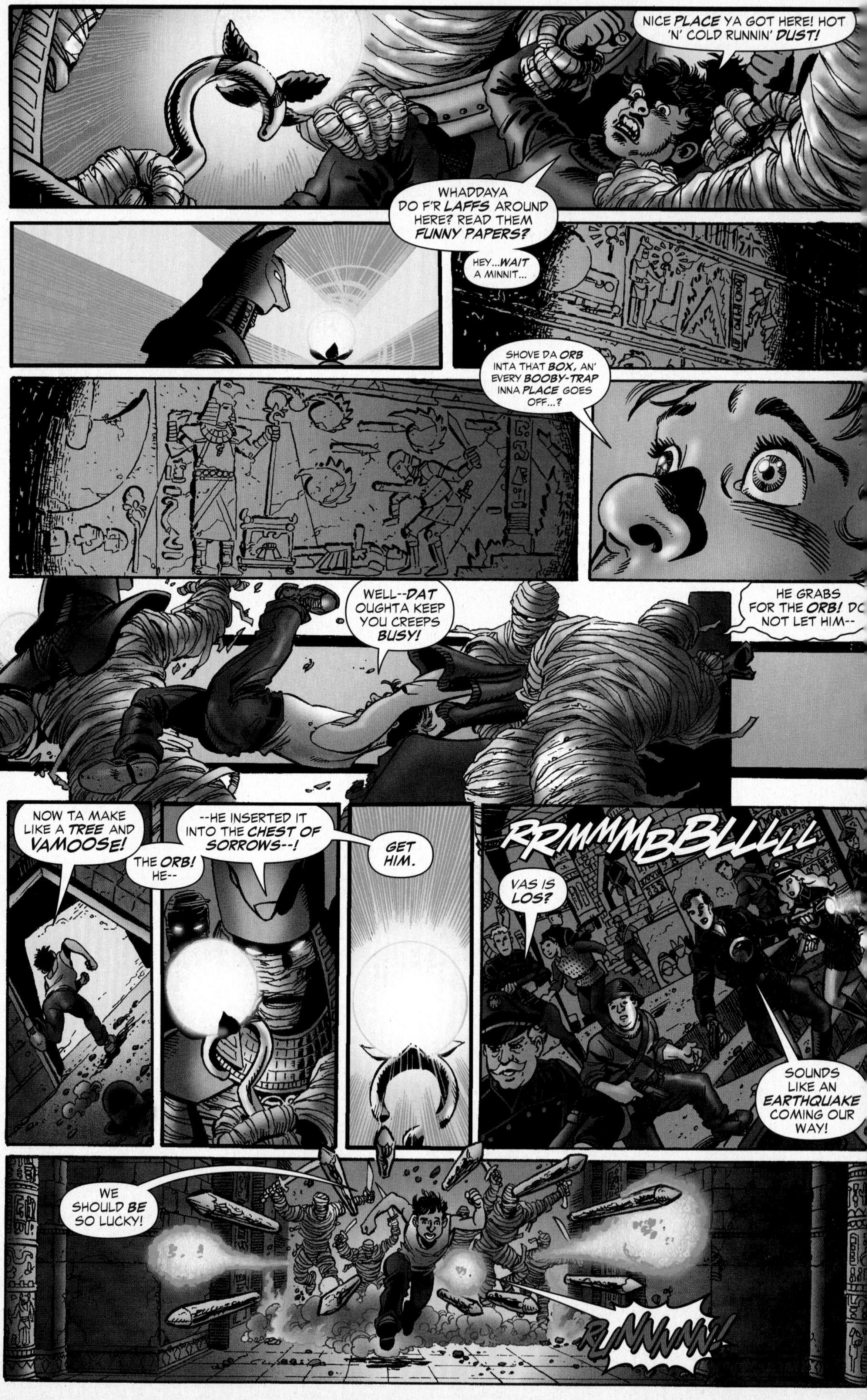
NICE PLACE YA GOT HERE! HOT 'N' COLD RUNNIN' DUST!
WHADDAYA DO F'R LAFFS AROUND HERE? READ THEM FUNNY PAPERS?
HEY...WAIT A MINNIT...
SHOVE DA ORB INTA THAT BOX, AN' EVERY BOOBY-TRAP INNA PLACE GOES OFF...?
WELL--DAT OUGHTA KEEP YOU CREEPS BUSY!
HE GRABS FOR THE ORB! DO NOT LET HIM--
NOW TA MAKE LIKE A TREE AND VAMOOSE!
THE ORB! HE--
--HE INSERTED IT INTO THE CHEST OF SORROWS--!
GET HIM.
RRMMMBBLLLLL
VAS IS LOS?
SOUNDS LIKE AN EARTHQUAKE COMING OUR WAY!
WE SHOULD BE SO LUCKY!
RUNNNN!

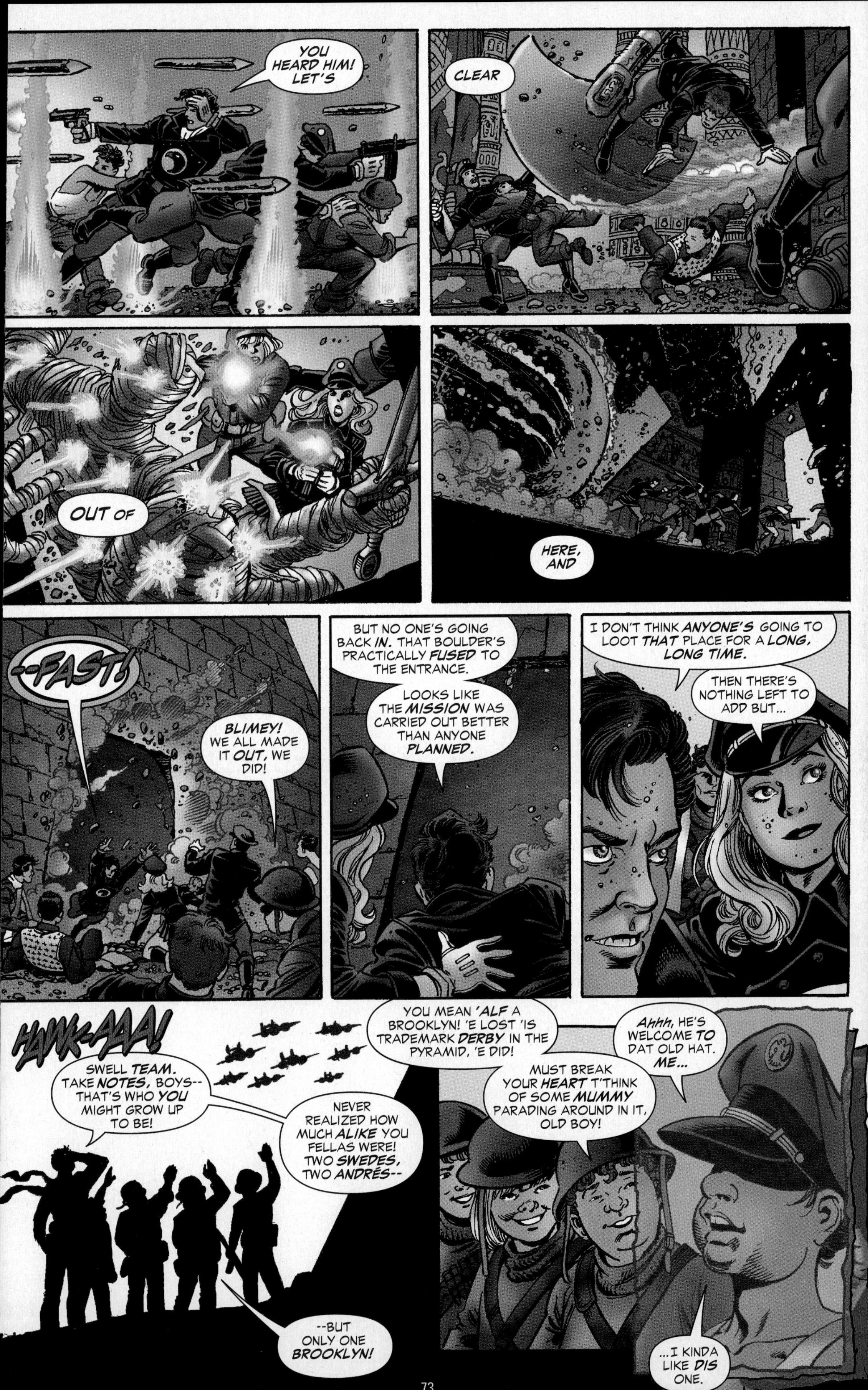
YOU HEARD HIM! LET'S
CLEAR
OUT OF
HERE, AND
--FAST!
BLIMEY! WE ALL MADE IT OUT, WE DID!
BUT NO ONE'S GOING BACK IN. THAT BOULDER'S PRACTICALLY FUSED TO THE ENTRANCE.
LOOKS LIKE THE MISSION WAS CARRIED OUT BETTER THAN ANYONE PLANNED.
I DON'T THINK ANYONE'S GOING TO LOOT THAT PLACE FOR A LONG, LONG TIME.
THEN THERE'S NOTHING LEFT TO ADD BUT...
HAWK-AAA!
SWELL TEAM. TAKE NOTES, BOYS--THAT'S WHO YOU MIGHT GROW UP TO BE!
NEVER REALIZED HOW MUCH ALIKE YOU FELLAS WERE! TWO SWEDES, TWO ANDRÉS--
--BUT ONLY ONE BROOKLYN!
YOU MEAN 'ALF A BROOKLYN! 'E LOST 'IS TRADEMARK DERBY IN THE PYRAMID, 'E DID!
MUST BREAK YOUR HEART T'THINK OF SOME MUMMY PARADING AROUND IN IT, OLD BOY!
Ahhh, HE'S WELCOME TO DAT OLD HAT. ME...
...I KINDA LIKE DIS ONE.

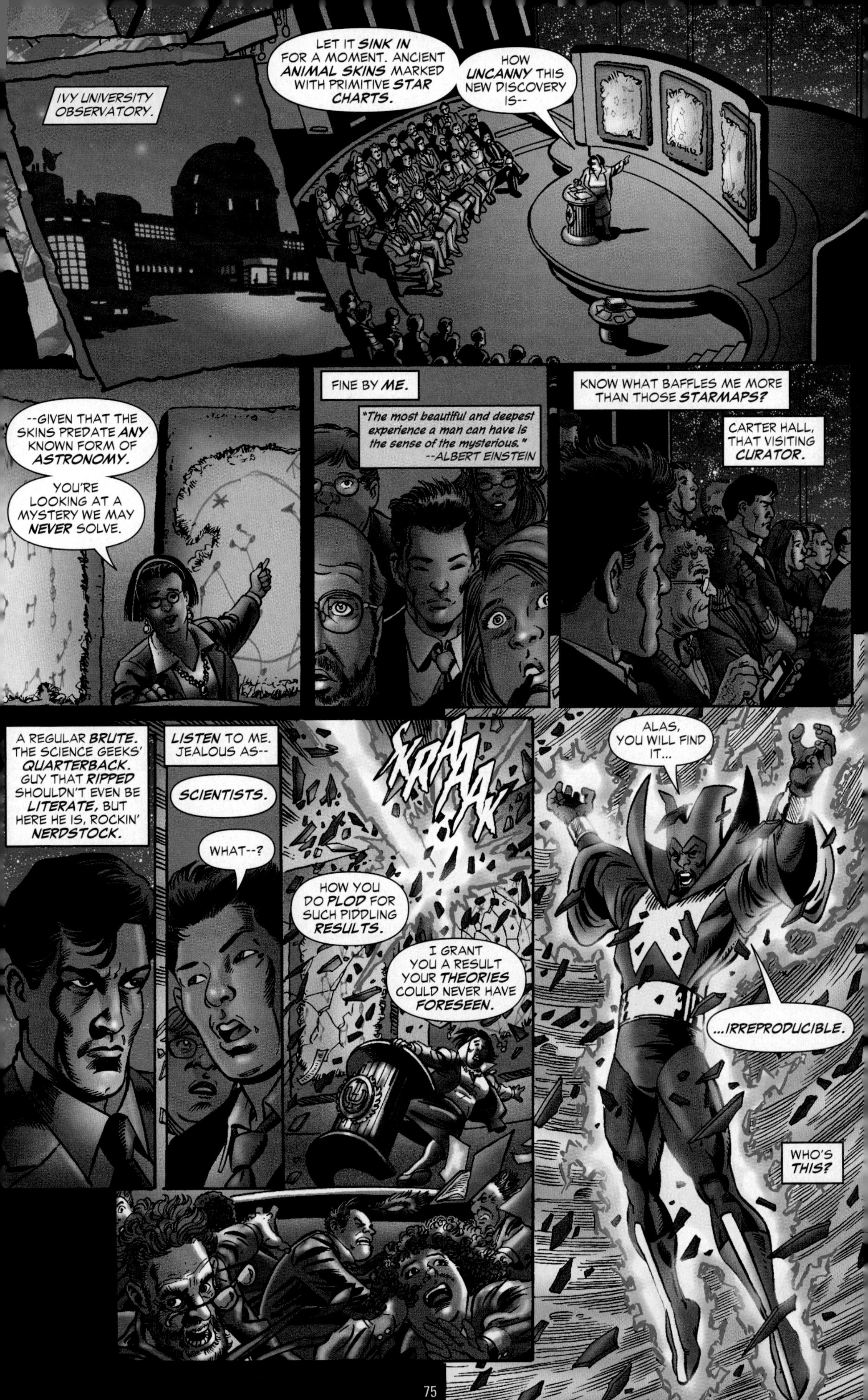
IVY UNIVERSITY OBSERVATORY.
LET IT SINK IN FOR A MOMENT. ANCIENT ANIMAL SKINS MARKED WITH PRIMITIVE STAR CHARTS.
HOW UNCANNY THIS NEW DISCOVERY IS--
--GIVEN THAT THE SKINS PREDATE ANY KNOWN FORM OF ASTRONOMY.
YOU'RE LOOKING AT A MYSTERY WE MAY NEVER SOLVE.
FINE BY ME.
"The most beautiful and deepest experience a man can have is the sense of the mysterious." --ALBERT EINSTEIN
KNOW WHAT BAFFLES ME MORE THAN THOSE STARMAPS?
CARTER HALL, THAT VISITING CURATOR.
A REGULAR BRUTE. THE SCIENCE GEEKS' QUARTERBACK. GUY THAT RIPPED SHOULDN'T EVEN BE LITERATE, BUT HERE HE IS, ROCKIN' NERDSTOCK.
LISTEN TO ME. JEALOUS AS--
SCIENTISTS.
WHAT--?
KRAAAAK
HOW YOU DO PLOD FOR SUCH PIDDLING RESULTS.
I GRANT YOU A RESULT YOUR THEORIES COULD NEVER HAVE FORESEEN.
ALAS, YOU WILL FIND IT...
...IRREPRODUCIBLE.
WHO'S THIS?

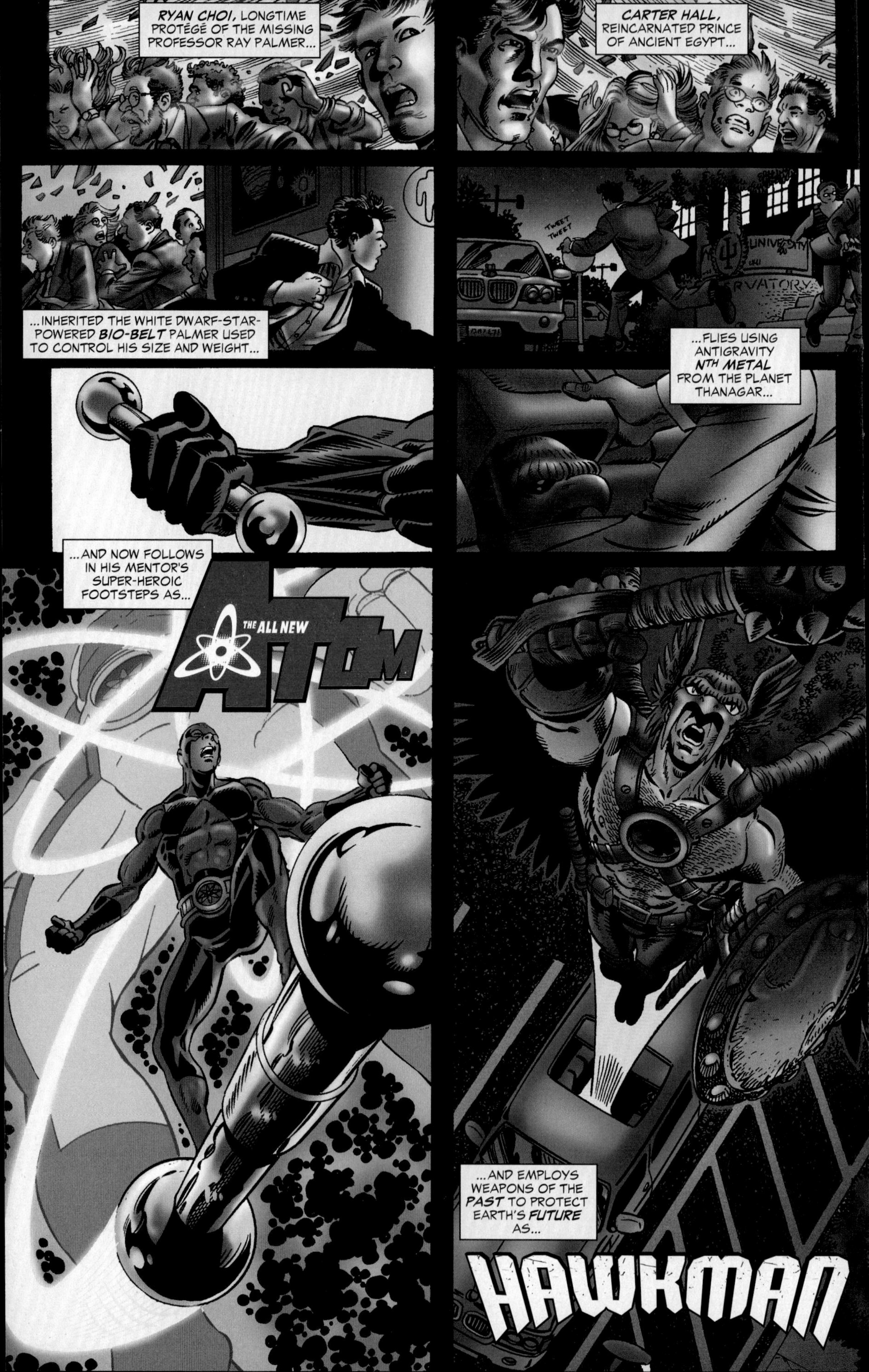
RYAN CHOI, LONGTIME PROTÉGÉ OF THE MISSING PROFESSOR RAY PALMER...
CARTER HALL, REINCARNATED PRINCE OF ANCIENT EGYPT...
...INHERITED THE WHITE DWARF-STAR-POWERED BIO-BELT PALMER USED TO CONTROL HIS SIZE AND WEIGHT...
TWEET TWEET
...FLIES USING ANTIGRAVITY NTH METAL FROM THE PLANET THANAGAR...
...AND NOW FOLLOWS IN HIS MENTOR'S SUPER-HEROIC FOOTSTEPS AS...
THE ALL NEW ATOM
...AND EMPLOYS WEAPONS OF THE PAST TO PROTECT EARTH'S FUTURE AS...
HAWKMAN

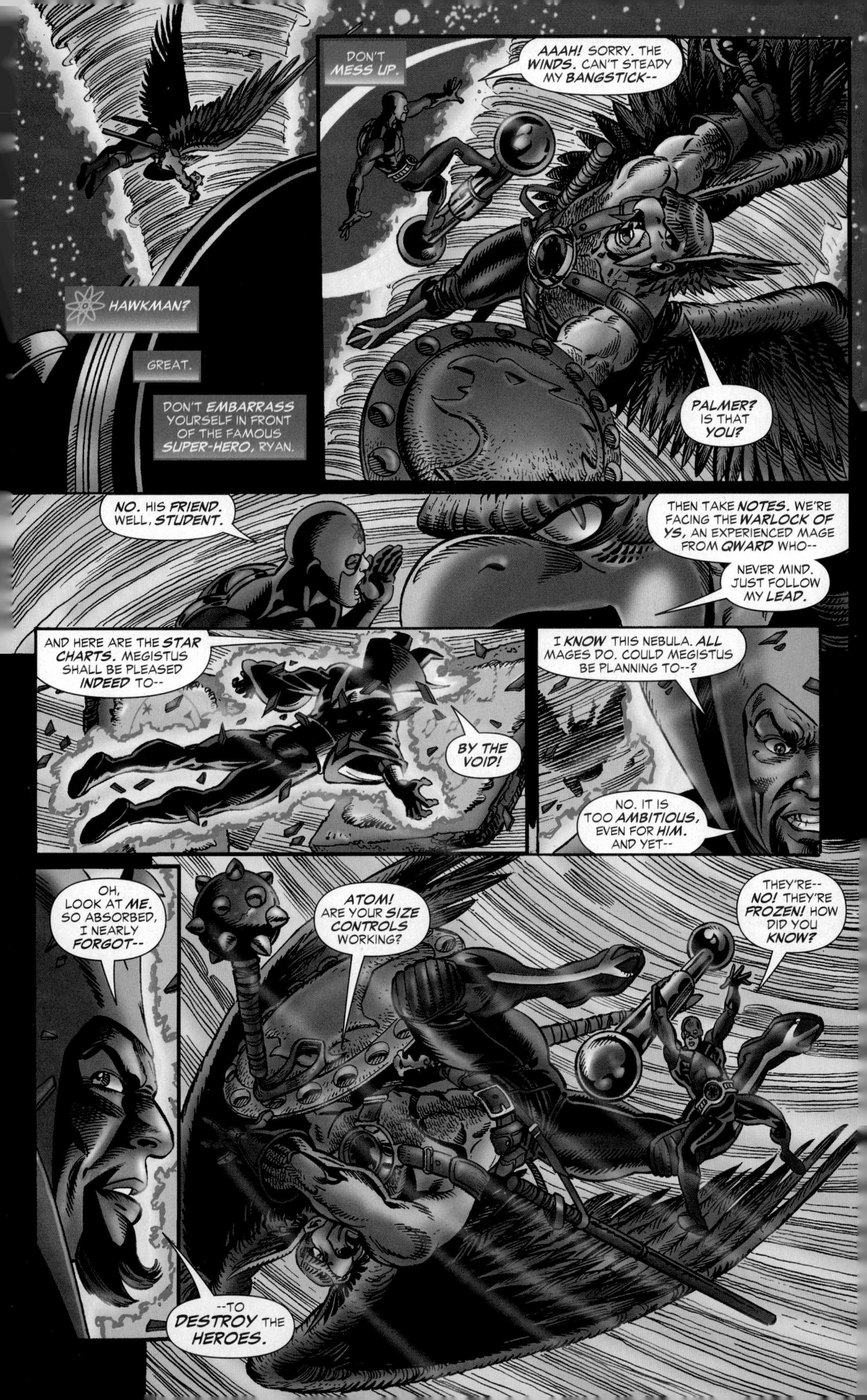
HAWKMAN?
GREAT.
DON'T EMBARRASS YOURSELF IN FRONT OF THE FAMOUS SUPER-HERO, RYAN.
DON'T MESS UP.
AAAH! SORRY. THE WINDS. CAN'T STEADY MY BANGSTICK--
PALMER? IS THAT YOU?
NO. HIS FRIEND. WELL, STUDENT.
THEN TAKE NOTES. WE'RE FACING THE WARLOCK OF YS, AN EXPERIENCED MAGE FROM QWARD WHO--
NEVER MIND. JUST FOLLOW MY LEAD.
AND HERE ARE THE STAR CHARTS. MEGISTUS SHALL BE PLEASED INDEED TO--
BY THE VOID!
I KNOW THIS NEBULA. ALL MAGES DO. COULD MEGISTUS BE PLANNING TO--?
NO. IT IS TOO AMBITIOUS, EVEN FOR HIM. AND YET--
OH, LOOK AT ME. SO ABSORBED, I NEARLY FORGOT--
--TO DESTROY THE HEROES.
ATOM! ARE YOUR SIZE CONTROLS WORKING?
THEY'RE-- NO! THEY'RE FROZEN! HOW DID YOU KNOW?

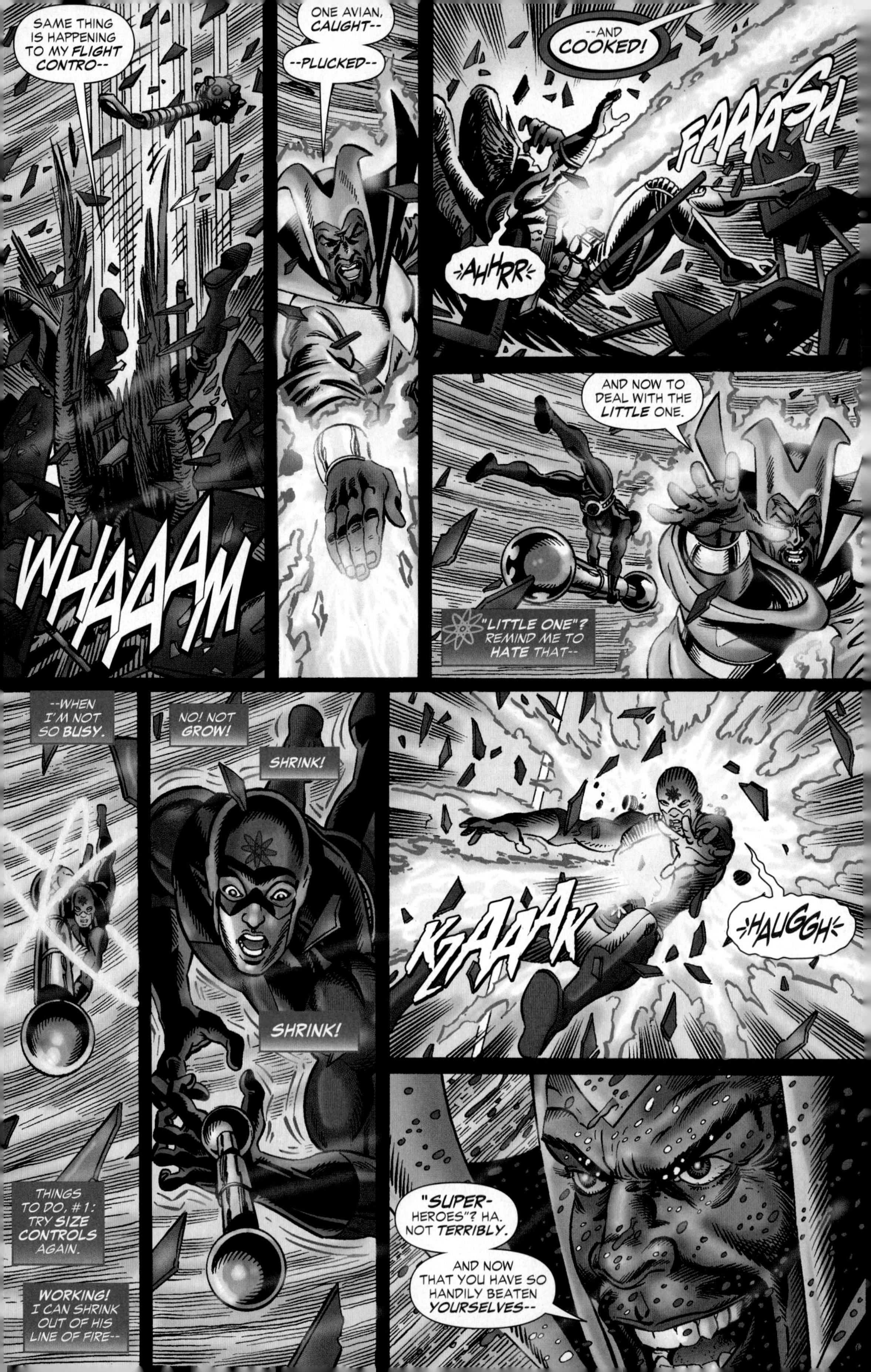
SAME THING IS HAPPENING TO MY FLIGHT CONTRO--
WHAAAAM
ONE AVIAN, CAUGHT--
--PLUCKED--
--AND COOKED!
FAAAASH
AHHRR
AND NOW TO DEAL WITH THE LITTLE ONE.
"LITTLE ONE"? REMIND ME TO HATE THAT--
--WHEN I'M NOT SO BUSY.
THINGS TO DO, #1: TRY SIZE CONTROLS AGAIN.
WORKING! I CAN SHRINK OUT OF HIS LINE OF FIRE--
NO! NOT GROW!
SHRINK!
SHRINK!
KZAAAK
HAUGGH
"SUPER-HEROES"? HA. NOT TERRIBLY.
AND NOW THAT YOU HAVE SO HANDILY BEATEN YOURSELVES--

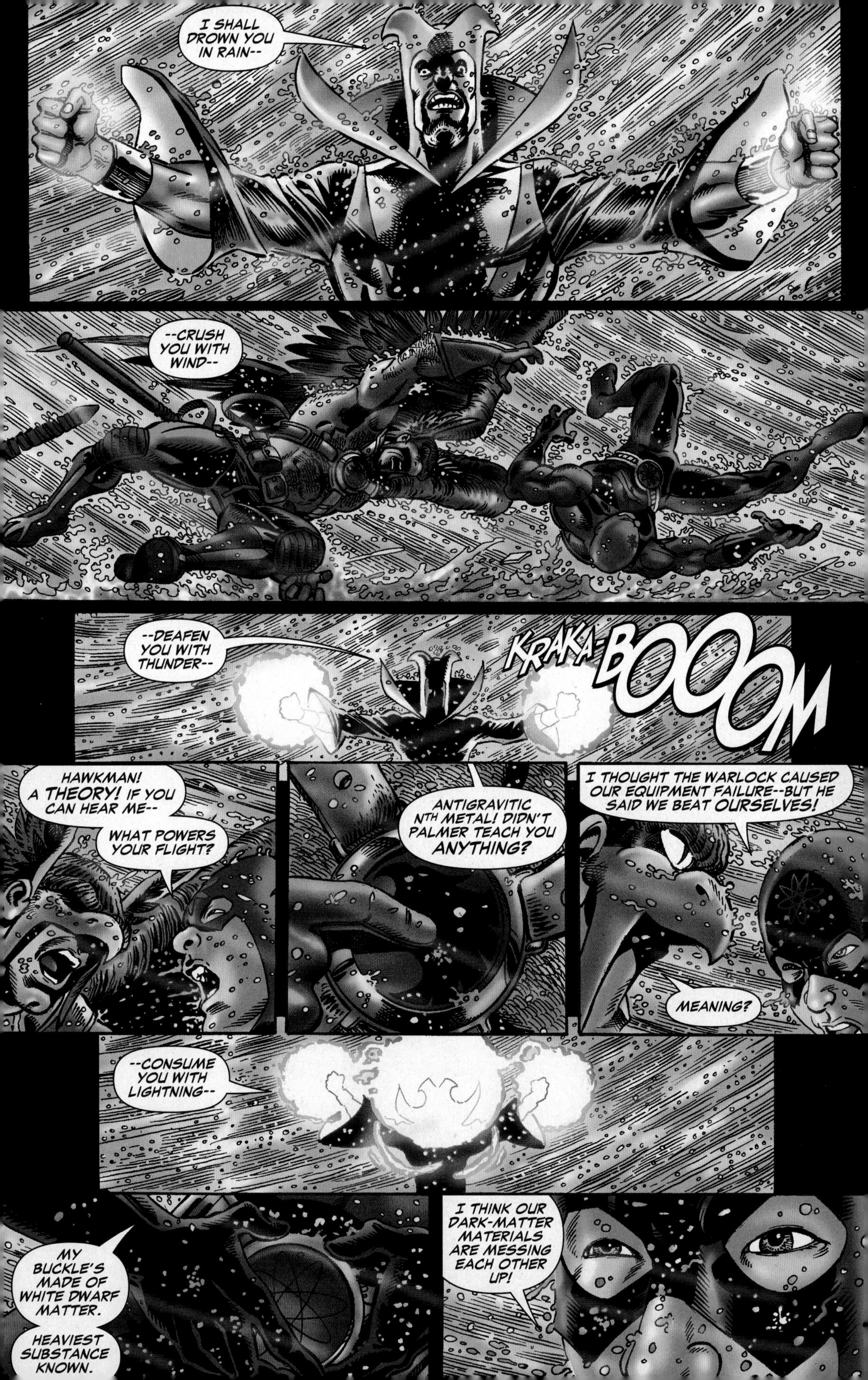
I SHALL DROWN YOU IN RAIN--
--CRUSH YOU WITH WIND--
--DEAFEN YOU WITH THUNDER--
KRAKA-BOOOOM
HAWKMAN! A THEORY! IF YOU CAN HEAR ME--
WHAT POWERS YOUR FLIGHT?
ANTIGRAVITIC NTH METAL! DIDN'T PALMER TEACH YOU ANYTHING?
I THOUGHT THE WARLOCK CAUSED OUR EQUIPMENT FAILURE--BUT HE SAID WE BEAT OURSELVES!
MEANING?
--CONSUME YOU WITH LIGHTNING--
MY BUCKLE'S MADE OF WHITE DWARF MATTER.
HEAVIEST SUBSTANCE KNOWN.
I THINK OUR DARK-MATTER MATERIALS ARE MESSING EACH OTHER UP!

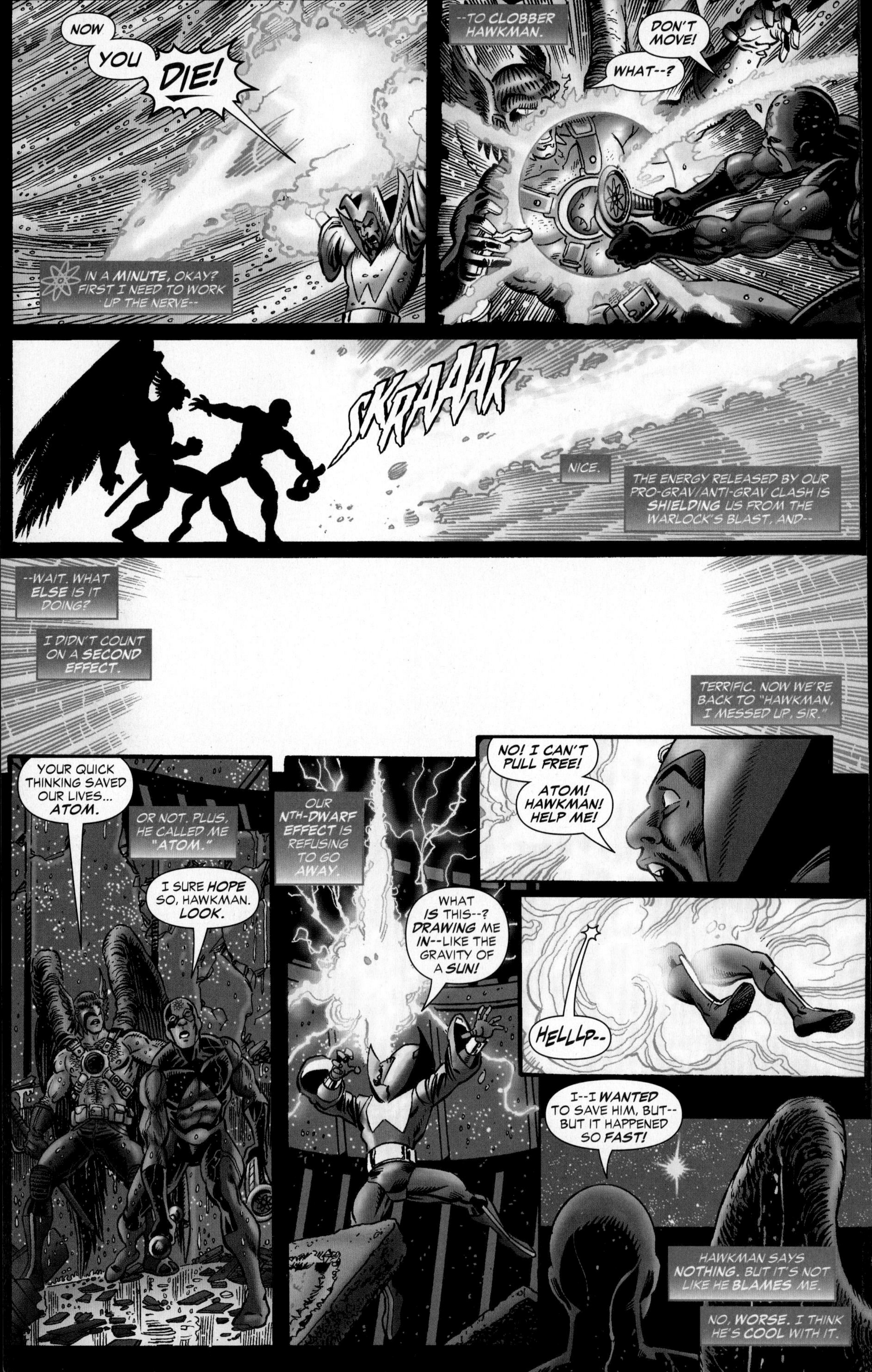
NOW
YOU
DIE!
IN A MINUTE, OKAY? FIRST I NEED TO WORK UP THE NERVE--
--TO CLOBBER HAWKMAN.
DON'T MOVE!
WHAT--?
SKRAAAK
NICE.
THE ENERGY RELEASED BY OUR PRO-GRAV/ANTI-GRAV CLASH IS SHIELDING US FROM THE WARLOCK'S BLAST, AND--
--WAIT. WHAT ELSE IS IT DOING?
I DIDN'T COUNT ON A SECOND EFFECT.
TERRIFIC. NOW WE'RE BACK TO "HAWKMAN, I MESSED UP, SIR."
YOUR QUICK THINKING SAVED OUR LIVES... ATOM.
OR NOT. PLUS, HE CALLED ME "ATOM."
I SURE HOPE SO, HAWKMAN. LOOK.
OUR NTH-DWARF EFFECT IS REFUSING TO GO AWAY.
WHAT IS THIS--? DRAWING ME IN--LIKE THE GRAVITY OF A SUN!
NO! I CAN'T PULL FREE!
ATOM! HAWKMAN! HELP ME!
HELLLP--
I--I WANTED TO SAVE HIM, BUT--BUT IT HAPPENED SO FAST!
HAWKMAN SAYS NOTHING. BUT IT'S NOT LIKE HE BLAMES ME.
NO, WORSE. I THINK HE'S COOL WITH IT.

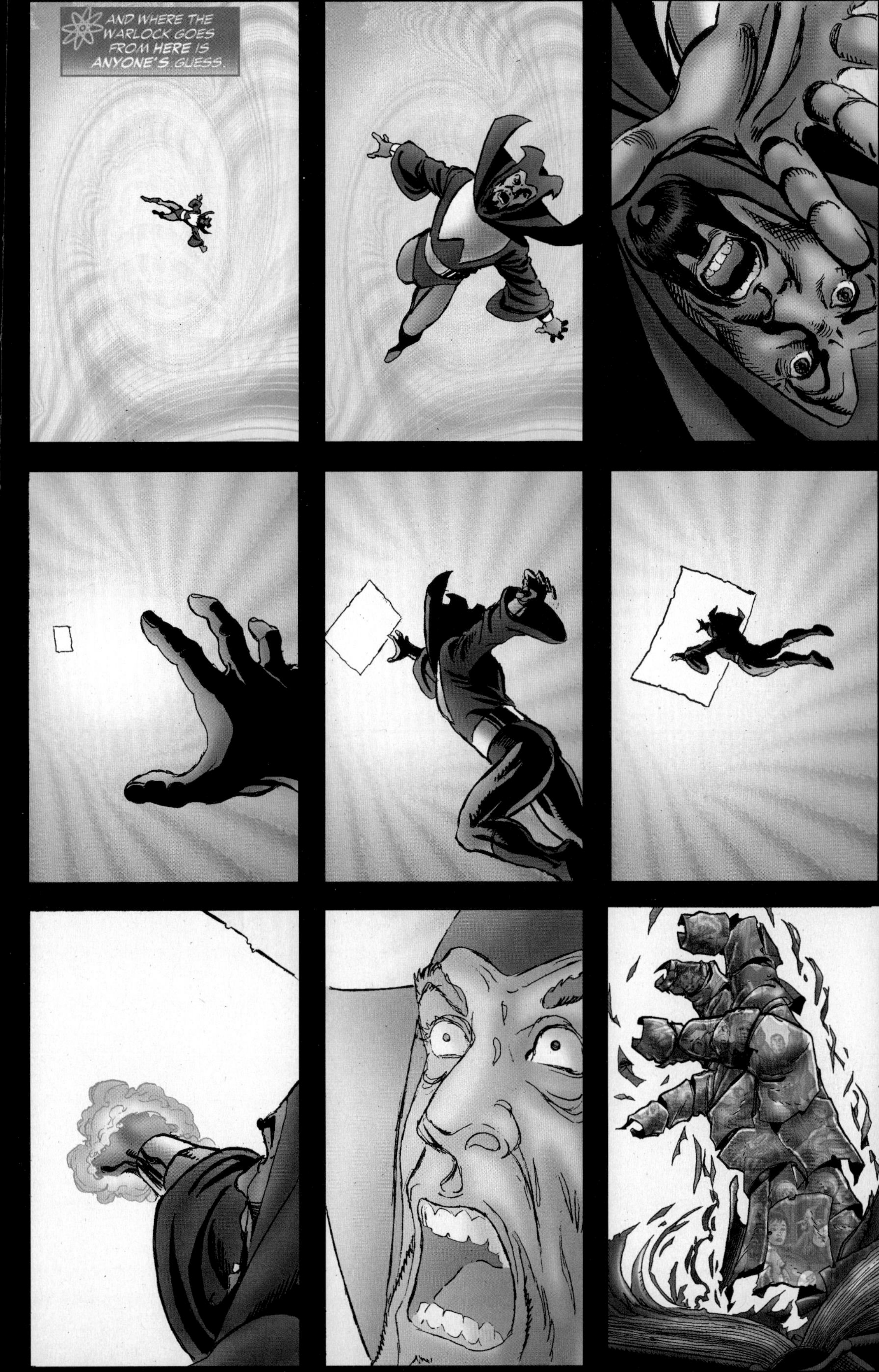
AND WHERE THE WARLOCK GOES FROM HERE IS ANYONE'S GUESS.

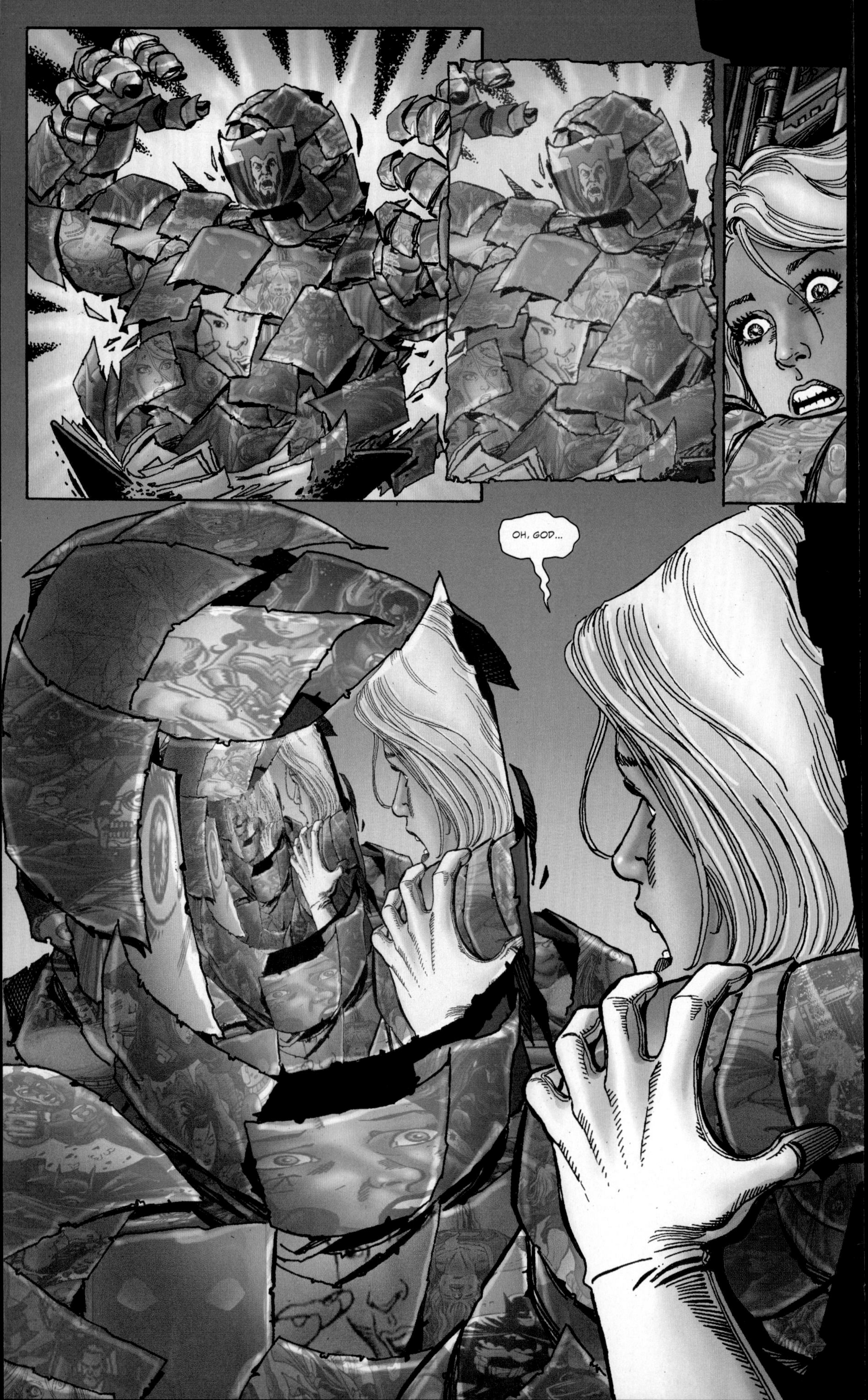
OH, GOD...

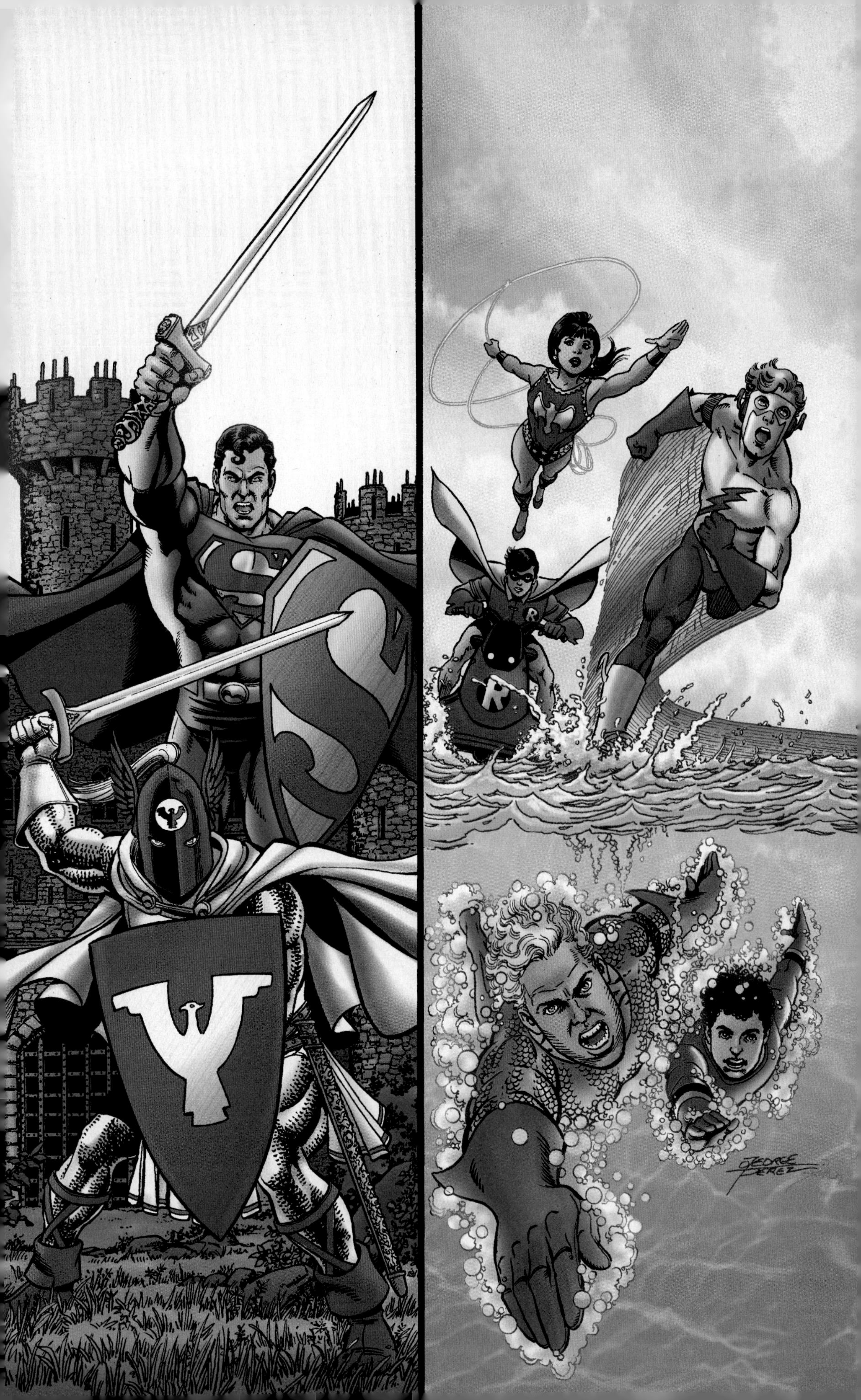
GEORGE PEREZ

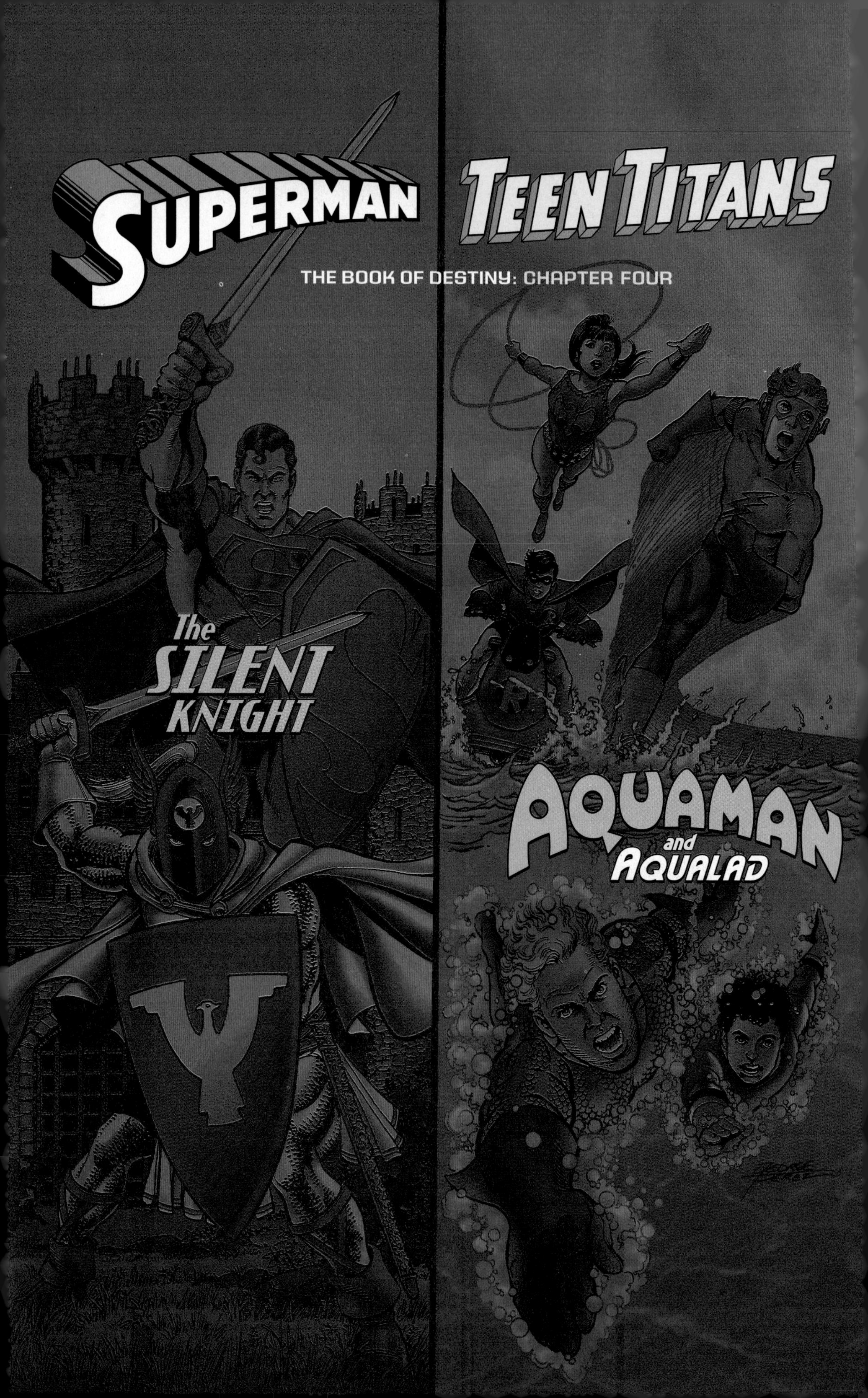
SUPERMAN
TEEN TITANS
THE BOOK OF DESTINY: CHAPTER FOUR
The SILENT KNIGHT
AQUAMAN and AQUALAD

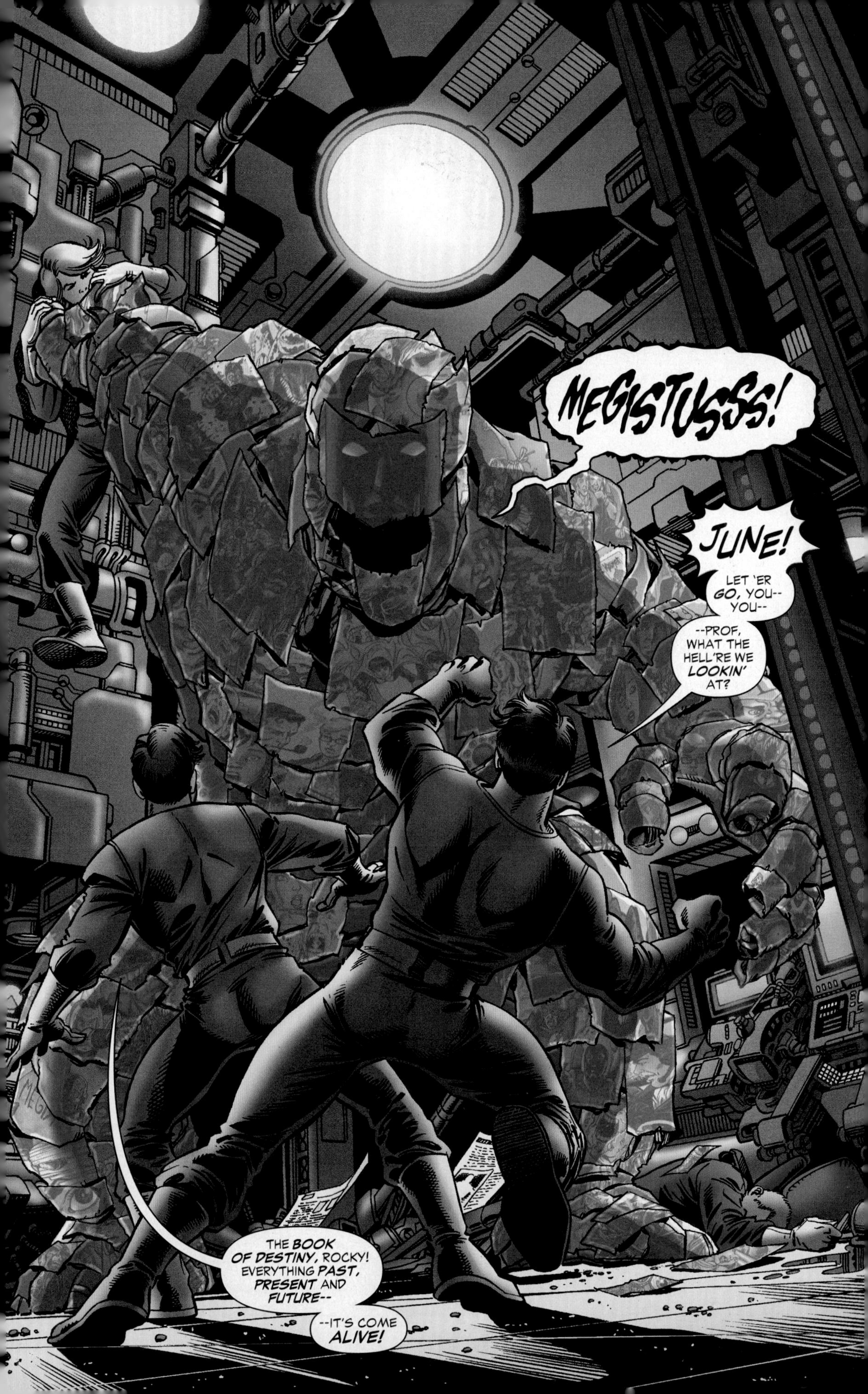
MEGISTUSSS!
JUNE!
LET 'ER GO, YOU-- YOU--
--PROF, WHAT THE HELL'RE WE LOOKIN' AT?
THE BOOK OF DESTINY, ROCKY! EVERYTHING PAST, PRESENT AND FUTURE--
--IT'S COME ALIVE!

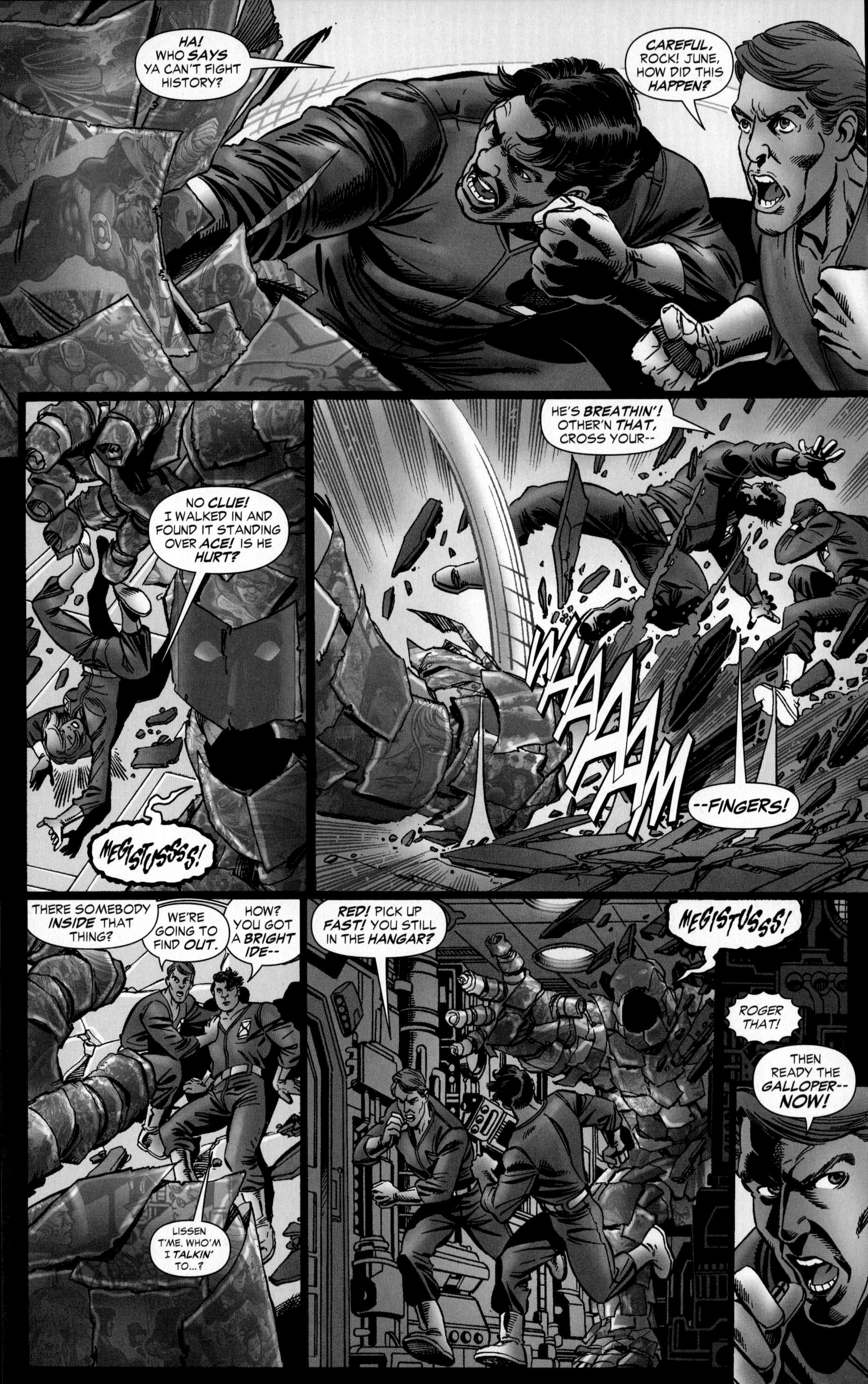
HA! WHO SAYS YA CAN'T FIGHT HISTORY?
CAREFUL, ROCK! JUNE, HOW DID THIS HAPPEN?
NO CLUE! I WALKED IN AND FOUND IT STANDING OVER ACE! IS HE HURT?
MEGISTUSSSS!
HE'S BREATHIN'! OTHER'N THAT, CROSS YOUR--
WHAAAAM
--FINGERS!
THERE SOMEBODY INSIDE THAT THING?
WE'RE GOING TO FIND OUT.
HOW? YOU GOT A BRIGHT IDE--
LISSEN T'ME. WHO'M I TALKIN' TO...?
RED! PICK UP FAST! YOU STILL IN THE HANGAR?
MEGISTUSSS!
ROGER THAT!
THEN READY THE GALLOPER-- NOW!

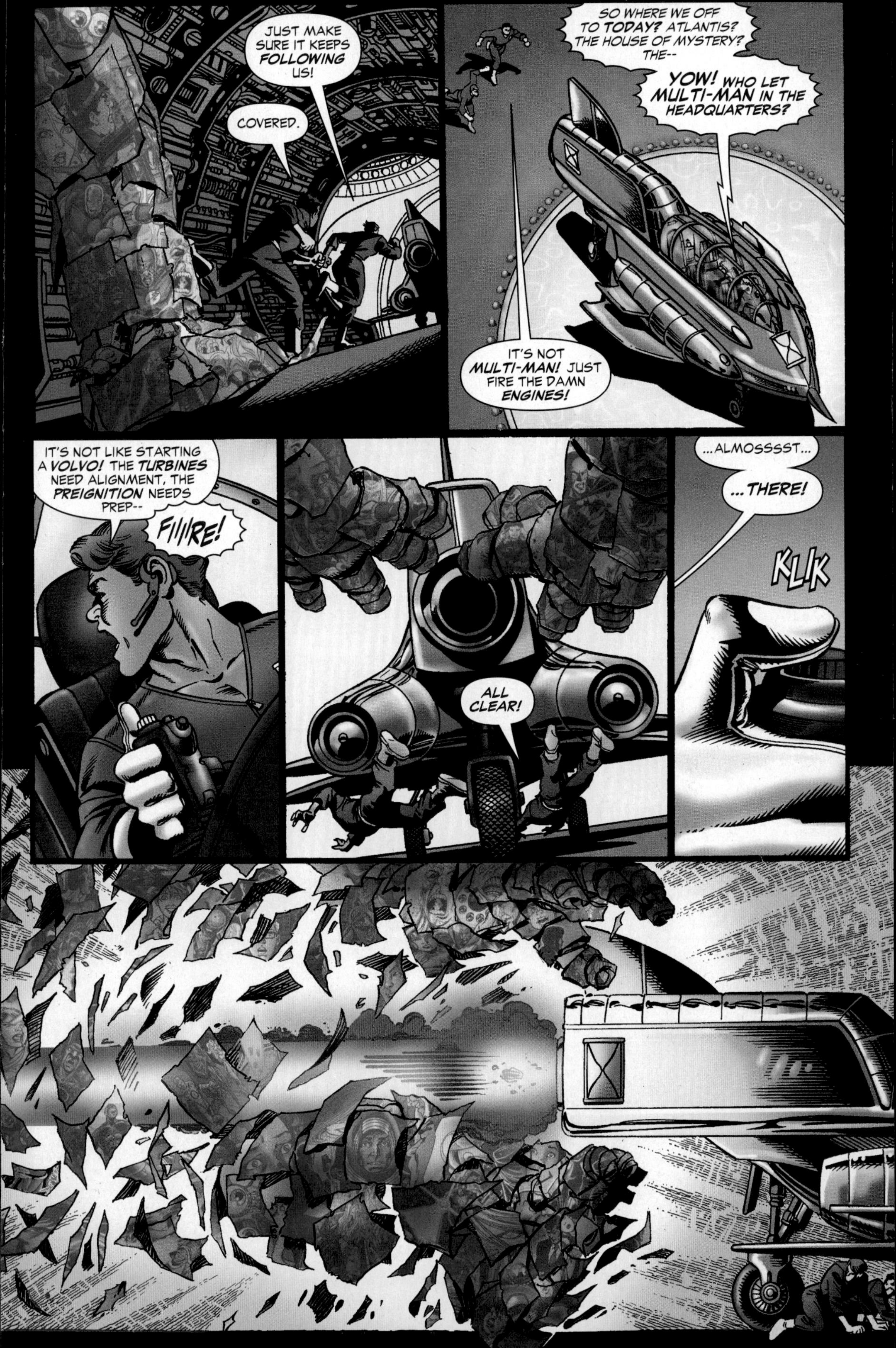
JUST MAKE SURE IT KEEPS FOLLOWING US!
COVERED.
SO WHERE WE OFF TO TODAY? ATLANTIS? THE HOUSE OF MYSTERY? THE--
YOW! WHO LET MULTI-MAN IN THE HEADQUARTERS?
IT'S NOT MULTI-MAN! JUST FIRE THE DAMN ENGINES!
IT'S NOT LIKE STARTING A VOLVO! THE TURBINES NEED ALIGNMENT, THE PREIGNITION NEEDS PREP--
FIIIRE!
ALL CLEAR!
...ALMOSSSST...
...THERE!
KLIK

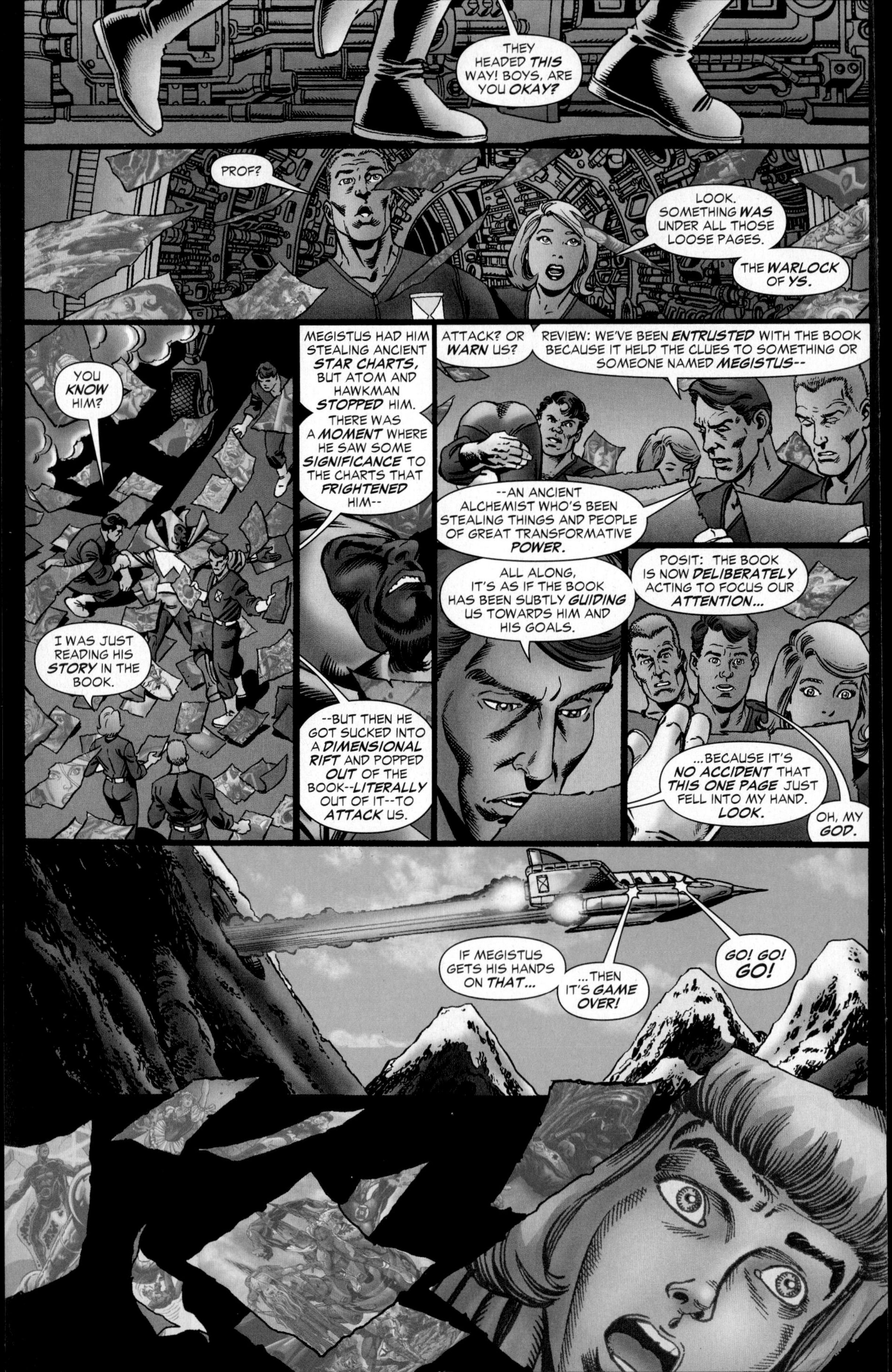
THEY HEADED THIS WAY! BOYS, ARE YOU OKAY?
PROF?
LOOK. SOMETHING WAS UNDER ALL THOSE LOOSE PAGES.
THE WARLOCK OF YS.
YOU KNOW HIM?
I WAS JUST READING HIS STORY IN THE BOOK.
MEGISTUS HAD HIM STEALING ANCIENT STAR CHARTS, BUT ATOM AND HAWKMAN STOPPED HIM. THERE WAS A MOMENT WHERE HE SAW SOME SIGNIFICANCE TO THE CHARTS THAT FRIGHTENED HIM--
--BUT THEN HE GOT SUCKED INTO A DIMENSIONAL RIFT AND POPPED OUT OF THE BOOK--LITERALLY OUT OF IT--TO ATTACK US.
ATTACK? OR WARN US?
REVIEW: WE'VE BEEN ENTRUSTED WITH THE BOOK BECAUSE IT HELD THE CLUES TO SOMETHING OR SOMEONE NAMED MEGISTUS--
--AN ANCIENT ALCHEMIST WHO'S BEEN STEALING THINGS AND PEOPLE OF GREAT TRANSFORMATIVE POWER.
ALL ALONG, IT'S AS IF THE BOOK HAS BEEN SUBTLY GUIDING US TOWARDS HIM AND HIS GOALS.
POSIT: THE BOOK IS NOW DELIBERATELY ACTING TO FOCUS OUR ATTENTION...
...BECAUSE IT'S NO ACCIDENT THAT THIS ONE PAGE JUST FELL INTO MY HAND. LOOK.
OH, MY GOD.
IF MEGISTUS GETS HIS HANDS ON THAT...
...THEN IT'S GAME OVER!
GO! GO! GO!

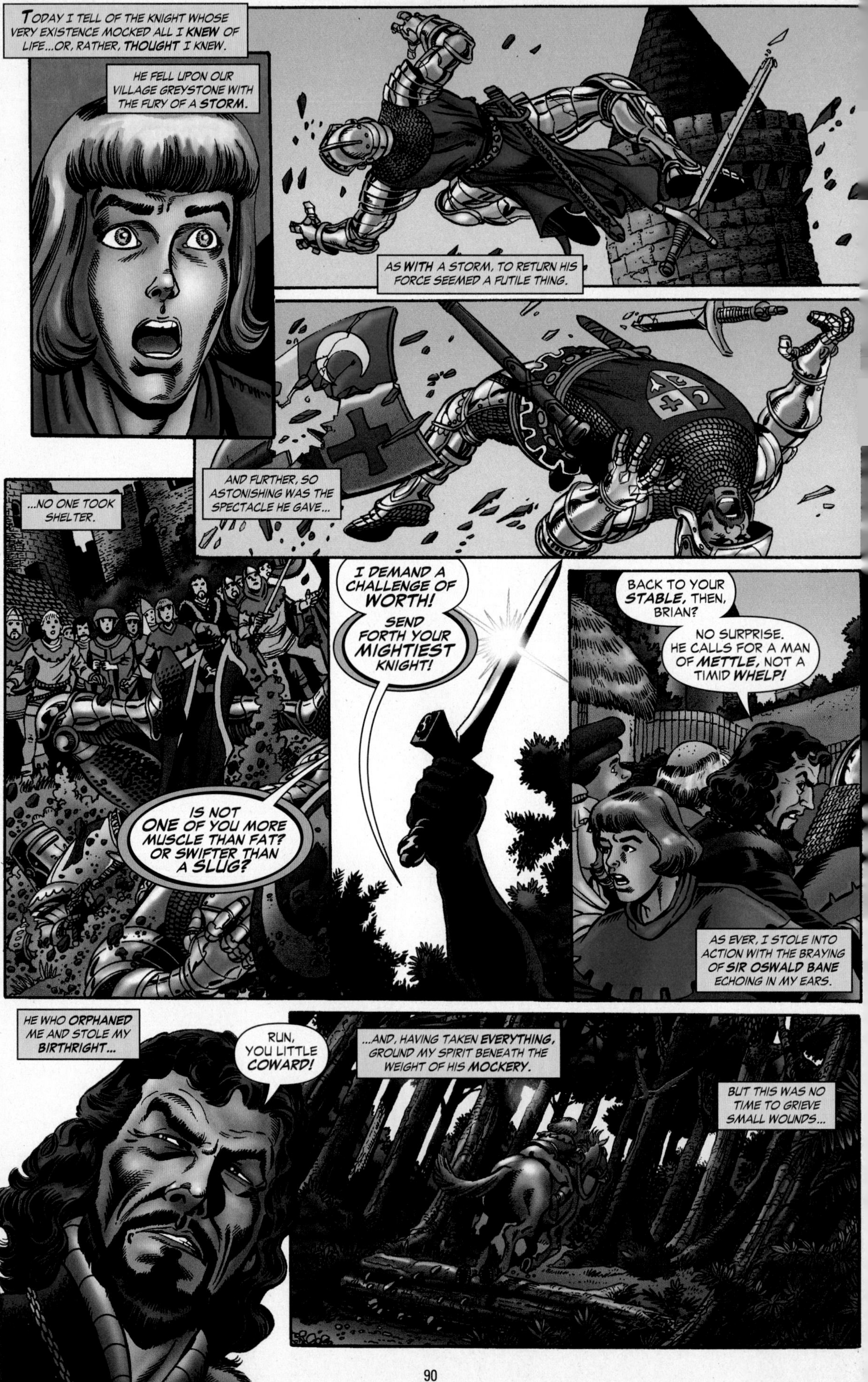
TODAY I TELL OF THE KNIGHT WHOSE VERY EXISTENCE MOCKED ALL I KNEW OF LIFE...OR, RATHER, THOUGHT I KNEW.
HE FELL UPON OUR VILLAGE GREYSTONE WITH THE FURY OF A STORM.
AS WITH A STORM, TO RETURN HIS FORCE SEEMED A FUTILE THING.
AND FURTHER, SO ASTONISHING WAS THE SPECTACLE HE GAVE...
...NO ONE TOOK SHELTER.
IS NOT ONE OF YOU MORE MUSCLE THAN FAT? OR SWIFTER THAN A SLUG?
I DEMAND A CHALLENGE OF WORTH!
SEND FORTH YOUR MIGHTIEST KNIGHT!
BACK TO YOUR STABLE, THEN, BRIAN?
NO SURPRISE. HE CALLS FOR A MAN OF METTLE, NOT A TIMID WHELP!
AS EVER, I STOLE INTO ACTION WITH THE BRAYING OF SIR OSWALD BANE ECHOING IN MY EARS.
HE WHO ORPHANED ME AND STOLE MY BIRTHRIGHT...
RUN, YOU LITTLE COWARD!
...AND, HAVING TAKEN EVERYTHING, GROUND MY SPIRIT BENEATH THE WEIGHT OF HIS MOCKERY.
BUT THIS WAS NO TIME TO GRIEVE SMALL WOUNDS...

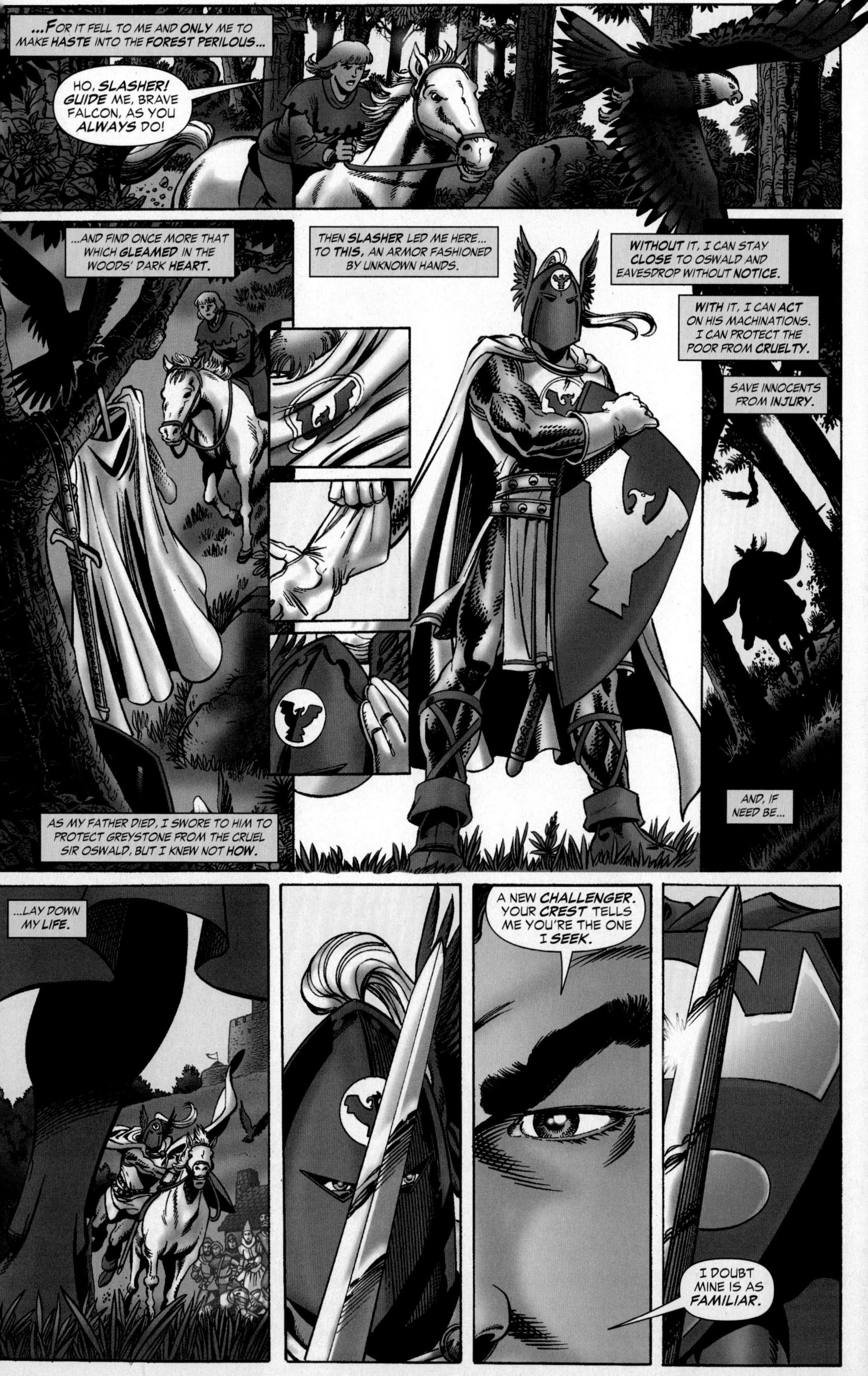
...FOR IT FELL TO ME AND ONLY ME TO MAKE HASTE INTO THE FOREST PERILOUS...
HO, SLASHER! GUIDE ME, BRAVE FALCON, AS YOU ALWAYS DO!
...AND FIND ONCE MORE THAT WHICH GLEAMED IN THE WOODS' DARK HEART.
AS MY FATHER DIED, I SWORE TO HIM TO PROTECT GREYSTONE FROM THE CRUEL SIR OSWALD, BUT I KNEW NOT HOW.
THEN SLASHER LED ME HERE... TO THIS, AN ARMOR FASHIONED BY UNKNOWN HANDS.
WITHOUT IT, I CAN STAY CLOSE TO OSWALD AND EAVESDROP WITHOUT NOTICE.
WITH IT, I CAN ACT ON HIS MACHINATIONS. I CAN PROTECT THE POOR FROM CRUELTY.
SAVE INNOCENTS FROM INJURY.
AND, IF NEED BE...
...LAY DOWN MY LIFE.
A NEW CHALLENGER. YOUR CREST TELLS ME YOU'RE THE ONE I SEEK.
I DOUBT MINE IS AS FAMILIAR.

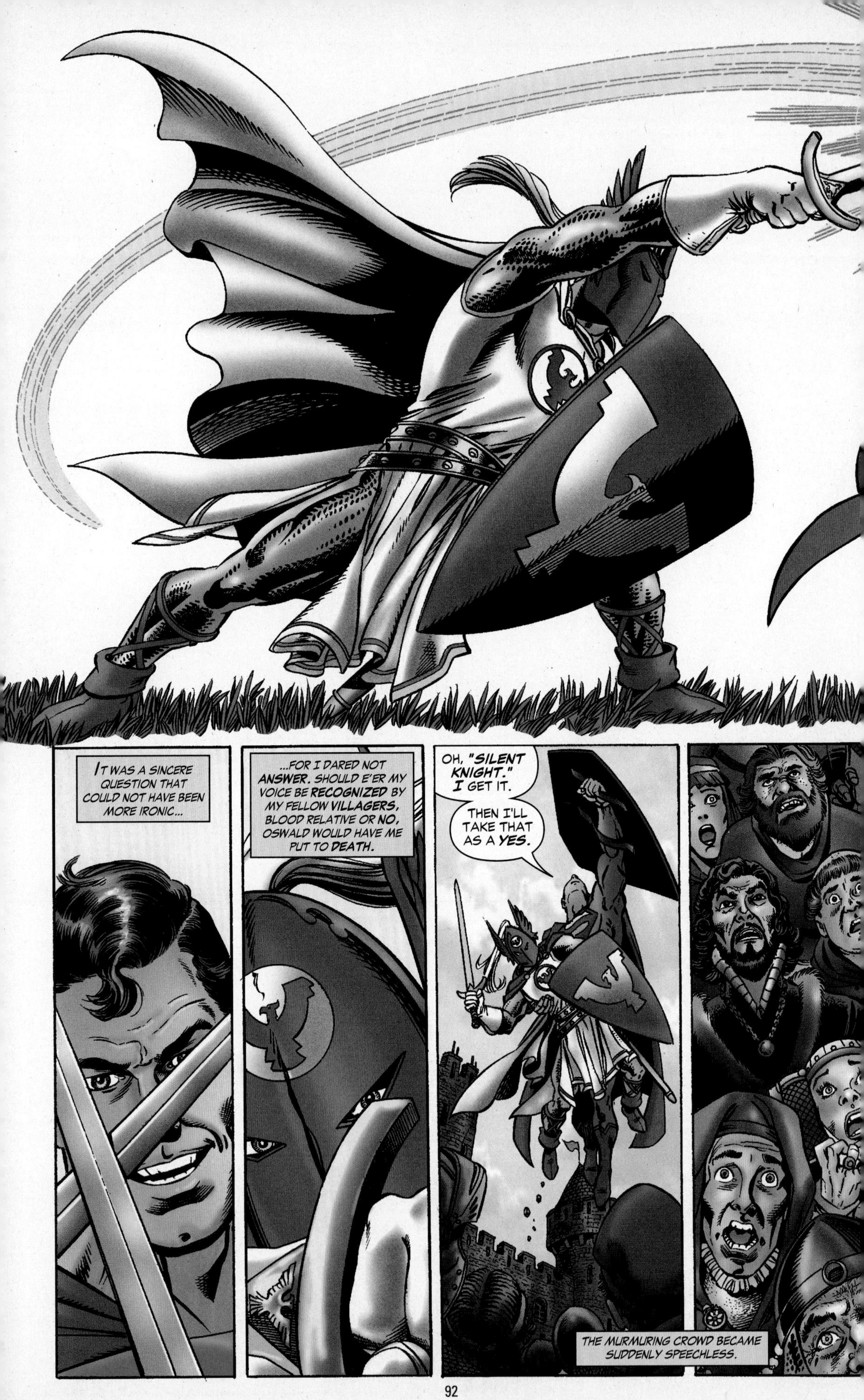
IT WAS A SINCERE QUESTION THAT COULD NOT HAVE BEEN MORE IRONIC...
...FOR I DARED NOT ANSWER. SHOULD E'ER MY VOICE BE RECOGNIZED BY MY FELLOW VILLAGERS, BLOOD RELATIVE OR NO, OSWALD WOULD HAVE ME PUT TO DEATH.
OH, "SILENT KNIGHT." I GET IT.
THEN I'LL TAKE THAT AS A YES.
THE MURMURING CROWD BECAME SUDDENLY SPEECHLESS.

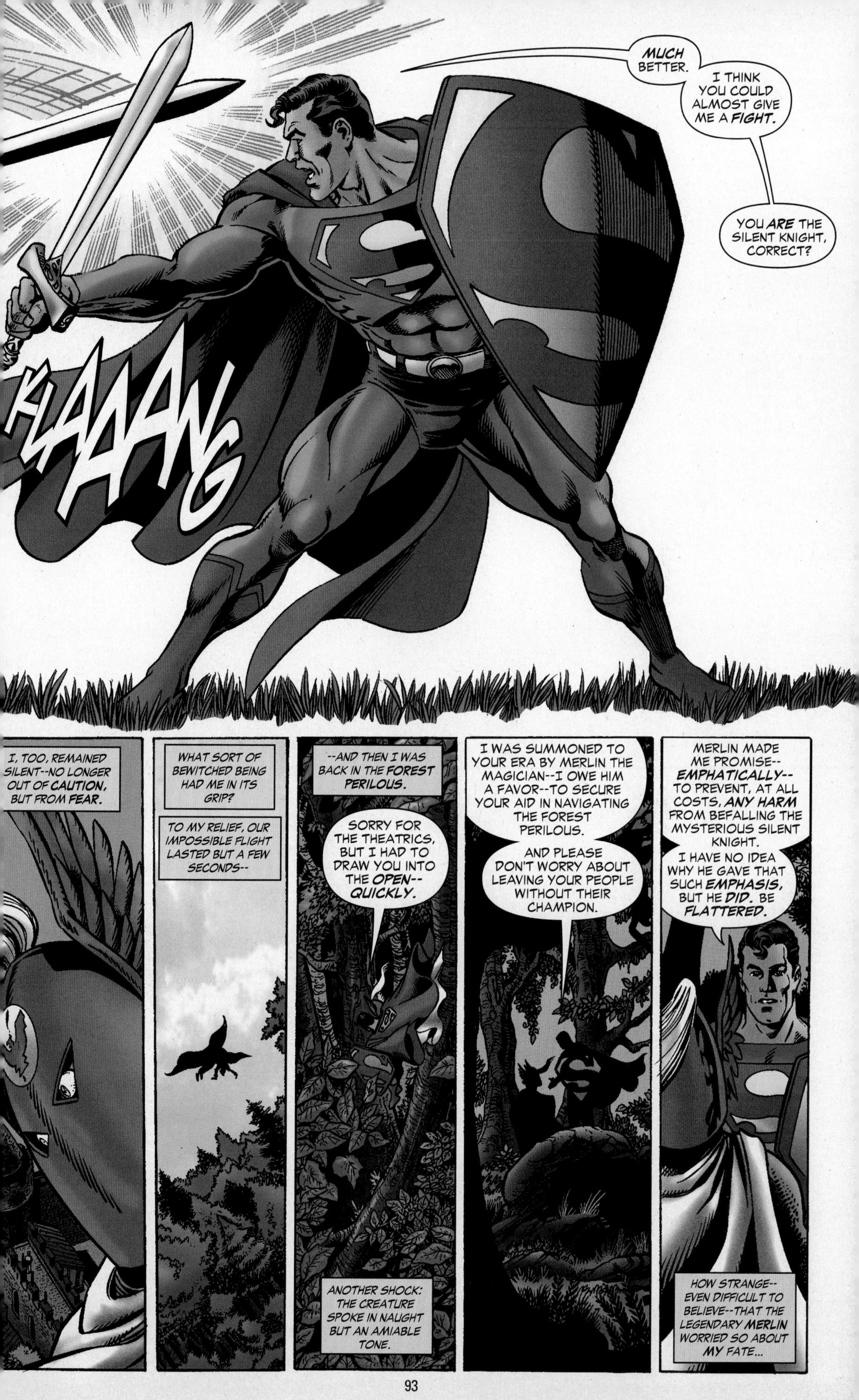
MUCH BETTER.
I THINK YOU COULD ALMOST GIVE ME A FIGHT.
YOU ARE THE SILENT KNIGHT, CORRECT?
KLAAANG
I, TOO, REMAINED SILENT--NO LONGER OUT OF CAUTION, BUT FROM FEAR.
WHAT SORT OF BEWITCHED BEING HAD ME IN ITS GRIP?
TO MY RELIEF, OUR IMPOSSIBLE FLIGHT LASTED BUT A FEW SECONDS--
--AND THEN I WAS BACK IN THE FOREST PERILOUS.
SORRY FOR THE THEATRICS, BUT I HAD TO DRAW YOU INTO THE OPEN--QUICKLY.
ANOTHER SHOCK: THE CREATURE SPOKE IN NAUGHT BUT AN AMIABLE TONE.
I WAS SUMMONED TO YOUR ERA BY MERLIN THE MAGICIAN--I OWE HIM A FAVOR--TO SECURE YOUR AID IN NAVIGATING THE FOREST PERILOUS.
AND PLEASE DON'T WORRY ABOUT LEAVING YOUR PEOPLE WITHOUT THEIR CHAMPION.
MERLIN MADE ME PROMISE--EMPHATICALLY--TO PREVENT, AT ALL COSTS, ANY HARM FROM BEFALLING THE MYSTERIOUS SILENT KNIGHT.
I HAVE NO IDEA WHY HE GAVE THAT SUCH EMPHASIS, BUT HE DID. BE FLATTERED.
HOW STRANGE--EVEN DIFFICULT TO BELIEVE--THAT THE LEGENDARY MERLIN WORRIED SO ABOUT MY FATE...

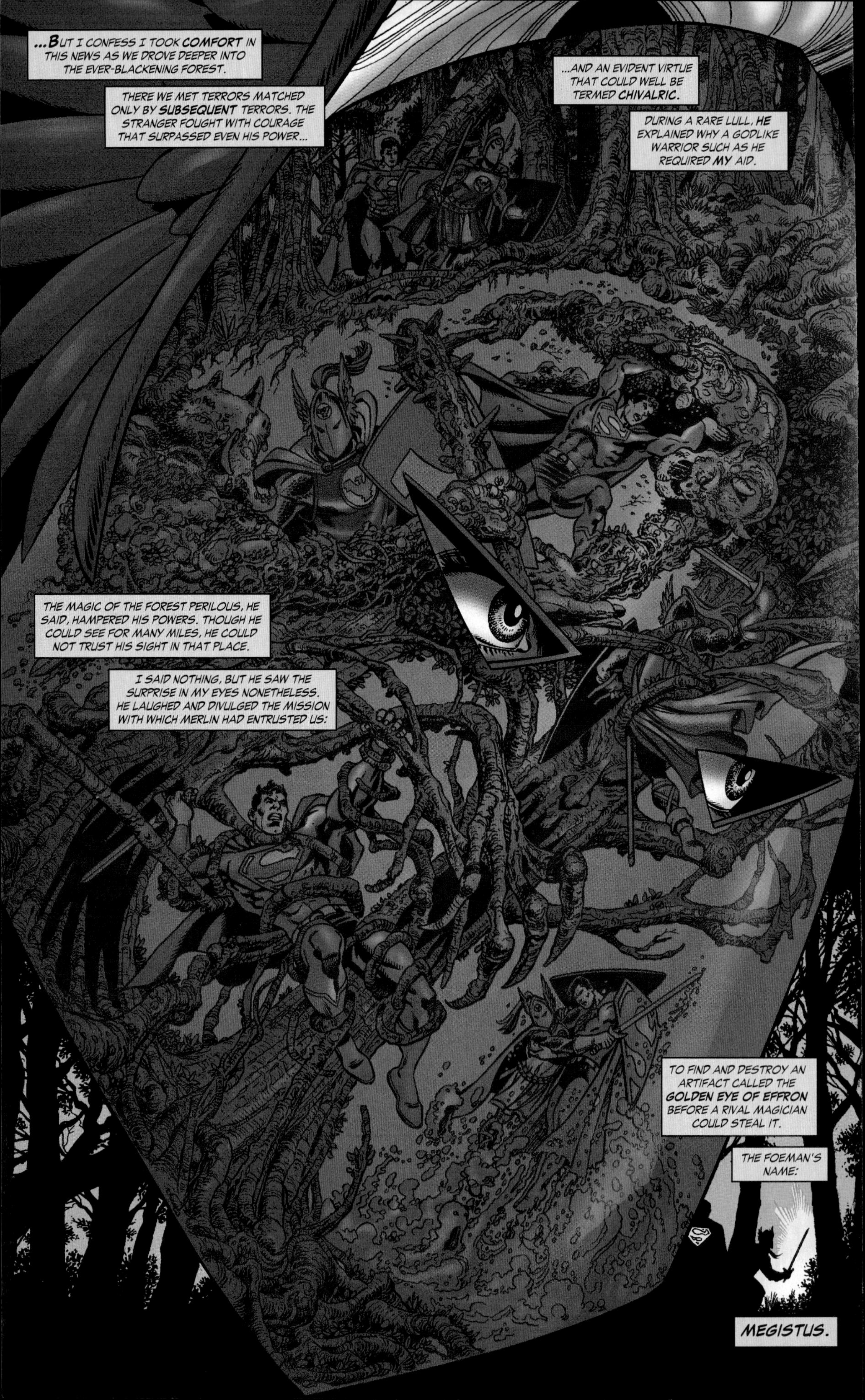
...BUT I CONFESS I TOOK COMFORT IN THIS NEWS AS WE DROVE DEEPER INTO THE EVER-BLACKENING FOREST.
THERE WE MET TERRORS MATCHED ONLY BY SUBSEQUENT TERRORS. THE STRANGER FOUGHT WITH COURAGE THAT SURPASSED EVEN HIS POWER...
...AND AN EVIDENT VIRTUE THAT COULD WELL BE TERMED CHIVALRIC.
DURING A RARE LULL, HE EXPLAINED WHY A GODLIKE WARRIOR SUCH AS HE REQUIRED MY AID.
THE MAGIC OF THE FOREST PERILOUS, HE SAID, HAMPERED HIS POWERS. THOUGH HE COULD SEE FOR MANY MILES, HE COULD NOT TRUST HIS SIGHT IN THAT PLACE.
I SAID NOTHING, BUT HE SAW THE SURPRISE IN MY EYES NONETHELESS. HE LAUGHED AND DIVULGED THE MISSION WITH WHICH MERLIN HAD ENTRUSTED US:
TO FIND AND DESTROY AN ARTIFACT CALLED THE GOLDEN EYE OF EFFRON BEFORE A RIVAL MAGICIAN COULD STEAL IT.
THE FOEMAN'S NAME:
MEGISTUS.

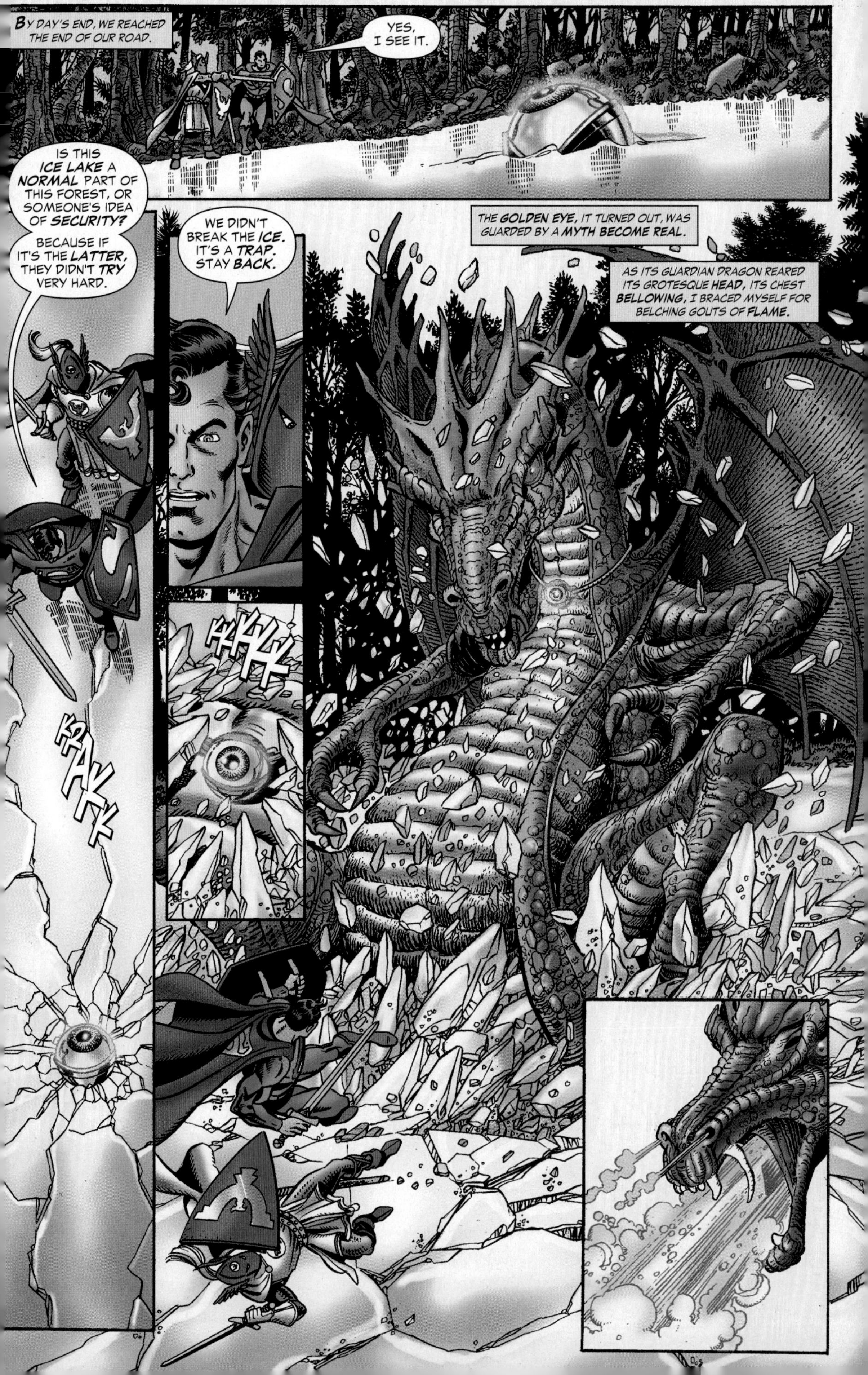
BY DAY'S END, WE REACHED THE END OF OUR ROAD.
YES, I SEE IT.
IS THIS ICE LAKE A NORMAL PART OF THIS FOREST, OR SOMEONE'S IDEA OF SECURITY?
BECAUSE IF IT'S THE LATTER, THEY DIDN'T TRY VERY HARD.
WE DIDN'T BREAK THE ICE. IT'S A TRAP. STAY BACK.
KRAKK
KRAKKK
THE GOLDEN EYE, IT TURNED OUT, WAS GUARDED BY A MYTH BECOME REAL.
AS ITS GUARDIAN DRAGON REARED ITS GROTESQUE HEAD, ITS CHEST BELLOWING, I BRACED MYSELF FOR BELCHING GOUTS OF FLAME.

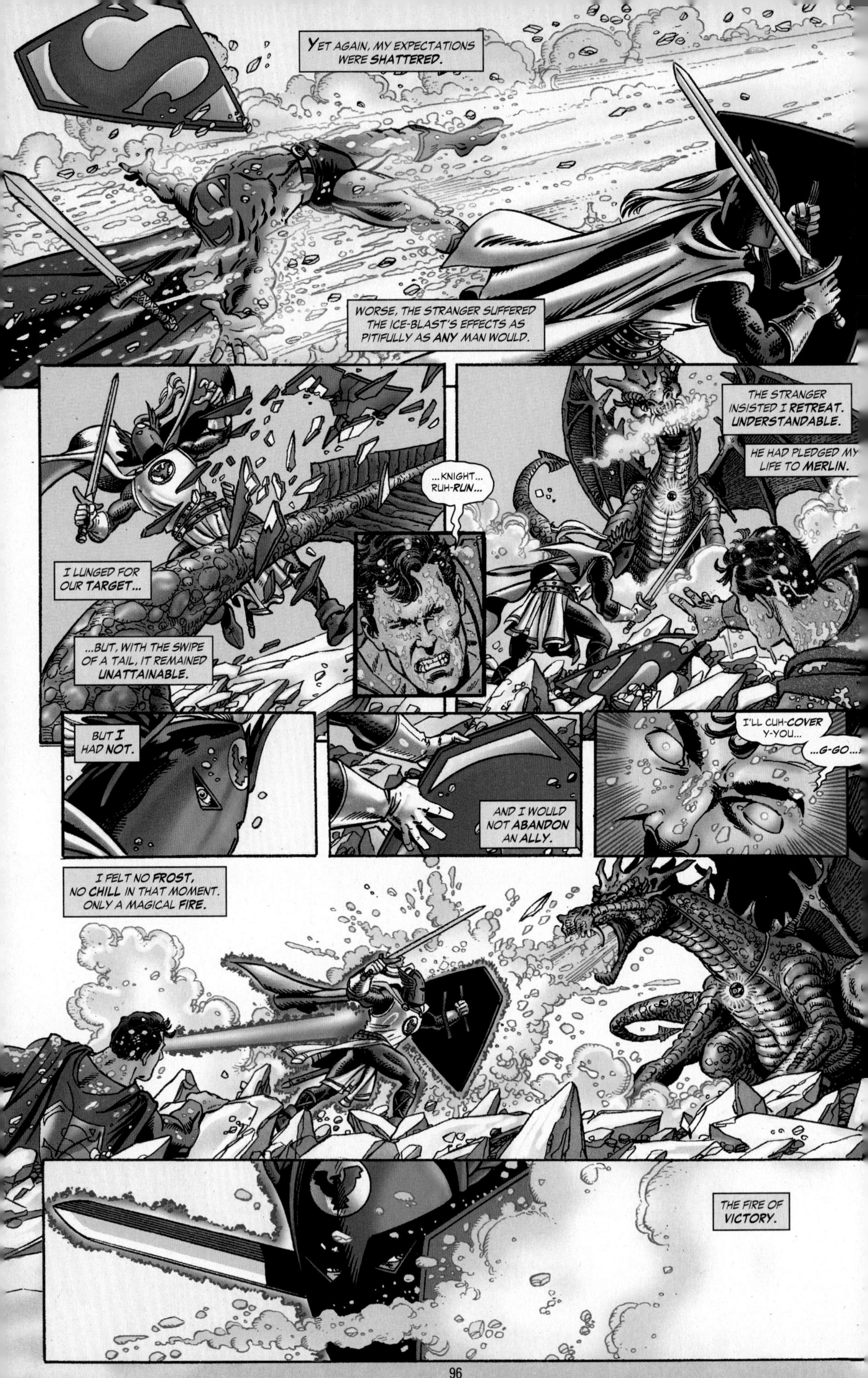
YET AGAIN, MY EXPECTATIONS WERE SHATTERED.
WORSE, THE STRANGER SUFFERED THE ICE-BLAST'S EFFECTS AS PITIFULLY AS ANY MAN WOULD.
I LUNGED FOR OUR TARGET...
...BUT, WITH THE SWIPE OF A TAIL, IT REMAINED UNATTAINABLE.
...KNIGHT... RUH-RUN...
THE STRANGER INSISTED I RETREAT. UNDERSTANDABLE.
HE HAD PLEDGED MY LIFE TO MERLIN.
BUT I HAD NOT.
AND I WOULD NOT ABANDON AN ALLY.
I'LL CUH-COVER Y-YOU...
...G-GO...
I FELT NO FROST, NO CHILL IN THAT MOMENT. ONLY A MAGICAL FIRE.
THE FIRE OF VICTORY.

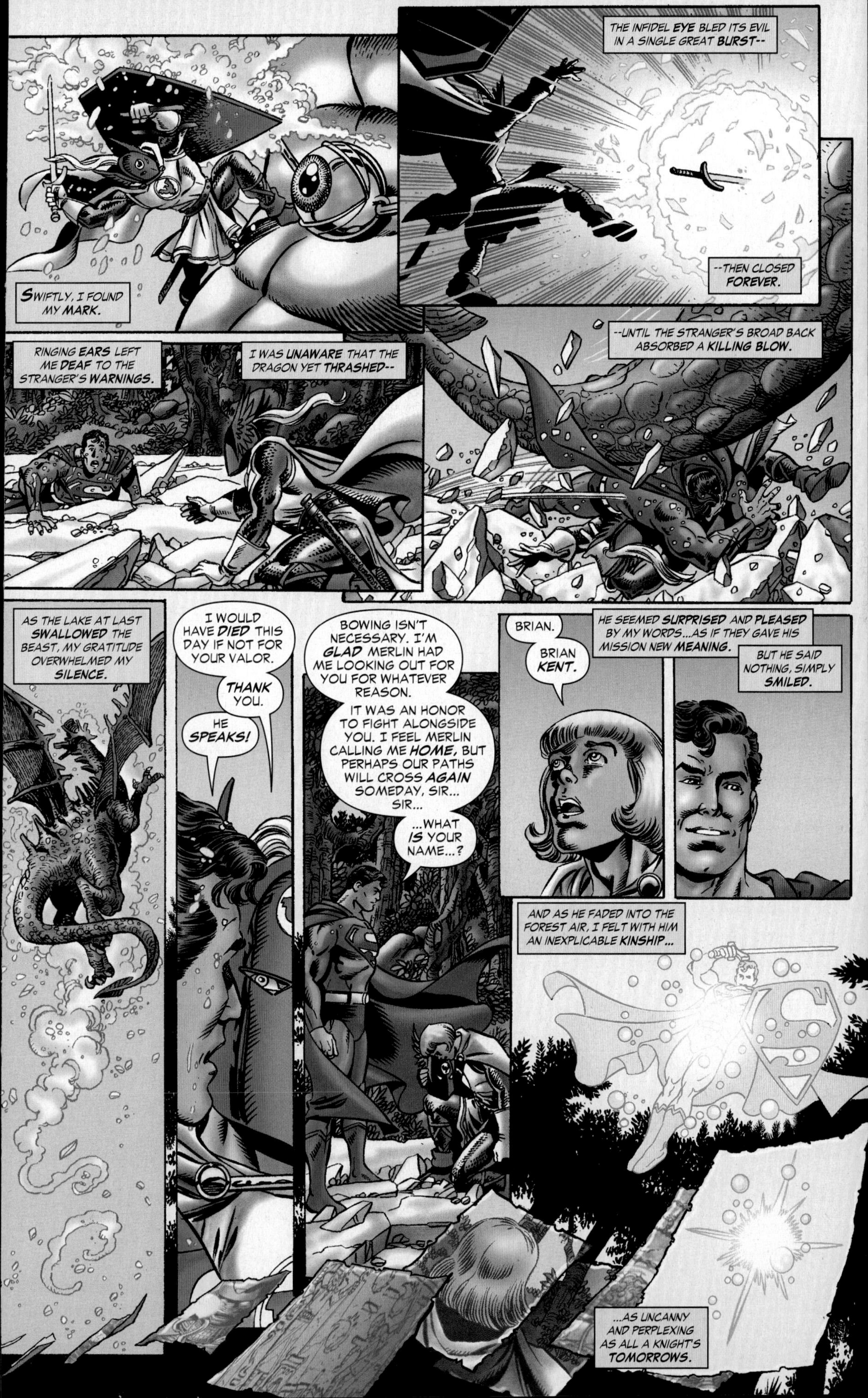
SWIFTLY, I FOUND MY MARK.
THE INFIDEL EYE BLED ITS EVIL IN A SINGLE GREAT BURST--
--THEN CLOSED FOREVER.
RINGING EARS LEFT ME DEAF TO THE STRANGER'S WARNINGS.
I WAS UNAWARE THAT THE DRAGON YET THRASHED--
--UNTIL THE STRANGER'S BROAD BACK ABSORBED A KILLING BLOW.
AS THE LAKE AT LAST SWALLOWED THE BEAST, MY GRATITUDE OVERWHELMED MY SILENCE.
I WOULD HAVE DIED THIS DAY IF NOT FOR YOUR VALOR.
THANK YOU.
HE SPEAKS!
BOWING ISN'T NECESSARY. I'M GLAD MERLIN HAD ME LOOKING OUT FOR YOU FOR WHATEVER REASON.
IT WAS AN HONOR TO FIGHT ALONGSIDE YOU. I FEEL MERLIN CALLING ME HOME, BUT PERHAPS OUR PATHS WILL CROSS AGAIN SOMEDAY, SIR... SIR...
...WHAT IS YOUR NAME...?
BRIAN.
BRIAN KENT.
HE SEEMED SURPRISED AND PLEASED BY MY WORDS...AS IF THEY GAVE HIS MISSION NEW MEANING.
BUT HE SAID NOTHING, SIMPLY SMILED.
AND AS HE FADED INTO THE FOREST AIR, I FELT WITH HIM AN INEXPLICABLE KINSHIP...
...AS UNCANNY AND PERPLEXING AS ALL A KNIGHT'S TOMORROWS.

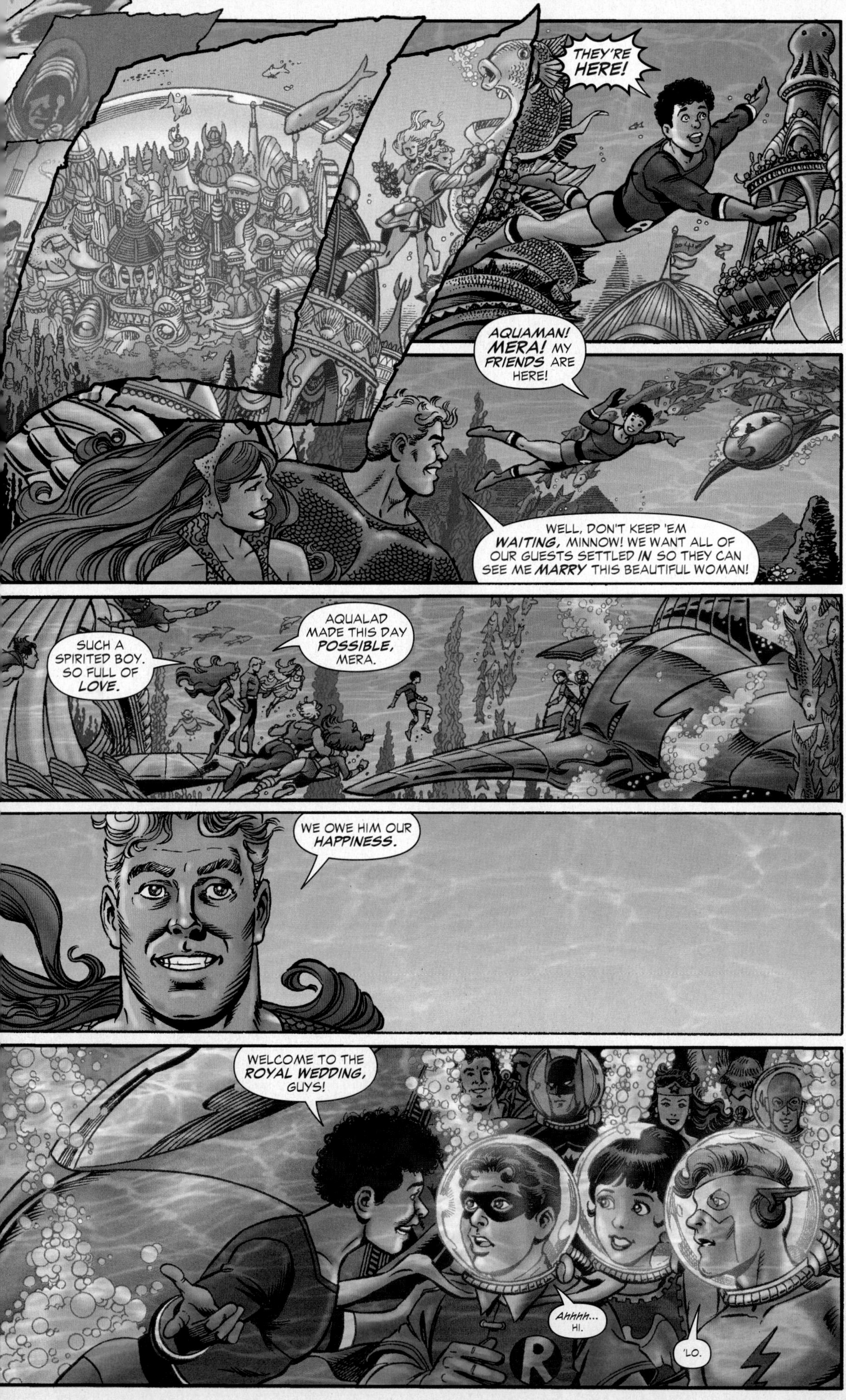
THEY'RE HERE!
AQUAMAN! MERA! MY FRIENDS ARE HERE!
WELL, DON'T KEEP 'EM WAITING, MINNOW! WE WANT ALL OF OUR GUESTS SETTLED IN SO THEY CAN SEE ME MARRY THIS BEAUTIFUL WOMAN!
SUCH A SPIRITED BOY. SO FULL OF LOVE.
AQUALAD MADE THIS DAY POSSIBLE, MERA.
WE OWE HIM OUR HAPPINESS.
WELCOME TO THE ROYAL WEDDING, GUYS!
Ahhhh... HI.
'LO.

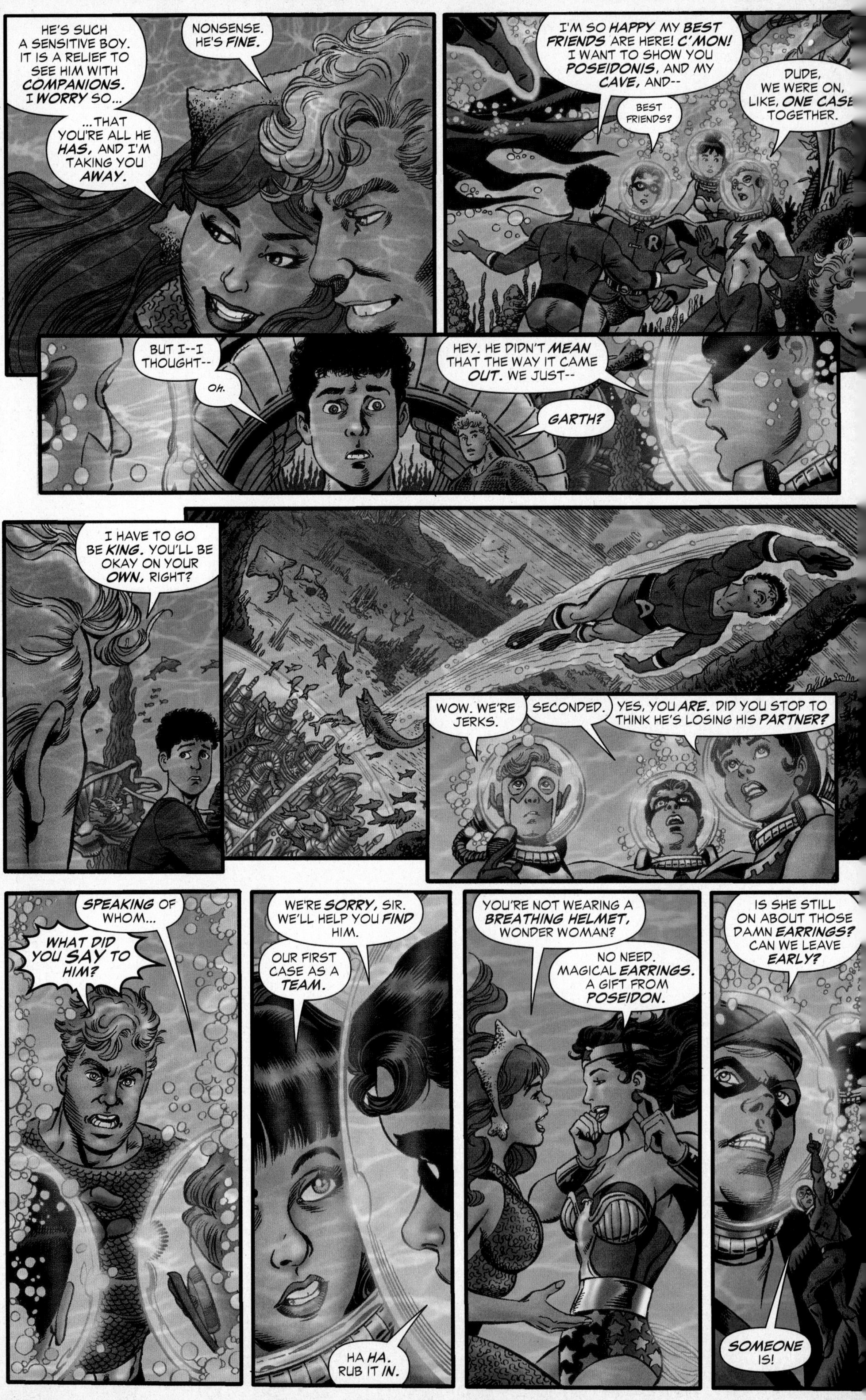
HE'S SUCH A SENSITIVE BOY. IT IS A RELIEF TO SEE HIM WITH COMPANIONS. I WORRY SO...
NONSENSE. HE'S FINE.
...THAT YOU'RE ALL HE HAS, AND I'M TAKING YOU AWAY.
I'M SO HAPPY MY BEST FRIENDS ARE HERE! C'MON! I WANT TO SHOW YOU POSEIDONIS, AND MY CAVE, AND--
BEST FRIENDS?
DUDE, WE WERE ON, LIKE, ONE CASE TOGETHER.
BUT I--I THOUGHT--
Oh.
HEY. HE DIDN'T MEAN THAT THE WAY IT CAME OUT. WE JUST--
GARTH?
I HAVE TO GO BE KING. YOU'LL BE OKAY ON YOUR OWN, RIGHT?
WOW. WE'RE JERKS.
SECONDED.
YES, YOU ARE. DID YOU STOP TO THINK HE'S LOSING HIS PARTNER?
SPEAKING OF WHOM...
WHAT DID YOU SAY TO HIM?
WE'RE SORRY, SIR. WE'LL HELP YOU FIND HIM.
OUR FIRST CASE AS A TEAM.
HA HA. RUB IT IN.
YOU'RE NOT WEARING A BREATHING HELMET, WONDER WOMAN?
NO NEED. MAGICAL EARRINGS. A GIFT FROM POSEIDON.
IS SHE STILL ON ABOUT THOSE DAMN EARRINGS? CAN WE LEAVE EARLY?
SOMEONE IS!

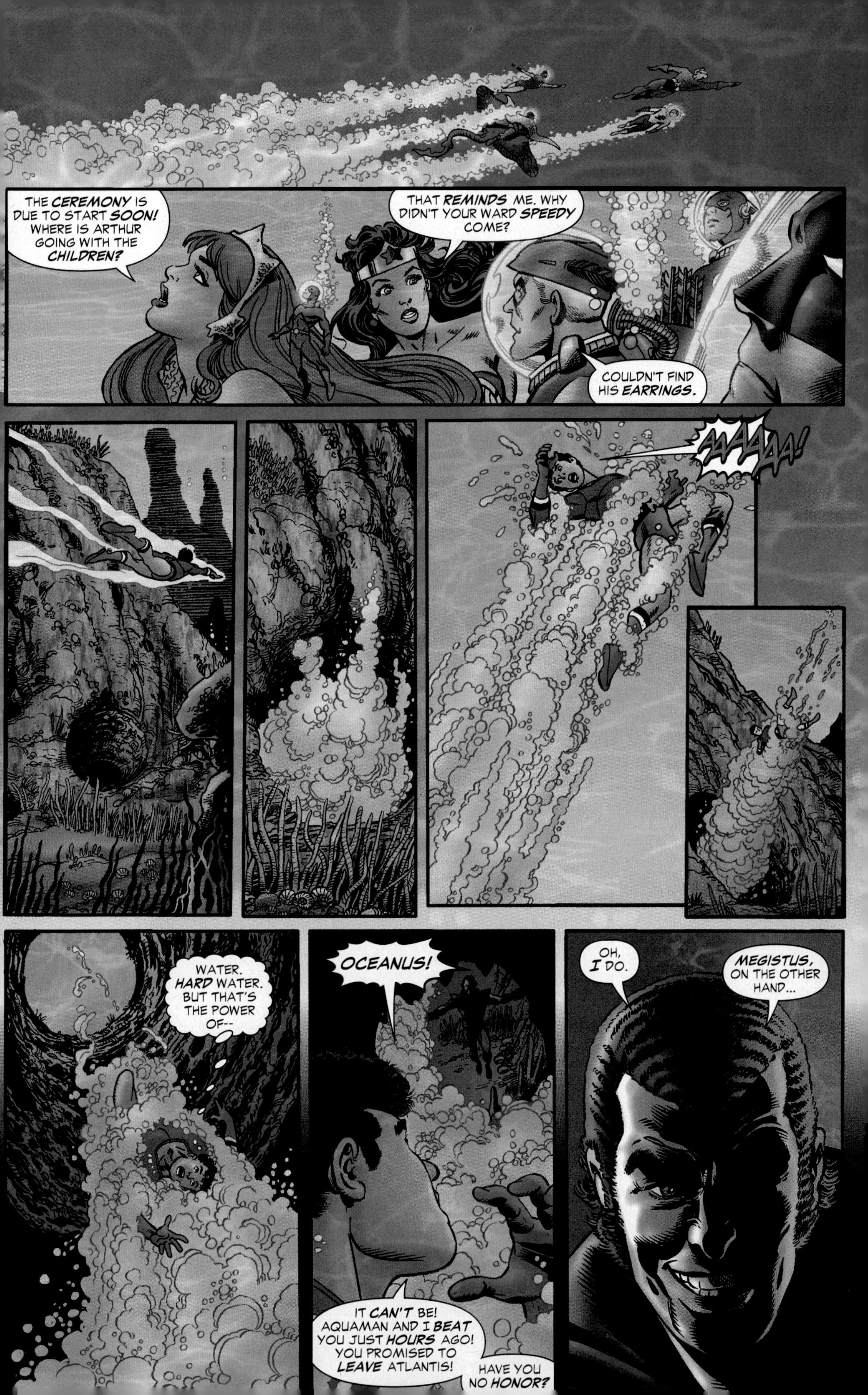
THE CEREMONY IS DUE TO START SOON! WHERE IS ARTHUR GOING WITH THE CHILDREN?
THAT REMINDS ME. WHY DIDN'T YOUR WARD SPEEDY COME?
COULDN'T FIND HIS EARRINGS.
AAAAAA!
WATER. HARD WATER. BUT THAT'S THE POWER OF--
OCEANUS!
IT CAN'T BE! AQUAMAN AND I BEAT YOU JUST HOURS AGO! YOU PROMISED TO LEAVE ATLANTIS!
HAVE YOU NO HONOR?
OH, I DO.
MEGISTUS, ON THE OTHER HAND...

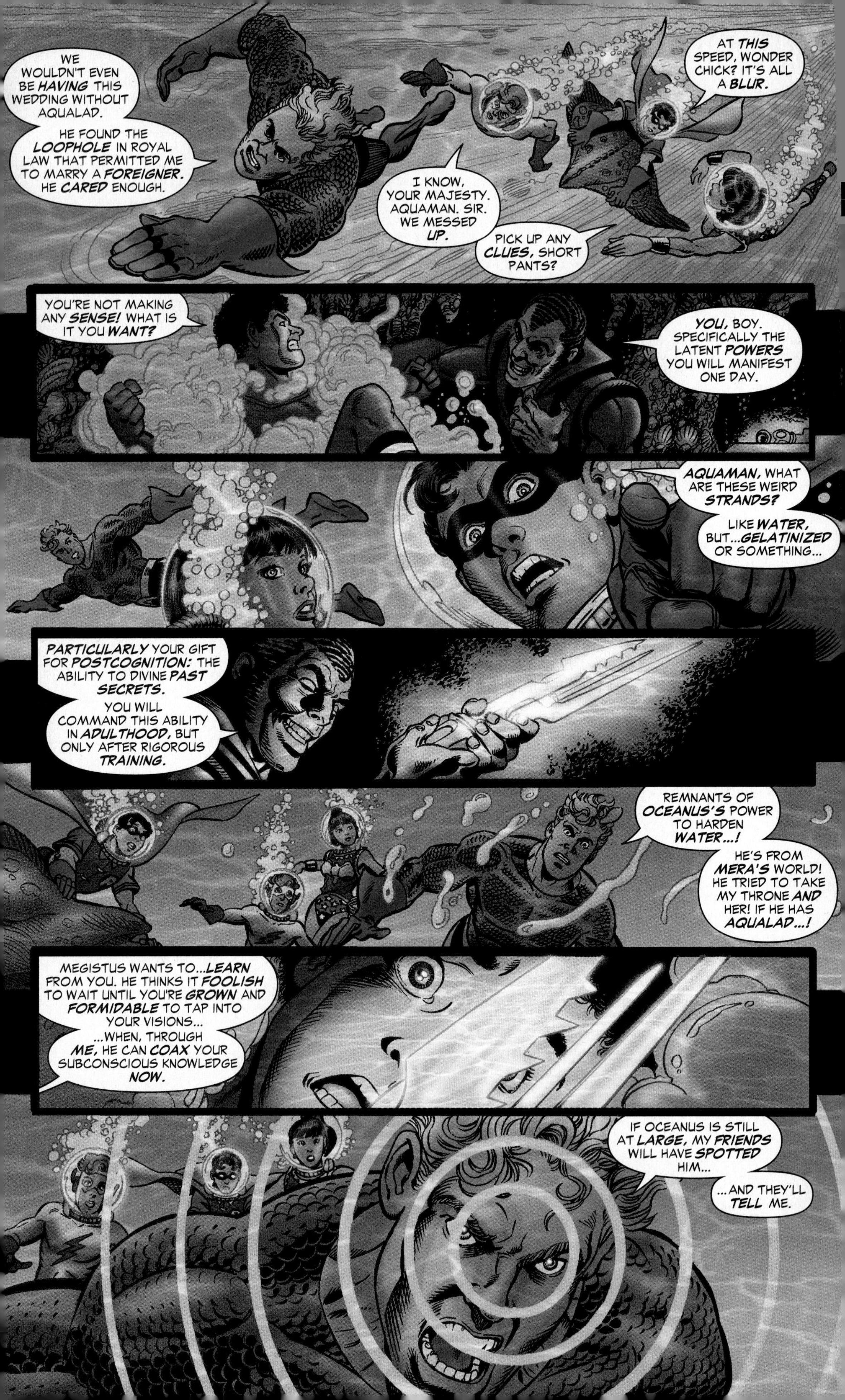
WE WOULDN'T EVEN BE HAVING THIS WEDDING WITHOUT AQUALAD.
HE FOUND THE LOOPHOLE IN ROYAL LAW THAT PERMITTED ME TO MARRY A FOREIGNER. HE CARED ENOUGH.
AT THIS SPEED, WONDER CHICK? IT'S ALL A BLUR.
I KNOW, YOUR MAJESTY. AQUAMAN. SIR. WE MESSED UP.
PICK UP ANY CLUES, SHORT PANTS?
YOU'RE NOT MAKING ANY SENSE! WHAT IS IT YOU WANT?
YOU, BOY. SPECIFICALLY THE LATENT POWERS YOU WILL MANIFEST ONE DAY.
AQUAMAN, WHAT ARE THESE WEIRD STRANDS?
LIKE WATER, BUT...GELATINIZED OR SOMETHING...
PARTICULARLY YOUR GIFT FOR POSTCOGNITION: THE ABILITY TO DIVINE PAST SECRETS.
YOU WILL COMMAND THIS ABILITY IN ADULTHOOD, BUT ONLY AFTER RIGOROUS TRAINING.
REMNANTS OF OCEANUS'S POWER TO HARDEN WATER...!
HE'S FROM MERA'S WORLD! HE TRIED TO TAKE MY THRONE AND HER! IF HE HAS AQUALAD...!
MEGISTUS WANTS TO...LEARN FROM YOU. HE THINKS IT FOOLISH TO WAIT UNTIL YOU'RE GROWN AND FORMIDABLE TO TAP INTO YOUR VISIONS...
...WHEN, THROUGH ME, HE CAN COAX YOUR SUBCONSCIOUS KNOWLEDGE NOW.
IF OCEANUS IS STILL AT LARGE, MY FRIENDS WILL HAVE SPOTTED HIM...
...AND THEY'LL TELL ME.

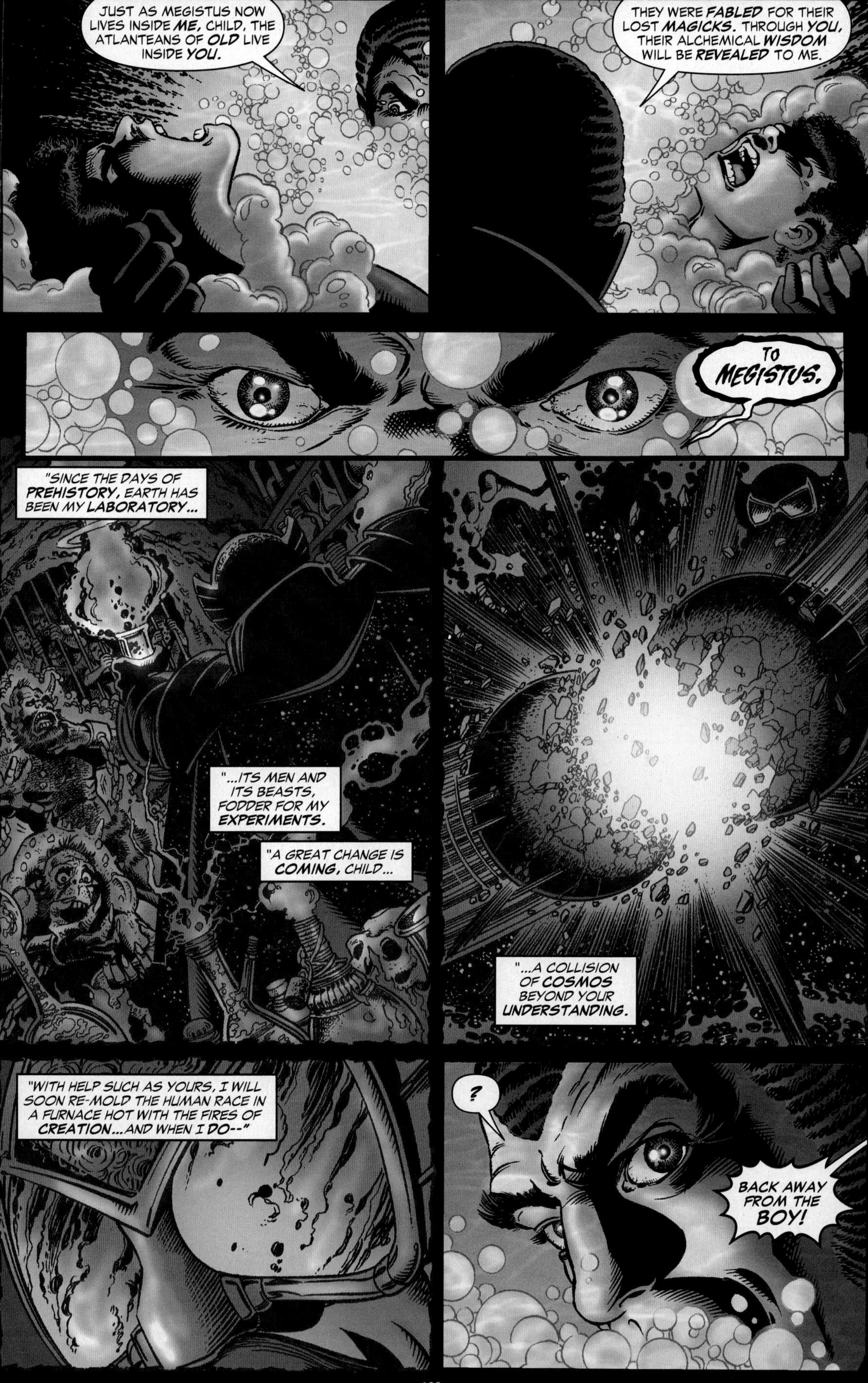
JUST AS MEGISTUS NOW LIVES INSIDE ME, CHILD, THE ATLANTEANS OF OLD LIVE INSIDE YOU.
THEY WERE FABLED FOR THEIR LOST MAGICKS. THROUGH YOU, THEIR ALCHEMICAL WISDOM WILL BE REVEALED TO ME.
TO MEGISTUS.
"SINCE THE DAYS OF PREHISTORY, EARTH HAS BEEN MY LABORATORY...
"...ITS MEN AND ITS BEASTS, FODDER FOR MY EXPERIMENTS.
"A GREAT CHANGE IS COMING, CHILD...
"...A COLLISION OF COSMOS BEYOND YOUR UNDERSTANDING.
"WITH HELP SUCH AS YOURS, I WILL SOON RE-MOLD THE HUMAN RACE IN A FURNACE HOT WITH THE FIRES OF CREATION...AND WHEN I DO--"
?
BACK AWAY FROM THE BOY!

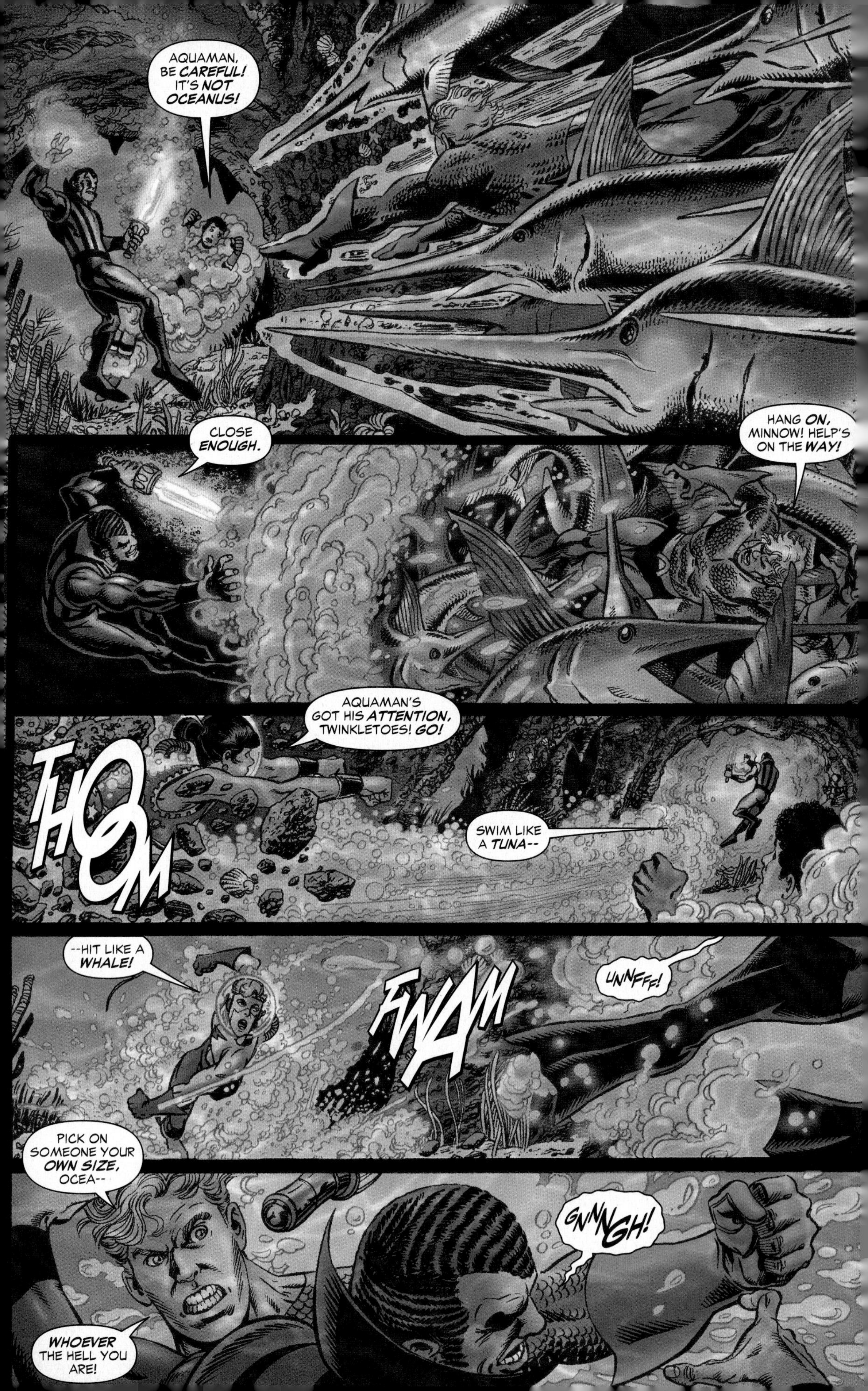
AQUAMAN, BE CAREFUL! IT'S NOT OCEANUS!
CLOSE ENOUGH.
HANG ON, MINNOW! HELP'S ON THE WAY!
THOOM
AQUAMAN'S GOT HIS ATTENTION, TWINKLETOES! GO!
SWIM LIKE A TUNA--
--HIT LIKE A WHALE!
FWAM
UNNFFF!
PICK ON SOMEONE YOUR OWN SIZE, OCEA--
GNNNGH!
WHOEVER THE HELL YOU ARE!

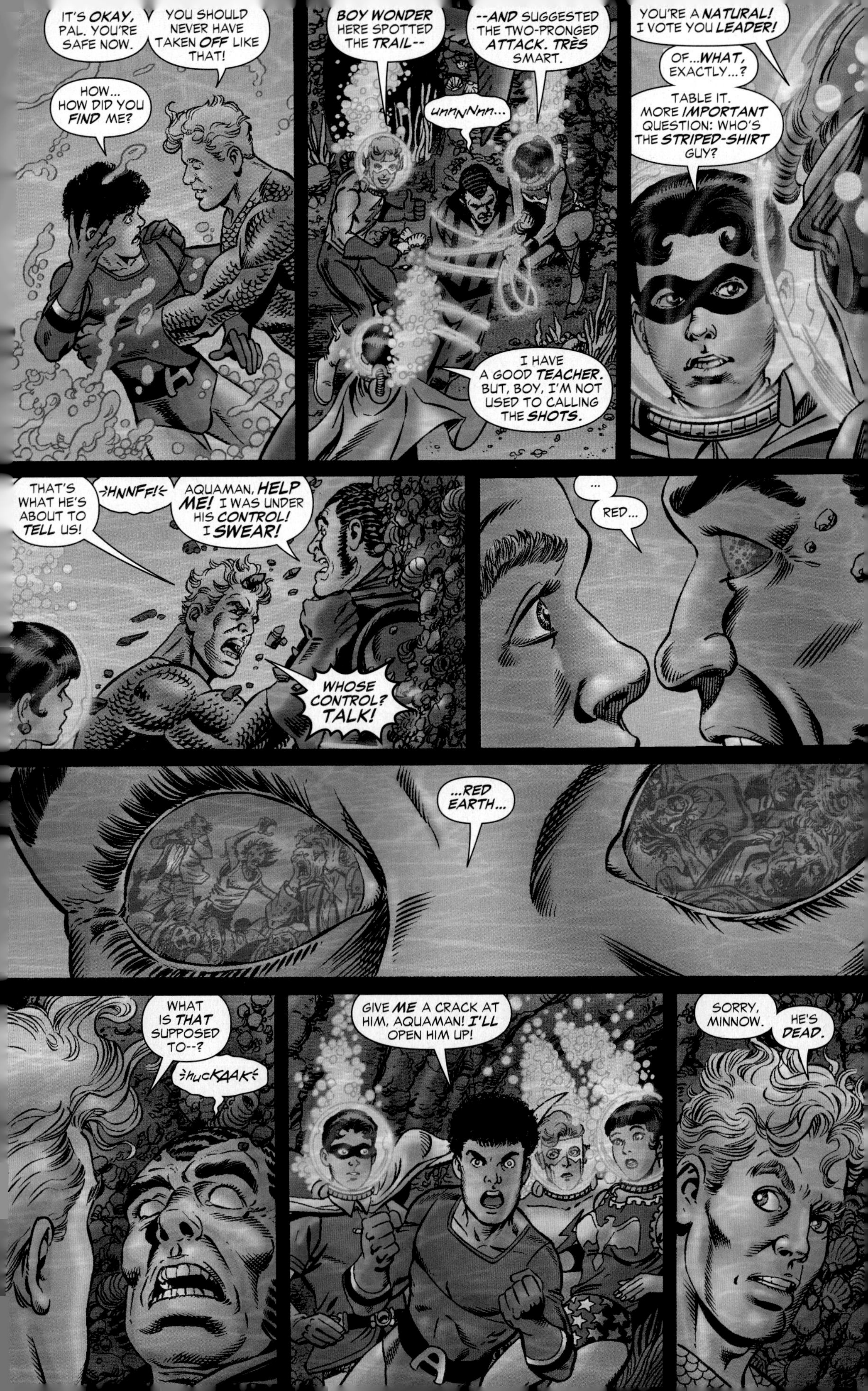
IT'S OKAY, PAL. YOU'RE SAFE NOW.
YOU SHOULD NEVER HAVE TAKEN OFF LIKE THAT!
HOW... HOW DID YOU FIND ME?
BOY WONDER HERE SPOTTED THE TRAIL--
--AND SUGGESTED THE TWO-PRONGED ATTACK. TRÈS SMART.
unnNNnn...
I HAVE A GOOD TEACHER. BUT, BOY, I'M NOT USED TO CALLING THE SHOTS.
YOU'RE A NATURAL! I VOTE YOU LEADER!
OF...WHAT, EXACTLY...?
TABLE IT. MORE IMPORTANT QUESTION: WHO'S THE STRIPED-SHIRT GUY?
THAT'S WHAT HE'S ABOUT TO TELL US!
HNNFF!
AQUAMAN, HELP ME! I WAS UNDER HIS CONTROL! I SWEAR!
WHOSE CONTROL? TALK!
...
RED...
...RED EARTH...
WHAT IS THAT SUPPOSED TO--?
hucKAAK
GIVE ME A CRACK AT HIM, AQUAMAN! I'LL OPEN HIM UP!
SORRY, MINNOW.
HE'S DEAD.

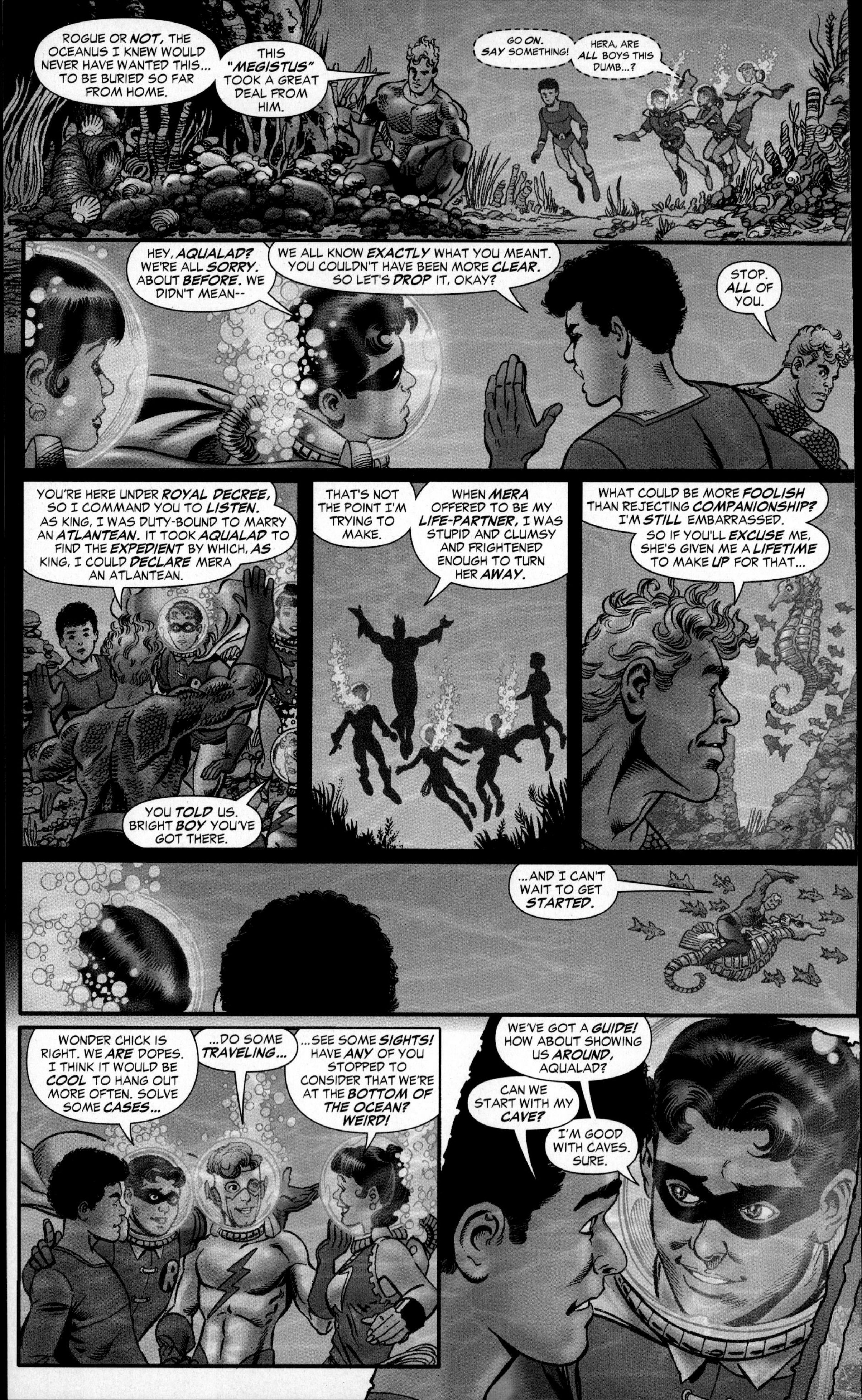
ROGUE OR NOT, THE OCEANUS I KNEW WOULD NEVER HAVE WANTED THIS... TO BE BURIED SO FAR FROM HOME.
THIS "MEGISTUS" TOOK A GREAT DEAL FROM HIM.
GO ON. SAY SOMETHING!
HERA, ARE ALL BOYS THIS DUMB...?
HEY, AQUALAD? WE'RE ALL SORRY. ABOUT BEFORE. WE DIDN'T MEAN--
WE ALL KNOW EXACTLY WHAT YOU MEANT. YOU COULDN'T HAVE BEEN MORE CLEAR. SO LET'S DROP IT, OKAY?
STOP. ALL OF YOU.
YOU'RE HERE UNDER ROYAL DECREE, SO I COMMAND YOU TO LISTEN. AS KING, I WAS DUTY-BOUND TO MARRY AN ATLANTEAN. IT TOOK AQUALAD TO FIND THE EXPEDIENT BY WHICH, AS KING, I COULD DECLARE MERA AN ATLANTEAN.
YOU TOLD US. BRIGHT BOY YOU'VE GOT THERE.
THAT'S NOT THE POINT I'M TRYING TO MAKE.
WHEN MERA OFFERED TO BE MY LIFE-PARTNER, I WAS STUPID AND CLUMSY AND FRIGHTENED ENOUGH TO TURN HER AWAY.
WHAT COULD BE MORE FOOLISH THAN REJECTING COMPANIONSHIP? I'M STILL EMBARRASSED.
SO IF YOU'LL EXCUSE ME, SHE'S GIVEN ME A LIFETIME TO MAKE UP FOR THAT...
...AND I CAN'T WAIT TO GET STARTED.
WONDER CHICK IS RIGHT. WE ARE DOPES. I THINK IT WOULD BE COOL TO HANG OUT MORE OFTEN. SOLVE SOME CASES...
...DO SOME TRAVELING...
...SEE SOME SIGHTS! HAVE ANY OF YOU STOPPED TO CONSIDER THAT WE'RE AT THE BOTTOM OF THE OCEAN? WEIRD!
WE'VE GOT A GUIDE! HOW ABOUT SHOWING US AROUND, AQUALAD?
CAN WE START WITH MY CAVE?
I'M GOOD WITH CAVES. SURE.

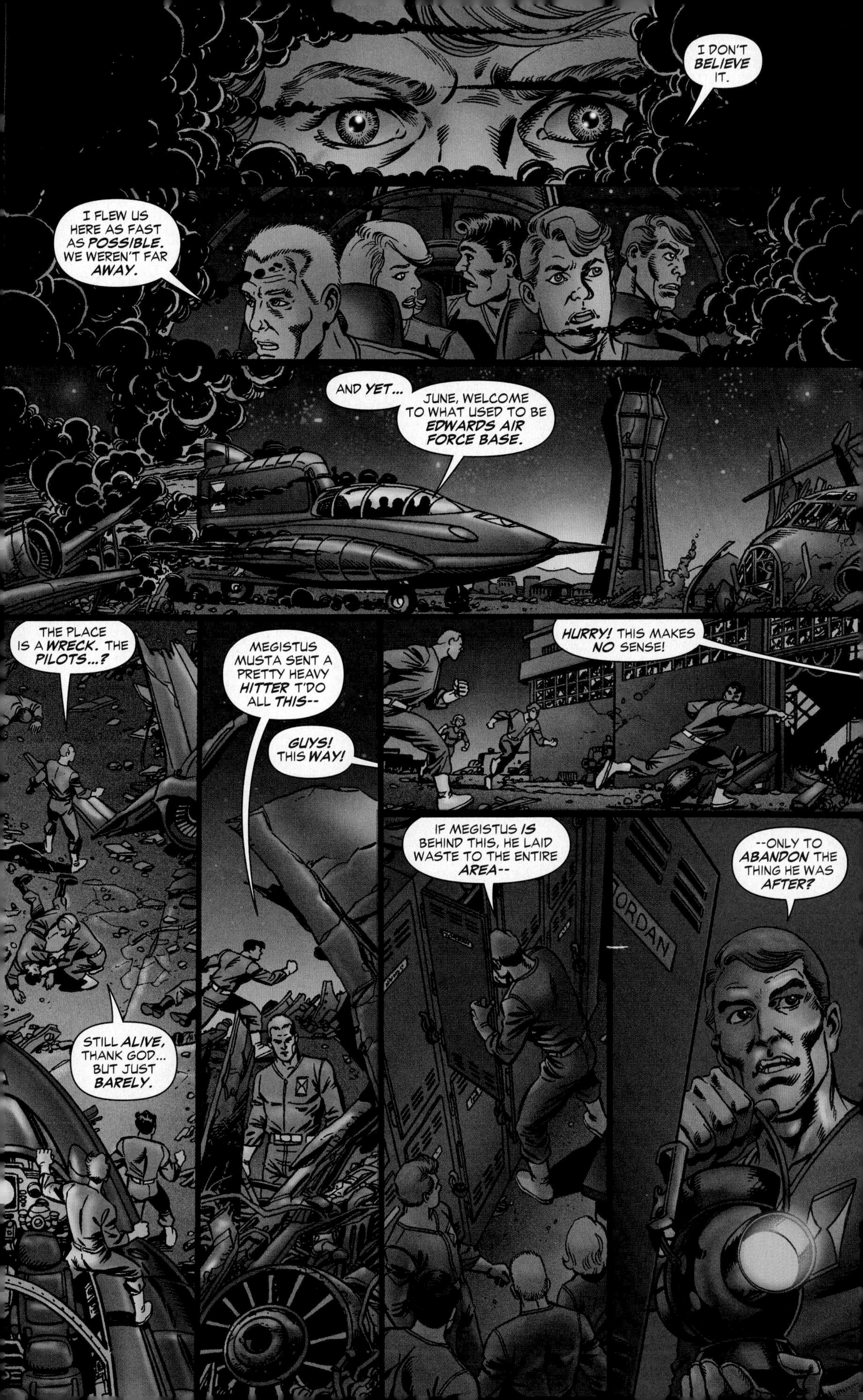
I DON'T BELIEVE IT.
I FLEW US HERE AS FAST AS POSSIBLE. WE WEREN'T FAR AWAY.
AND YET...
JUNE, WELCOME TO WHAT USED TO BE EDWARDS AIR FORCE BASE.
THE PLACE IS A WRECK. THE PILOTS...?
STILL ALIVE, THANK GOD... BUT JUST BARELY.
MEGISTUS MUSTA SENT A PRETTY HEAVY HITTER T'DO ALL THIS--
GUYS! THIS WAY!
HURRY! THIS MAKES NO SENSE!
IF MEGISTUS IS BEHIND THIS, HE LAID WASTE TO THE ENTIRE AREA--
--ONLY TO ABANDON THE THING HE WAS AFTER?
JORDAN

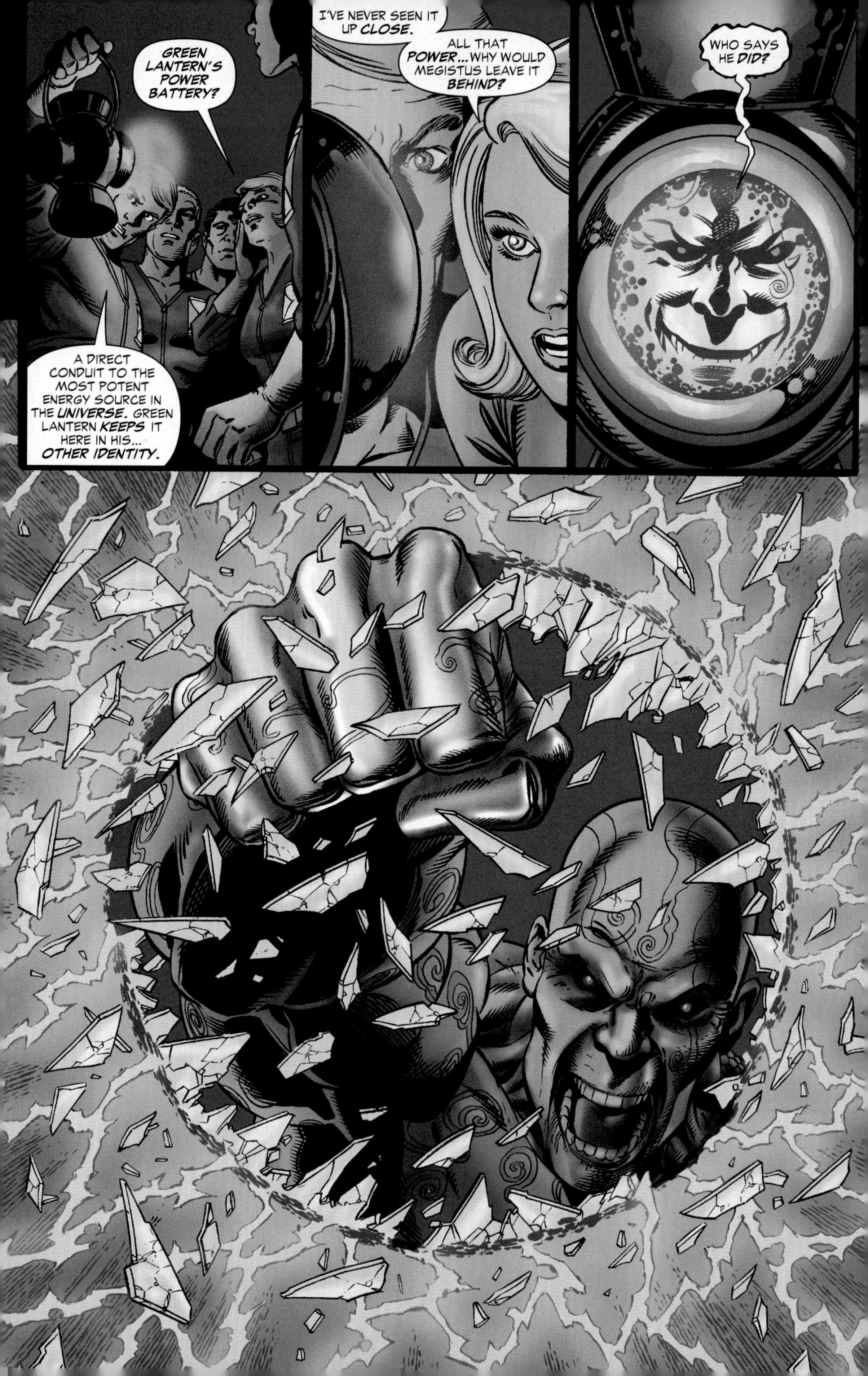
GREEN LANTERN'S POWER BATTERY?
A DIRECT CONDUIT TO THE MOST POTENT ENERGY SOURCE IN THE UNIVERSE. GREEN LANTERN KEEPS IT HERE IN HIS... OTHER IDENTITY.
I'VE NEVER SEEN IT UP CLOSE.
ALL THAT POWER... WHY WOULD MEGISTUS LEAVE IT BEHIND?
WHO SAYS HE DID?

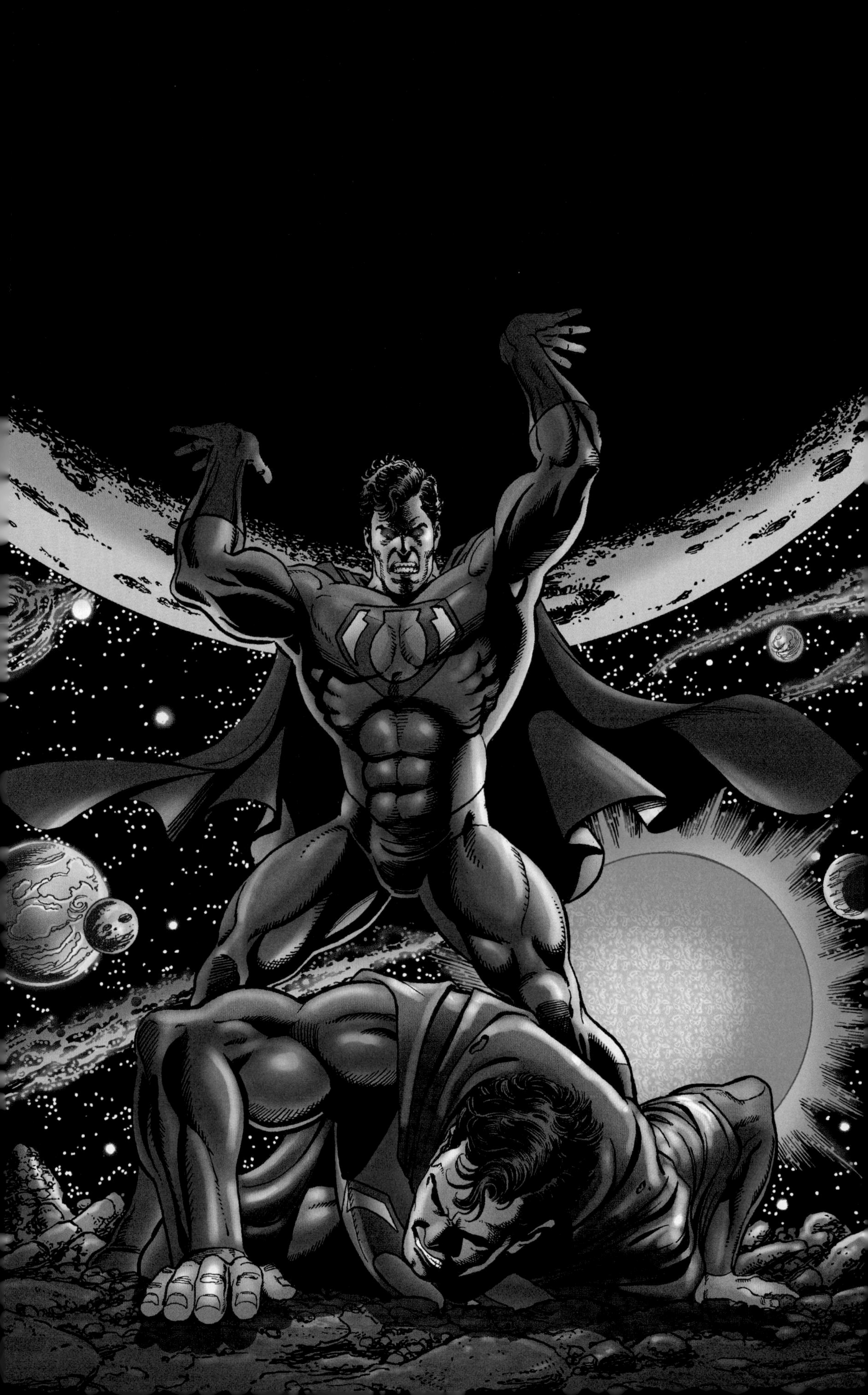

SUPERMAN and ULTRAMAN

THE BOOK OF DESTINY: CHAPTER FIVE

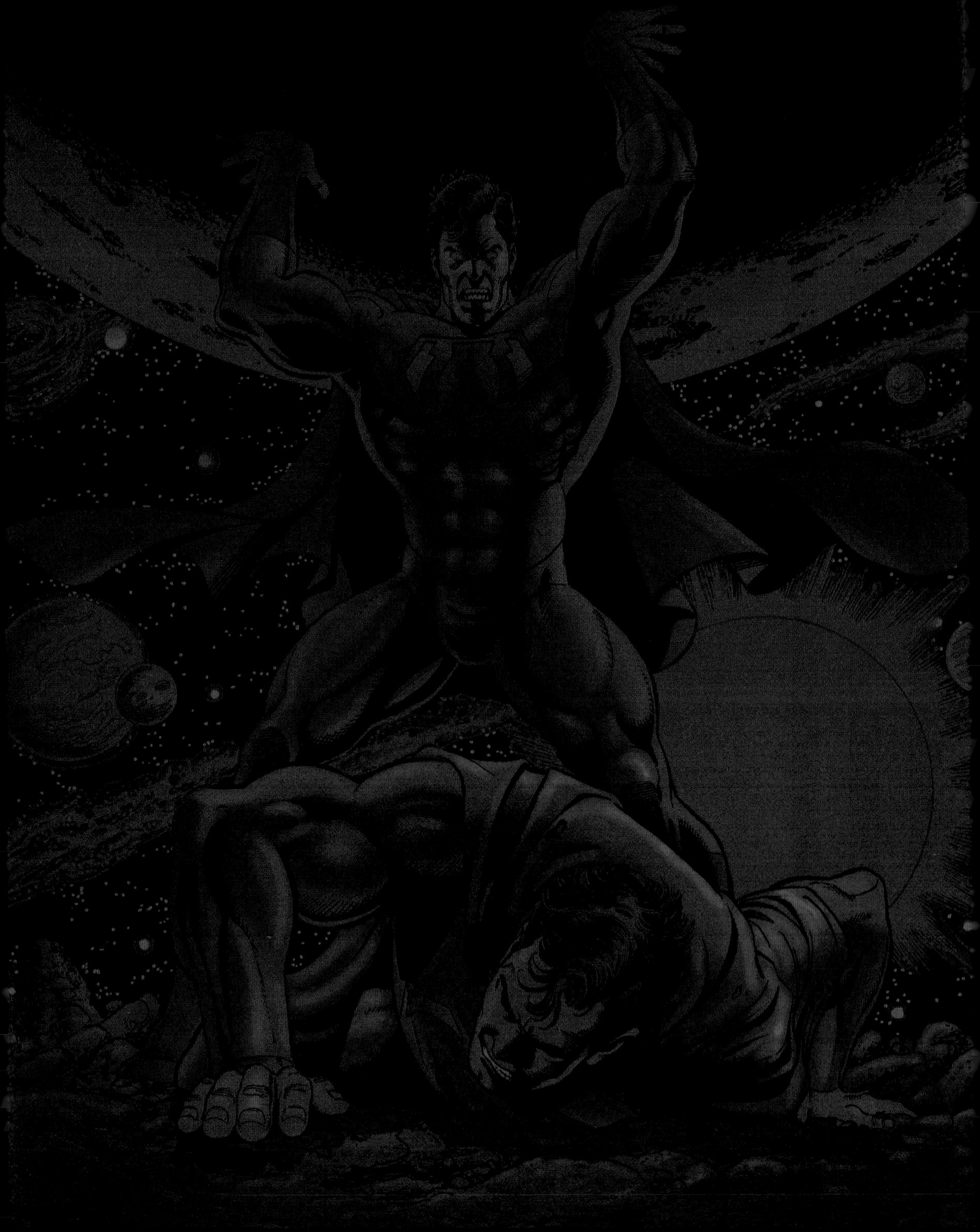

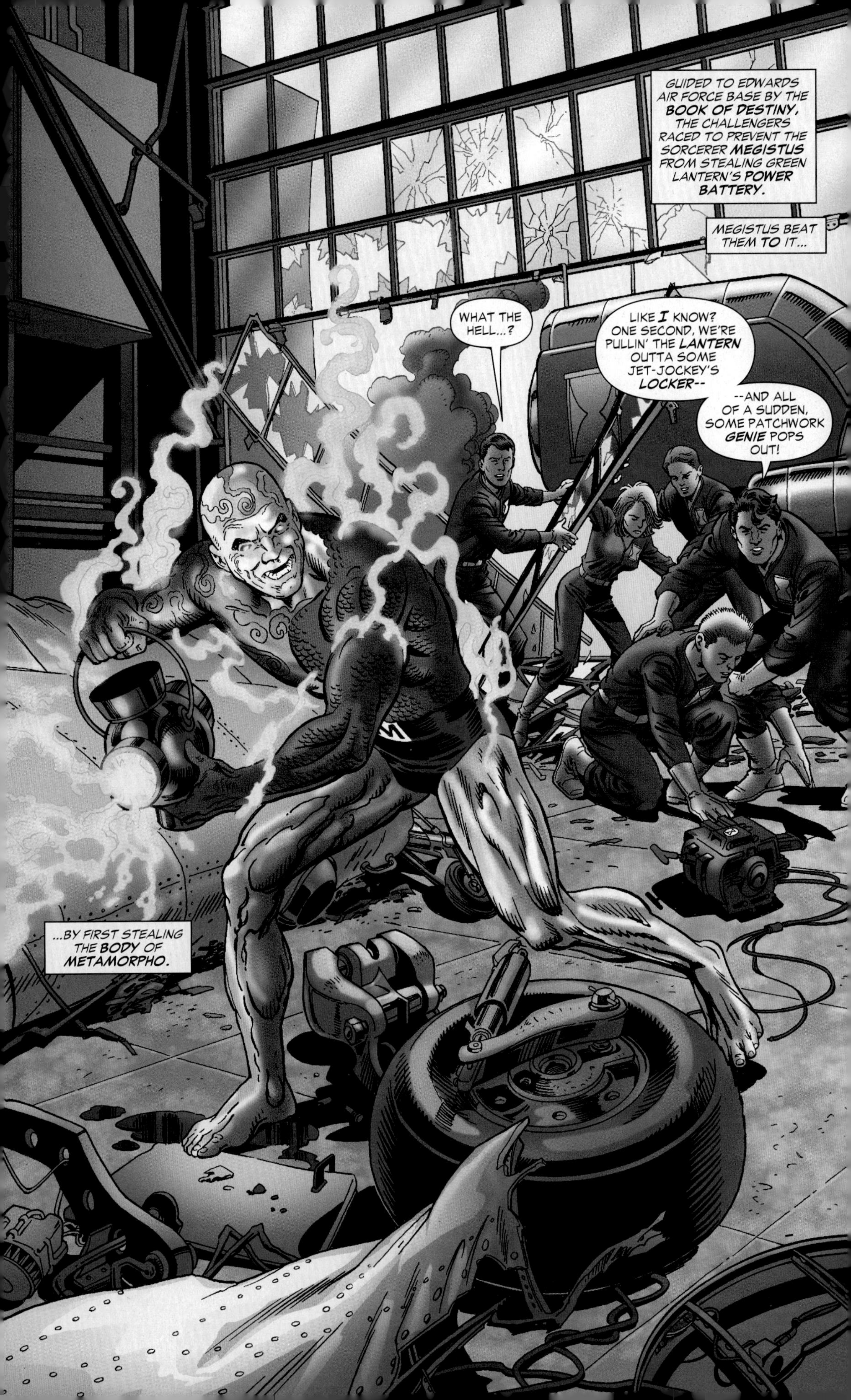
GUIDED TO EDWARDS AIR FORCE BASE BY THE BOOK OF DESTINY, THE CHALLENGERS RACED TO PREVENT THE SORCERER MEGISTUS FROM STEALING GREEN LANTERN'S POWER BATTERY.
MEGISTUS BEAT THEM TO IT...
WHAT THE HELL...?
LIKE I KNOW? ONE SECOND, WE'RE PULLIN' THE LANTERN OUTTA SOME JET-JOCKEY'S LOCKER--
--AND ALL OF A SUDDEN, SOME PATCHWORK GENIE POPS OUT!
...BY FIRST STEALING THE BODY OF METAMORPHO.

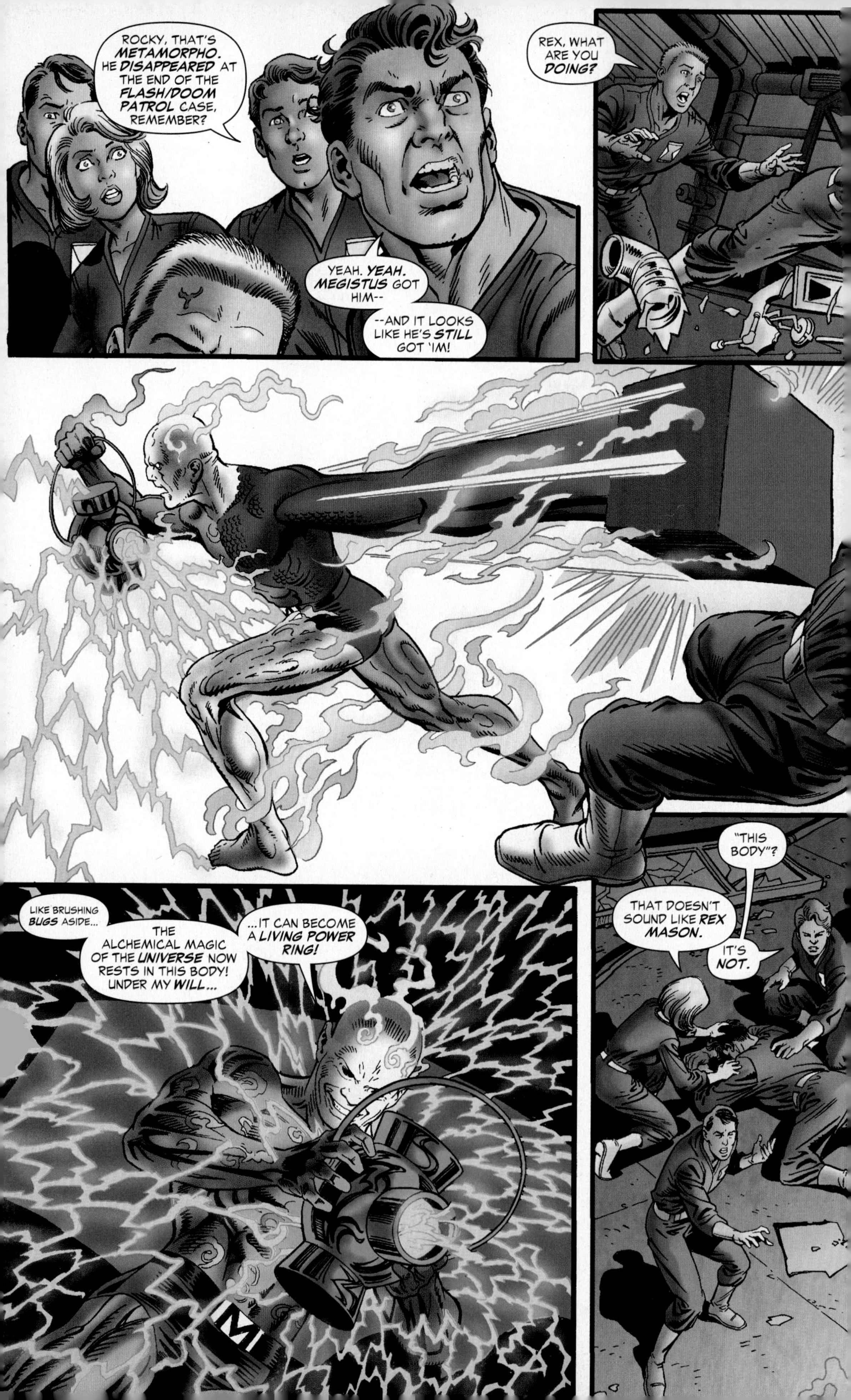
ROCKY, THAT'S METAMORPHO. HE DISAPPEARED AT THE END OF THE FLASH/DOOM PATROL CASE, REMEMBER?
YEAH. YEAH. MEGISTUS GOT HIM--
--AND IT LOOKS LIKE HE'S STILL GOT 'IM!
REX, WHAT ARE YOU DOING?
LIKE BRUSHING BUGS ASIDE...
THE ALCHEMICAL MAGIC OF THE UNIVERSE NOW RESTS IN THIS BODY! UNDER MY WILL...
...IT CAN BECOME A LIVING POWER RING!
"THIS BODY"?
THAT DOESN'T SOUND LIKE REX MASON.
IT'S NOT.

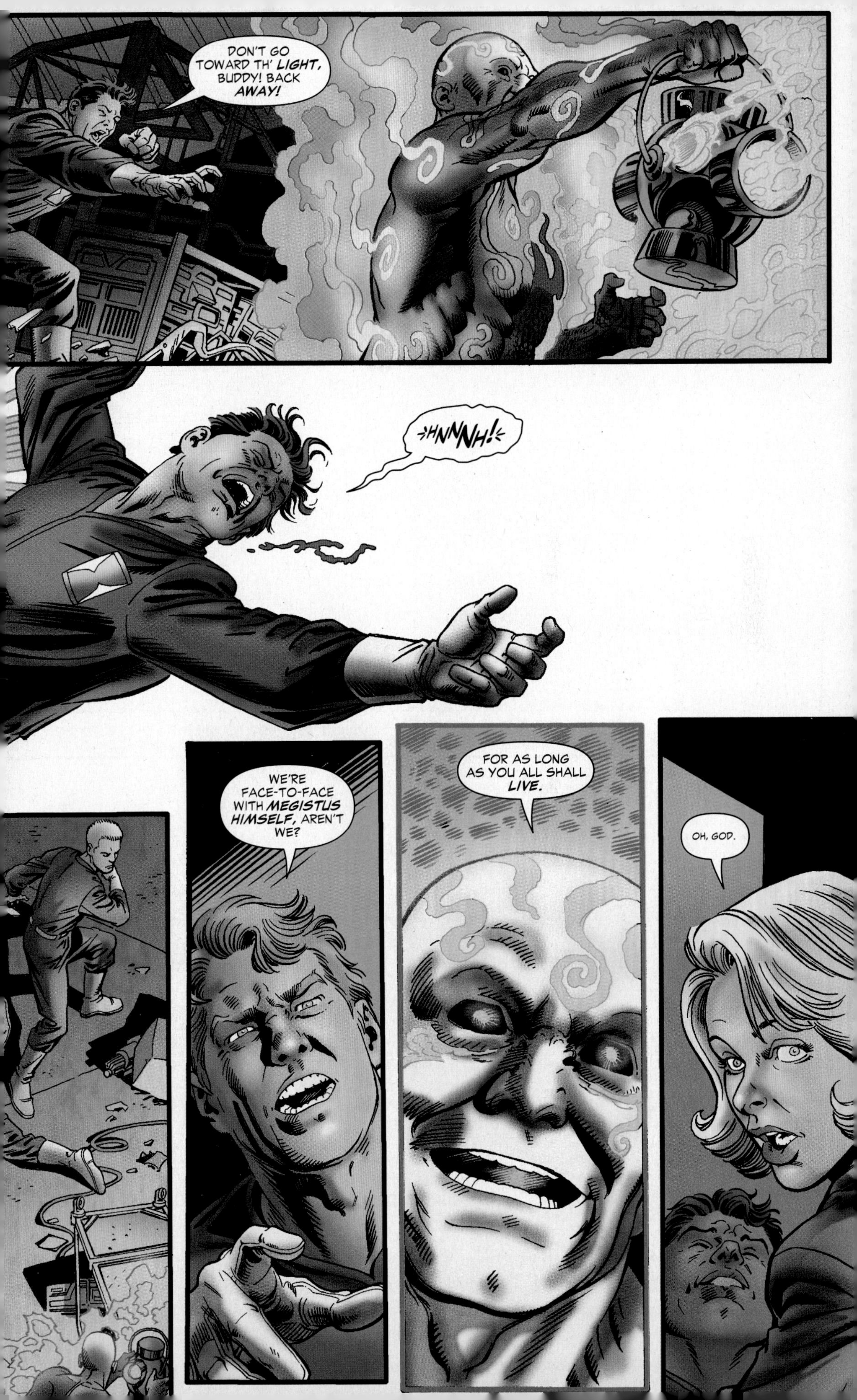
DON'T GO TOWARD TH' LIGHT, BUDDY! BACK AWAY!
HNNNH!
WE'RE FACE-TO-FACE WITH MEGISTUS HIMSELF, AREN'T WE?
FOR AS LONG AS YOU ALL SHALL LIVE.
OH, GOD.

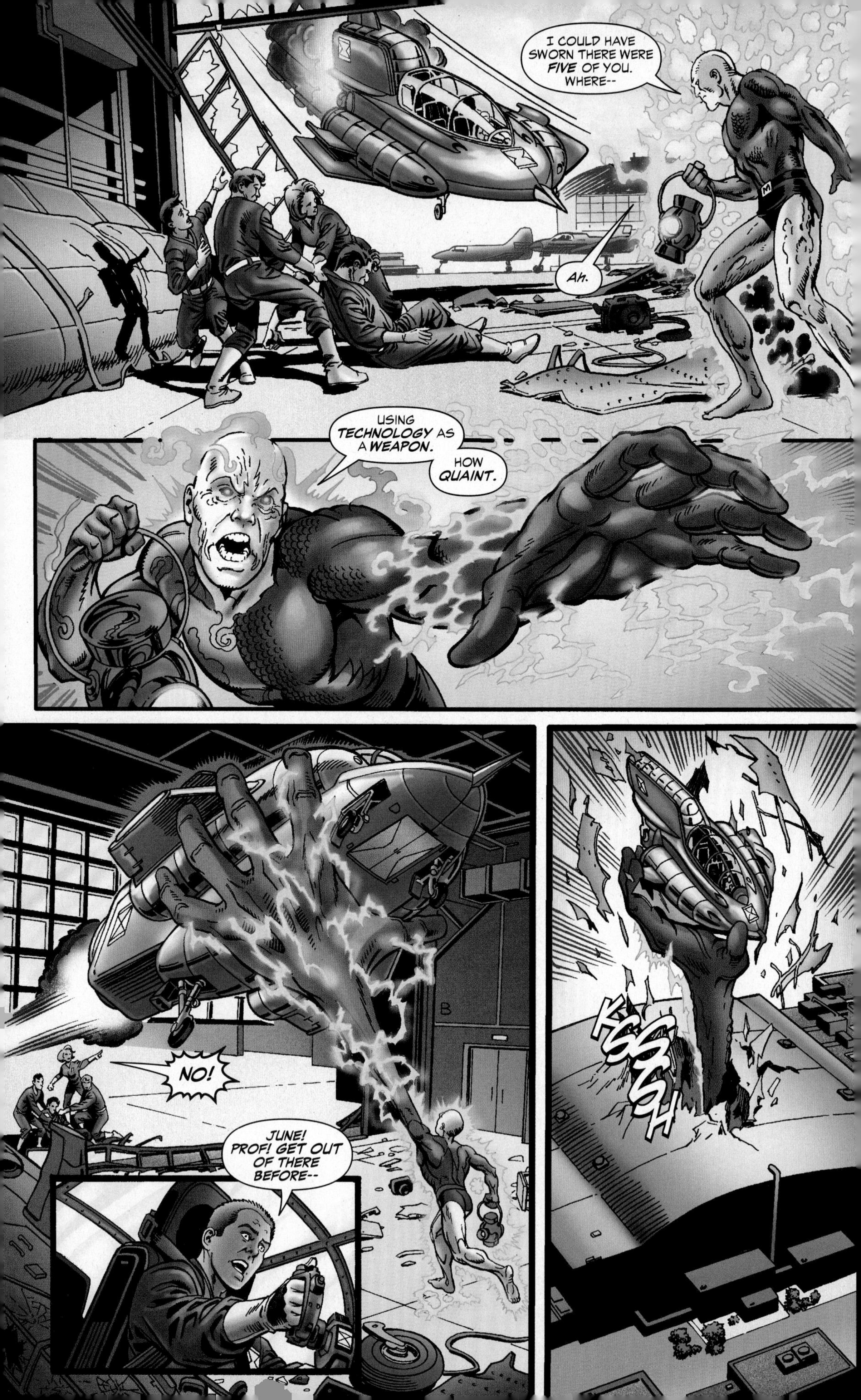
I COULD HAVE SWORN THERE WERE FIVE OF YOU. WHERE--
Ah.
USING TECHNOLOGY AS A WEAPON.
HOW QUAINT.
NO!
JUNE! PROF! GET OUT OF THERE BEFORE--
KSSSHH

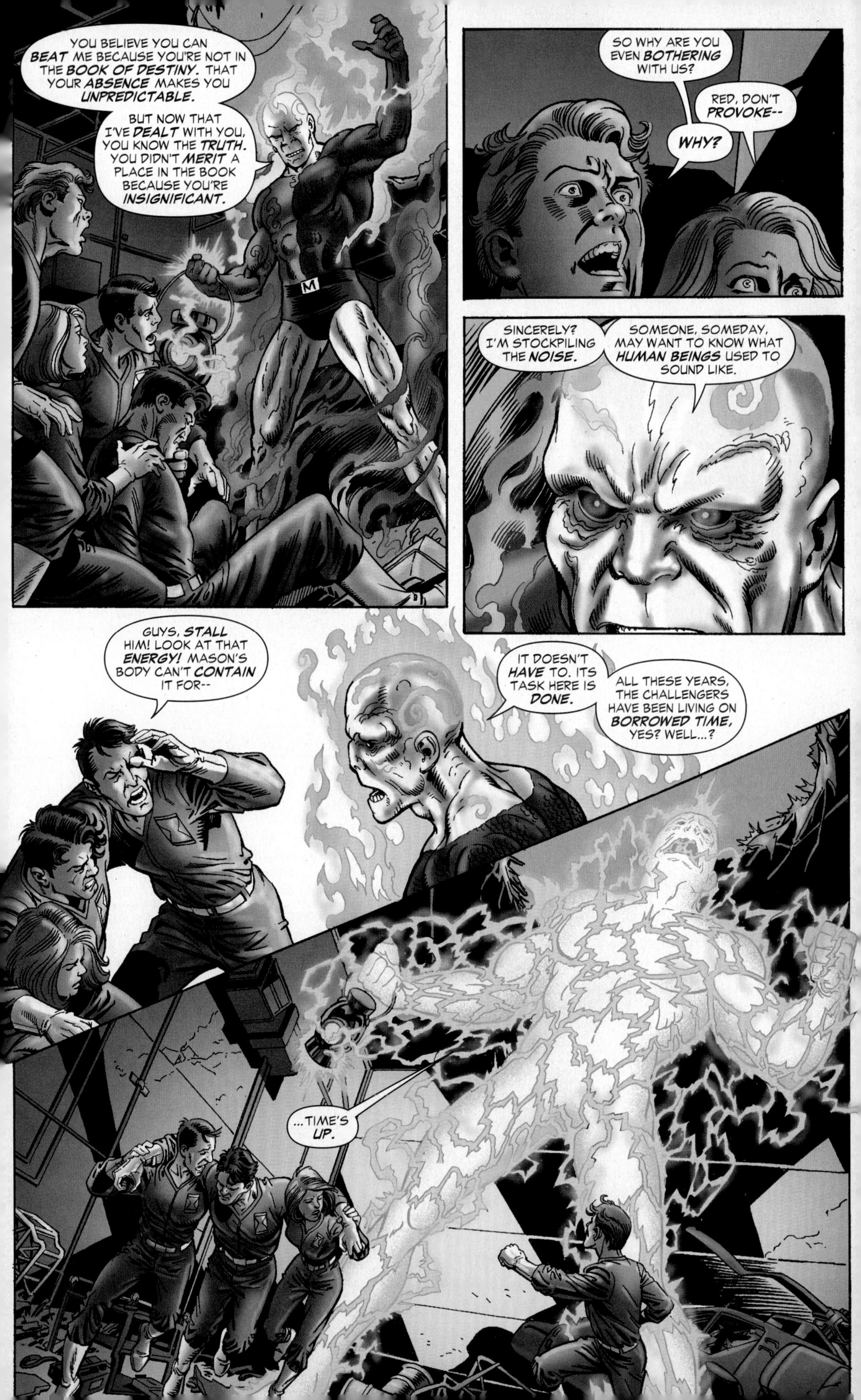
YOU BELIEVE YOU CAN BEAT ME BECAUSE YOU'RE NOT IN THE BOOK OF DESTINY. THAT YOUR ABSENCE MAKES YOU UNPREDICTABLE.
BUT NOW THAT I'VE DEALT WITH YOU, YOU KNOW THE TRUTH. YOU DIDN'T MERIT A PLACE IN THE BOOK BECAUSE YOU'RE INSIGNIFICANT.
M
SO WHY ARE YOU EVEN BOTHERING WITH US?
RED, DON'T PROVOKE--
WHY?
SINCERELY? I'M STOCKPILING THE NOISE.
SOMEONE, SOMEDAY, MAY WANT TO KNOW WHAT HUMAN BEINGS USED TO SOUND LIKE.
GUYS, STALL HIM! LOOK AT THAT ENERGY! MASON'S BODY CAN'T CONTAIN IT FOR--
IT DOESN'T HAVE TO. ITS TASK HERE IS DONE.
ALL THESE YEARS, THE CHALLENGERS HAVE BEEN LIVING ON BORROWED TIME, YES? WELL...?
...TIME'S UP.

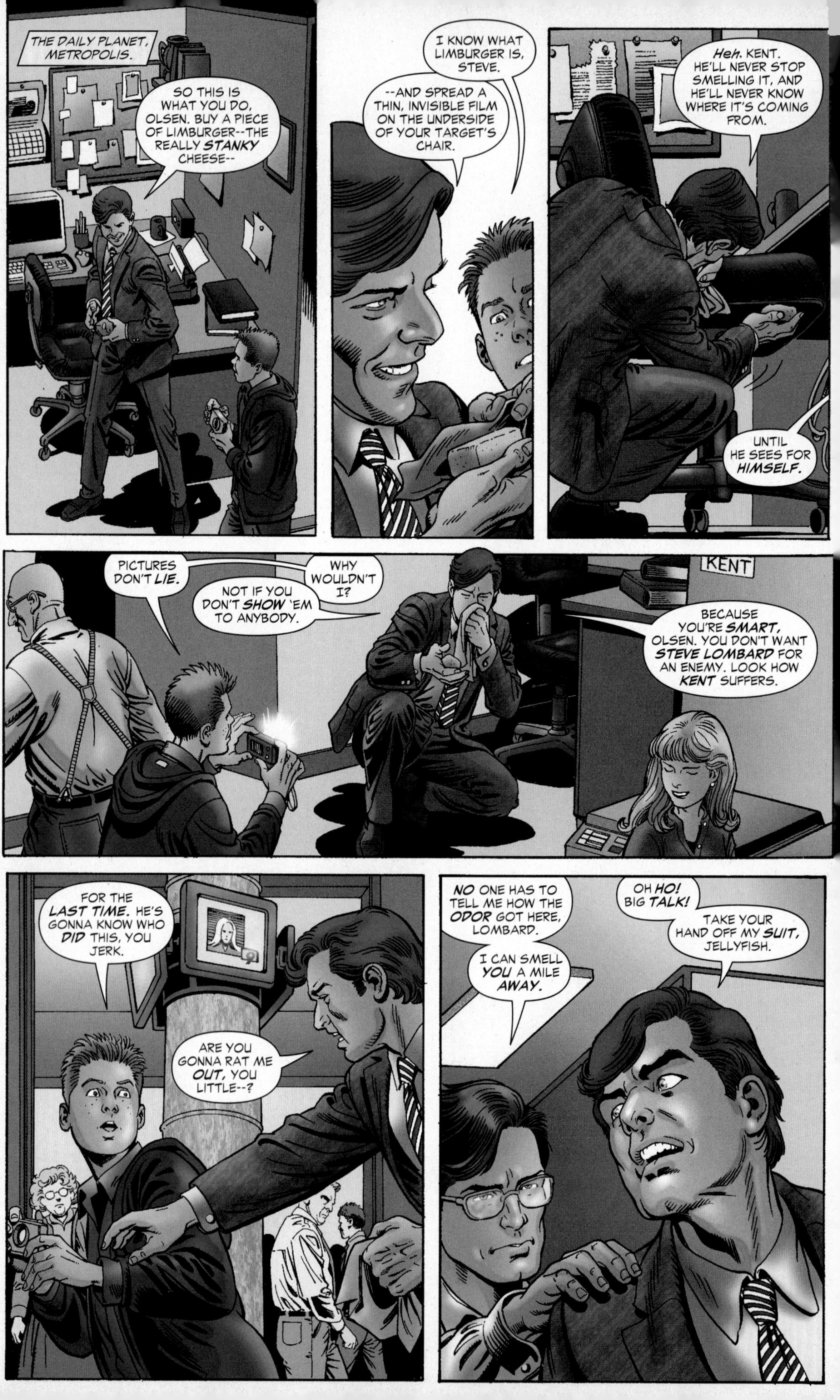
THE DAILY PLANET, METROPOLIS.
SO THIS IS WHAT YOU DO, OLSEN. BUY A PIECE OF LIMBURGER--THE REALLY STANKY CHEESE--
I KNOW WHAT LIMBURGER IS, STEVE.
--AND SPREAD A THIN, INVISIBLE FILM ON THE UNDERSIDE OF YOUR TARGET'S CHAIR.
Heh. KENT. HE'LL NEVER STOP SMELLING IT, AND HE'LL NEVER KNOW WHERE IT'S COMING FROM.
UNTIL HE SEES FOR HIMSELF.
PICTURES DON'T LIE.
WHY WOULDN'T I?
NOT IF YOU DON'T SHOW 'EM TO ANYBODY.
KENT
BECAUSE YOU'RE SMART, OLSEN. YOU DON'T WANT STEVE LOMBARD FOR AN ENEMY. LOOK HOW KENT SUFFERS.
FOR THE LAST TIME. HE'S GONNA KNOW WHO DID THIS, YOU JERK.
ARE YOU GONNA RAT ME OUT, YOU LITTLE--?
NO ONE HAS TO TELL ME HOW THE ODOR GOT HERE, LOMBARD.
I CAN SMELL YOU A MILE AWAY.
OH HO! BIG TALK!
TAKE YOUR HAND OFF MY SUIT, JELLYFISH.

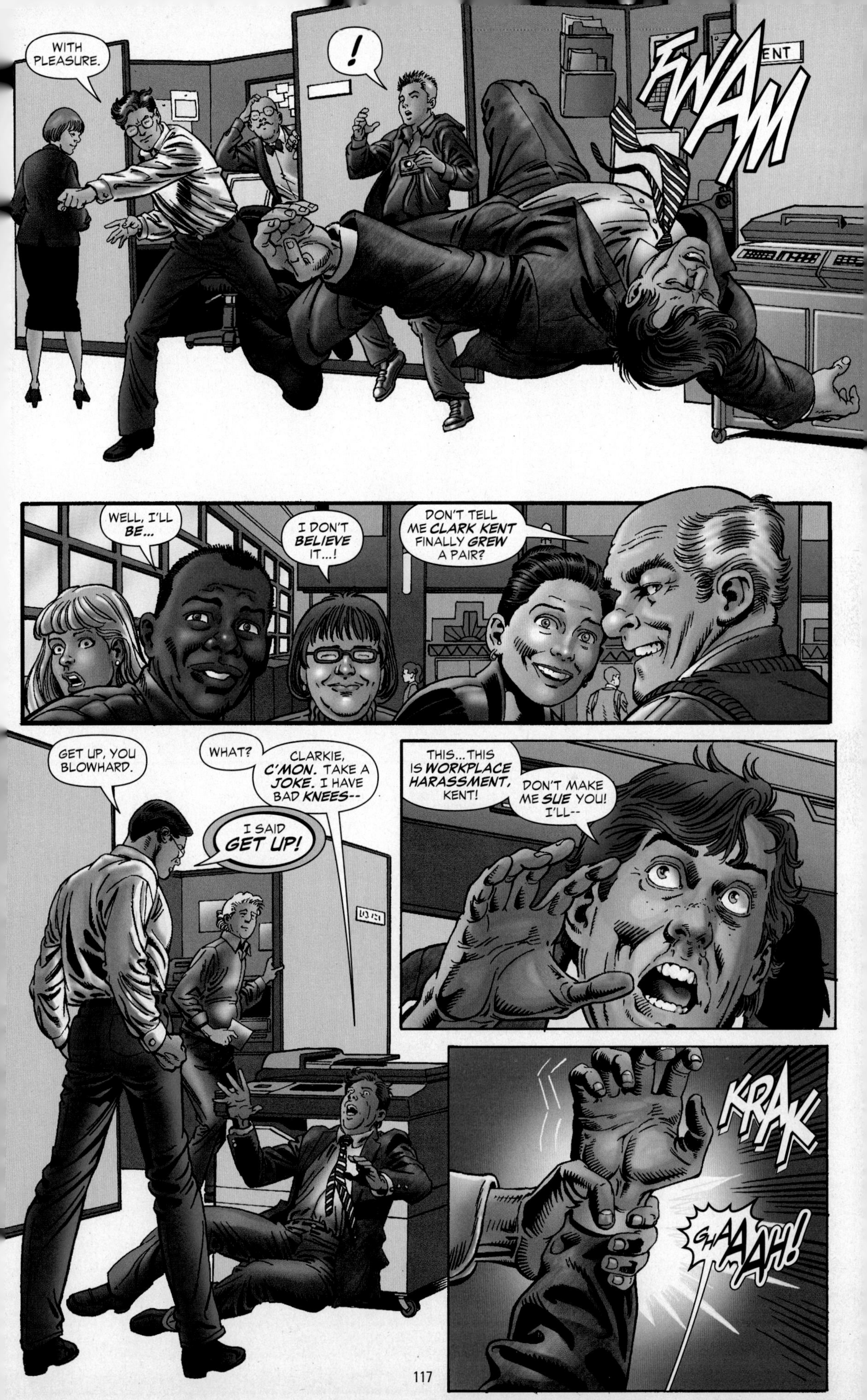
WITH PLEASURE.
!
FWAM
WELL, I'LL BE...
I DON'T BELIEVE IT...!
DON'T TELL ME CLARK KENT FINALLY GREW A PAIR?
GET UP, YOU BLOWHARD.
WHAT?
CLARKIE, C'MON. TAKE A JOKE. I HAVE BAD KNEES--
I SAID GET UP!
THIS...THIS IS WORKPLACE HARASSMENT, KENT!
DON'T MAKE ME SUE YOU! I'LL--
KRAK
GHAAAAH!

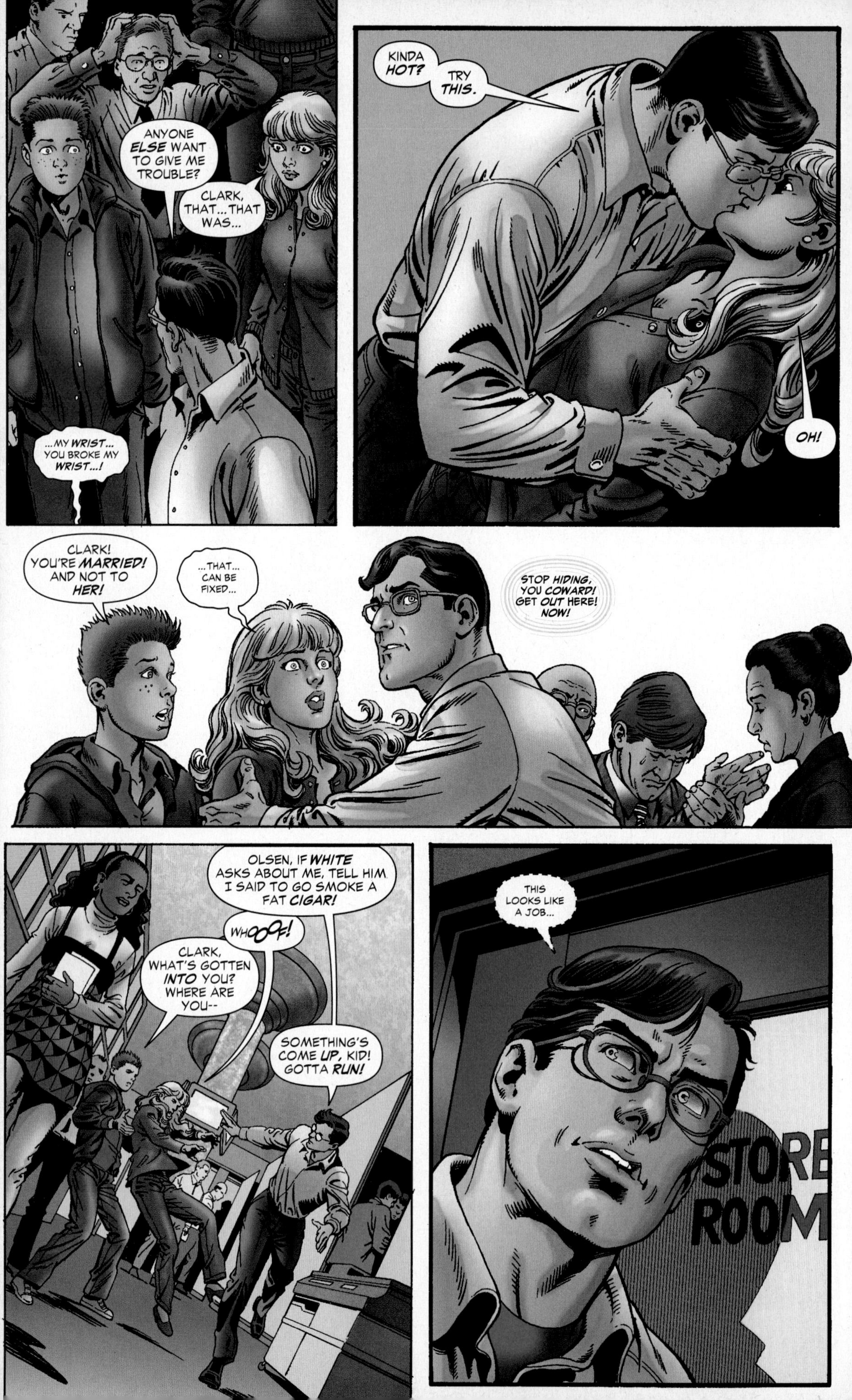
ANYONE ELSE WANT TO GIVE ME TROUBLE?
CLARK, THAT...THAT WAS...
...MY WRIST... YOU BROKE MY WRIST...!
KINDA HOT?
TRY THIS.
OH!
CLARK! YOU'RE MARRIED! AND NOT TO HER!
...THAT... CAN BE FIXED...
STOP HIDING, YOU COWARD! GET OUT HERE! NOW!
OLSEN, IF WHITE ASKS ABOUT ME, TELL HIM I SAID TO GO SMOKE A FAT CIGAR!
WHOOOF!
CLARK, WHAT'S GOTTEN INTO YOU? WHERE ARE YOU--
SOMETHING'S COME UP, KID! GOTTA RUN!
THIS LOOKS LIKE A JOB...
STORE ROOM

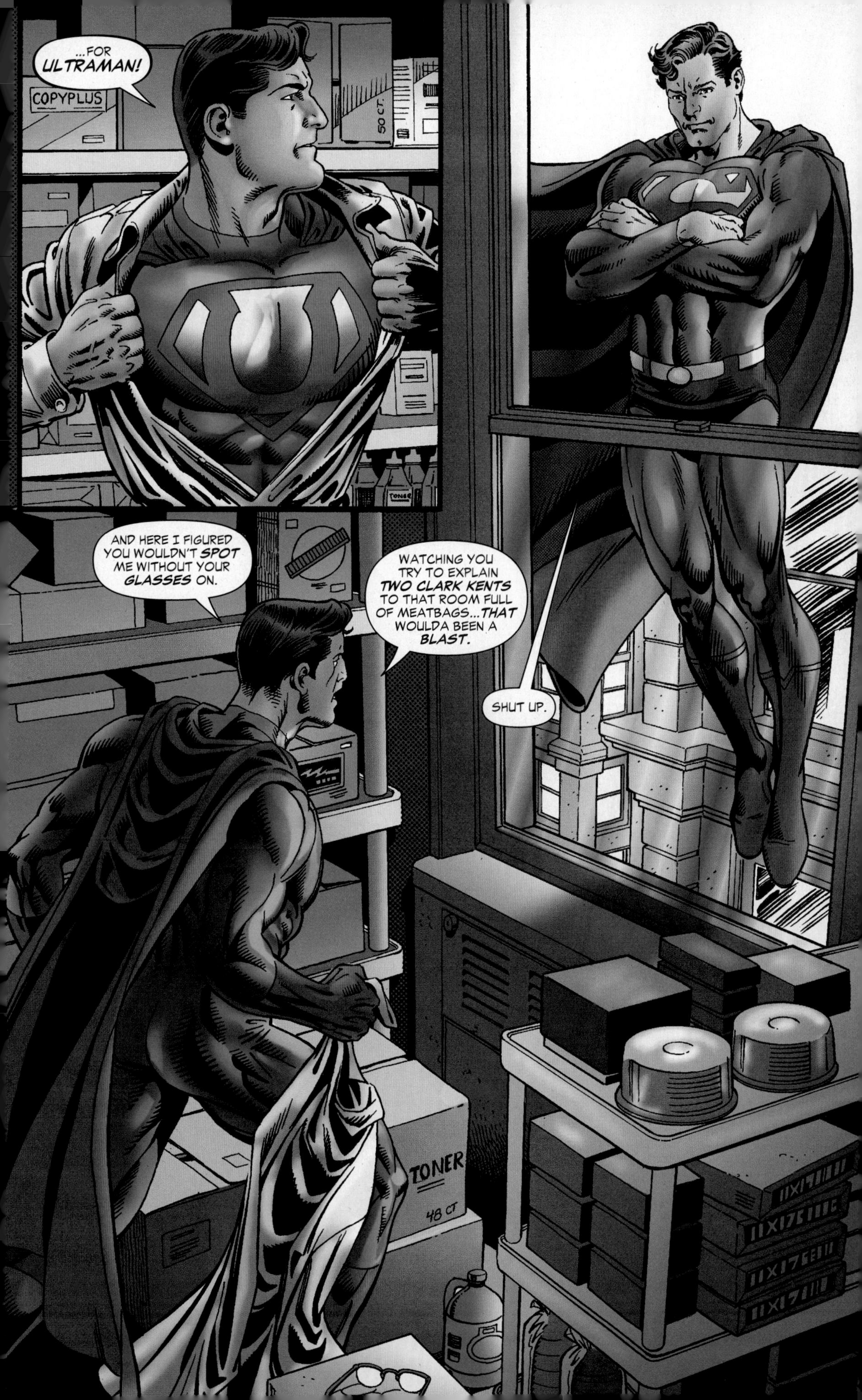

...FOR ULTRAMAN!
COPYPLUS
50 CT.
TONER
AND HERE I FIGURED YOU WOULDN'T SPOT ME WITHOUT YOUR GLASSES ON.
WATCHING YOU TRY TO EXPLAIN TWO CLARK KENTS TO THAT ROOM FULL OF MEATBAGS...THAT WOULDA BEEN A BLAST.
SHUT UP.
TONER
48 CT

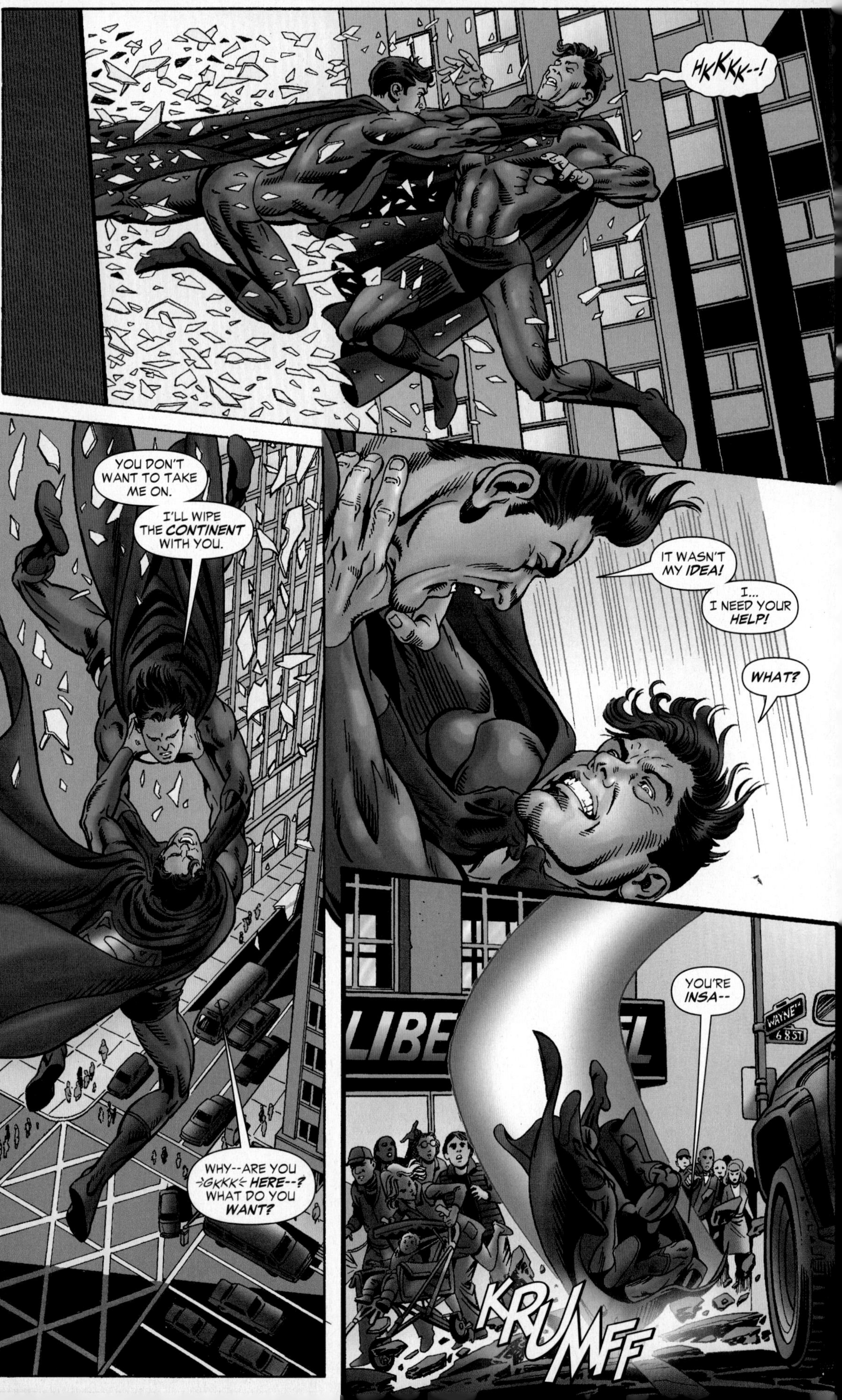
HKKKK--!
YOU DON'T WANT TO TAKE ME ON.
I'LL WIPE THE CONTINENT WITH YOU.
WHY--ARE YOU ~GKKK~ HERE--? WHAT DO YOU WANT?
IT WASN'T MY IDEA!
I... I NEED YOUR HELP!
WHAT?
YOU'RE INSA--
WAYNE
68 ST
KRUMFF

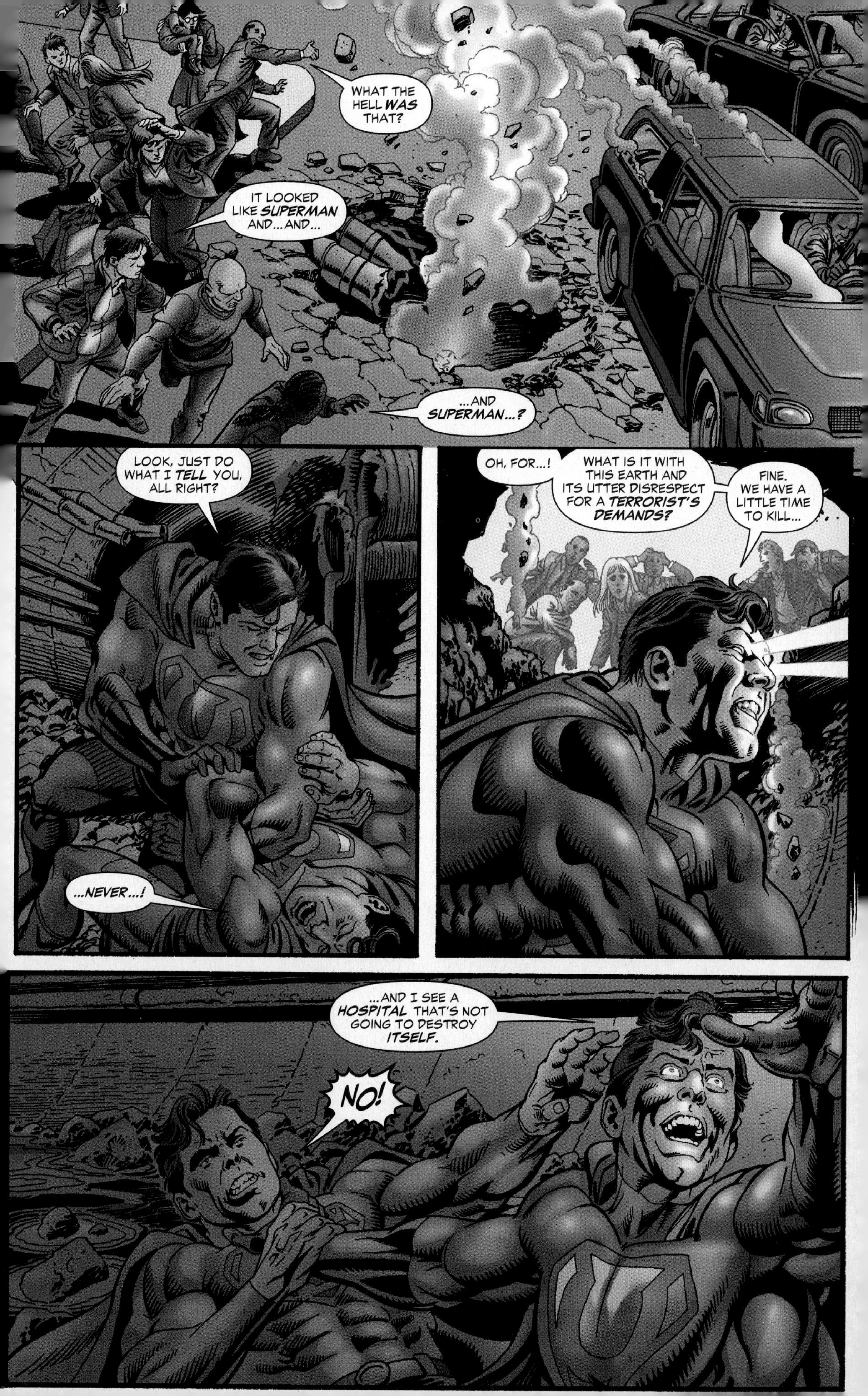
WHAT THE HELL WAS THAT?
IT LOOKED LIKE SUPERMAN AND... AND...
...AND SUPERMAN...?
LOOK, JUST DO WHAT I TELL YOU, ALL RIGHT?
...NEVER...!
OH, FOR...!
WHAT IS IT WITH THIS EARTH AND ITS UTTER DISRESPECT FOR A TERRORIST'S DEMANDS?
FINE. WE HAVE A LITTLE TIME TO KILL...
...AND I SEE A HOSPITAL THAT'S NOT GOING TO DESTROY ITSELF.
NO!

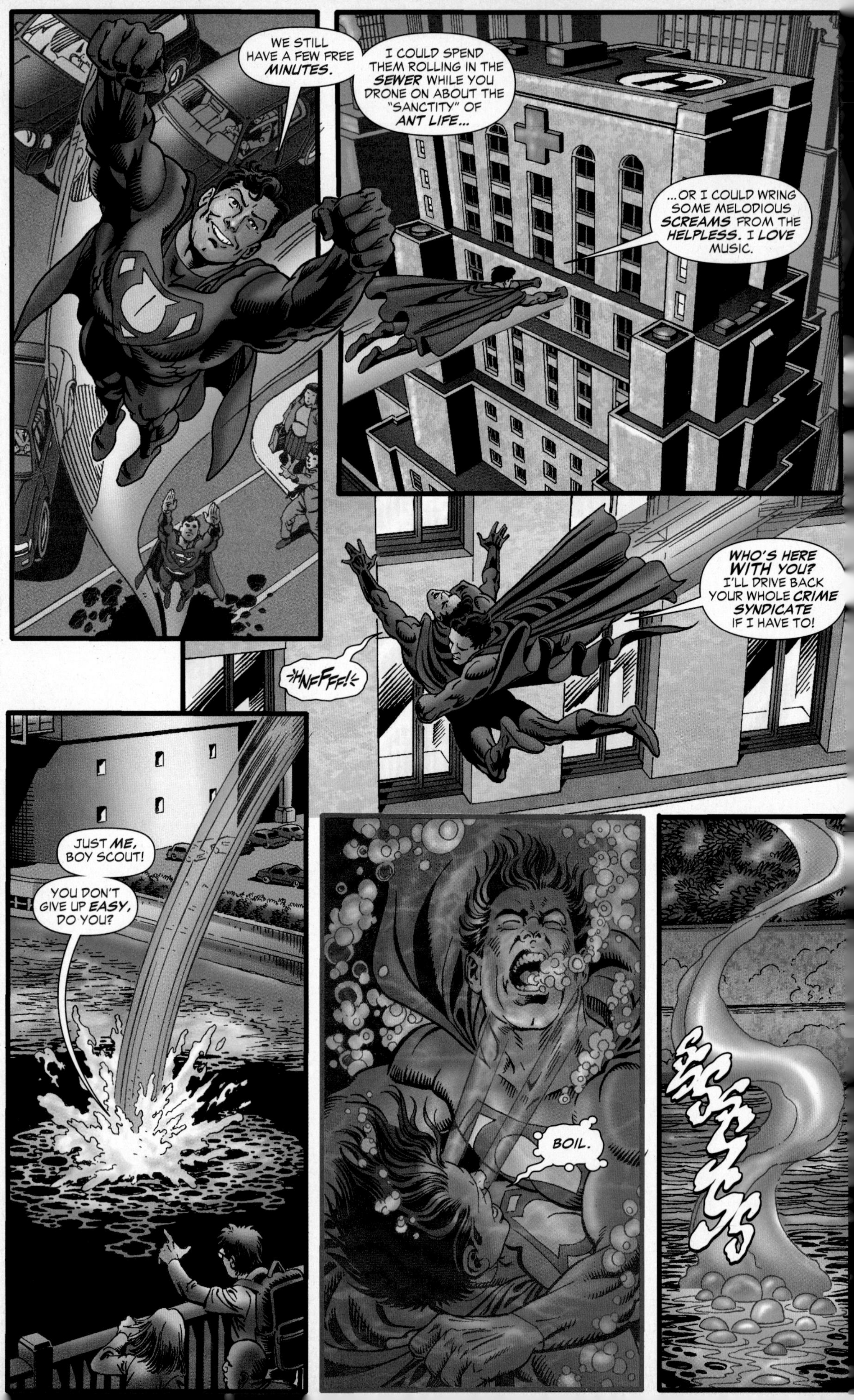
WE STILL HAVE A FEW FREE MINUTES.
I COULD SPEND THEM ROLLING IN THE SEWER WHILE YOU DRONE ON ABOUT THE "SANCTITY" OF ANT LIFE...
...OR I COULD WRING SOME MELODIOUS SCREAMS FROM THE HELPLESS. I LOVE MUSIC.
WHO'S HERE WITH YOU? I'LL DRIVE BACK YOUR WHOLE CRIME SYNDICATE IF I HAVE TO!
HNFFFF!
JUST ME, BOY SCOUT!
YOU DON'T GIVE UP EASY, DO YOU?
BOIL.

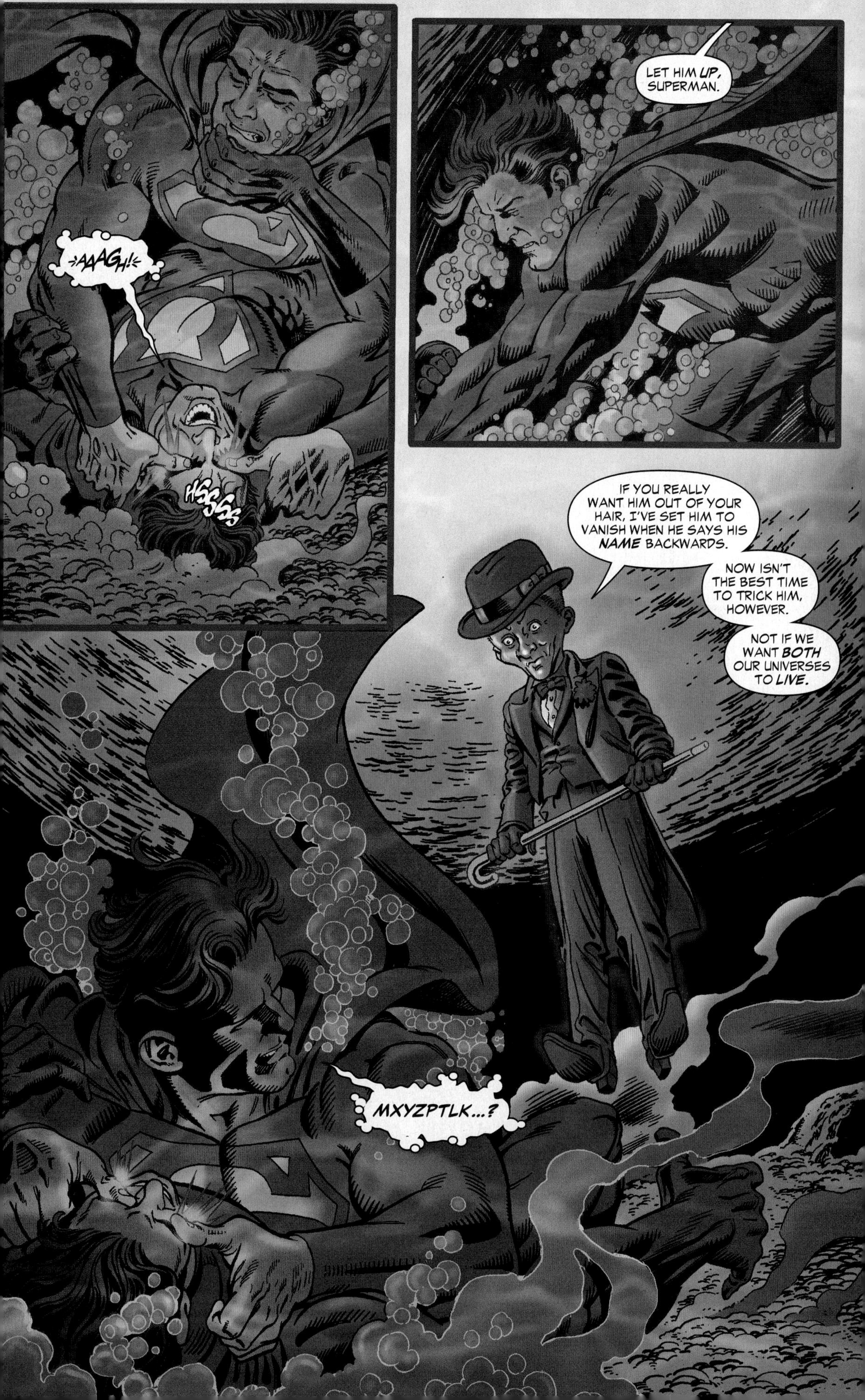
AAAGH!
HSSSSS
LET HIM UP, SUPERMAN.
IF YOU REALLY WANT HIM OUT OF YOUR HAIR, I'VE SET HIM TO VANISH WHEN HE SAYS HIS NAME BACKWARDS.
NOW ISN'T THE BEST TIME TO TRICK HIM, HOWEVER.
NOT IF WE WANT BOTH OUR UNIVERSES TO LIVE.
MXYZPTLK...?

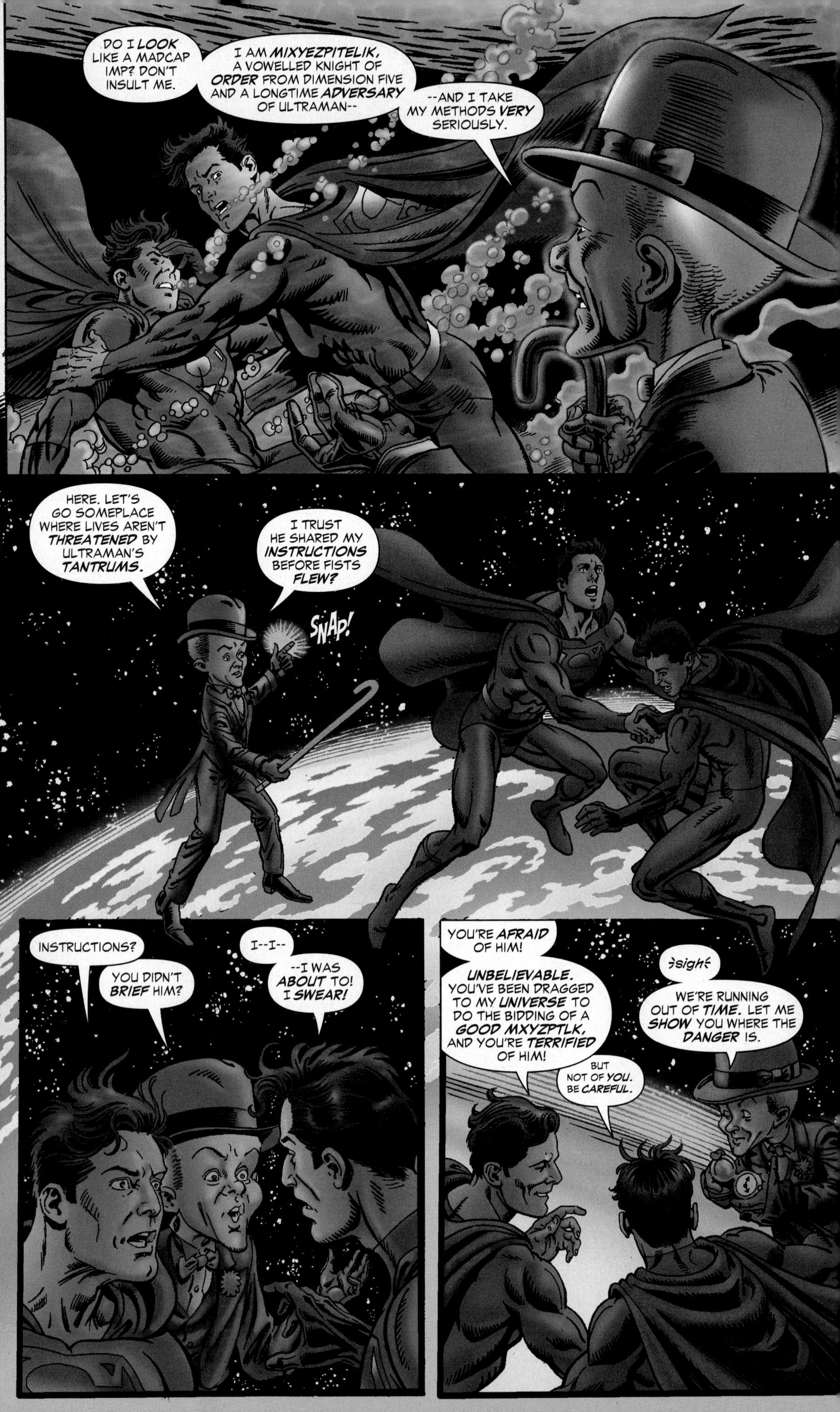
DO I LOOK LIKE A MADCAP IMP? DON'T INSULT ME.
I AM MIXYEZPITELIK, A VOWELLED KNIGHT OF ORDER FROM DIMENSION FIVE AND A LONGTIME ADVERSARY OF ULTRAMAN--
--AND I TAKE MY METHODS VERY SERIOUSLY.
HERE. LET'S GO SOMEPLACE WHERE LIVES AREN'T THREATENED BY ULTRAMAN'S TANTRUMS.
I TRUST HE SHARED MY INSTRUCTIONS BEFORE FISTS FLEW?
SNAP!
INSTRUCTIONS?
YOU DIDN'T BRIEF HIM?
I--I--
--I WAS ABOUT TO! I SWEAR!
YOU'RE AFRAID OF HIM!
UNBELIEVABLE. YOU'VE BEEN DRAGGED TO MY UNIVERSE TO DO THE BIDDING OF A GOOD MXYZPTLK, AND YOU'RE TERRIFIED OF HIM!
BUT NOT OF YOU. BE CAREFUL.
sigh
WE'RE RUNNING OUT OF TIME. LET ME SHOW YOU WHERE THE DANGER IS.

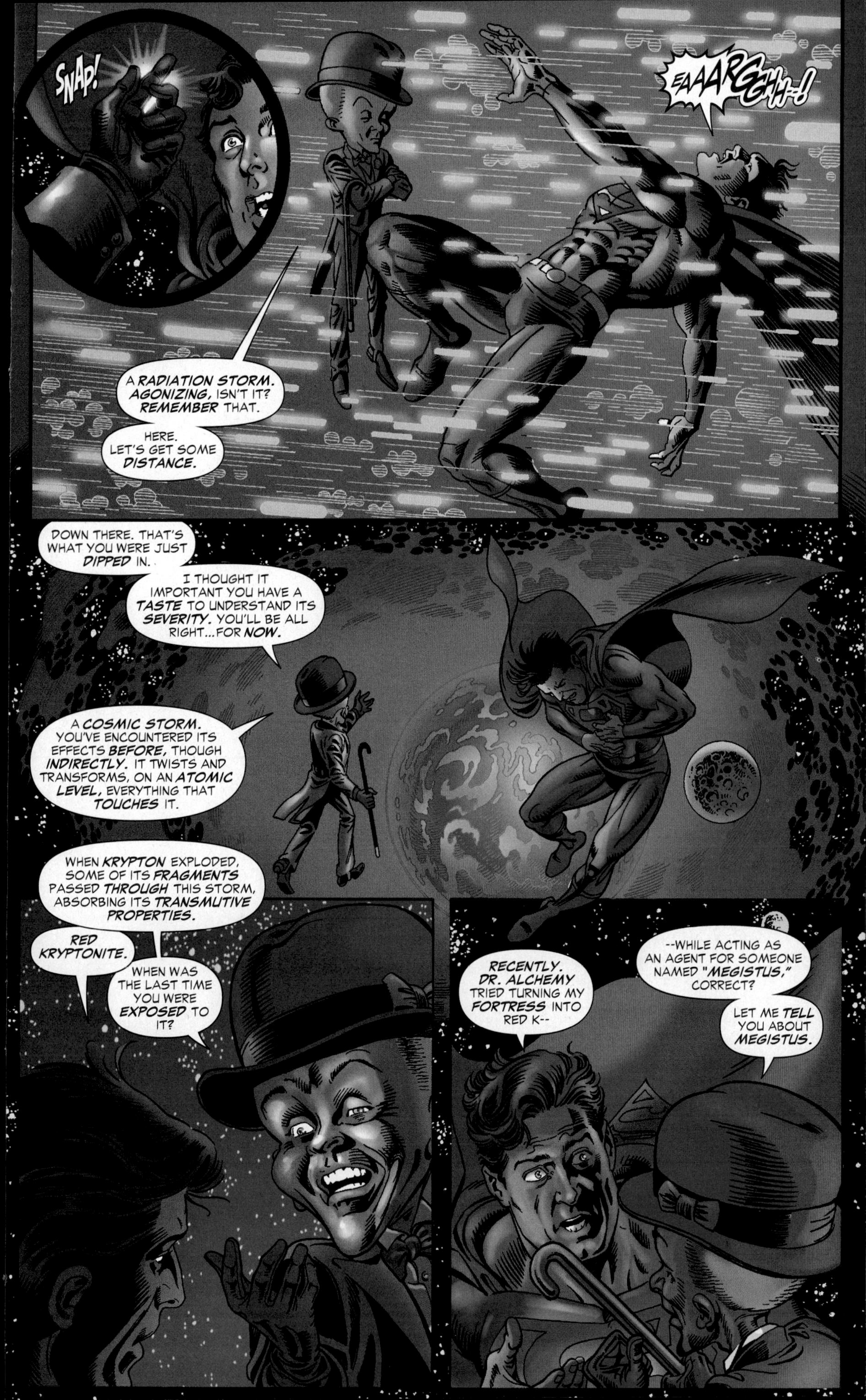
SNAP!
EAAARGHH--!
A RADIATION STORM. AGONIZING, ISN'T IT? REMEMBER THAT.
HERE. LET'S GET SOME DISTANCE.
DOWN THERE. THAT'S WHAT YOU WERE JUST DIPPED IN.
I THOUGHT IT IMPORTANT YOU HAVE A TASTE TO UNDERSTAND ITS SEVERITY. YOU'LL BE ALL RIGHT...FOR NOW.
A COSMIC STORM. YOU'VE ENCOUNTERED ITS EFFECTS BEFORE, THOUGH INDIRECTLY. IT TWISTS AND TRANSFORMS, ON AN ATOMIC LEVEL, EVERYTHING THAT TOUCHES IT.
WHEN KRYPTON EXPLODED, SOME OF ITS FRAGMENTS PASSED THROUGH THIS STORM, ABSORBING ITS TRANSMUTIVE PROPERTIES.
RED KRYPTONITE.
WHEN WAS THE LAST TIME YOU WERE EXPOSED TO IT?
RECENTLY. DR. ALCHEMY TRIED TURNING MY FORTRESS INTO RED K--
--WHILE ACTING AS AN AGENT FOR SOMEONE NAMED "MEGISTUS," CORRECT?
LET ME TELL YOU ABOUT MEGISTUS.

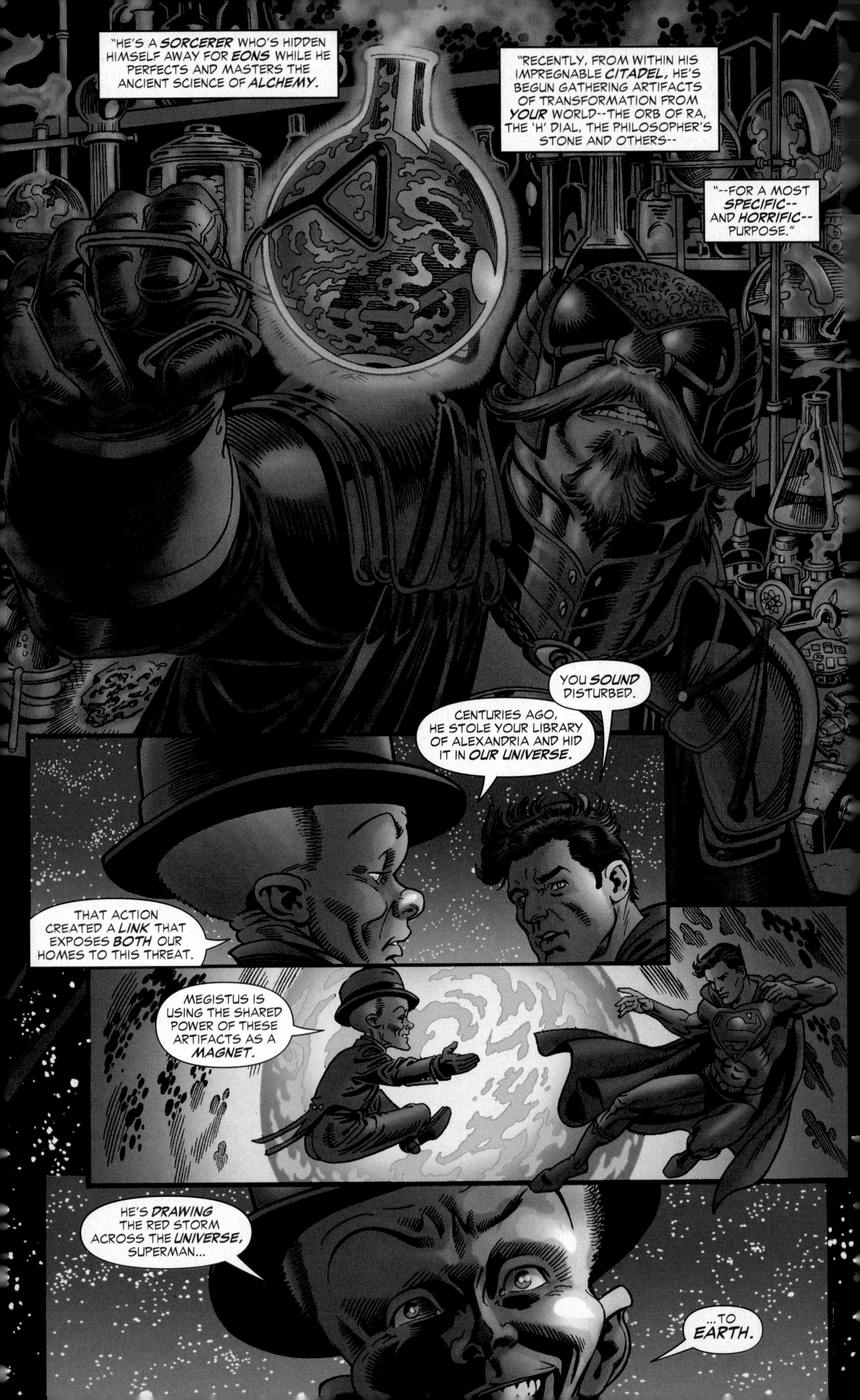
"HE'S A SORCERER WHO'S HIDDEN HIMSELF AWAY FOR EONS WHILE HE PERFECTS AND MASTERS THE ANCIENT SCIENCE OF ALCHEMY.
"RECENTLY, FROM WITHIN HIS IMPREGNABLE CITADEL, HE'S BEGUN GATHERING ARTIFACTS OF TRANSFORMATION FROM YOUR WORLD--THE ORB OF RA, THE 'H' DIAL, THE PHILOSOPHER'S STONE AND OTHERS--
"--FOR A MOST SPECIFIC-- AND HORRIFIC-- PURPOSE."
YOU SOUND DISTURBED.
CENTURIES AGO, HE STOLE YOUR LIBRARY OF ALEXANDRIA AND HID IT IN OUR UNIVERSE.
THAT ACTION CREATED A LINK THAT EXPOSES BOTH OUR HOMES TO THIS THREAT.
MEGISTUS IS USING THE SHARED POWER OF THESE ARTIFACTS AS A MAGNET.
HE'S DRAWING THE RED STORM ACROSS THE UNIVERSE, SUPERMAN...
...TO EARTH.

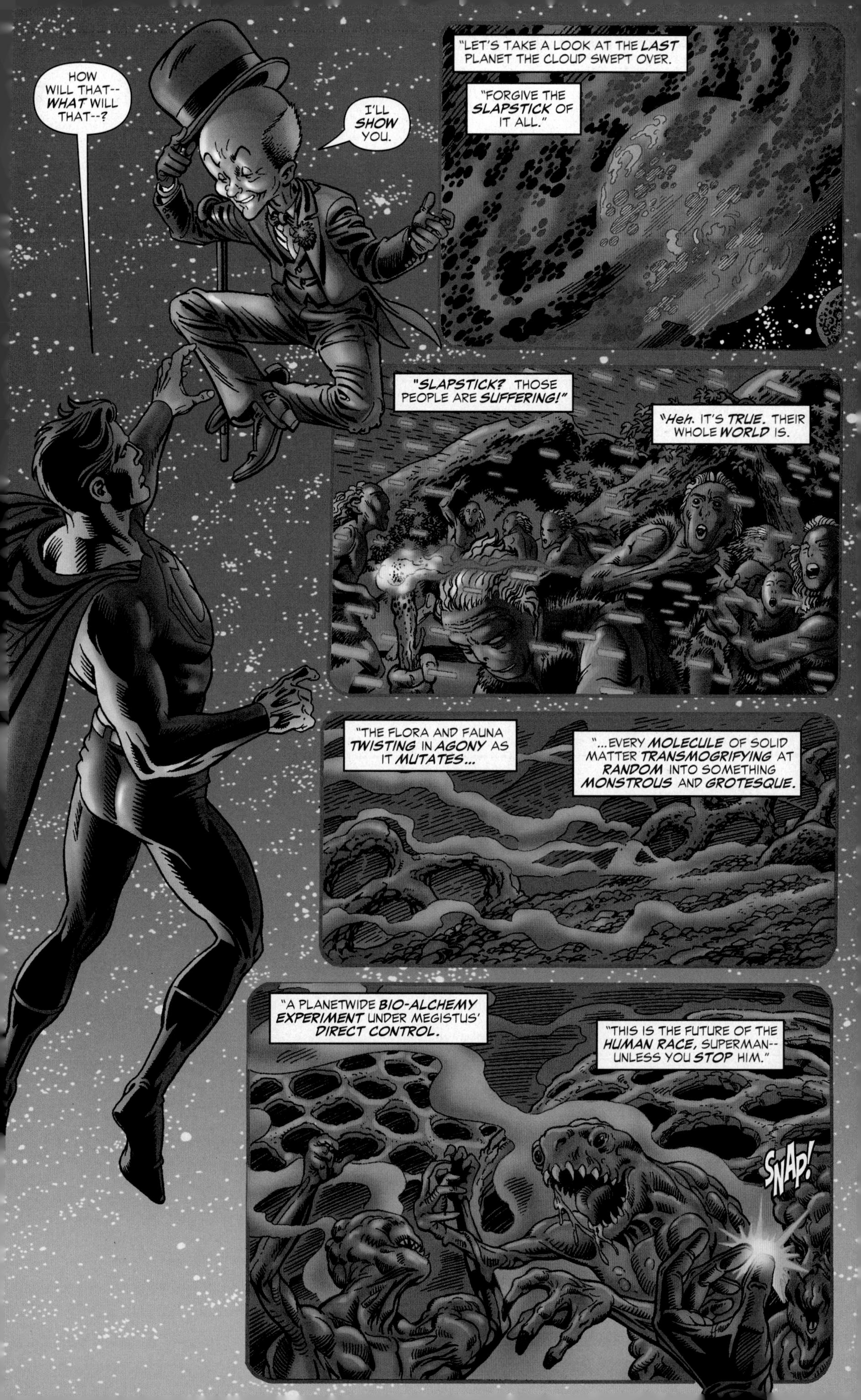
HOW WILL THAT-- WHAT WILL THAT--?
I'LL SHOW YOU.
"LET'S TAKE A LOOK AT THE LAST PLANET THE CLOUD SWEPT OVER.
"FORGIVE THE SLAPSTICK OF IT ALL."
"SLAPSTICK? THOSE PEOPLE ARE SUFFERING!"
"Heh. IT'S TRUE. THEIR WHOLE WORLD IS.
"THE FLORA AND FAUNA TWISTING IN AGONY AS IT MUTATES...
"...EVERY MOLECULE OF SOLID MATTER TRANSMOGRIFYING AT RANDOM INTO SOMETHING MONSTROUS AND GROTESQUE.
"A PLANETWIDE BIO-ALCHEMY EXPERIMENT UNDER MEGISTUS' DIRECT CONTROL.
"THIS IS THE FUTURE OF THE HUMAN RACE, SUPERMAN-- UNLESS YOU STOP HIM."
SNAP!

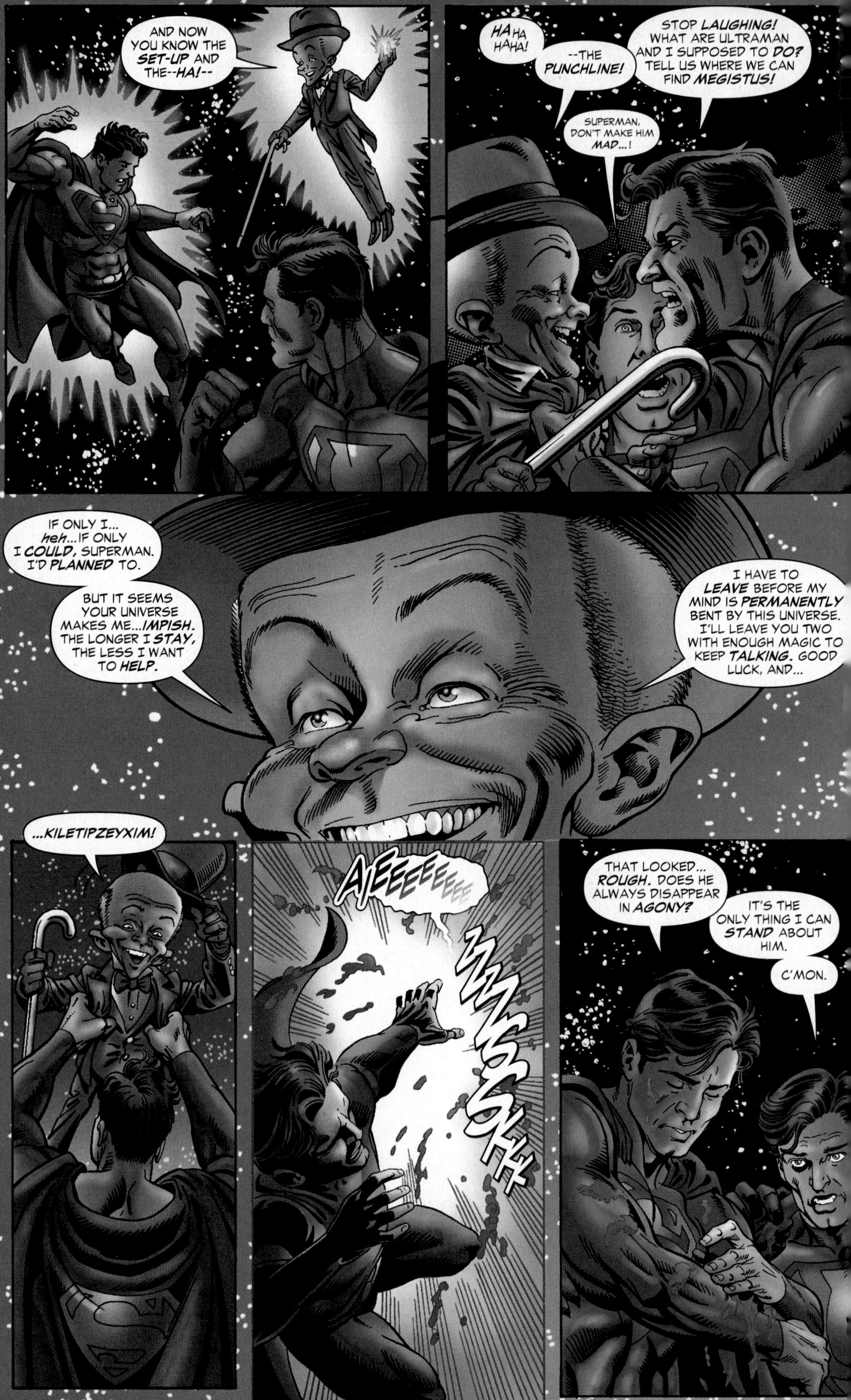
AND NOW YOU KNOW THE SET-UP AND THE--HA!--
HA HA HAHA!
--THE PUNCHLINE!
STOP LAUGHING! WHAT ARE ULTRAMAN AND I SUPPOSED TO DO? TELL US WHERE WE CAN FIND MEGISTUS!
SUPERMAN, DON'T MAKE HIM MAD...!
IF ONLY I... heh...IF ONLY I COULD, SUPERMAN. I'D PLANNED TO.
BUT IT SEEMS YOUR UNIVERSE MAKES ME...IMPISH. THE LONGER I STAY, THE LESS I WANT TO HELP.
I HAVE TO LEAVE BEFORE MY MIND IS PERMANENTLY BENT BY THIS UNIVERSE. I'LL LEAVE YOU TWO WITH ENOUGH MAGIC TO KEEP TALKING. GOOD LUCK, AND...
...KILETIPZEYXIM!
AIEEEEEEEE
ZZWSSKKK
THAT LOOKED... ROUGH. DOES HE ALWAYS DISAPPEAR IN AGONY?
IT'S THE ONLY THING I CAN STAND ABOUT HIM.
C'MON.

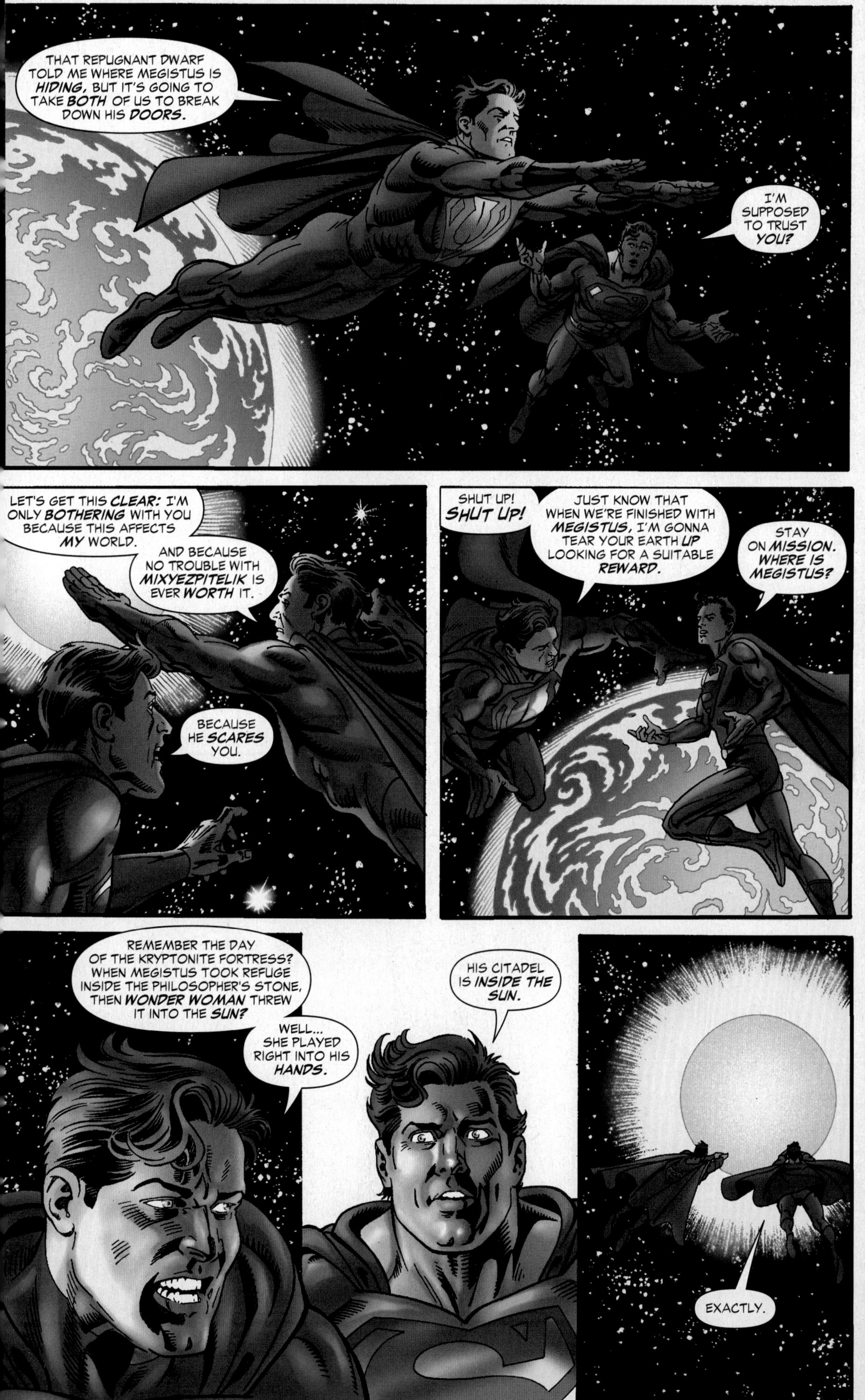
THAT REPUGNANT DWARF TOLD ME WHERE MEGISTUS IS HIDING, BUT IT'S GOING TO TAKE BOTH OF US TO BREAK DOWN HIS DOORS.
I'M SUPPOSED TO TRUST YOU?
LET'S GET THIS CLEAR: I'M ONLY BOTHERING WITH YOU BECAUSE THIS AFFECTS MY WORLD.
AND BECAUSE NO TROUBLE WITH MIXYEZPITELIK IS EVER WORTH IT.
BECAUSE HE SCARES YOU.
SHUT UP! SHUT UP!
JUST KNOW THAT WHEN WE'RE FINISHED WITH MEGISTUS, I'M GONNA TEAR YOUR EARTH UP LOOKING FOR A SUITABLE REWARD.
STAY ON MISSION. WHERE IS MEGISTUS?
REMEMBER THE DAY OF THE KRYPTONITE FORTRESS? WHEN MEGISTUS TOOK REFUGE INSIDE THE PHILOSOPHER'S STONE, THEN WONDER WOMAN THREW IT INTO THE SUN?
WELL... SHE PLAYED RIGHT INTO HIS HANDS.
HIS CITADEL IS INSIDE THE SUN.
EXACTLY.

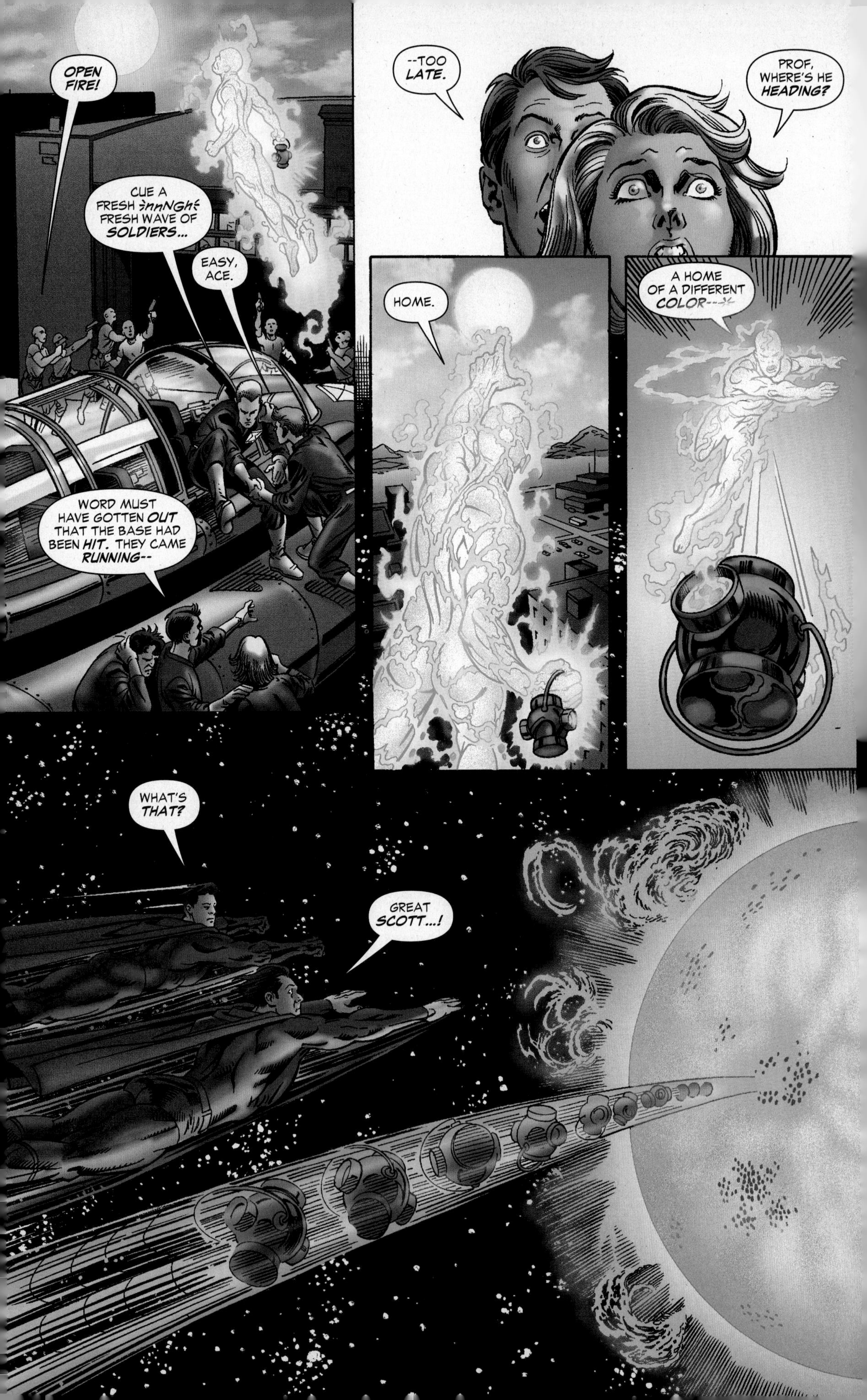
OPEN FIRE!
CUE A FRESH ;nnNgh; FRESH WAVE OF SOLDIERS...
EASY, ACE.
WORD MUST HAVE GOTTEN OUT THAT THE BASE HAD BEEN HIT. THEY CAME RUNNING--
--TOO LATE.
PROF, WHERE'S HE HEADING?
HOME.
A HOME OF A DIFFERENT COLOR--
WHAT'S THAT?
GREAT SCOTT...!

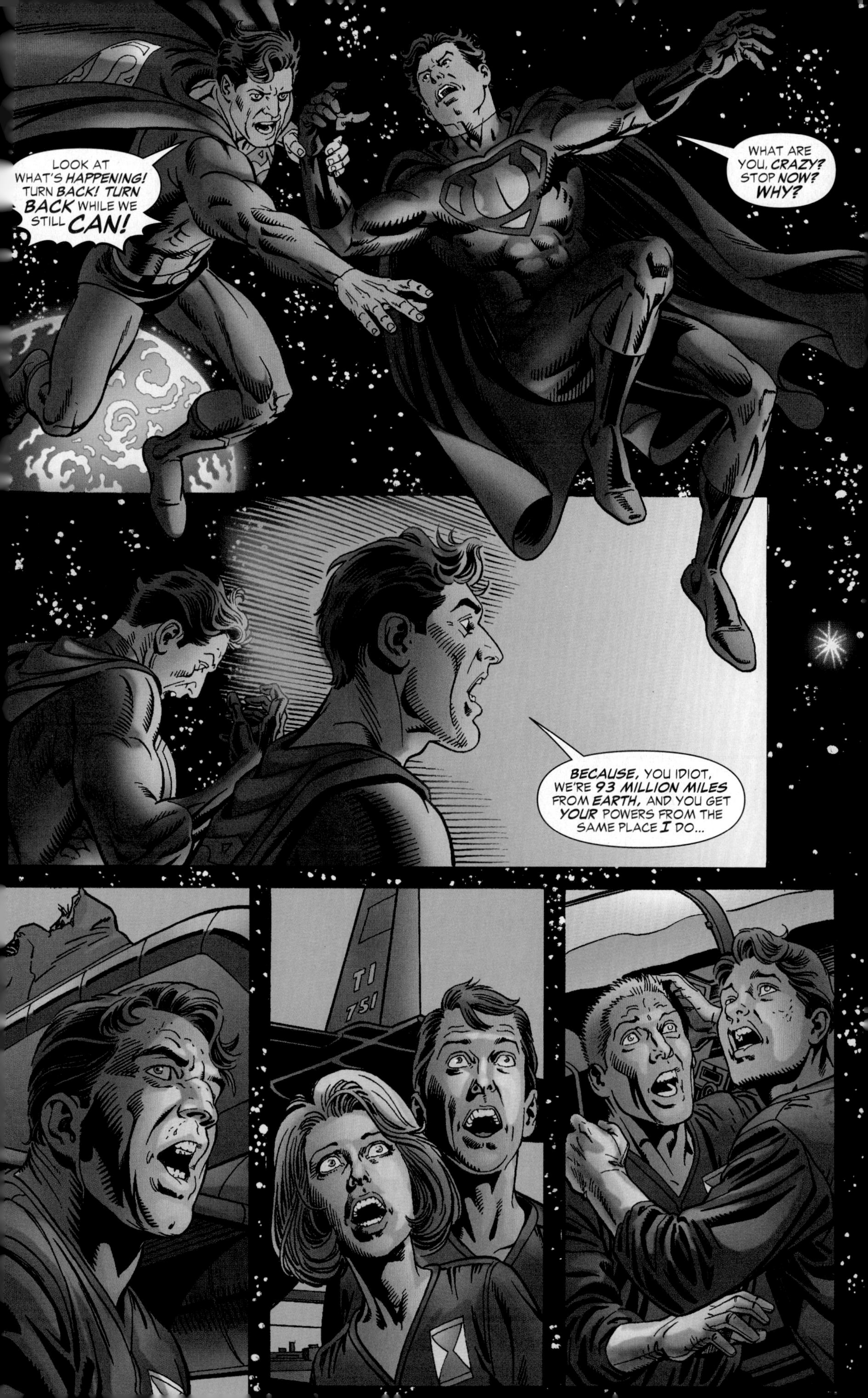
LOOK AT WHAT'S HAPPENING! TURN BACK! TURN BACK WHILE WE STILL CAN!
WHAT ARE YOU, CRAZY? STOP NOW? WHY?
BECAUSE, YOU IDIOT, WE'RE 93 MILLION MILES FROM EARTH, AND YOU GET YOUR POWERS FROM THE SAME PLACE I DO...
TI 751

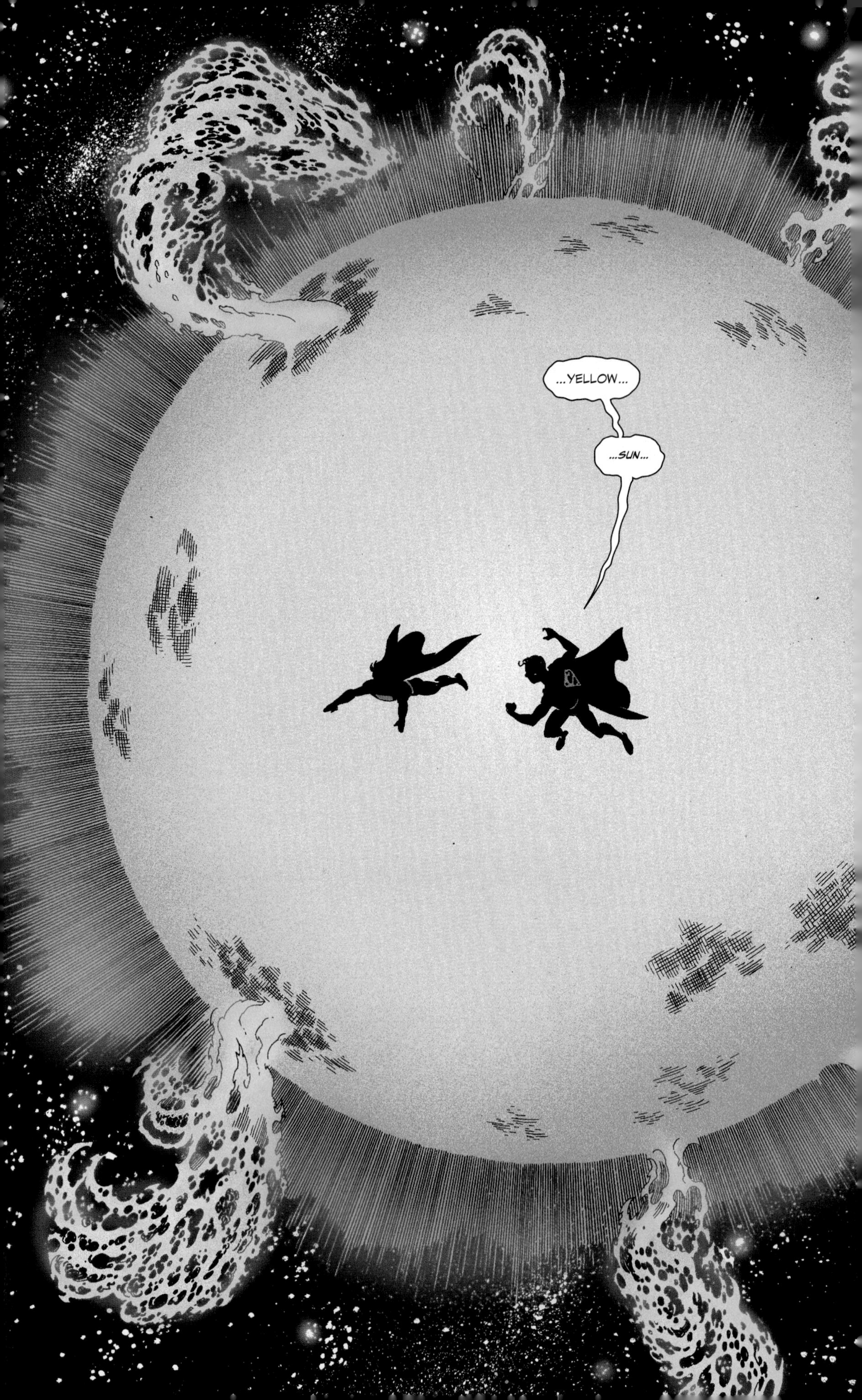
...YELLOW...
...SUN...

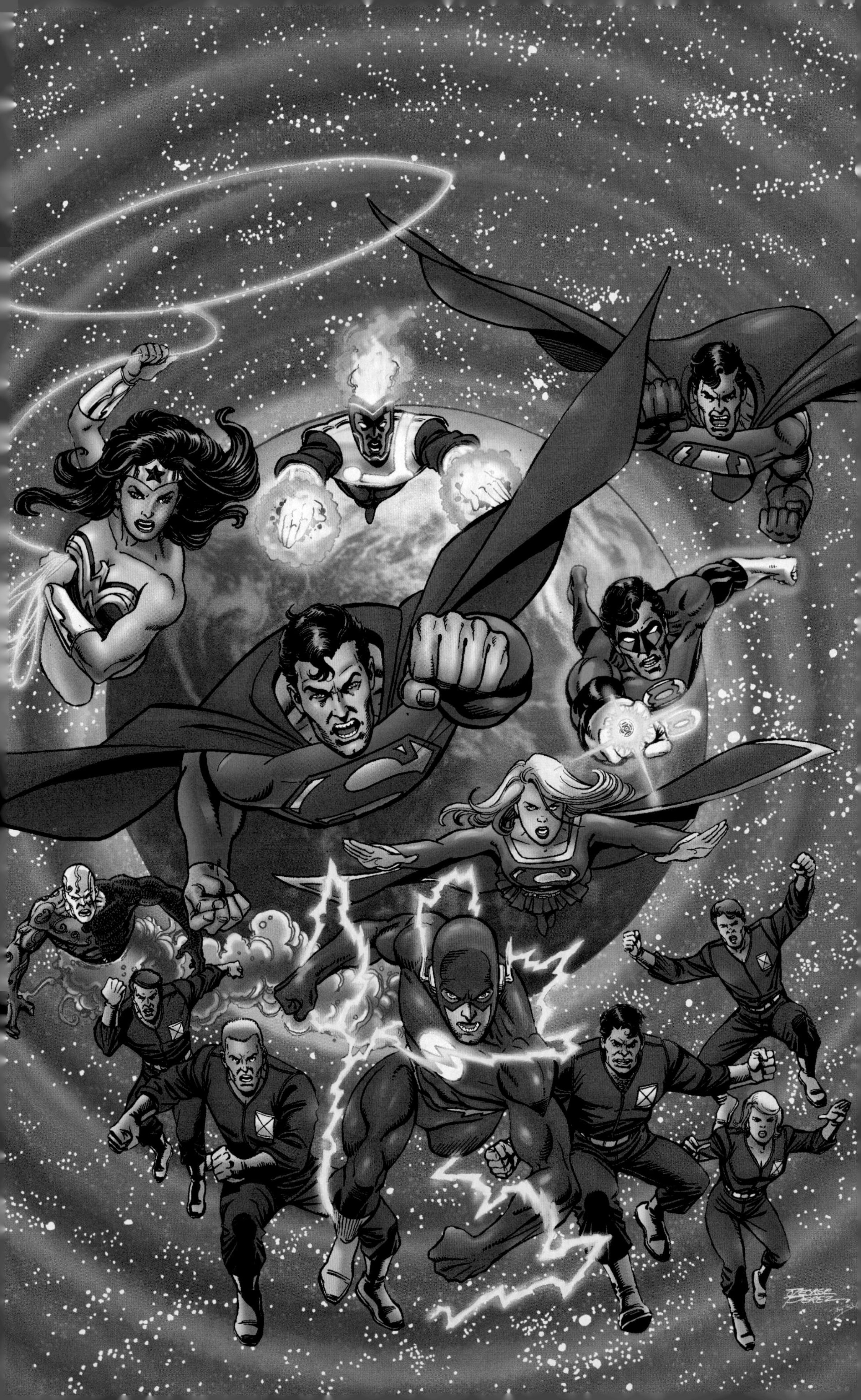

the BRAVE and the BOLD

THE BOOK OF DESTINY: CHAPTER SIX: SUNSTROKE

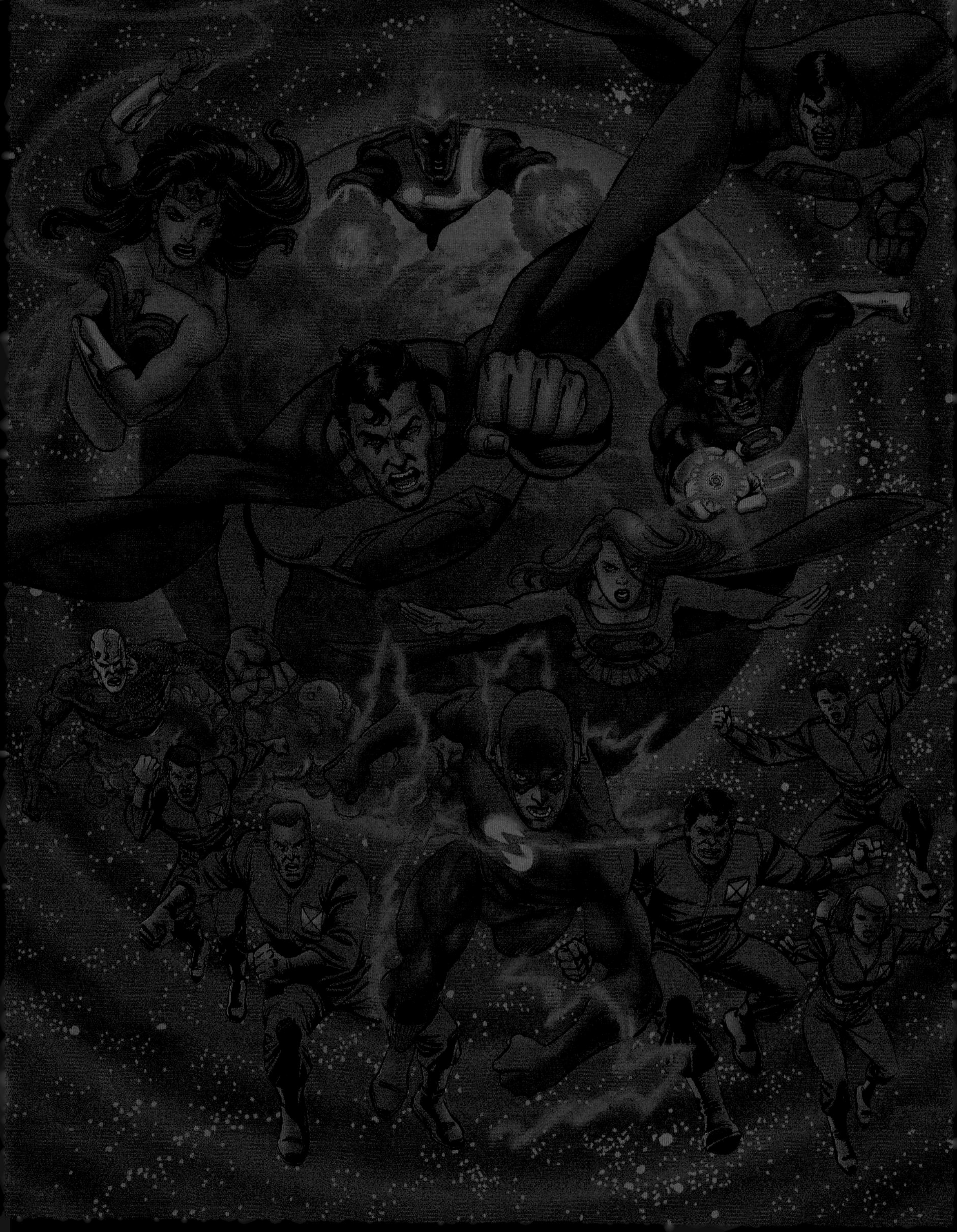

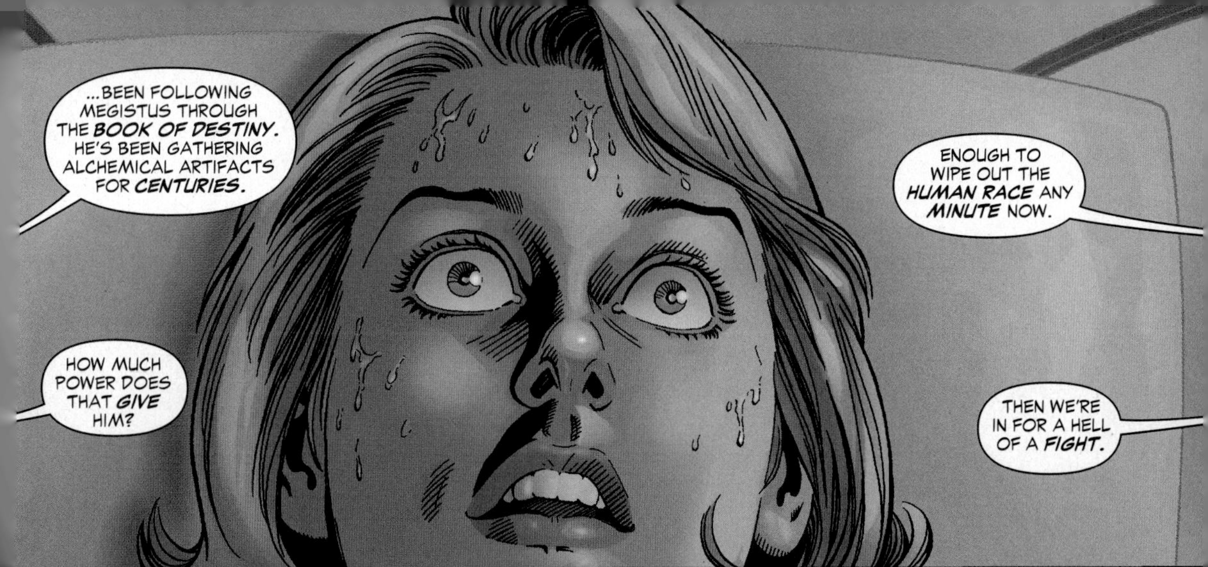
...BEEN FOLLOWING MEGISTUS THROUGH THE BOOK OF DESTINY. HE'S BEEN GATHERING ALCHEMICAL ARTIFACTS FOR CENTURIES.
ENOUGH TO WIPE OUT THE HUMAN RACE ANY MINUTE NOW.
HOW MUCH POWER DOES THAT GIVE HIM?
THEN WE'RE IN FOR A HELL OF A FIGHT.

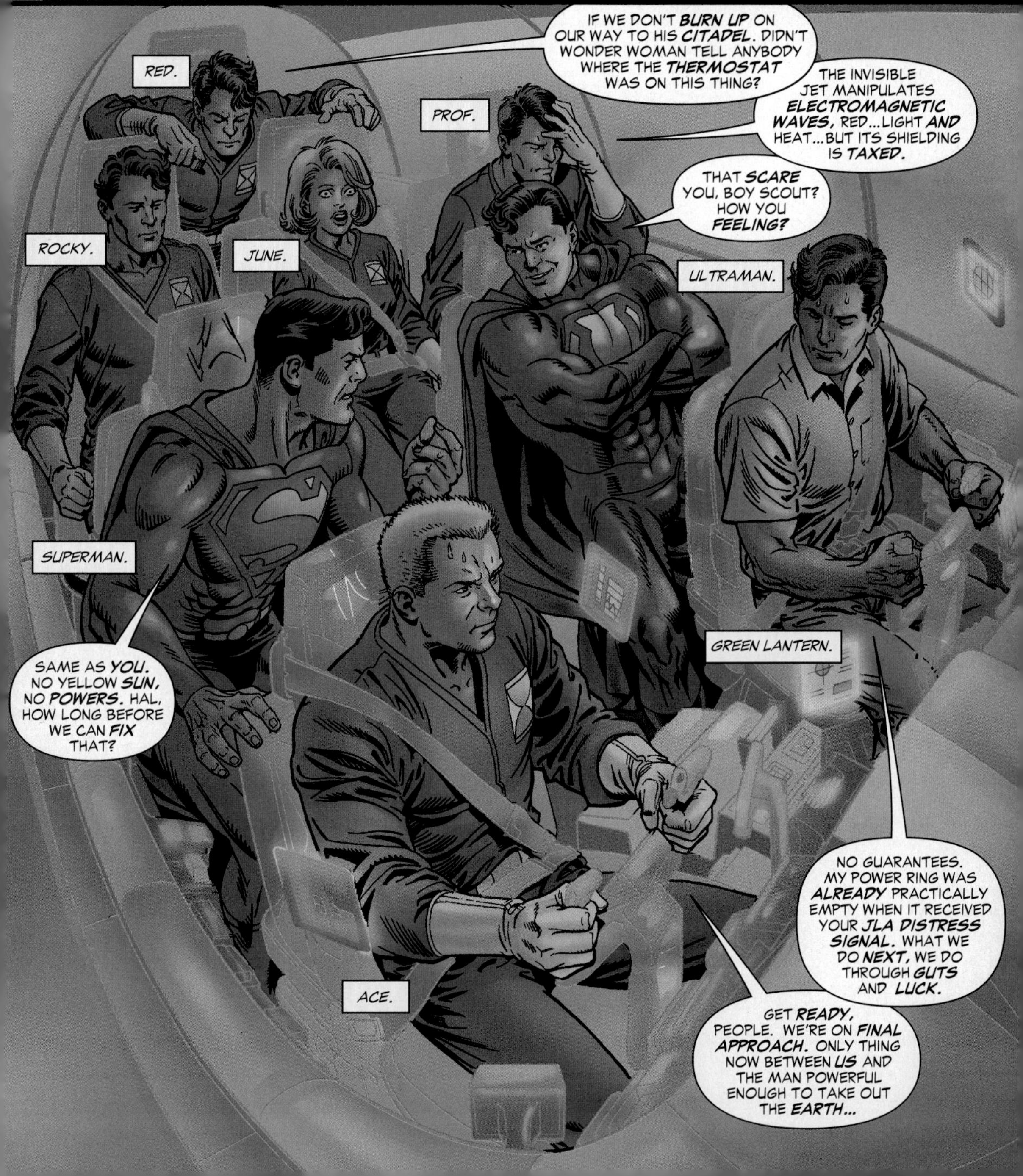
RED.
IF WE DON'T BURN UP ON OUR WAY TO HIS CITADEL. DIDN'T WONDER WOMAN TELL ANYBODY WHERE THE THERMOSTAT WAS ON THIS THING?
PROF.
THE INVISIBLE JET MANIPULATES ELECTROMAGNETIC WAVES, RED...LIGHT AND HEAT...BUT ITS SHIELDING IS TAXED.
THAT SCARE YOU, BOY SCOUT? HOW YOU FEELING?
ROCKY.
JUNE.
ULTRAMAN.
SUPERMAN.
SAME AS YOU. NO YELLOW SUN, NO POWERS. HAL, HOW LONG BEFORE WE CAN FIX THAT?
GREEN LANTERN.
NO GUARANTEES. MY POWER RING WAS ALREADY PRACTICALLY EMPTY WHEN IT RECEIVED YOUR JLA DISTRESS SIGNAL. WHAT WE DO NEXT, WE DO THROUGH GUTS AND LUCK.
ACE.
GET READY, PEOPLE. WE'RE ON FINAL APPROACH. ONLY THING NOW BETWEEN US AND THE MAN POWERFUL ENOUGH TO TAKE OUT THE EARTH...

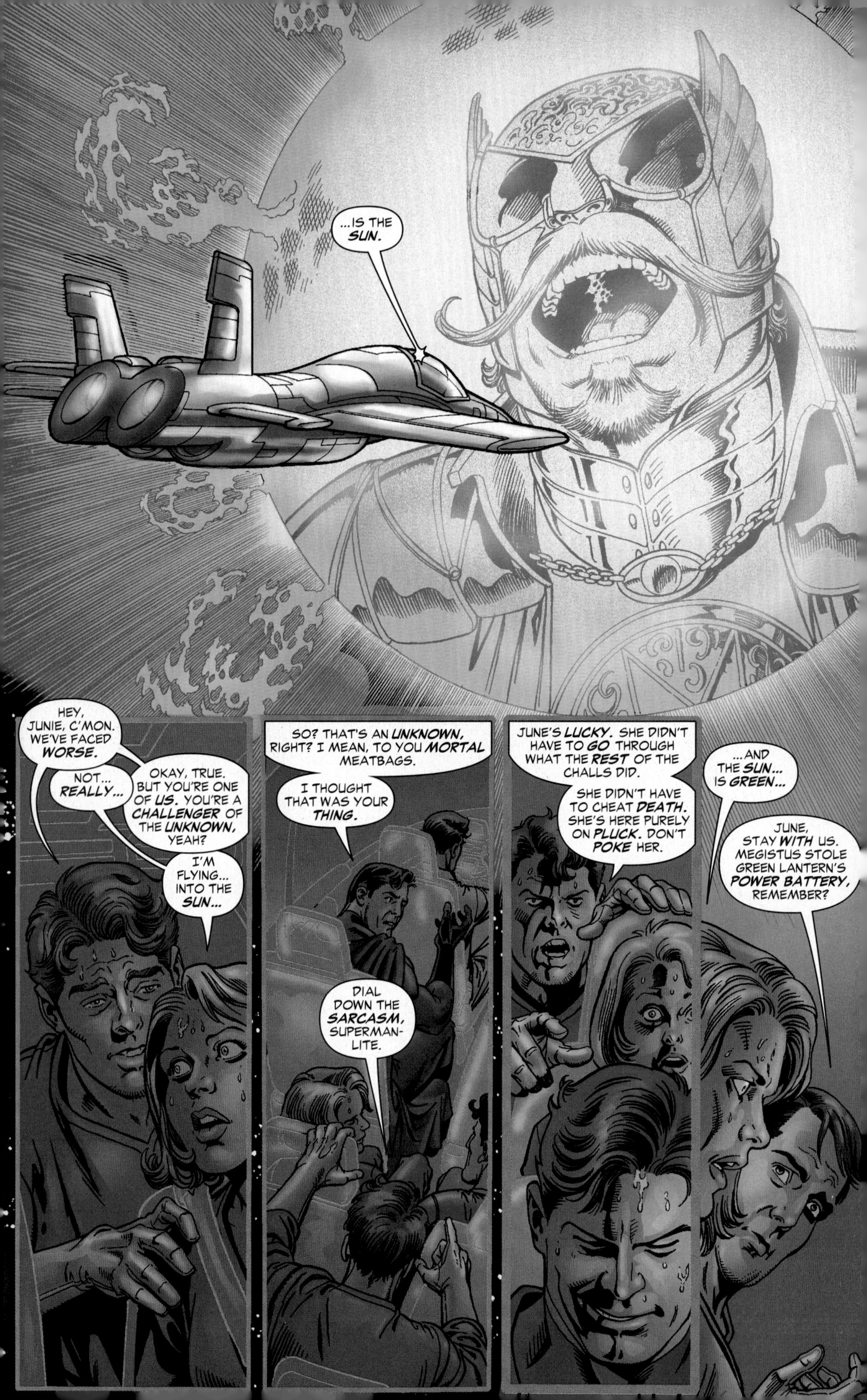
...IS THE SUN.
HEY, JUNIE, C'MON. WE'VE FACED WORSE.
NOT... REALLY...
OKAY, TRUE. BUT YOU'RE ONE OF US. YOU'RE A CHALLENGER OF THE UNKNOWN, YEAH?
I'M FLYING... INTO THE SUN...
SO? THAT'S AN UNKNOWN, RIGHT? I MEAN, TO YOU MORTAL MEATBAGS.
I THOUGHT THAT WAS YOUR THING.
DIAL DOWN THE SARCASM, SUPERMAN-LITE.
JUNE'S LUCKY. SHE DIDN'T HAVE TO GO THROUGH WHAT THE REST OF THE CHALLS DID.
SHE DIDN'T HAVE TO CHEAT DEATH. SHE'S HERE PURELY ON PLUCK. DON'T POKE HER.
...AND THE SUN... IS GREEN...
JUNE, STAY WITH US. MEGISTUS STOLE GREEN LANTERN'S POWER BATTERY, REMEMBER?

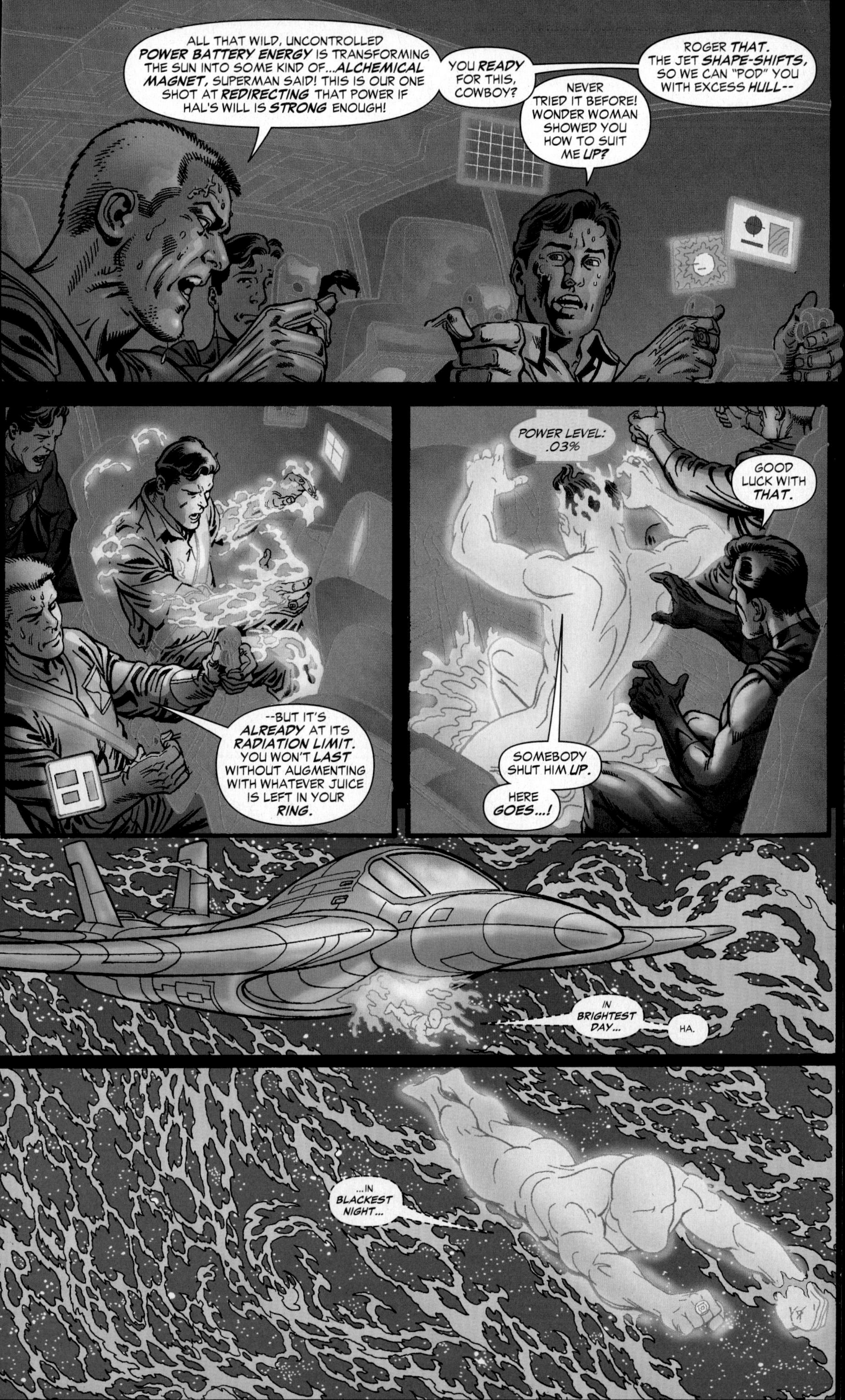
ALL THAT WILD, UNCONTROLLED POWER BATTERY ENERGY IS TRANSFORMING THE SUN INTO SOME KIND OF...ALCHEMICAL MAGNET, SUPERMAN SAID! THIS IS OUR ONE SHOT AT REDIRECTING THAT POWER IF HAL'S WILL IS STRONG ENOUGH!
YOU READY FOR THIS, COWBOY?
NEVER TRIED IT BEFORE! WONDER WOMAN SHOWED YOU HOW TO SUIT ME UP?
ROGER THAT. THE JET SHAPE-SHIFTS, SO WE CAN "POD" YOU WITH EXCESS HULL--
--BUT IT'S ALREADY AT ITS RADIATION LIMIT. YOU WON'T LAST WITHOUT AUGMENTING WITH WHATEVER JUICE IS LEFT IN YOUR RING.
POWER LEVEL: .03%
GOOD LUCK WITH THAT.
SOMEBODY SHUT HIM UP.
HERE GOES...!
IN BRIGHTEST DAY...
HA.
...IN BLACKEST NIGHT...

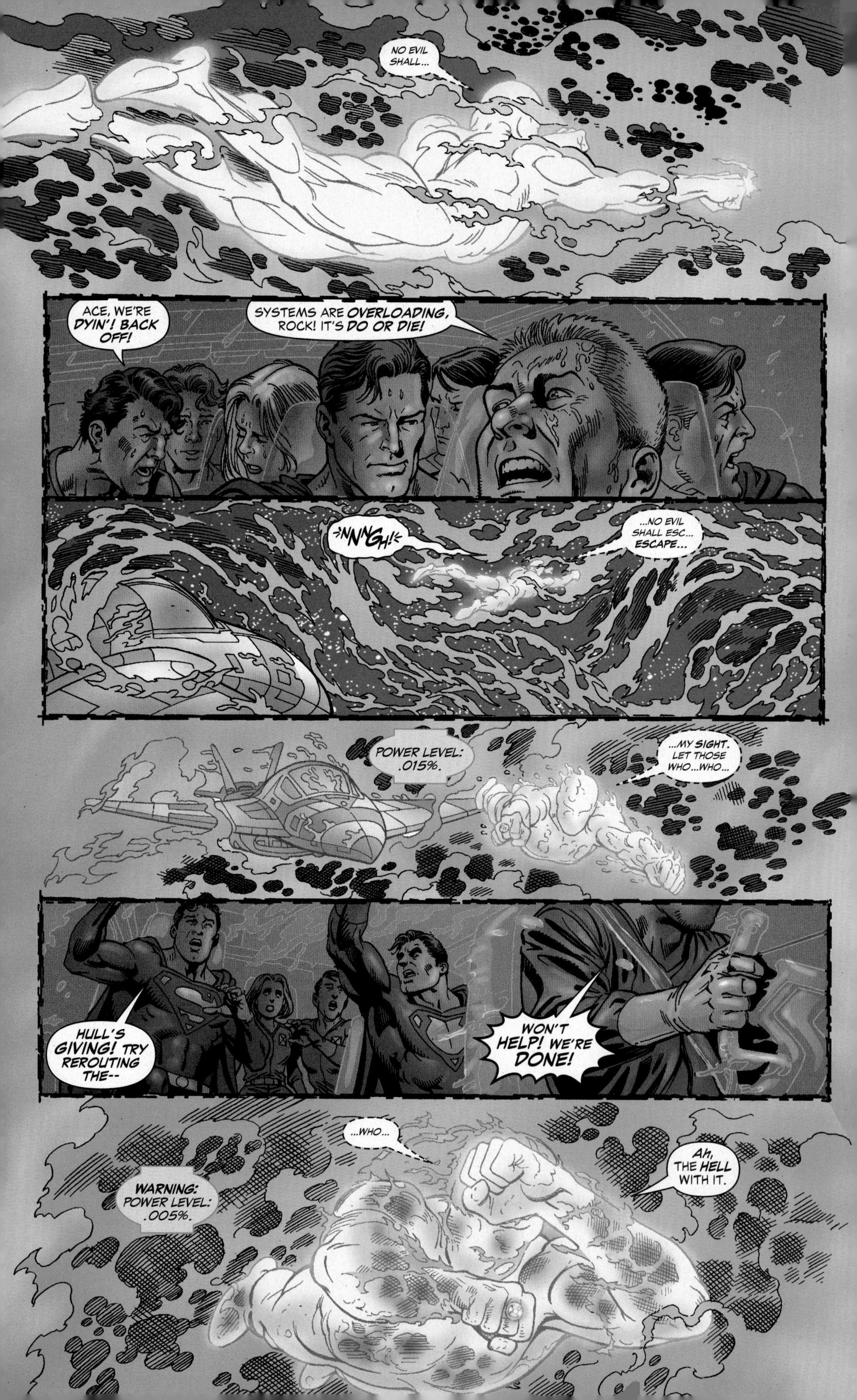
NO EVIL SHALL...
ACE, WE'RE DYIN'! BACK OFF!
SYSTEMS ARE OVERLOADING, ROCK! IT'S DO OR DIE!
NNNGH!
...NO EVIL SHALL ESC... ESCAPE...
POWER LEVEL: .015%.
...MY SIGHT. LET THOSE WHO...WHO...
HULL'S GIVING! TRY REROUTING THE--
WON'T HELP! WE'RE DONE!
...WHO...
WARNING: POWER LEVEL: .005%.
Ah, THE HELL WITH IT.

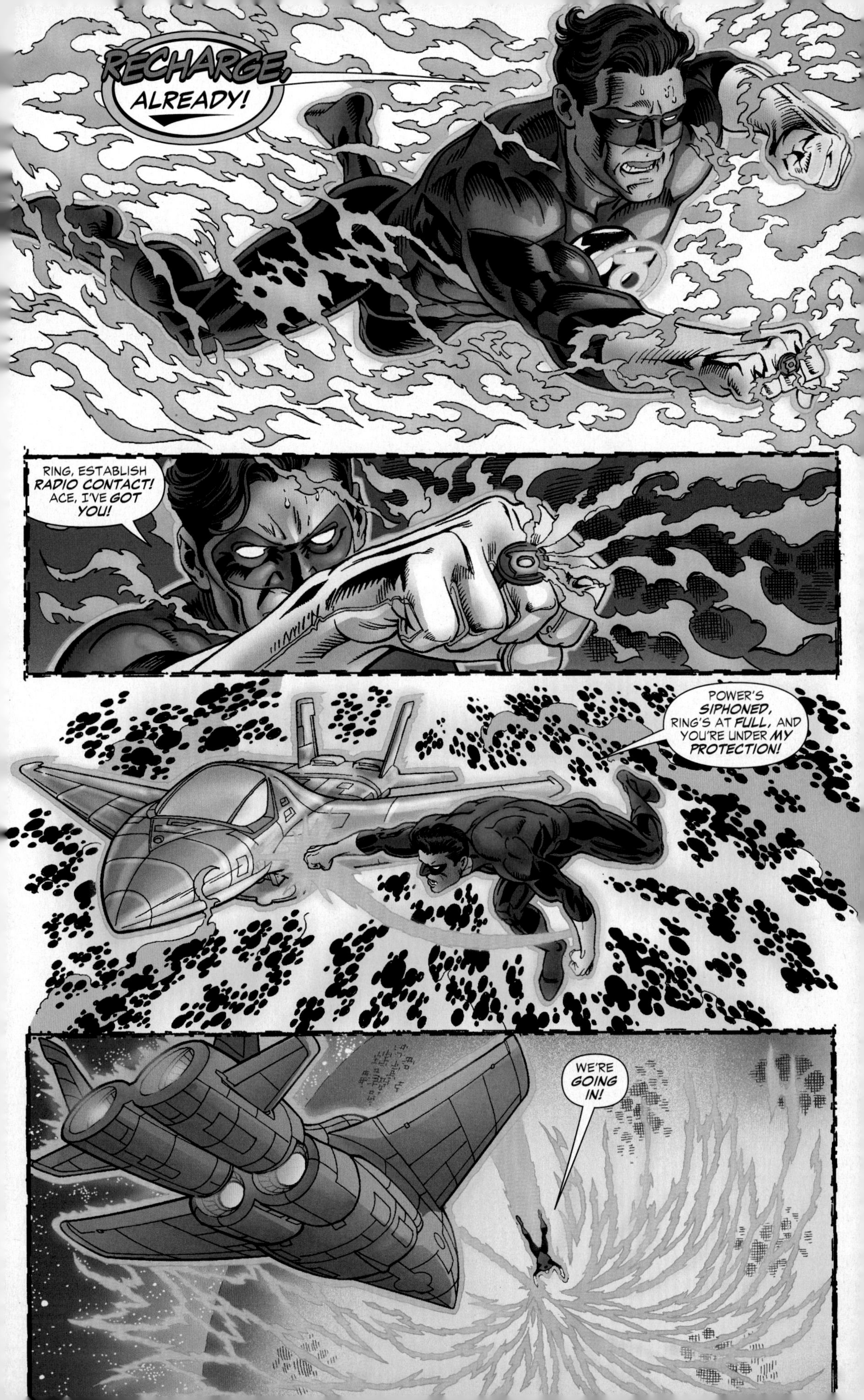
RECHARGE, ALREADY!
RING, ESTABLISH RADIO CONTACT! ACE, I'VE GOT YOU!
POWER'S SIPHONED, RING'S AT FULL, AND YOU'RE UNDER MY PROTECTION!
WE'RE GOING IN!

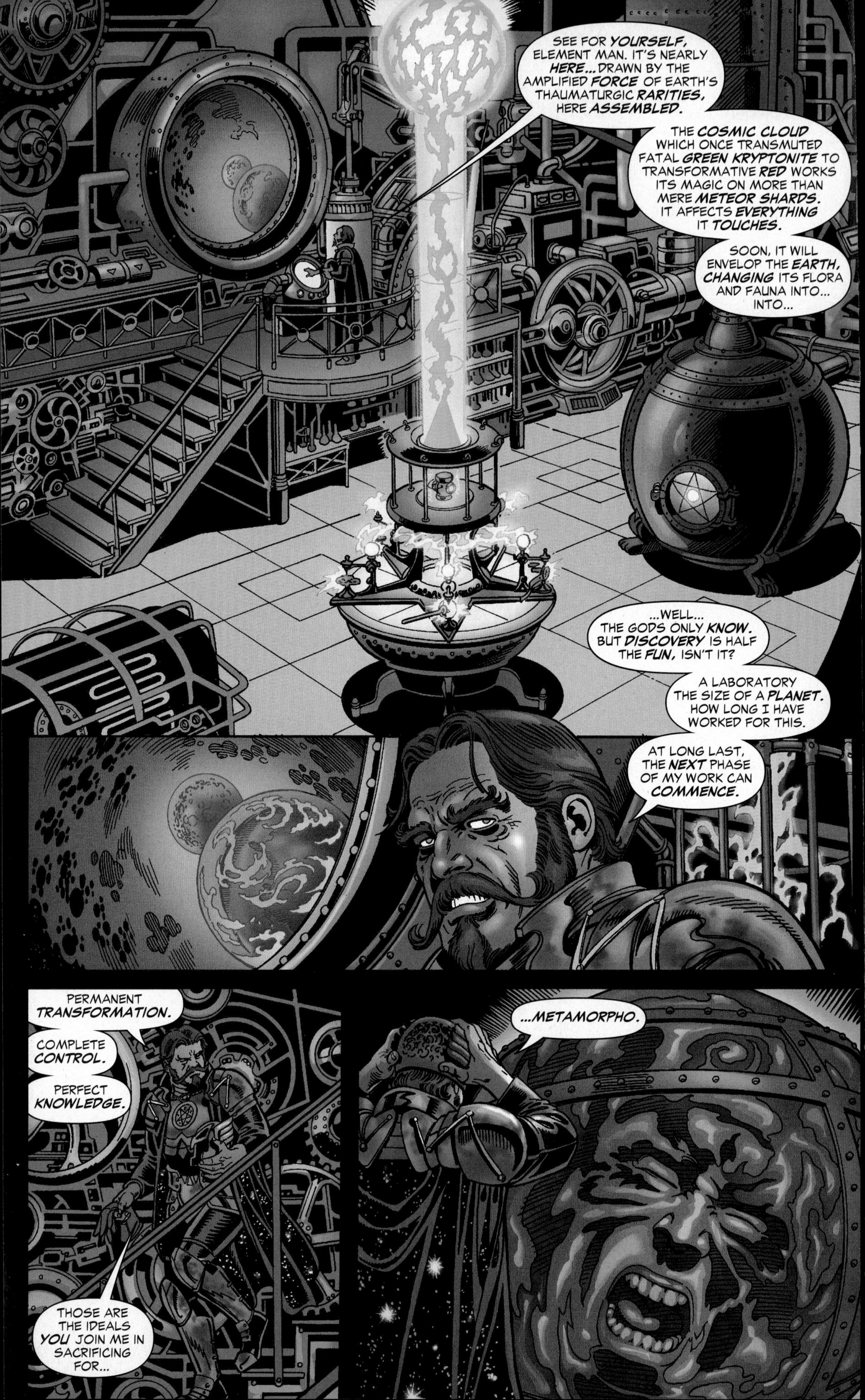
SEE FOR YOURSELF, ELEMENT MAN. IT'S NEARLY HERE... DRAWN BY THE AMPLIFIED FORCE OF EARTH'S THAUMATURGIC RARITIES, HERE ASSEMBLED.
THE COSMIC CLOUD WHICH ONCE TRANSMUTED FATAL GREEN KRYPTONITE TO TRANSFORMATIVE RED WORKS ITS MAGIC ON MORE THAN MERE METEOR SHARDS. IT AFFECTS EVERYTHING IT TOUCHES.
SOON, IT WILL ENVELOP THE EARTH, CHANGING ITS FLORA AND FAUNA INTO... INTO...
...WELL... THE GODS ONLY KNOW. BUT DISCOVERY IS HALF THE FUN, ISN'T IT?
A LABORATORY THE SIZE OF A PLANET. HOW LONG I HAVE WORKED FOR THIS.
AT LONG LAST, THE NEXT PHASE OF MY WORK CAN COMMENCE.
PERMANENT TRANSFORMATION.
COMPLETE CONTROL.
PERFECT KNOWLEDGE.
THOSE ARE THE IDEALS YOU JOIN ME IN SACRIFICING FOR...
...METAMORPHO.

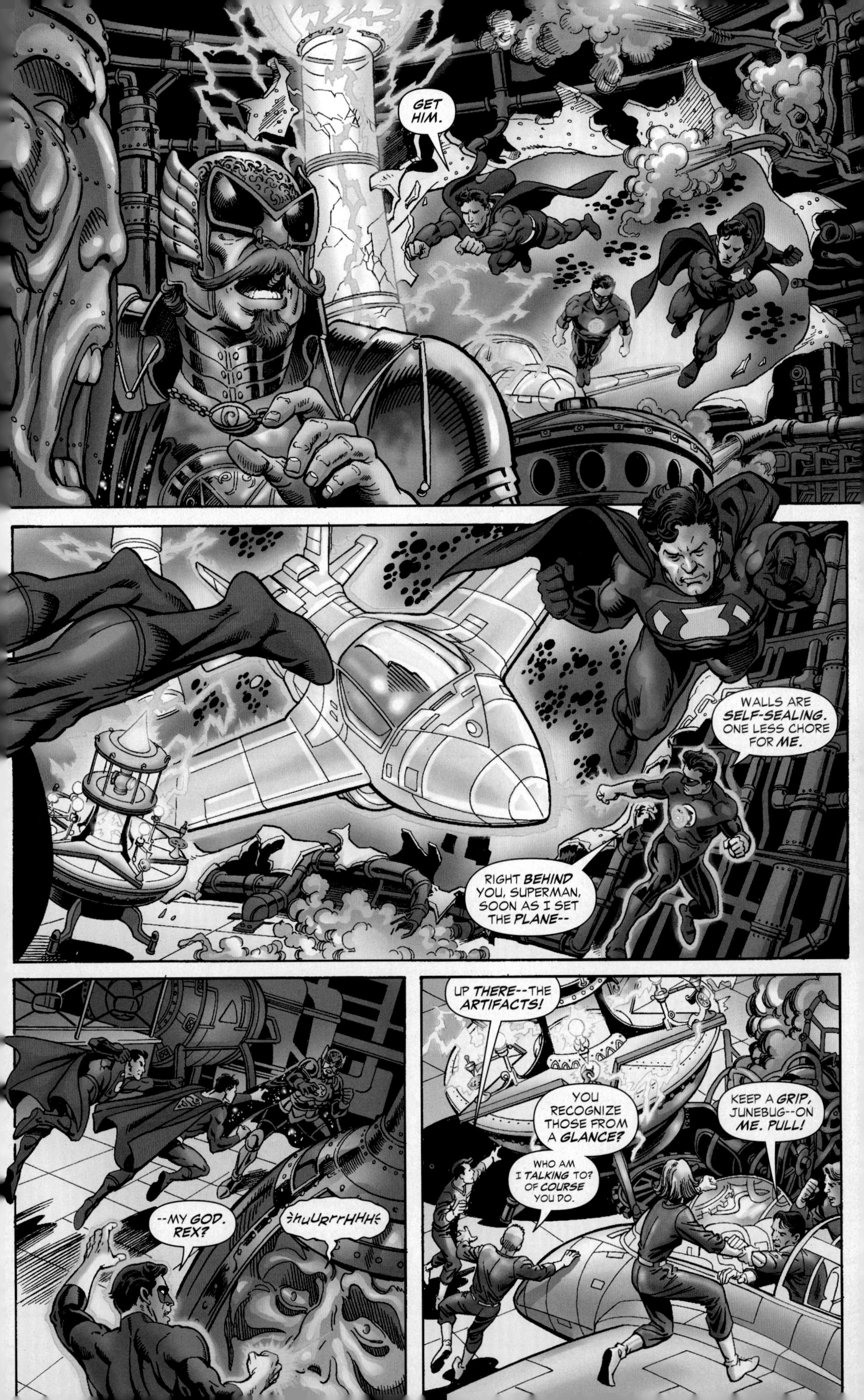
GET HIM.
WALLS ARE SELF-SEALING. ONE LESS CHORE FOR ME.
RIGHT BEHIND YOU, SUPERMAN, SOON AS I SET THE PLANE--
--MY GOD. REX?
huUrrrHHH
UP THERE--THE ARTIFACTS!
YOU RECOGNIZE THOSE FROM A GLANCE?
WHO AM I TALKING TO? OF COURSE YOU DO.
KEEP A GRIP, JUNEBUG--ON ME. PULL!

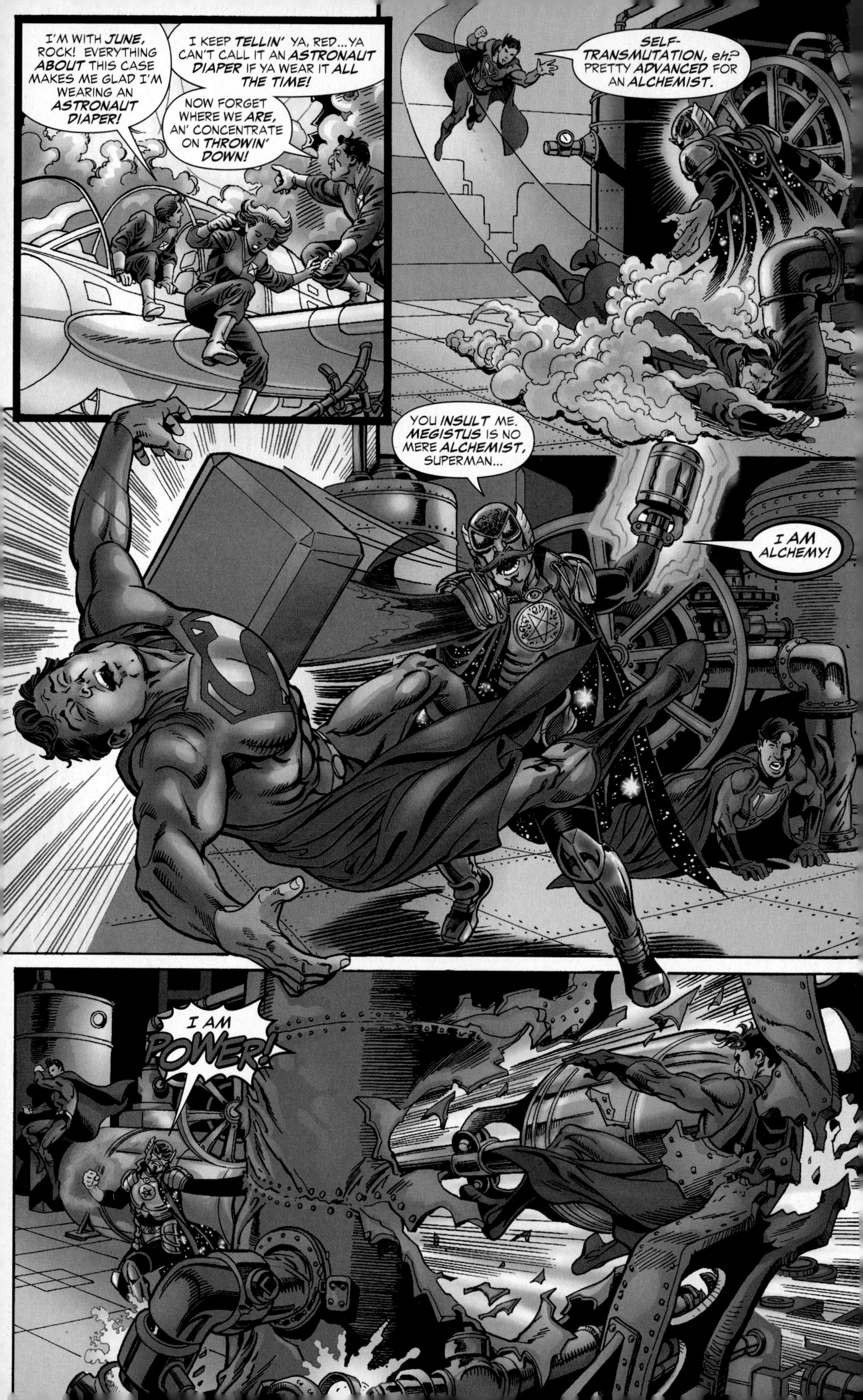

I'M WITH JUNE, ROCK! EVERYTHING ABOUT THIS CASE MAKES ME GLAD I'M WEARING AN ASTRONAUT DIAPER!
I KEEP TELLIN' YA, RED...YA CAN'T CALL IT AN ASTRONAUT DIAPER IF YA WEAR IT ALL THE TIME!
NOW FORGET WHERE WE ARE, AN' CONCENTRATE ON THROWIN' DOWN!
SELF-TRANSMUTATION, eh? PRETTY ADVANCED FOR AN ALCHEMIST.
YOU INSULT ME. MEGISTUS IS NO MERE ALCHEMIST, SUPERMAN...
I AM ALCHEMY!
I AM POWER!

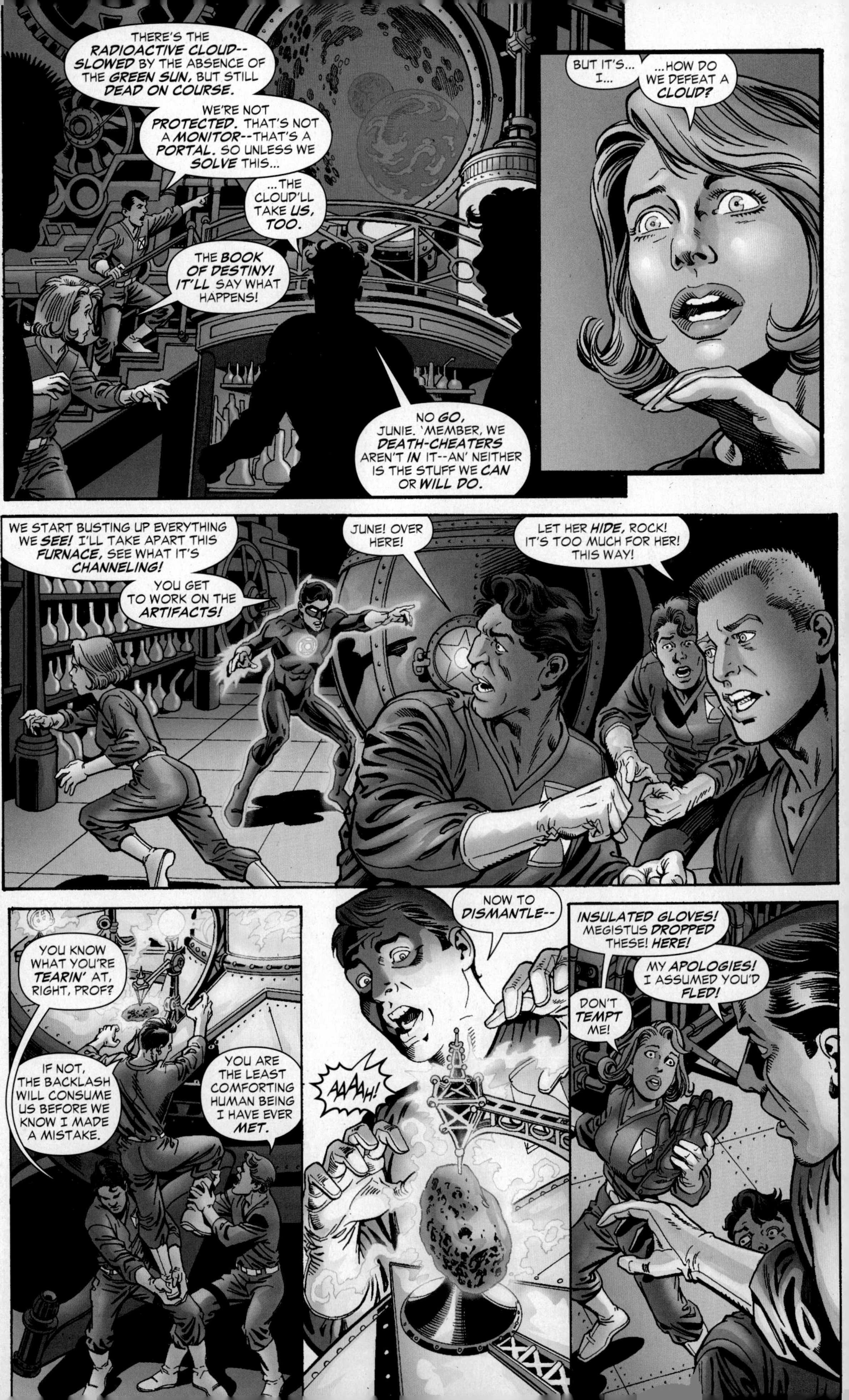
THERE'S THE RADIOACTIVE CLOUD--SLOWED BY THE ABSENCE OF THE GREEN SUN, BUT STILL DEAD ON COURSE.
WE'RE NOT PROTECTED. THAT'S NOT A MONITOR--THAT'S A PORTAL. SO UNLESS WE SOLVE THIS...
...THE CLOUD'LL TAKE US, TOO.
THE BOOK OF DESTINY! IT'LL SAY WHAT HAPPENS!
NO GO, JUNIE. 'MEMBER, WE DEATH-CHEATERS AREN'T IN IT--AN' NEITHER IS THE STUFF WE CAN OR WILL DO.
BUT IT'S... I...
...HOW DO WE DEFEAT A CLOUD?
WE START BUSTING UP EVERYTHING WE SEE! I'LL TAKE APART THIS FURNACE, SEE WHAT IT'S CHANNELING!
YOU GET TO WORK ON THE ARTIFACTS!
JUNE! OVER HERE!
LET HER HIDE, ROCK! IT'S TOO MUCH FOR HER! THIS WAY!
YOU KNOW WHAT YOU'RE TEARIN' AT, RIGHT, PROF?
IF NOT, THE BACKLASH WILL CONSUME US BEFORE WE KNOW I MADE A MISTAKE.
YOU ARE THE LEAST COMFORTING HUMAN BEING I HAVE EVER MET.
NOW TO DISMANTLE--
AAAAH!
INSULATED GLOVES! MEGISTUS DROPPED THESE! HERE!
MY APOLOGIES! I ASSUMED YOU'D FLED!
DON'T TEMPT ME!

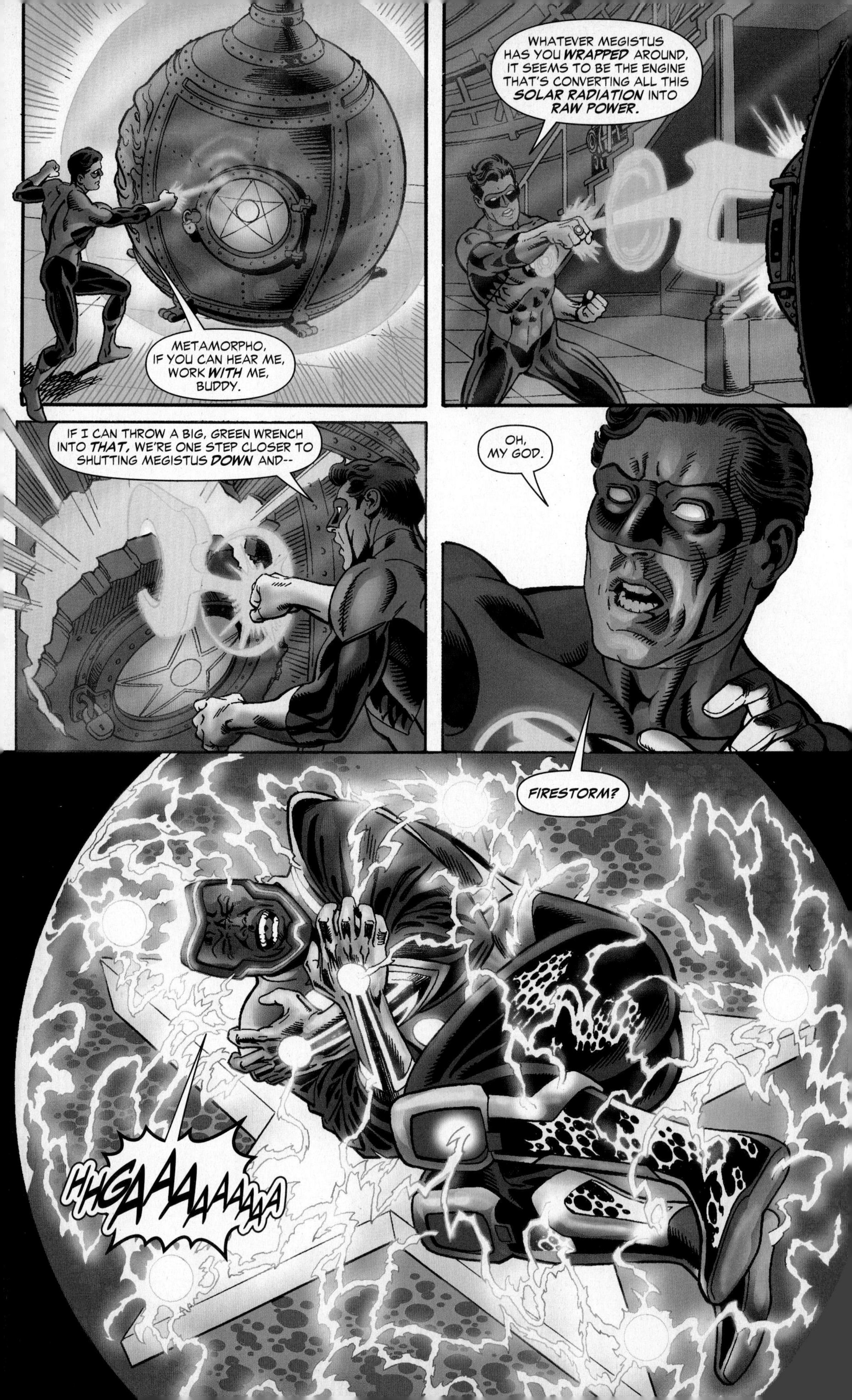
METAMORPHO, IF YOU CAN HEAR ME, WORK WITH ME, BUDDY.
WHATEVER MEGISTUS HAS YOU WRAPPED AROUND, IT SEEMS TO BE THE ENGINE THAT'S CONVERTING ALL THIS SOLAR RADIATION INTO RAW POWER.
IF I CAN THROW A BIG, GREEN WRENCH INTO THAT, WE'RE ONE STEP CLOSER TO SHUTTING MEGISTUS DOWN AND--
OH, MY GOD.
FIRESTORM?
HHGAAAAAAAA

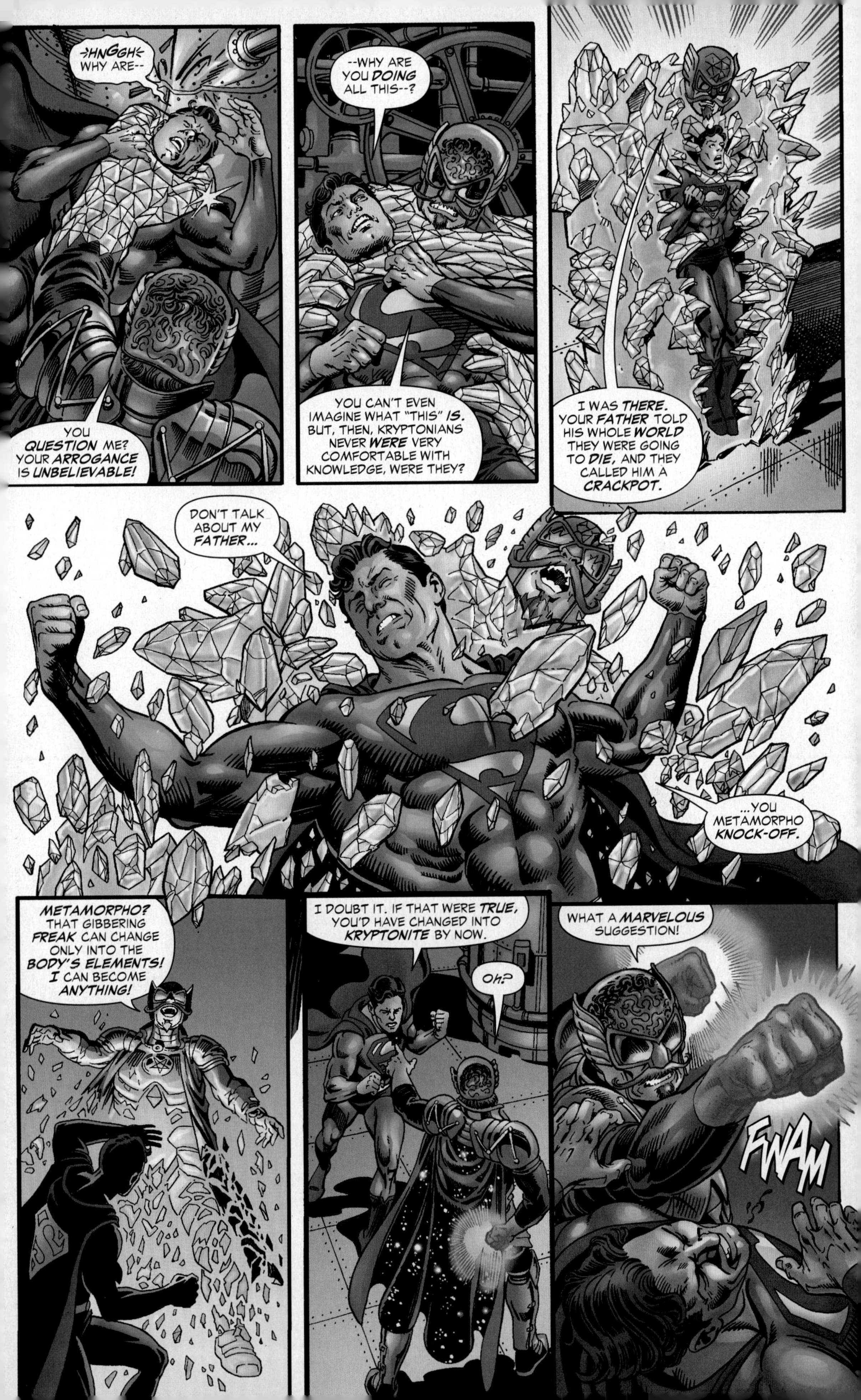

HNGGH WHY ARE--
YOU QUESTION ME? YOUR ARROGANCE IS UNBELIEVABLE!
--WHY ARE YOU DOING ALL THIS--?
YOU CAN'T EVEN IMAGINE WHAT "THIS" IS. BUT, THEN, KRYPTONIANS NEVER WERE VERY COMFORTABLE WITH KNOWLEDGE, WERE THEY?
I WAS THERE. YOUR FATHER TOLD HIS WHOLE WORLD THEY WERE GOING TO DIE, AND THEY CALLED HIM A CRACKPOT.
DON'T TALK ABOUT MY FATHER...
...YOU METAMORPHO KNOCK-OFF.
METAMORPHO? THAT GIBBERING FREAK CAN CHANGE ONLY INTO THE BODY'S ELEMENTS! I CAN BECOME ANYTHING!
I DOUBT IT. IF THAT WERE TRUE, YOU'D HAVE CHANGED INTO KRYPTONITE BY NOW.
Oh?
WHAT A MARVELOUS SUGGESTION!
FWAM

PROF, **HURRY!**

THE **RED CLOUD'S** REACHED THE **NORTHERN HEMISPHERE--**

"--AND I THINK IT'S **ALREADY TOUCHING DOWN!**"

FLASH?

NINE HUNDRED **SIX**...905...

HEY! IT'S **WONDER WOMAN!**

...814... 792...

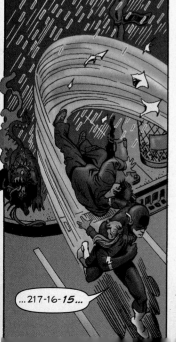

...217-16-**15**...

...**THREE**... **TWO**...

...ONE...**ZERO!** THANK YOU, **SPEED-OF-MERCURY WOMAN!** SUPERMAN FIGURED WE'D NEED YOU ON THE FRONT LINES!

EVERY RESIDENT'S **ACCOUNTED FOR** AND **SHELTERED--**

--BUT THAT'S ONLY **ONE TOWN!**

AND THE CLOUD'S TENDRILS ARE **SPREADING!**

CENTER

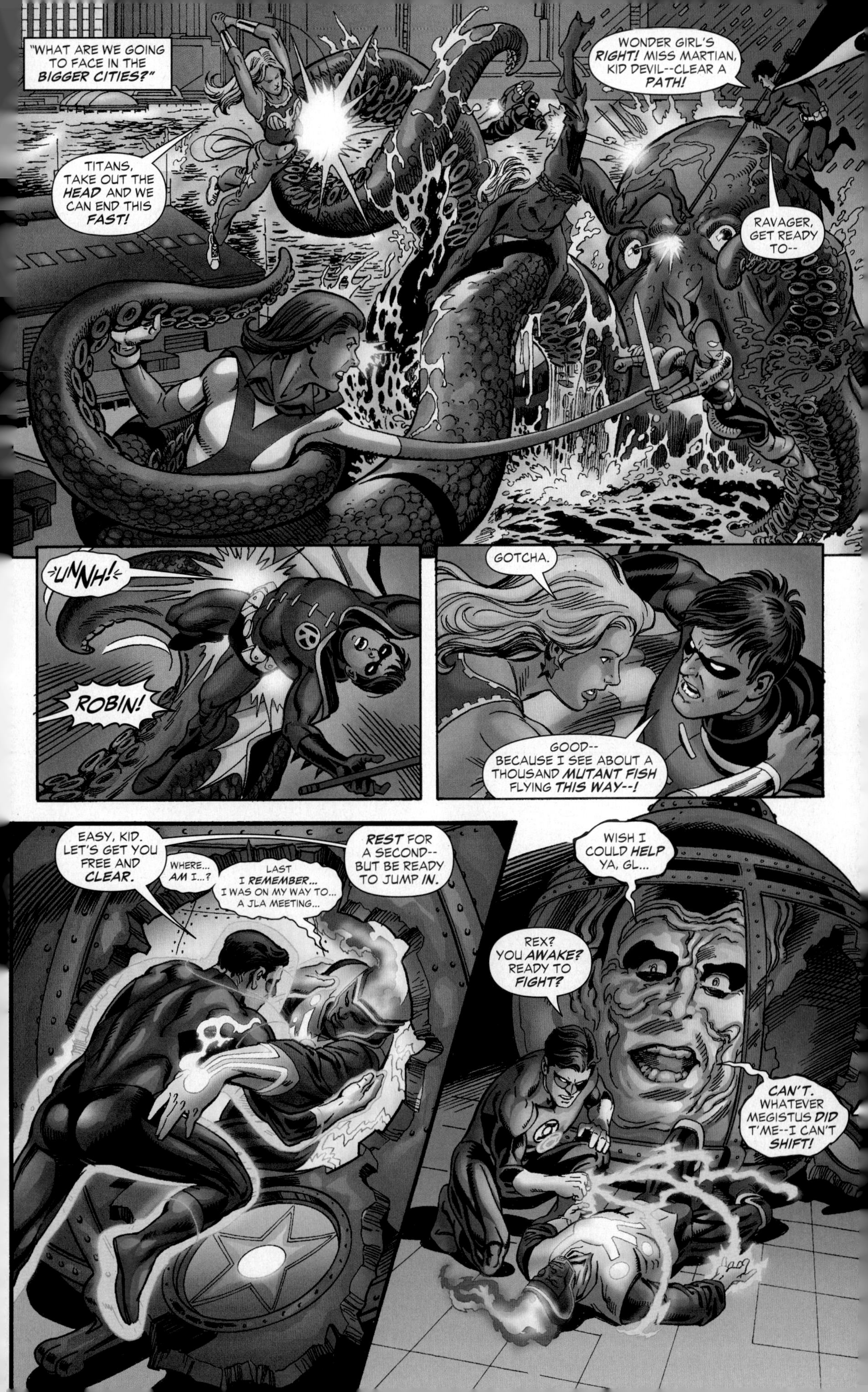
"WHAT ARE WE GOING TO FACE IN THE BIGGER CITIES?"
WONDER GIRL'S RIGHT! MISS MARTIAN, KID DEVIL--CLEAR A PATH!
TITANS, TAKE OUT THE HEAD AND WE CAN END THIS FAST!
RAVAGER, GET READY TO--
UNNH!
ROBIN!
GOTCHA.
GOOD-- BECAUSE I SEE ABOUT A THOUSAND MUTANT FISH FLYING THIS WAY--!
EASY, KID. LET'S GET YOU FREE AND CLEAR.
WHERE... AM I...?
LAST I REMEMBER... I WAS ON MY WAY TO... A JLA MEETING...
REST FOR A SECOND-- BUT BE READY TO JUMP IN.
WISH I COULD HELP YA, GL...
REX? YOU AWAKE? READY TO FIGHT?
CAN'T. WHATEVER MEGISTUS DID T'ME--I CAN'T SHIFT!

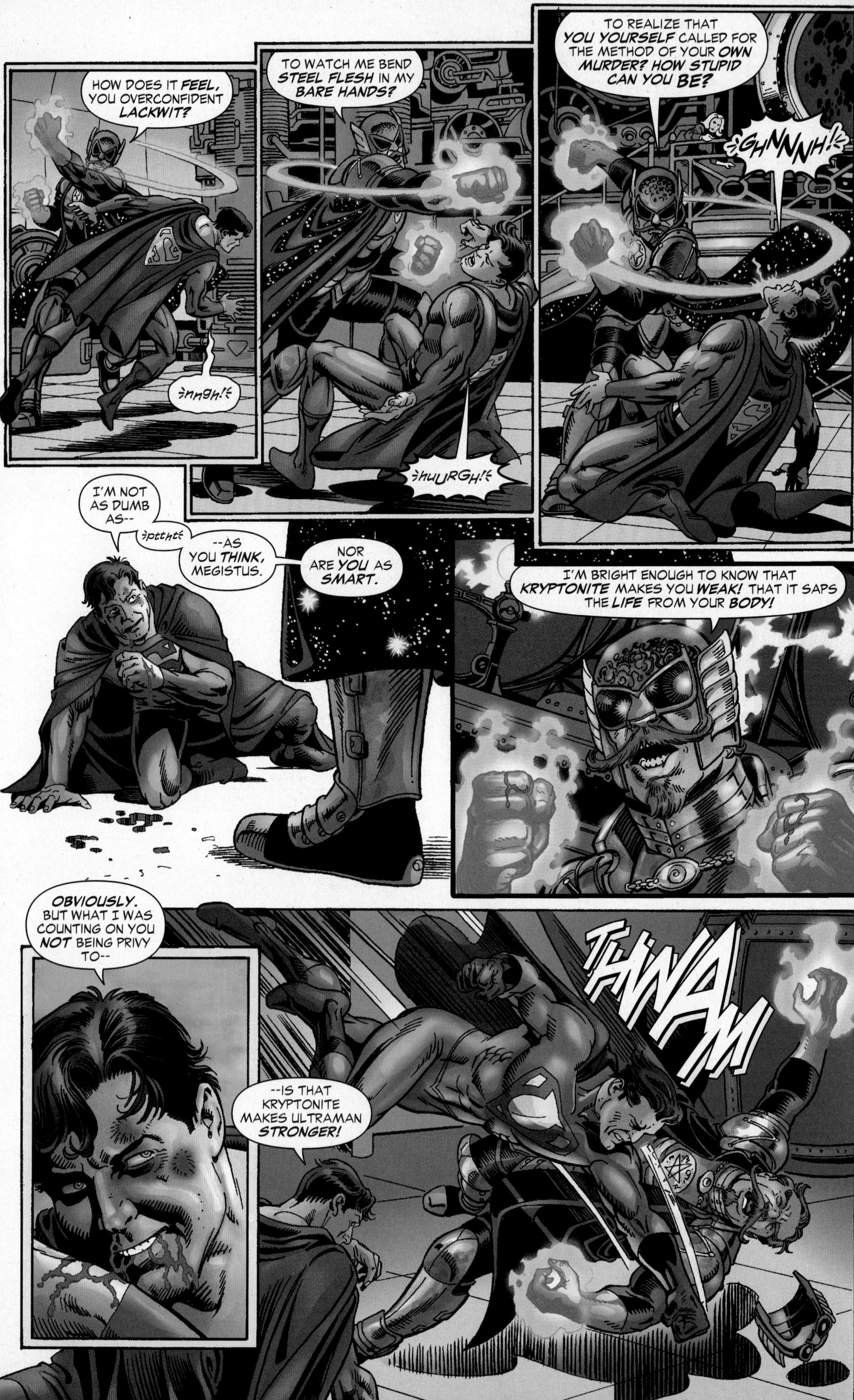
HOW DOES IT FEEL, YOU OVERCONFIDENT LACKWIT?
nngh!
TO WATCH ME BEND STEEL FLESH IN MY BARE HANDS?
huURGH!
TO REALIZE THAT YOU YOURSELF CALLED FOR THE METHOD OF YOUR OWN MURDER? HOW STUPID CAN YOU BE?
GHNNNH!
I'M NOT AS DUMB AS--
pttht
--AS YOU THINK, MEGISTUS.
NOR ARE YOU AS SMART.
I'M BRIGHT ENOUGH TO KNOW THAT KRYPTONITE MAKES YOU WEAK! THAT IT SAPS THE LIFE FROM YOUR BODY!
OBVIOUSLY. BUT WHAT I WAS COUNTING ON YOU NOT BEING PRIVY TO--
--IS THAT KRYPTONITE MAKES ULTRAMAN STRONGER!
THWAM

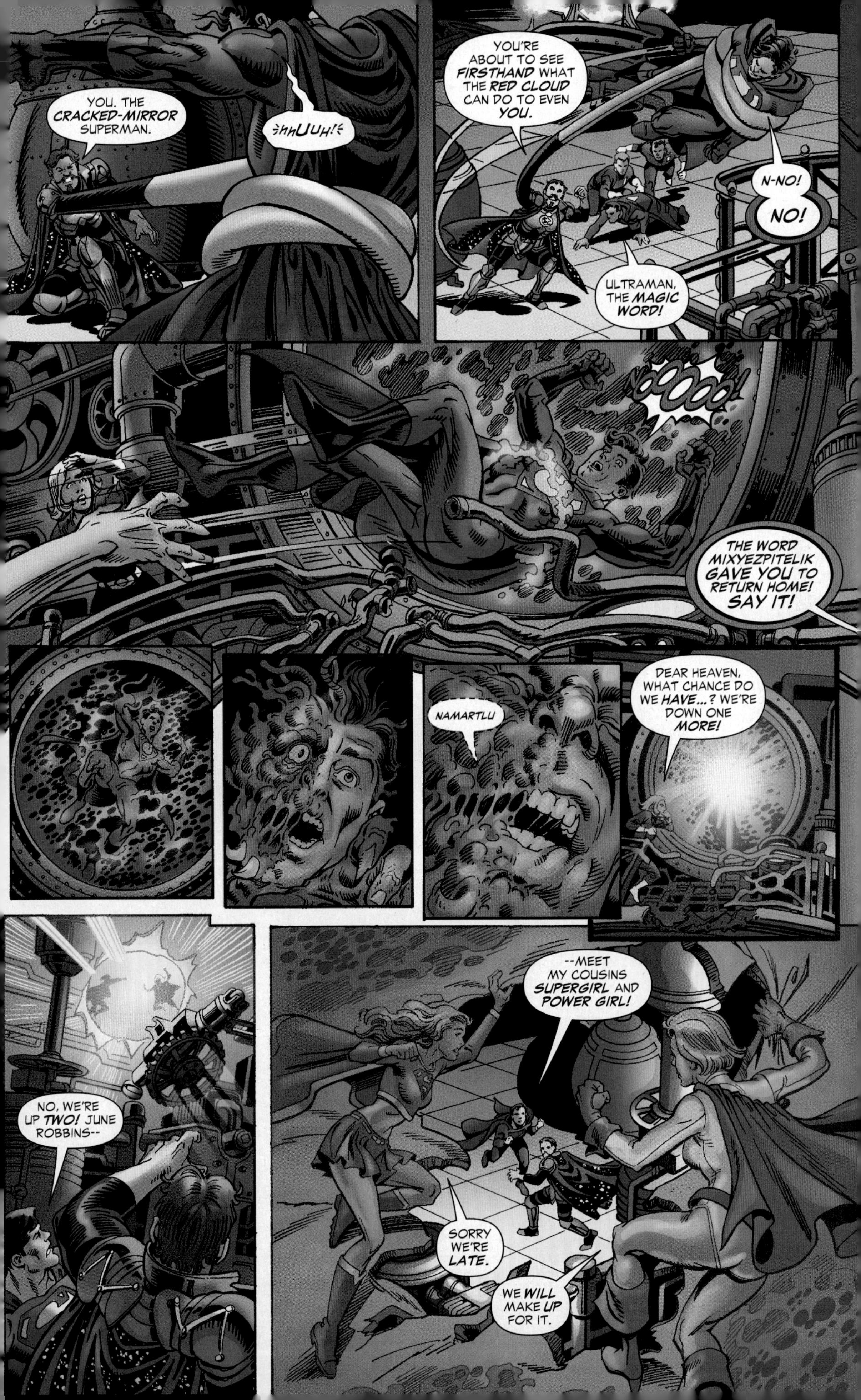
YOU. THE CRACKED-MIRROR SUPERMAN.
HHUUH!
YOU'RE ABOUT TO SEE FIRSTHAND WHAT THE RED CLOUD CAN DO TO EVEN YOU.
N-NO!
NO!
ULTRAMAN, THE MAGIC WORD!
NOOOOO!
THE WORD MIXYEZPITELIK GAVE YOU TO RETURN HOME! SAY IT!
NAMARTLU
DEAR HEAVEN, WHAT CHANCE DO WE HAVE...? WE'RE DOWN ONE MORE!
NO, WE'RE UP TWO! JUNE ROBBINS--
--MEET MY COUSINS SUPERGIRL AND POWER GIRL!
SORRY WE'RE LATE.
WE WILL MAKE UP FOR IT.

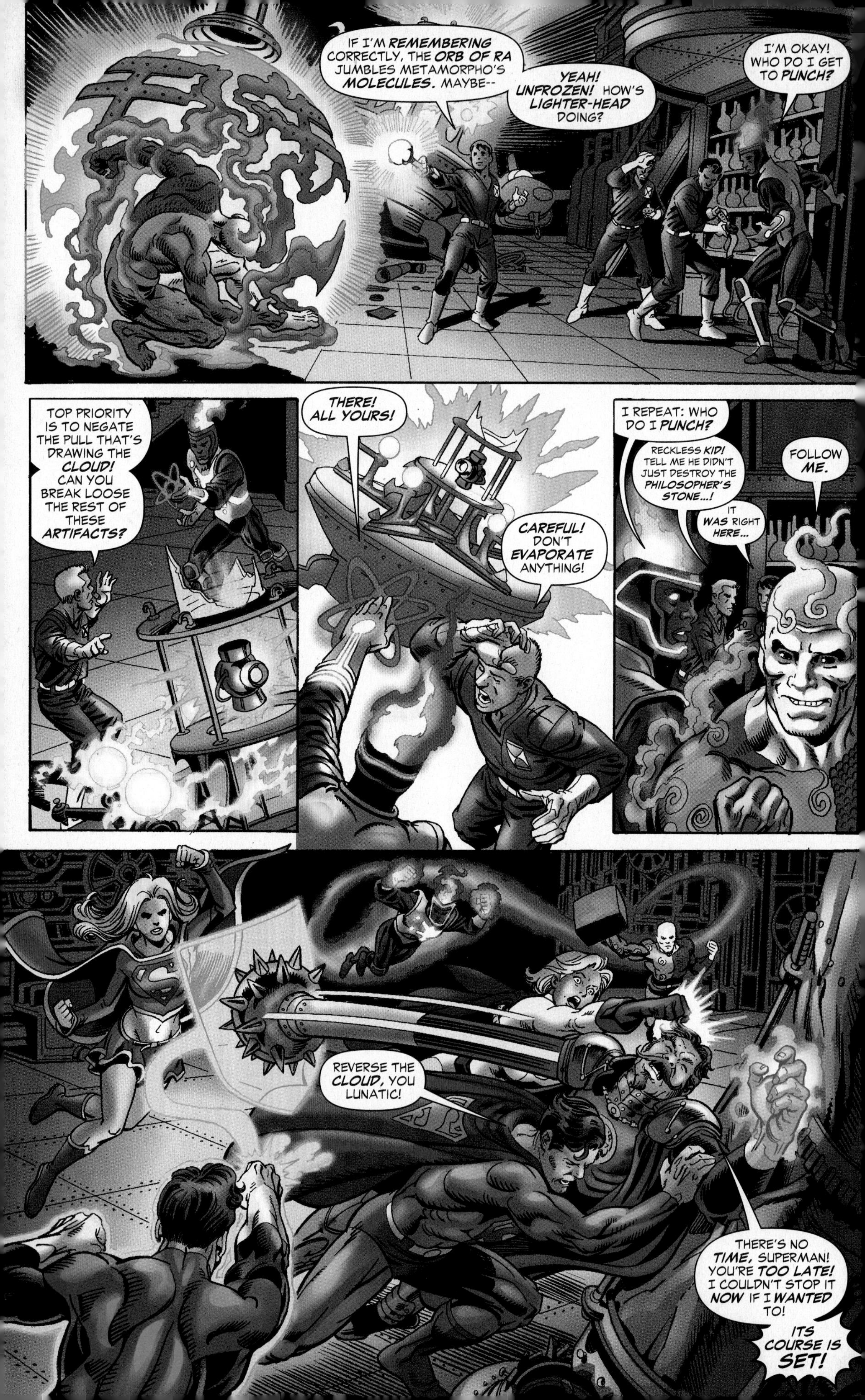
IF I'M REMEMBERING CORRECTLY, THE ORB OF RA JUMBLES METAMORPHO'S MOLECULES. MAYBE--
YEAH! UNFROZEN! HOW'S LIGHTER-HEAD DOING?
I'M OKAY! WHO DO I GET TO PUNCH?
TOP PRIORITY IS TO NEGATE THE PULL THAT'S DRAWING THE CLOUD! CAN YOU BREAK LOOSE THE REST OF THESE ARTIFACTS?
THERE! ALL YOURS!
CAREFUL! DON'T EVAPORATE ANYTHING!
I REPEAT: WHO DO I PUNCH?
RECKLESS KID! TELL ME HE DIDN'T JUST DESTROY THE PHILOSOPHER'S STONE...!
IT WAS RIGHT HERE...
FOLLOW ME.
REVERSE THE CLOUD, YOU LUNATIC!
THERE'S NO TIME, SUPERMAN! YOU'RE TOO LATE! I COULDN'T STOP IT NOW IF I WANTED TO!
ITS COURSE IS SET!

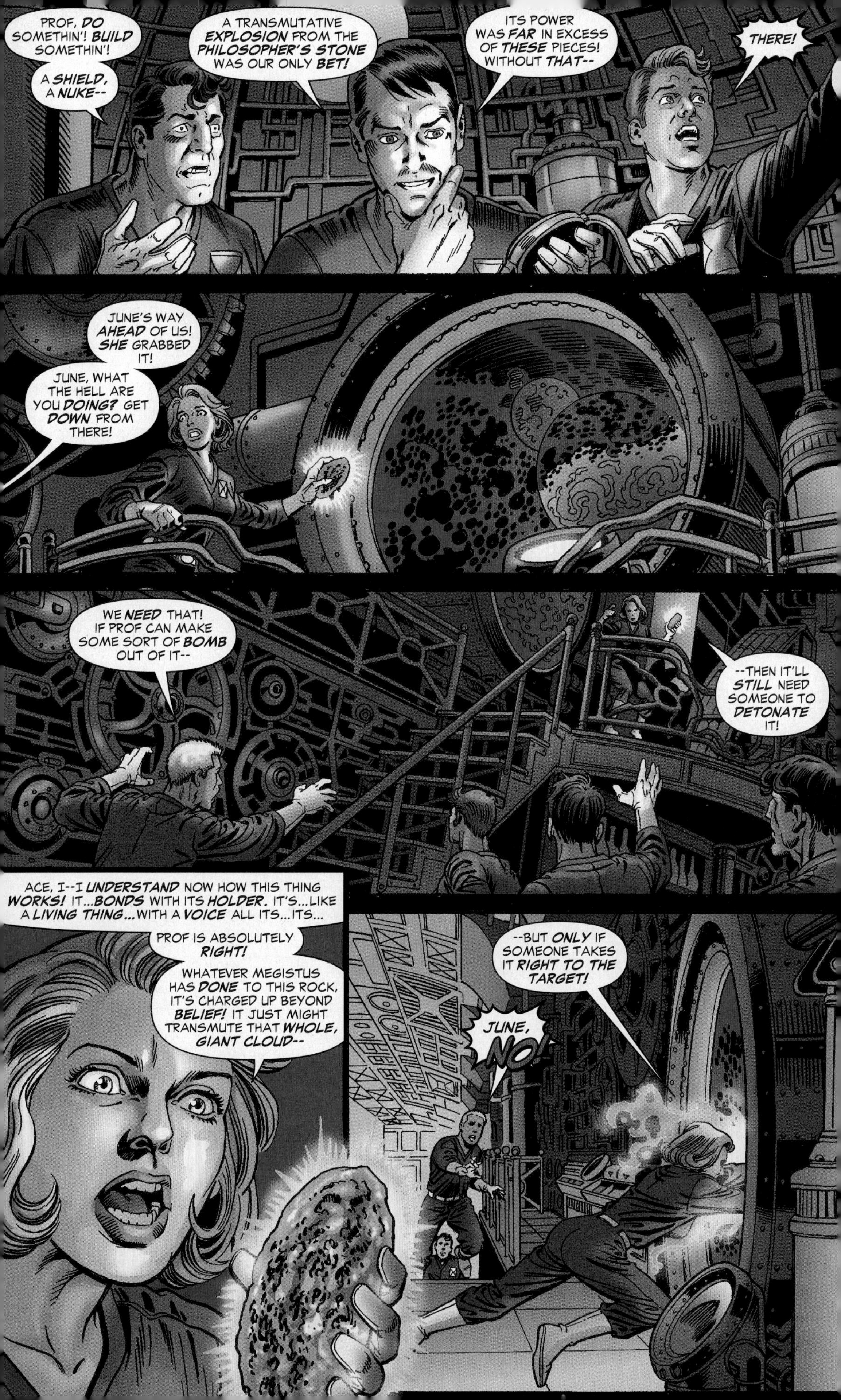
PROF, DO SOMETHIN'! BUILD SOMETHIN'!
A SHIELD, A NUKE--
A TRANSMUTATIVE EXPLOSION FROM THE PHILOSOPHER'S STONE WAS OUR ONLY BET!
ITS POWER WAS FAR IN EXCESS OF THESE PIECES! WITHOUT THAT--
THERE!
JUNE'S WAY AHEAD OF US! SHE GRABBED IT!
JUNE, WHAT THE HELL ARE YOU DOING? GET DOWN FROM THERE!
WE NEED THAT! IF PROF CAN MAKE SOME SORT OF BOMB OUT OF IT--
--THEN IT'LL STILL NEED SOMEONE TO DETONATE IT!
ACE, I--I UNDERSTAND NOW HOW THIS THING WORKS! IT...BONDS WITH ITS HOLDER. IT'S...LIKE A LIVING THING...WITH A VOICE ALL ITS...ITS...
PROF IS ABSOLUTELY RIGHT!
WHATEVER MEGISTUS HAS DONE TO THIS ROCK, IT'S CHARGED UP BEYOND BELIEF! IT JUST MIGHT TRANSMUTE THAT WHOLE, GIANT CLOUD--
--BUT ONLY IF SOMEONE TAKES IT RIGHT TO THE TARGET!
JUNE, NO!

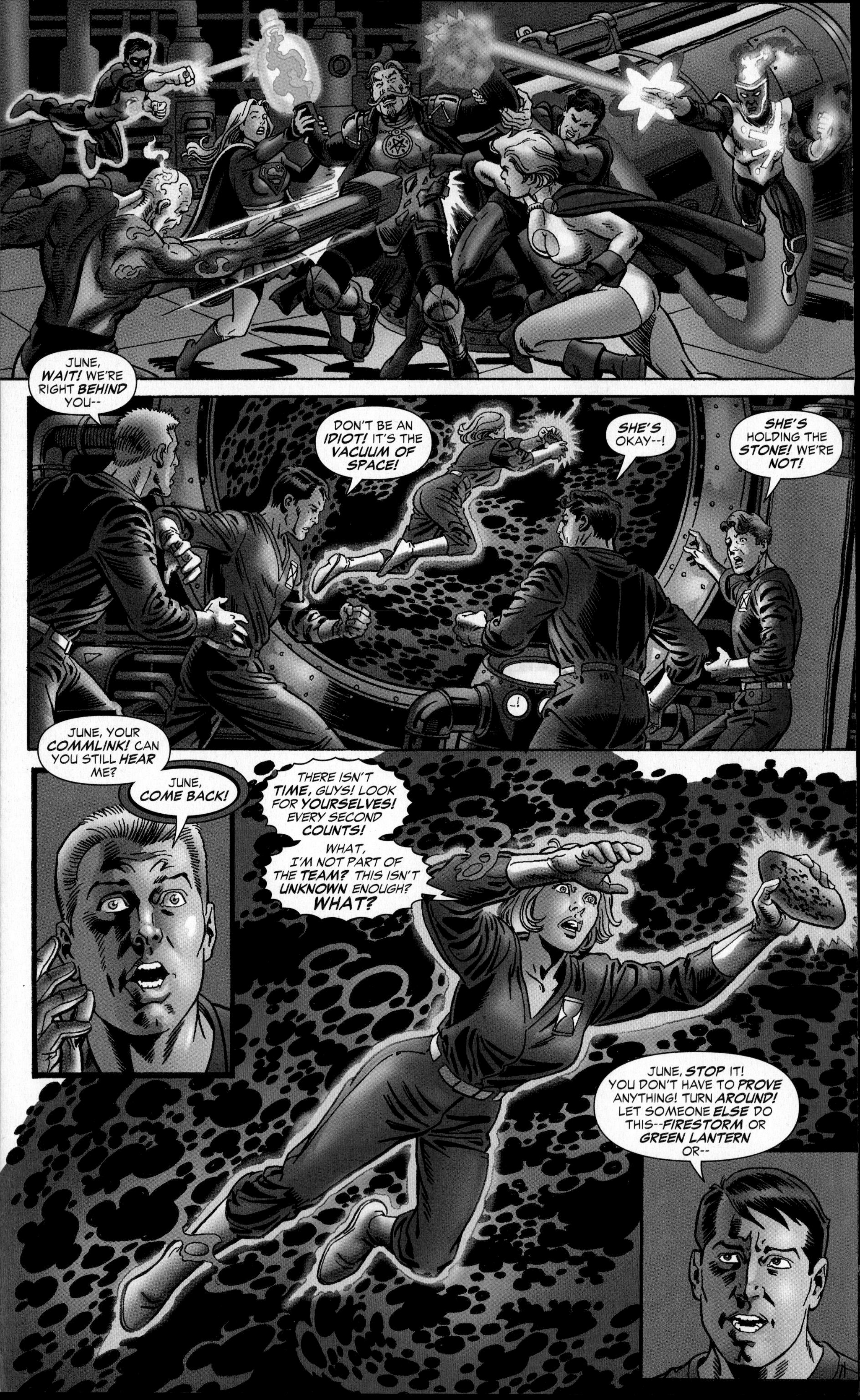
JUNE, WAIT! WE'RE RIGHT BEHIND YOU--
DON'T BE AN IDIOT! IT'S THE VACUUM OF SPACE!
SHE'S OKAY--!
SHE'S HOLDING THE STONE! WE'RE NOT!
JUNE, YOUR COMMLINK! CAN YOU STILL HEAR ME?
JUNE, COME BACK!
THERE ISN'T TIME, GUYS! LOOK FOR YOURSELVES! EVERY SECOND COUNTS!
WHAT, I'M NOT PART OF THE TEAM? THIS ISN'T UNKNOWN ENOUGH? WHAT?
JUNE, STOP IT! YOU DON'T HAVE TO PROVE ANYTHING! TURN AROUND! LET SOMEONE ELSE DO THIS--FIRESTORM OR GREEN LANTERN OR--

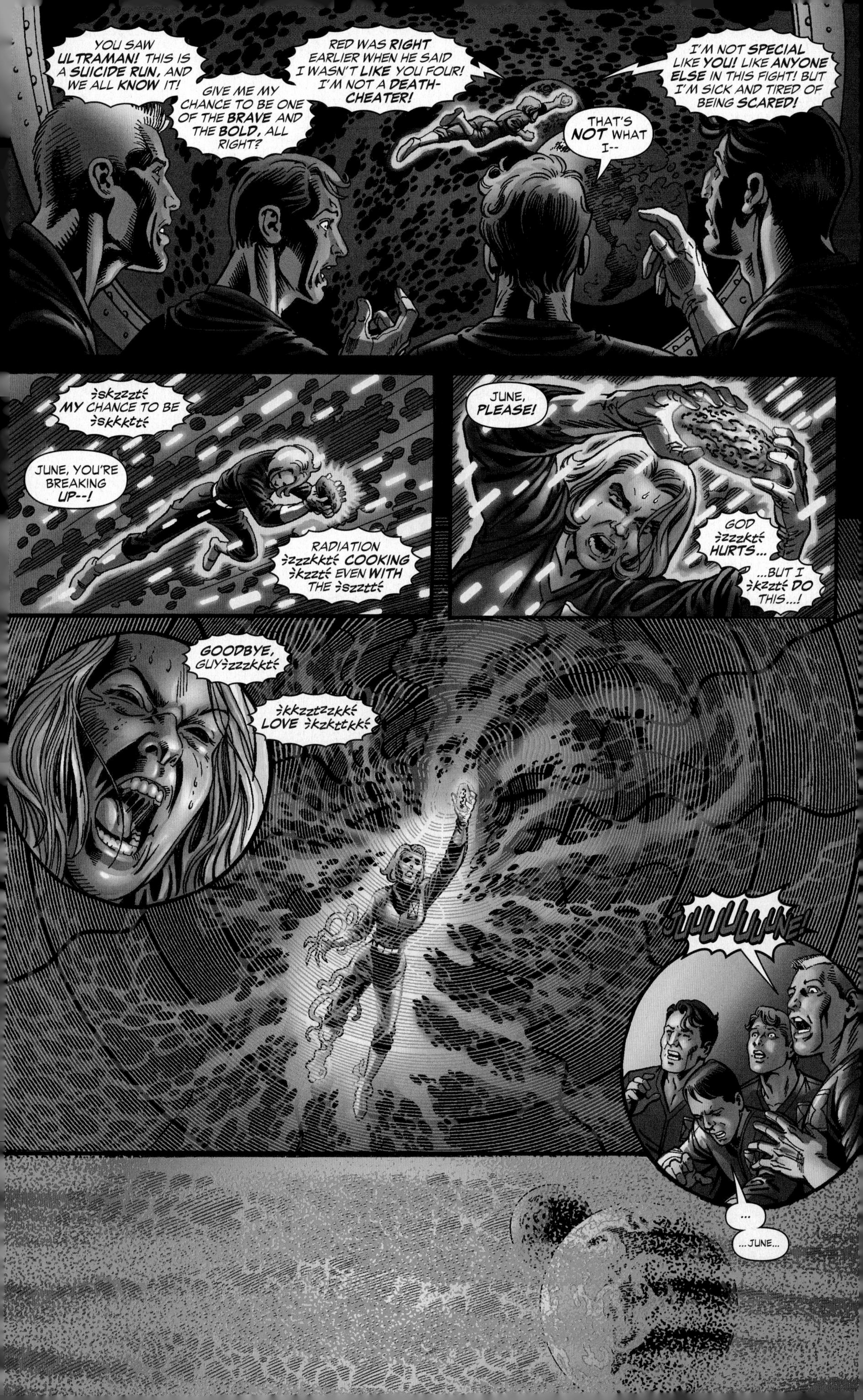
YOU SAW ULTRAMAN! THIS IS A SUICIDE RUN, AND WE ALL KNOW IT!
GIVE ME MY CHANCE TO BE ONE OF THE BRAVE AND THE BOLD, ALL RIGHT?
RED WAS RIGHT EARLIER WHEN HE SAID I WASN'T LIKE YOU FOUR! I'M NOT A DEATH-CHEATER!
THAT'S NOT WHAT I--
I'M NOT SPECIAL LIKE YOU! LIKE ANYONE ELSE IN THIS FIGHT! BUT I'M SICK AND TIRED OF BEING SCARED!
skzzzt MY CHANCE TO BE skkktt
JUNE, YOU'RE BREAKING UP--!
RADIATION zzzkkt COOKING kzzt EVEN WITH THE szzzt
JUNE, PLEASE!
GOD zzzkt HURTS...
...BUT I kzzt DO THIS...!
GOODBYE, GUY zzzkkt
kkzzzt zzkk LOVE kzktkk
JUUUUUUNE!
...
...JUNE...

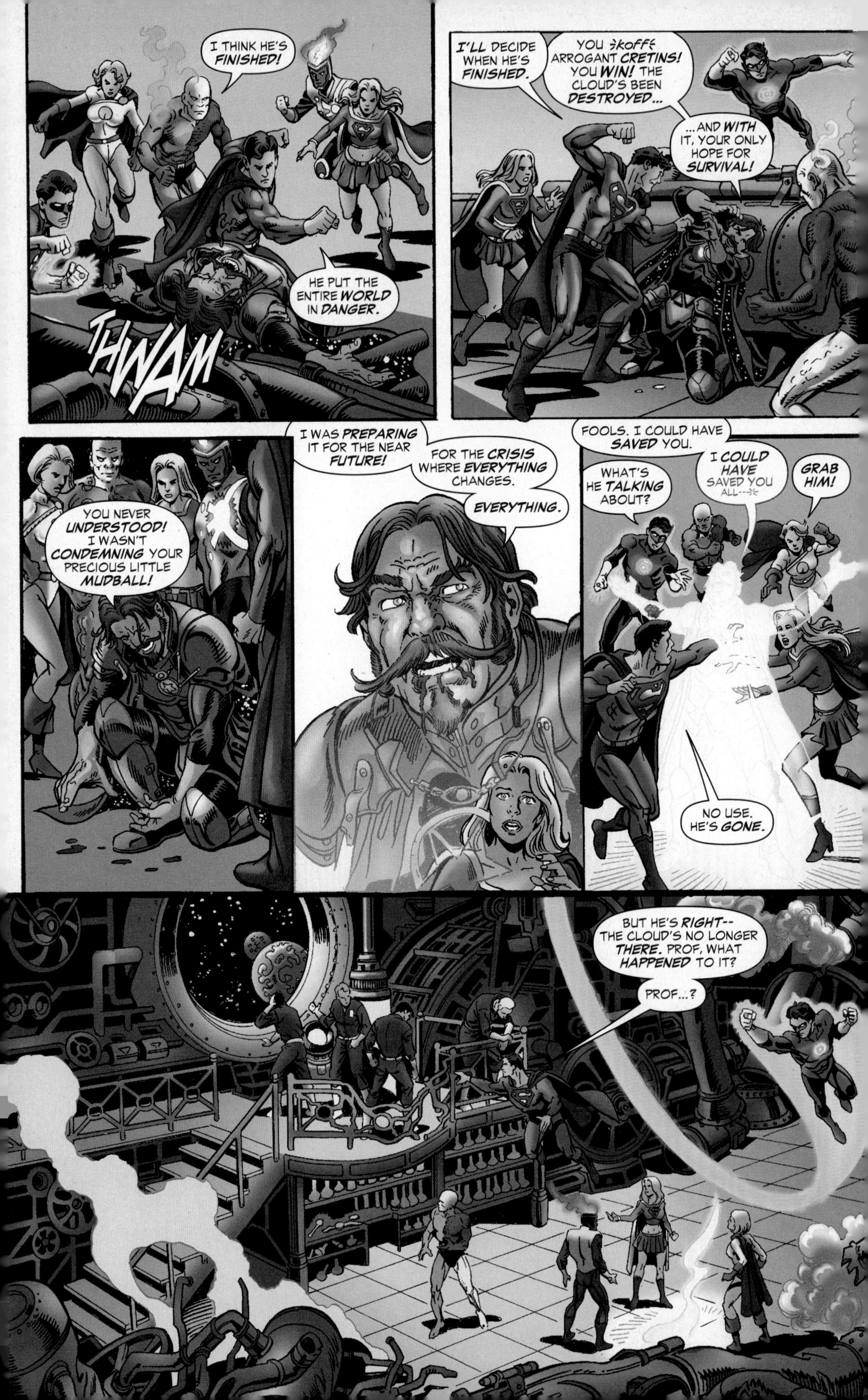
I THINK HE'S FINISHED!
HE PUT THE ENTIRE WORLD IN DANGER.
THWAM
I'LL DECIDE WHEN HE'S FINISHED.
YOU *KOFF* ARROGANT CRETINS! YOU WIN! THE CLOUD'S BEEN DESTROYED...
...AND WITH IT, YOUR ONLY HOPE FOR SURVIVAL!
YOU NEVER UNDERSTOOD! I WASN'T CONDEMNING YOUR PRECIOUS LITTLE MUDBALL!
I WAS PREPARING IT FOR THE NEAR FUTURE!
FOR THE CRISIS WHERE EVERYTHING CHANGES.
EVERYTHING.
FOOLS. I COULD HAVE SAVED YOU.
WHAT'S HE TALKING ABOUT?
I COULD HAVE SAVED YOU ALL--*
GRAB HIM!
NO USE. HE'S GONE.
BUT HE'S RIGHT-- THE CLOUD'S NO LONGER THERE. PROF, WHAT HAPPENED TO IT?
PROF...?

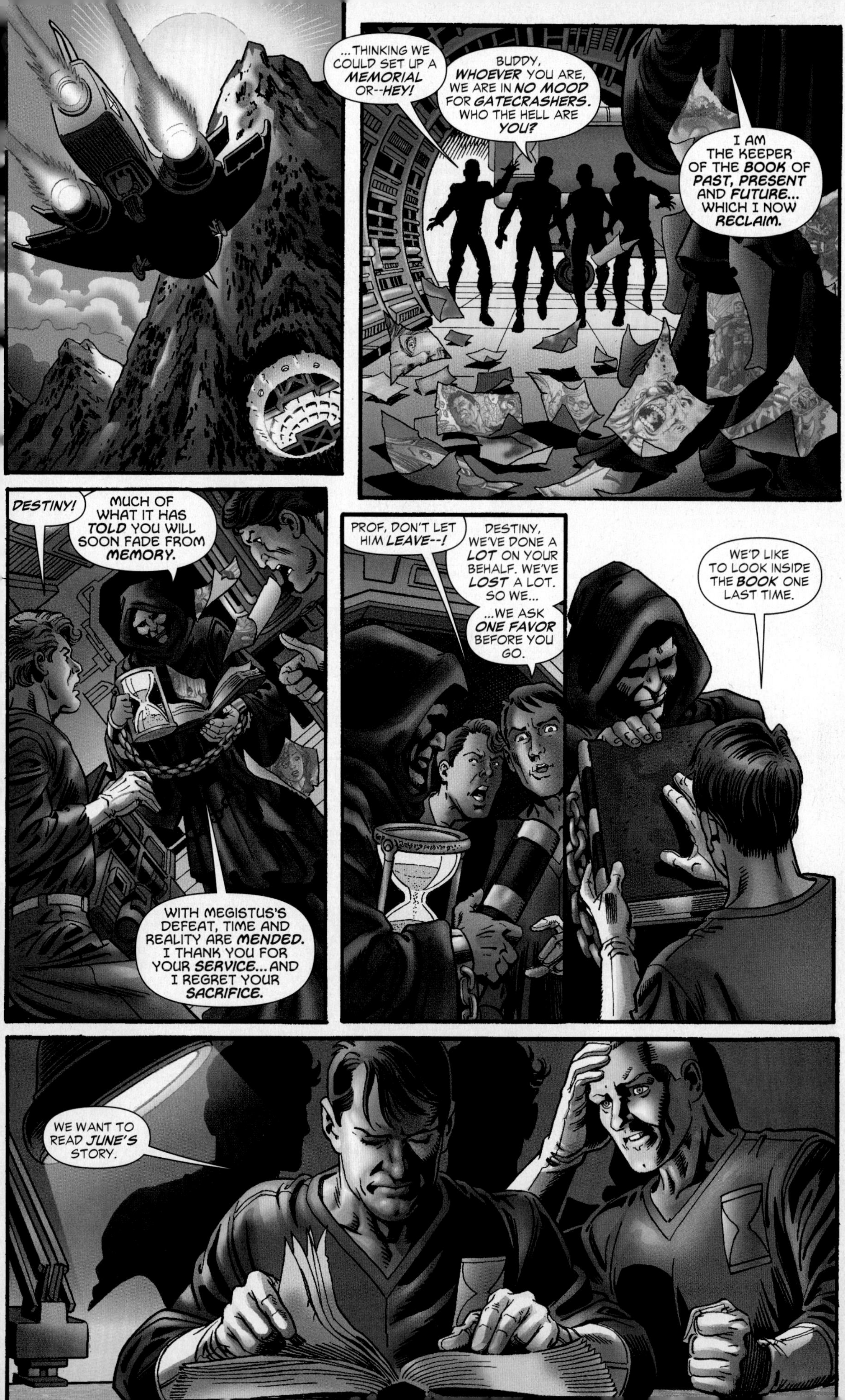
...THINKING WE COULD SET UP A MEMORIAL OR--HEY!
BUDDY, WHOEVER YOU ARE, WE ARE IN NO MOOD FOR GATECRASHERS. WHO THE HELL ARE YOU?
I AM THE KEEPER OF THE BOOK OF PAST, PRESENT AND FUTURE... WHICH I NOW RECLAIM.
DESTINY!
MUCH OF WHAT IT HAS TOLD YOU WILL SOON FADE FROM MEMORY.
WITH MEGISTUS'S DEFEAT, TIME AND REALITY ARE MENDED. I THANK YOU FOR YOUR SERVICE... AND I REGRET YOUR SACRIFICE.
PROF, DON'T LET HIM LEAVE--!
DESTINY, WE'VE DONE A LOT ON YOUR BEHALF. WE'VE LOST A LOT. SO WE...
...WE ASK ONE FAVOR BEFORE YOU GO.
WE'D LIKE TO LOOK INSIDE THE BOOK ONE LAST TIME.
WE WANT TO READ JUNE'S STORY.

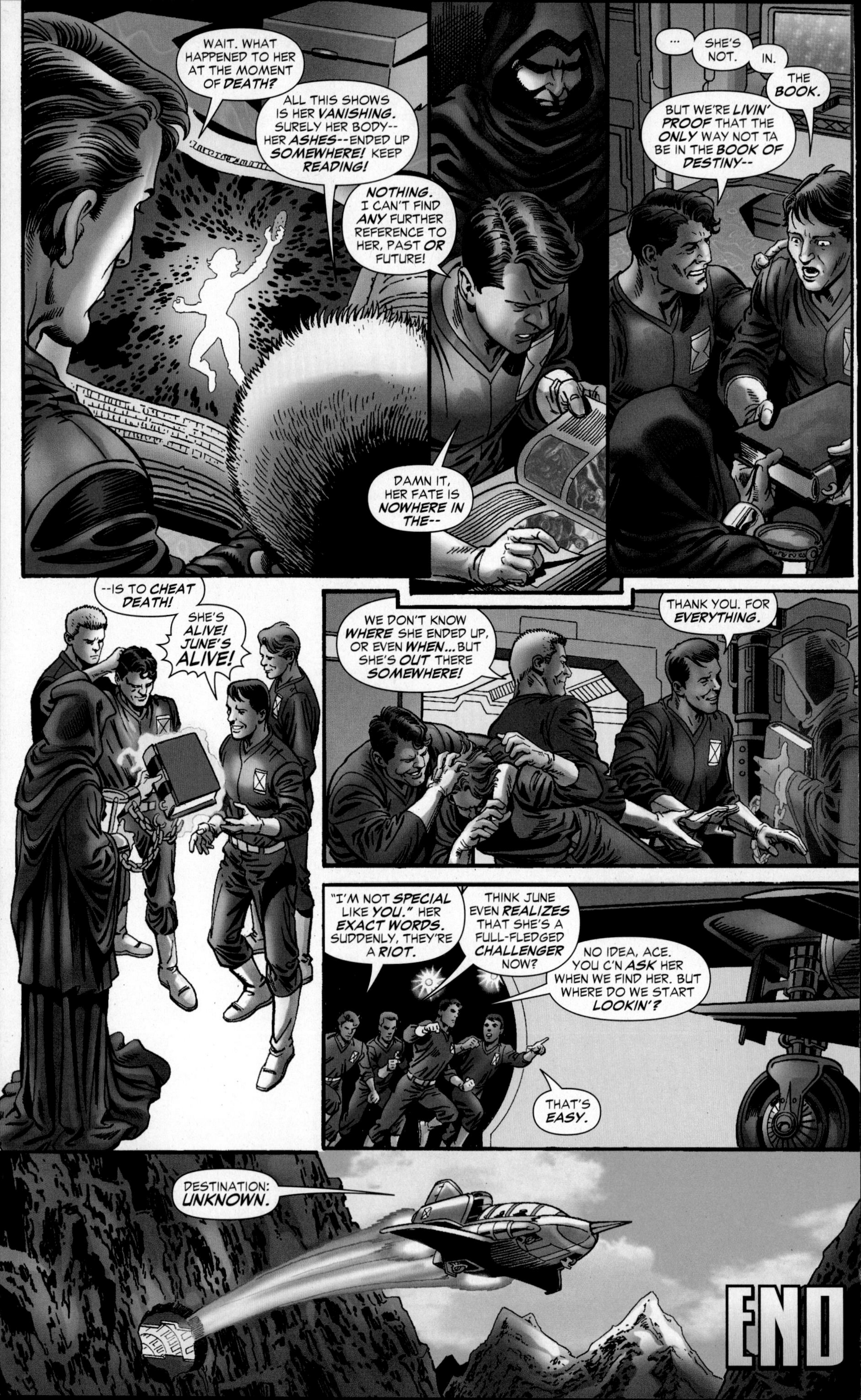
WAIT. WHAT HAPPENED TO HER AT THE MOMENT OF DEATH?
ALL THIS SHOWS IS HER VANISHING. SURELY HER BODY-- HER ASHES--ENDED UP SOMEWHERE! KEEP READING!
NOTHING. I CAN'T FIND ANY FURTHER REFERENCE TO HER, PAST OR FUTURE!
DAMN IT, HER FATE IS NOWHERE IN THE--
...
SHE'S NOT.
IN.
THE BOOK.
BUT WE'RE LIVIN' PROOF THAT THE ONLY WAY NOT TA BE IN THE BOOK OF DESTINY--
--IS TO CHEAT DEATH!
SHE'S ALIVE! JUNE'S ALIVE!
WE DON'T KNOW WHERE SHE ENDED UP, OR EVEN WHEN... BUT SHE'S OUT THERE SOMEWHERE!
THANK YOU. FOR EVERYTHING.
"I'M NOT SPECIAL LIKE YOU." HER EXACT WORDS. SUDDENLY, THEY'RE A RIOT.
THINK JUNE EVEN REALIZES THAT SHE'S A FULL-FLEDGED CHALLENGER NOW?
NO IDEA, ACE. YOU C'N ASK HER WHEN WE FIND HER. BUT WHERE DO WE START LOOKIN'?
THAT'S EASY.
DESTINATION: UNKNOWN.
END

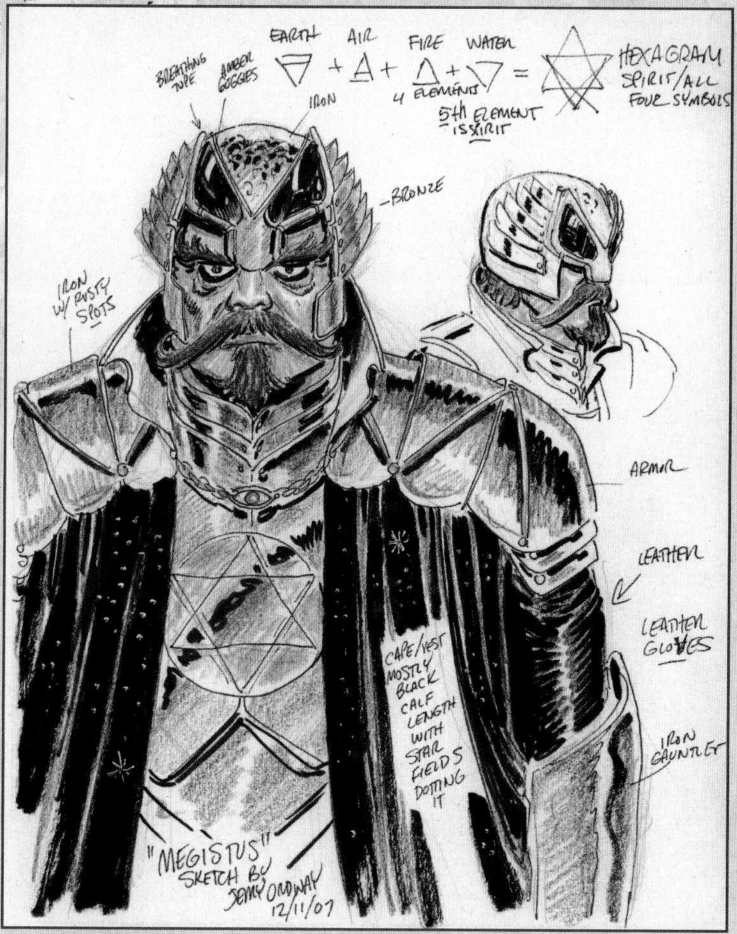
EARTH
AIR
FIRE
WATER
HEXAGRAM
SPIRIT/ALL
FOUR SYMBOLS
4 ELEMENTS
5TH ELEMENT
IS SPIRIT
BREATHING TUBE
AMBER GOGGLES
IRON
BRONZE
IRON
W/ RUSTY
SPOTS
ARMOR
LEATHER
LEATHER
GLOVES
IRON
GAUNTLET
CAPE/VEST
MOSTLY
BLACK
CALF
LENGTH
WITH
STAR
FIELDS
DOTTING
IT
"MEGISTUS"
SKETCH BY
JERRY ORDWAY
12/11/07

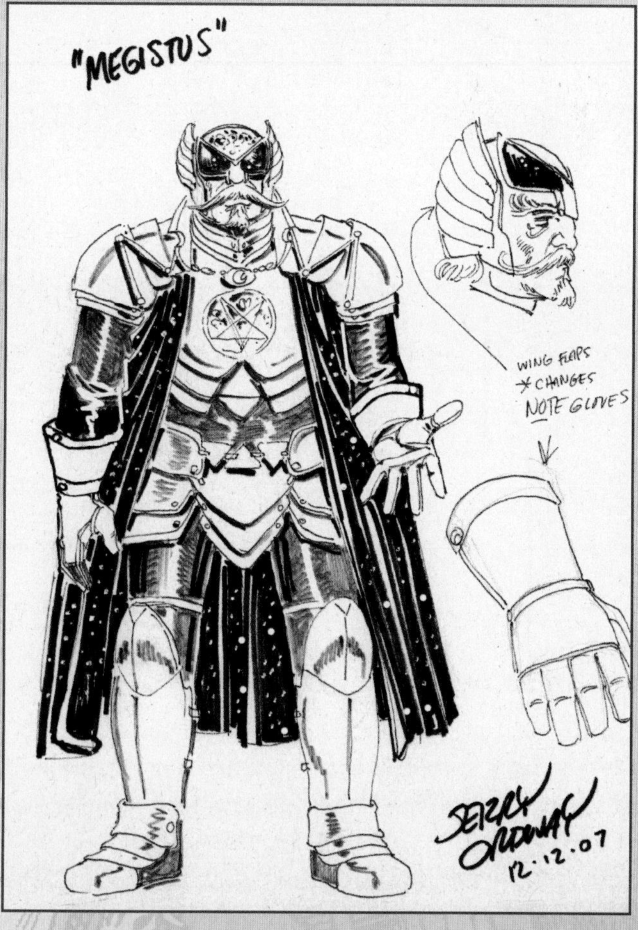
"MEGISTUS"
WING FLAPS
* CHANGES
NOTE GLOVES
JERRY
ORDWAY
12.12.07

Megistus sketches
by Jerry Ordway

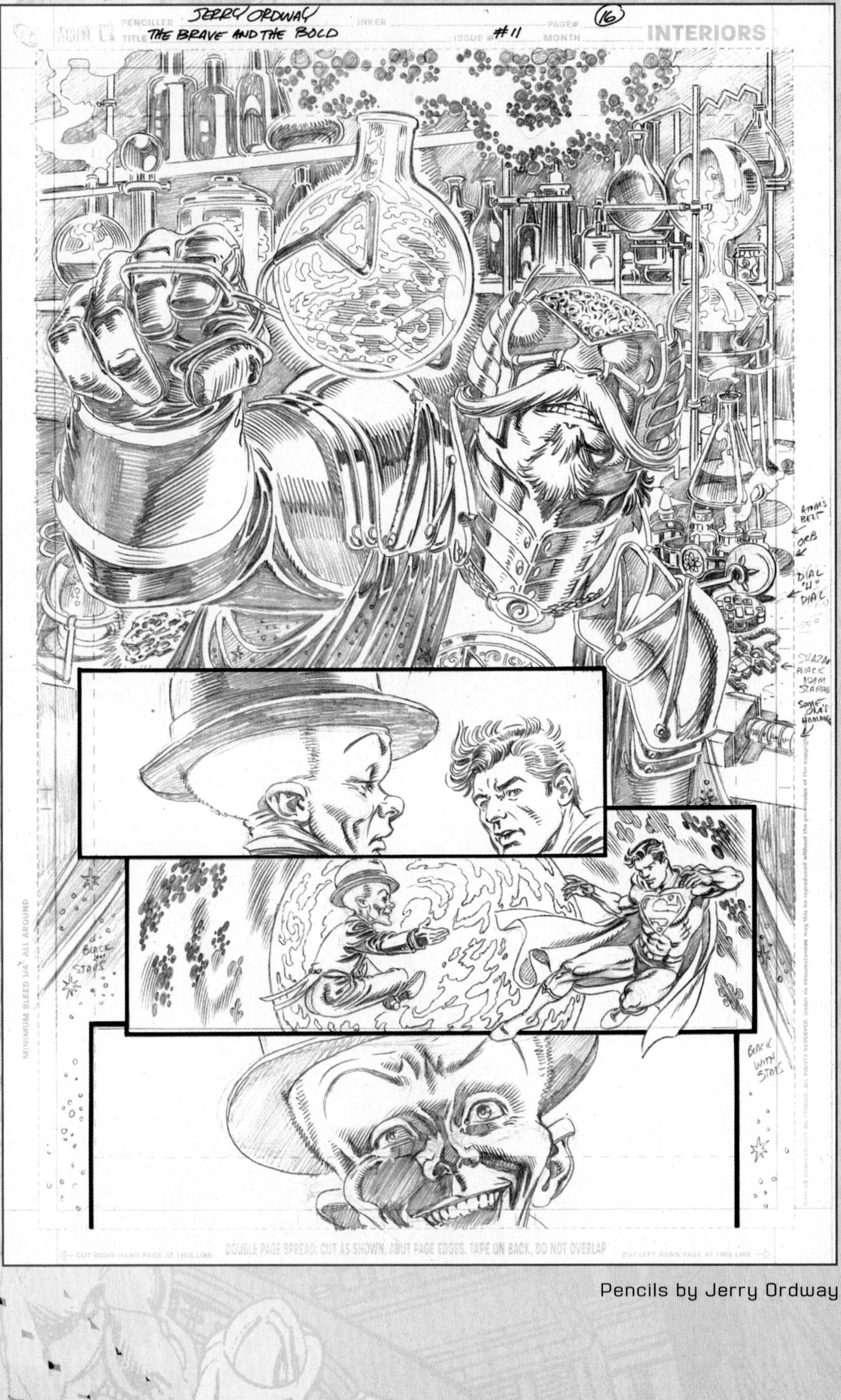
PENCILLER JERRY ORDWAY
INKER
PAGE# 16
TITLE THE BRAVE AND THE BOLD
ISSUE # #11
MONTH
INTERIORS
ATOM'S BELT
ORB
DIAL
"H" DIAL
SHAZAM BLACK ADAM SCARAB
SOME OLA'S HAMMER
BLACK WITH STARS
BLACK WITH STARS
MINIMUM BLEED 1/4" ALL AROUND
DOUBLE PAGE SPREAD: CUT AS SHOWN. ABUT PAGE EDGES. TAPE ON BACK. DO NOT OVERLAP

Pencils by Jerry Ordway

READ MORE ADVENTURES OF YOUR FAVORITE HEROES IN THESE COLLECTIONS FROM DC COMICS:

KINGDOM COME

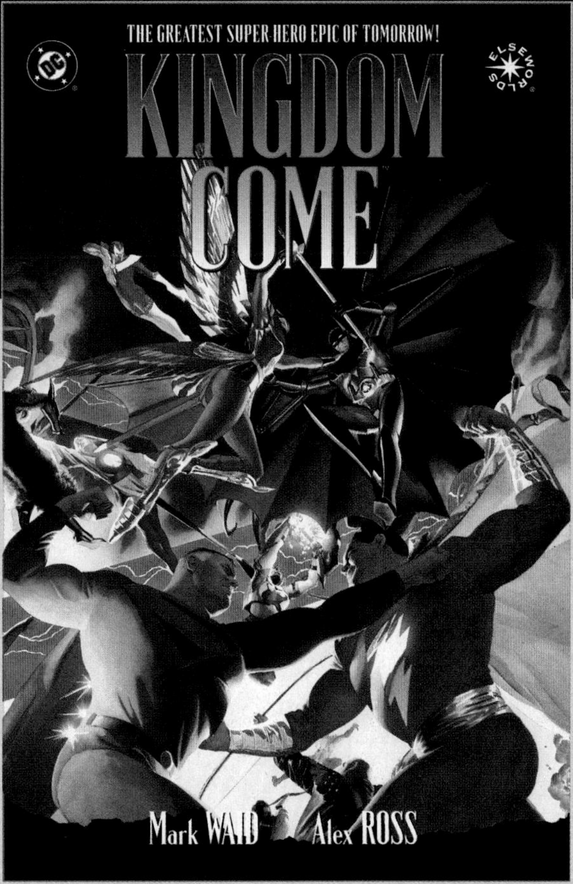
THE GREATEST SUPER-HERO EPIC OF TOMORROW!
KINGDOM COME
Mark WAID Alex ROSS

Mark Waid and **Alex Ross** deliver a grim tale of youth versus experience, tradition versus change and what defines a hero. KINGDOM COME is a riveting story pitting the old guard — Superman, Batman, Wonder Woman and their peers — against a new uncompromising generation.

WINNER OF FIVE EISNER AND HARVEY AWARDS, INCLUDING BEST LIMITED SERIES AND BEST ARTIST

IDENTITY CRISIS

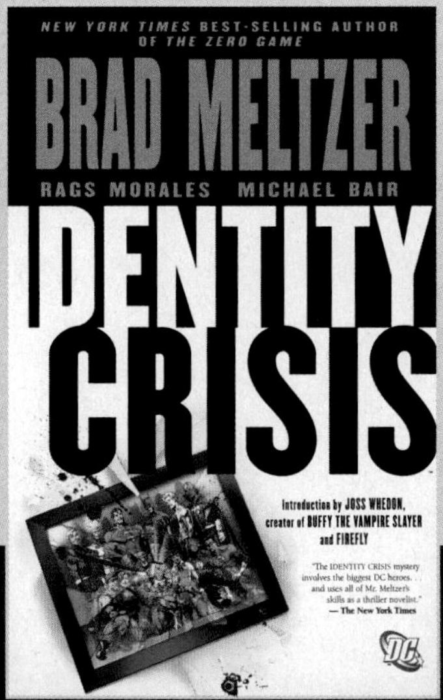
NEW YORK TIMES BEST-SELLING AUTHOR OF THE ZERO GAME
BRAD MELTZER
RAGS MORALES MICHAEL BAIR
IDENTITY CRISIS
Introduction by JOSS WHEDON, creator of BUFFY THE VAMPIRE SLAYER and FIREFLY

BRAD MELTZER
RAGS MORALES
MICHAEL BAIR

CRISIS ON INFINITE EARTHS

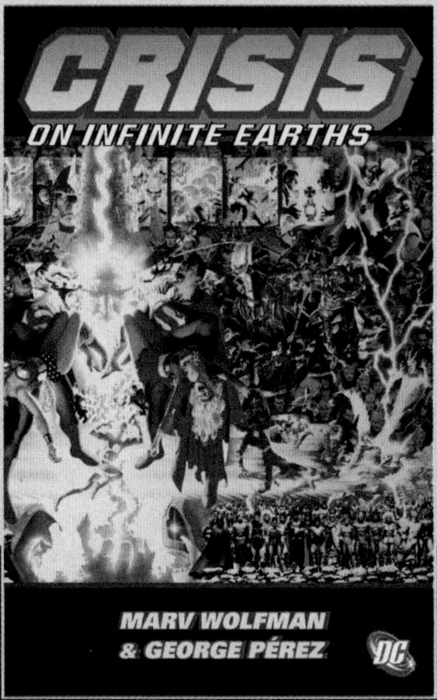
CRISIS ON INFINITE EARTHS
MARV WOLFMAN & GEORGE PÉREZ

MARV WOLFMAN
GEORGE PÉREZ

DC: THE NEW FRONTIER VOLUME 1

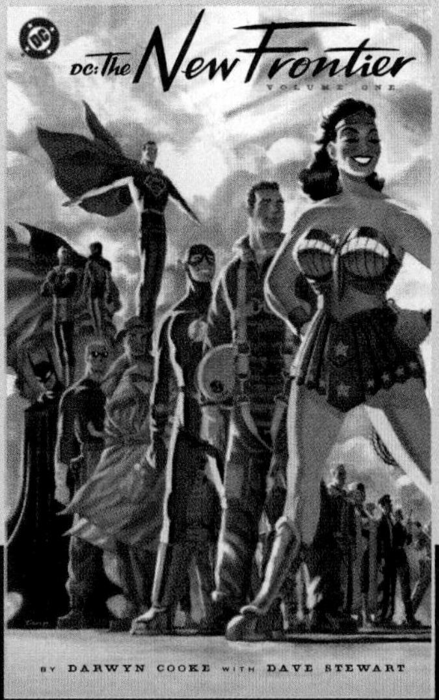
DC: The New Frontier
BY DARWYN COOKE WITH DAVE STEWART

DARWYN COOKE
DAVE STEWART

DON'T MISS THESE OTHER GREAT TITLES FROM AROUND THE **DCU!**

SUPERMAN:
BIRTHRIGHT

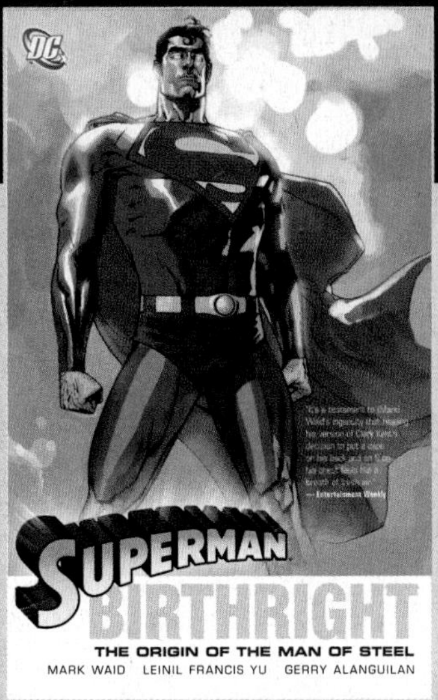
SUPERMAN
BIRTHRIGHT
THE ORIGIN OF THE MAN OF STEEL
MARK WAID LEINIL FRANCIS YU GERRY ALANGUILAN

MARK WAID
LEINIL FRANCIS YU
GERRY ALANGUILAN

BATMAN:
DARK VICTORY

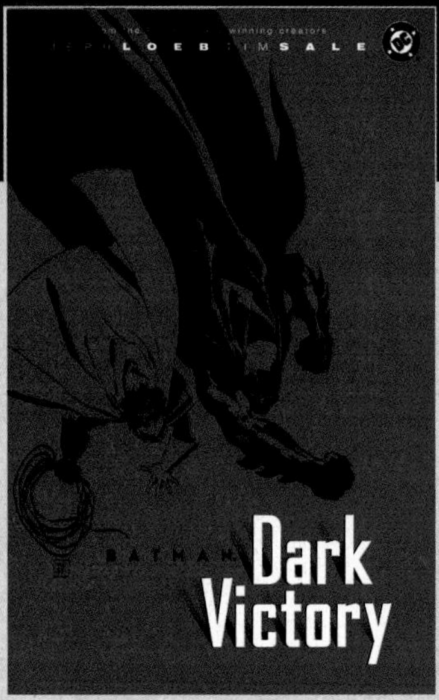
BATMAN
Dark Victory

JEPH LOEB
TIM SALE

WONDER WOMAN:
GODS AND MORTALS

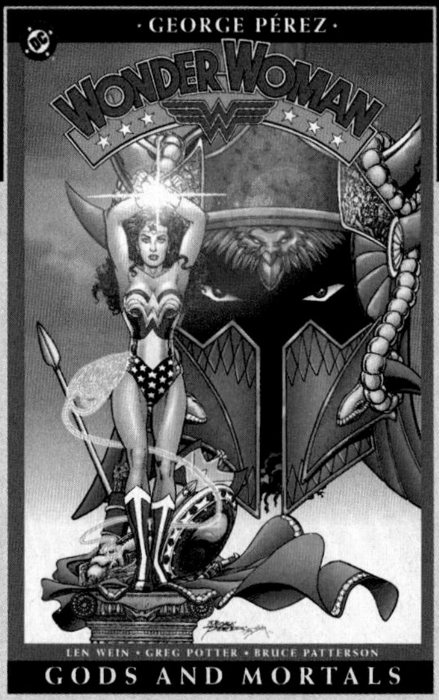
· GEORGE PÉREZ ·
WONDER WOMAN
LEN WEIN • GREG POTTER • BRUCE PATTERSON
GODS AND MORTALS

GEORGE PÉREZ
LEN WEIN/GREG POTTER
BRUCE PATTERSON

GREEN LANTERN:
NO FEAR

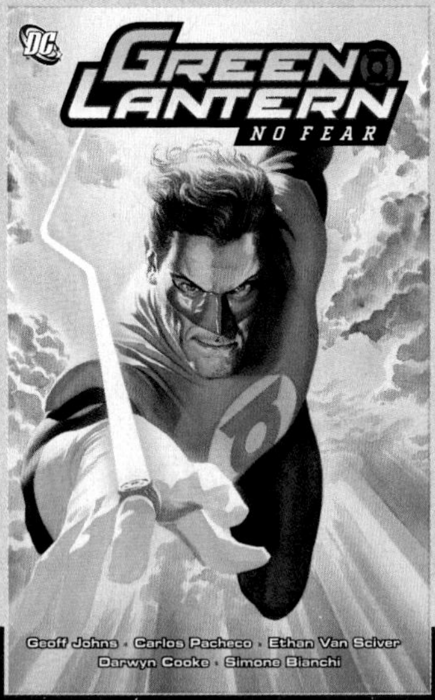
GREEN LANTERN
NO FEAR
Geoff Johns · Carlos Pacheco · Ethan Van Sciver
Darwyn Cooke · Simone Bianchi

GEOFF JOHNS
CARLOS PACHECO
ETHAN VAN SCIVER

GREEN ARROW:
QUIVER

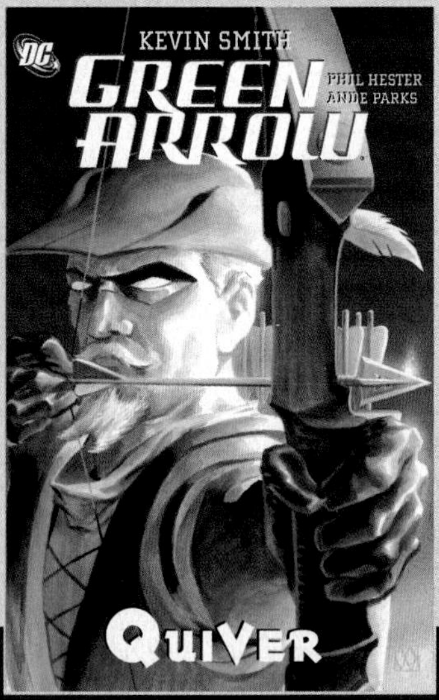
KEVIN SMITH
GREEN ARROW
PHIL HESTER
ANDE PARKS
QUIVER

KEVIN SMITH
PHIL HESTER
ANDE PARKS

TEEN TITANS:
A KID'S GAME

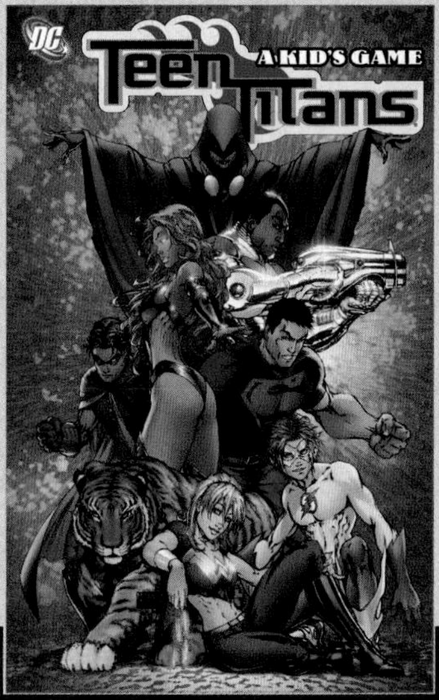
A KID'S GAME
Teen Titans

GEOFF JOHNS
MIKE McKONE

SEARCH THE GRAPHIC NOVELS SECTION OF
www.DCCOMICS.com
FOR ART AND INFORMATION ON ALL OF OUR BOOKS!